Integrated Management from E-Business Perspective

Concepts, Architectures and Methodologies

NETWORK AND SYSTEMS MANAGEMENT

Series Editor: Manu Malek
Stevens Institute of Technology
Hoboken, New Jersey

ACTIVE NETWORKS AND ACTIVE NETWORK MANAGEMENT: A Proactive Management Framework

Stephen F. Bush and Amit B. Kulkarni

BASIC CONCEPTS FOR MANAGING TELECOMMUNICATIONS NETWORKS: Copper to Sand to Glass to Air

Lawrence Bernstein and C. M. Yuhas

COOPERATIVE MANAGEMENT OF ENTERPRISE NETWORKS

Pradeep Ray

INTEGRATED MANAGEMENT FROM E-BUSINESS PERSPECTIVE: Concepts, Architectures and Methodologies

Pradeep Kumar Ray

MANAGING BUSINESS AND SERVICE NETWORKS

Lundy Lewis

Integrated Management from E-Business Perspective

Concepts, Architectures and Methodologies

Pradeep Kumar Ray
University of New South Wales
Sydney, Australia

SPRINGER SCIENCE+BUSINESS MEDIA, LLC

ISBN 978-1-4613-4918-1 ISBN 978-1-4615-0089-6 (eBook)
DOI 10.1007/978-1-4615-0089-6

Originally published by Kluwer Academic/Plenum Publishers, New York in 2003
Softcover reprint of the hardcover 1st edition 2003

http://www.wkap.nl/

10 9 8 7 6 5 4 3 2 1

A C.I.P. record for this book is available from the Library of Congress

Contents

Acknowledgements

I would like to sincerely acknowledge the contribution of some people who have played important roles in the completion of this book. Firstly, I would like to thank Manu Malek, the editor of the network and systems management series of Kluwer Academic/Plenum Publishing Corporation for encouraging me to write this book, and the reviewers (Lundy Lewis, Shri Goyal and Gabriel Jakobson) whose names were disclosed to me after the manuscript was revised based on their thoughtful suggestions. I must thank James Herman of Nervewire, USA for gracefully agreeing to let me use some of his presentation slides as part of this book. I am very much indebted to Albert Fuss of Intelligent Communication Software (ICS), Germany for allowing me to use some of the case studies conducted by ICS on service management (in Appendices 1 and 4 and in Chapter 2). I would like to thank Aprisma Technologies for assisting in various ways in the writing of this book. Thanks are due to many management professionsla, particularly Gora Sen Gupta for spending time in clarifying some of the ideas in this book.

Thanks are due to Gaele for helping with the proof reading and editorial corrections. I would like to thank my research students, Bao Hua Michael Liu and Lawrence Yao for helping me in compiling this book. Thanks are due to the Australian Research Council (ARC) for supporting this research partially through a SPIRT grant during 2000-2002. I must thank my employer, the University of New South Wales, Australia, for extending assistance towards writing this book partially through the SRG grant. Finally, I would like to thank my wife Kumkum for her understanding and for patiently bearing with me during the long and arduous process of writing this book. Thanks are due to my colleagues, parents, other family members, relatives and friends for providing all encouragement in this project.

Preface

E-business is transforming business around the world. The world-wide-web provides an extremely convenient, and cost-effective electronic medium for commercial activity, linking buyers, suppliers, and business intermediaries worldwide.

Due to the tremendous pace of movement in this electronic market, many well-known firms will be hard pressed to gain and retain market leadership. Hence the tolerance of error will be quite low for the methods and techniques used for this business. The success of firms in e-business will be critically dependent on their ability to manage and control e-business. Timeliness, format and accuracy of management information will be of great value.

While business enterprises will need to perform in this fiercely competitive environment, these firms will also have to cooperate with competition to provide an interoperable business environment for the benefit of all stakeholders, including customers, and collaborating firms. Standards in e-business management can play a critical role in this dimension of e-business development.

Thanks to the changing business environment, such as the deregulation of the telecommunication industry, it is important to provide an integration of organizational business processes with network and systems management. For example, these days huge amounts (worth millions of dollars) of stocks are traded daily over the Internet. Any down time of networked services may result in huge losses to concerned organizations. As telemedicine technology grows, the networked computing system in medical environments may become directly responsible for lives saved. These are different forms of e-businesses, such as e-healthcare, and e-government that need to be managed effectively.

The subject of network and systems management has evolved greatly over the last few years. It has attracted people from disciplines such as Telecommunications, Software Engineering, Network Technology and Artificial Intelligence. Recently, there have also been major developments in the management of applications and services, as evidenced by the release of a number of commercial products and books in this area. The integration of network and systems management with applications and services management is expressed as *integrated management.* In view of the similarities of many of the problems of integrated management to e-business management, a number of management platform vendors are in the process of adapting and bringing out products for the e-business management market. However, the problem of e-business management needs to be addressed in a top-down fashion. There is a need for a balanced understanding of the business perspectives as well as the technology perspectives. This book addresses this important niche market.

It may be noted that the term *e-businesses* is considered more general than e-commerce, which is popularly associated with the business of selling popular items (e.g., CDs, books, and shares) over the Internet, also known as the Business to Consumer (B2C) aspect of e-business. So e-business involves Business to Business (B2B), and Consumer to Consumer (C2C) aspects in addition to the B2C notion of e-commerce. Since many of the e-commerce technologies are being used in e-business, this book has used the terms e-commerce and e-business interchangeably in some sections. E-commerce and e-business systems are deployed using modern Information Technology (IT) that relies heavily on the protocols, standards and tools for the development and operation of networked applications over the Internet. Many software services are now emerging to facilitate the process of e-business application development. These services are mostly object-oriented and help reduce the complexity of applications for e-businesses. These services (used in many e-business applications) could exist at various levels in the e-business environment. For example, they could be Internet application services, such as email, FTP, and WWW, or they could be specialized services for security and management. These services are described in this book using a number of interchangeable terms, such as *e-business services, e-commerce services, e-services, and IT services.*

This book is organized into five parts and four appendices. These five parts present the five viewpoints of Integrated Management from E-Business Perspectives, namely

1. Business Viewpoint

2. Methodology and Process Viewpoint
3. Architectural Viewpoint
4. Technology and Standards Viewpoint
5. Collaboration Viewpoint

Each part has been sub divided into two chapters.

Part 1 (Chapters 1 and 2) provides a brief review of concepts and models related to integrated management, and e-business environments. Although Chapter 1 touches upon major concepts in this area, it is not intended to provide a tutorial on e-business environments. Chapter 2 highlights the four key management dimensions for e-business; people, organization, process, and technology.

Part 2 (Chapters 3 and 4) discusses the problem of e-business service development from a technology-independent perspective. The objective of Chapter 3 is to show the need for a holistic perspective on e-business services, integrating business processes with appropriate techniques to assist in the quantification of qualitative business parameters, such as service quality. Chapter 4 presents an approach to the study of the management of diverse services through a common 8-stage methodology. The chapter concludes with a methodology for e-business management based on software engineering. Like many management texts, this part of the book emphasizes models and concepts that are applicable to various types of businesses (including telecommunications). The concepts are illustrated using examples from e-healthcare.

While a methodology gives a general guideline for development, architecture is needed to realize the design through software building blocks. Hence Part 3 (Chapters 5 and 6) discusses architectures for e-business management in a top-down manner. The discussion covers various viewpoints on e-business management, namely the Process View, Transaction View, and the Infrastructure View. This encompasses a number of different areas of modern information technology. For example, the Process View is studied as part of Computer Supported Cooperative Work (CSCW). The Transaction View is discussed as part of transaction processing and database systems, and standards (Chapter 5), and the Infrastructure View maps e-business management to management of the underlying networks, systems and applications through the concept of Service Level Management (Chapter 6).

Part 4 (Chapters 7 and 8) discusses various emerging technologies and standards covering the entire e-business constituent areas discussed in Part 3. While Chapter 7 discusses various network, systems and application management standards, Chapter 8 discusses the integration of these standards, and some other emerging standards for a practical e-business management solution, illustrated by a case study of e-business in telecommunication industry (e-telco).

Part 5 (Chapters 9 and 10) of this book integrates the concepts presented in Parts 1-4 to develop a new methodology for the development of e-business management solutions. This is based on recent developments in CSCW and software engineering. This methodology is called Cooperative Management Methodology for E-business Networks and Services (CoMENS), which is an extension of CoMEN discussed in this author's book, *Cooperative Management of Enterprise Networks*, published by Kluwer Academic/Plenum Publishers in May 2000. Chapter 9 presents various conceptual building blocks of CoMENS methodology, and Chapter 10 illustrates CoMENS with a case study in the telecommunication service business.

Four appendices supplement these chapters. Appendix 1 presents a case study, which illustrates how an e-business infrastructure management solution can be realized by integrating products of network management, systems management, and service management.

Appendix-2 discusses the e-business management guideline (being used by many telecom service providers) from the Tele-Management Forum (TMF). This guideline, called Telcom Operations Map (TOM) consists of three major processes, namely Fulfillment, Assurance and Billing.

Appendix 3 shows how the CoMENS scenario analysis may be applied to analyze an e-business management scenario.

Appendix 4 illustrates a practical multi-vendor solution for Service Level Management based on commercially available products.

This book may be useful in different ways to network and systems management professionals wishing to know about e-business management, business managers wishing to understand the issues in e-business management, software system developers, and students and researchers of Business Information Systems, Telecommunications Engineering, Computer Science (networking), and Software Engineering. Readers may take different sequences of chapters for reading, depending on the objectives of the study. For example, a Business Information systems student may skip Part 4. A Telecommunication-Engineering student may skip Part 2.

Pradeep Kumar Ray

April 2002

PART -1

BUSINESS VIEWPOINT

Chapter 1. E-Business Environment

E-business refers to a broader definition of Electronic Commerce, not just the buying and selling of goods and services, but also servicing customers, collaborating with business partners, and conducting electronic transactions within an organization[24].

The worldwide proliferation of the Internet (and networked computing) has led to the growth of business communication over the electronic computer communication networks. This in turn has led to the growth of electronic commerce involving the advertisement and sale of goods and services from business firms to consumers over the network. This has been followed by more ways of conducting business over the Internet, such as business-to-business, business-to-employees, and people-to-people transactions, realizing more potent forms of e-business.

E-business has created a new revolution in business due to faster transactions, lower costs, higher flexibility, and extensive, global reach. However, these advantages come at a cost that mainly consists of a perceived reduction in security and privacy, and the difficulties of managing e-business. As a lot has already been written pertaining to the improvement of the security infrastructure of e-business, this book focuses only on management problems and their solutions.

In the recent past the world has seen a flurry of activities towards the development and implementation of efficient, and generic business models for e-business. Some of the popular models include Supply Chain Management (SCM), and Customer Relationship Management (CRM). Once e-business systems are deployed extensively, organizations will face the question of how to manage e-businesses from the standpoint of configurations, operations, security, performance, and quality. Although efforts are being made towards the development of standards for interoperable e-business frameworks, such as ebXML, Rosettanet, etc., little work has been done on management frameworks for e-businesses. This book provides an overview of management issues of e-business in Chapter 2.

Chapter 1 addresses the following questions:

- What is e-business?
- How can e-businesses be modeled and analyzed?
- What do e-business applications and infrastructures look like?

1.1 Evolution of E-Business

Before we discuss e-business issues, it is necessary to look at the evolution of business management paradigms. Management is a multi-disciplinary subject with inputs from Mathematics, Statistics, Economics, Psychology, Industrial Engineering, Sociology, and Computer Science. Many books on management point to three stages of the Industrial Revolution, i.e., the Agricultural Era, the Mechanical-Engine Age, and the Information Age. We are now in the Information Age. As shown in Figure 1, the Information Age has evolved quite rapidly since the 1960s. It was preceded by the dominance of classical and administrative/bureaucratic theories of management. In general management theories can be categorized into three main schools[14]:

- Technical- Rational
- Behavioral
- Cognitive

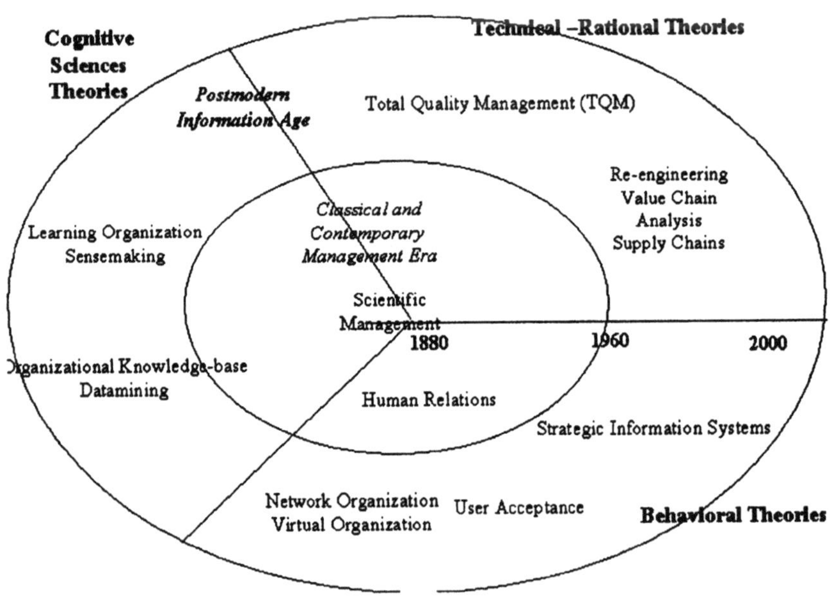

Figure 1. Evolution of Management Theories[18]

The Technical-Rational School focuses on planning, coordination, decision-making and control. It has borrowed knowledge from significant areas, such as Total Quality Management (TQM), Business Process Re-engineering, and Value Chain Analysis. The school believes a management process can be studied and improved mainly by breaking it down into smaller processes, and aggregating the results (just as in many other technical/scientific disciplines, such as Physics and Chemistry)[18].

The Behavioral Science School is important to any course in business or management. It considers the human and organizational behavior issues that concern business productivity. This area has reported a number of empirical observations on how organizations actually behave or what mangers actually do on the job, as opposed to what they say they do. There have been some interesting studies as part of Strategic Information Systems, and Network/virtual Organizations. Modern Psychology, Economics, and Political Science have greatly influenced developments in this area[18].

The Cognitive Sciences School believes that the success of emerging and future businesses will largely depend on the efficiency of organizational processes for acquisition, dissemination and adoption of knowledge. This school relies heavily on developments in Cognitive Science (e.g., sense-making), Networked Information Systems and Information Technology (particularly on the developments in Internet-based electronic commerce, government and health). This book aims at familiarizing readers with a range of concepts, models and methodologies required to manage services/products in the knowledge-based economy. There are also references to the postulates of the two other schools of thought (e.g., TQM, Re-engineering).

E-business is now a fast growing area with inputs from different disciplines and walks of life, including entrepreneurs, large multinational companies, managers, engineers, accountants, housewives, artists, medical practitioners, lawyers, and government officials. Hence there are a number of different perspectives of e-business [24].

- *From a business perspective*, e-business is the delivery of goods, services, information, or payments over computer networks or by any other electronic means. This perspective is also concerned with the business models, and the roles of different stakeholders, and interactions amongst them as discussed in Part 1, Chapters 1 and 2.
- *From a service perspective*, e-business may be viewed as a tool that addresses the desire of firms, consumers and management to cut service costs while improving the quality of goods and increasing the speed of service delivery. This toolkit appears as a set of online middleware services, also known as e-services, in the form of reusable high-level software. This is discussed in Part 2, Chapters 3 and 4.
- *From an architectural perspective*, e-business infrastructure involves a plethora of frameworks, architectures, and protocols to address different types of issues including development, deployment, management and security of e-business. These mechanisms are implemented using

different software and middleware building blocks. This is discussed in Part 3, Chapters 5 and 6.

- *From a standards and technology perspective*, e-business involves interoperability of different communication protocols, middleware, hardware, software and content. Standards play a crucial role in providing the interoperability amongst these different elements of e-business. This is discussed in Part 4, Chapters 7 and 8.
- *From a collaborations perspective*, e-business is the framework for inter- and intra-organizational collaboration, including workflows. It is extremely important to understand the needs and means of supporting collaboration amongst human roles and software entities. This is discussed in Part 5, Chapters 9 & 10.

1.1.1 The Economics of E-Business

Economists view a business through theories on firms and transactions costs. These theories postulate that the role of a firm in an economic system is to make sure that a transaction cost is less within the firm than if it were carried out through the market. The cost of a transaction within a firm is brought down by increasing capital, or by increasing labor (number of employees). Information Technology (IT) helps in reducing this cost for the same capital investment with less number of employees[18]. E-business extends this economic advantage of IT to transactions within and across organizations. In the modern information economy, firms are trying to extract maximum advantage from IT through information systems.

As shown in Figure 2, e-business extends the benefit of IT to firms in another dimension that is shown as a trade-off between richness and reach in a business interaction. This traditional inverse relation between richness and reach forces a firm's management to establish the geographical presence of the firm close to the market[2]. This in turn creates a barrier for new entrants to the market. However, e-business helps achieve better richness of business interaction irrespective of the geographical location of the firm but this removes any barriers for competition.

Economists define the role of a business manager of a firm by the term 'agent' and the agency (managerial) cost increases with the size of the firm (number of employees). E-business reduces agency cost through electronic processes and electronic agent as discussed in Section 1.1.2.

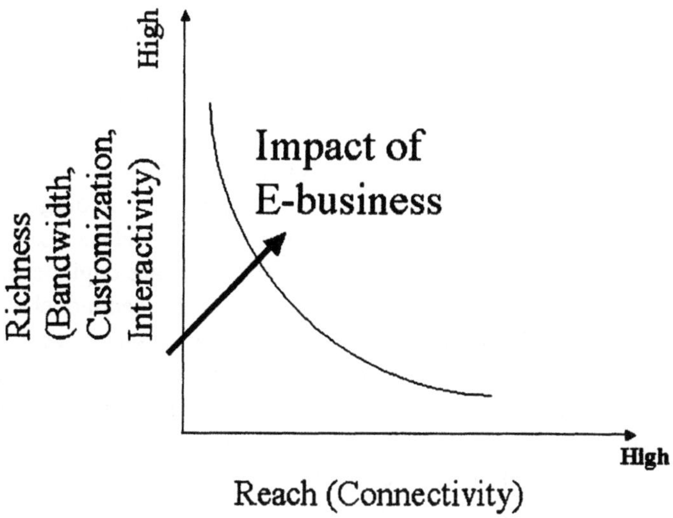

Figure 2. Impact of E-business on firms[2]

Hence enterprises all over the world are fast moving towards adopting e-business to stay competitive in this dynamic marketplace. There are several types of e-businesses depending on the type of business sector, such as e-commerce (buying and selling over electronic media), e-health (treatment of patients over network), and e-government (administration of governments over network). Here are some of the examples of real world e-businesses:

- Shopping online is an increasingly popular activity. At the close of 1999, nearly 55 million people (60 percent of Internet users) were shopping online[7].
- Delta Airlines planned to spend $100 million in 2000 on software and infrastructure to establish its web site, in expectation of a revenue of $1 billion in ticket sales through electronic media (compared with a tiny fraction in 1998)[12].
- It took 62 days for the IC chip manufacturer, Texas Instruments (TI), to complete an e-procurement software implementation in 1999. This project is expected to generate $20 million annual savings in material procurement[12].
- The French government deployed the Teletel/Minitel videotext system in 1979, and by 1995 Minitel provided 26,000 government services [9]. While the Australian government has pledged to move all its services online within 2002, the British government has announced that it would move all its services online by 2005, opening a market worth approximately $18 billion in UK[27].

- In Australia, the New South Wales government has announced that all patients and healthcare providers will be linked through an integrated Electronic Health Record (EHR) system by 2003. This necessitates a sophisticated network security infrastructure called Public Key Infrastructure (PKI)[5].

The challenges of e-business are slow implementations, higher complexity of interdependent business processes and technologies, and scarce skilled resources. Unpredictable implementation delays have been endemic in many software projects. Researchers in software engineering are working on ways to solve this problem. However, the second challenge facing the deployment of e-business is that business processes have become more complex as the number of participants and technologies has increased. Successful development and deployment of e-business solutions requires integrated business processes, including networks of business teams, technology vendors, business partners, systems integrators, and software developers. New software applications, legacy systems, web contents, incompatible technology platforms and protocols, frequent changes, and ongoing updates to application software all add layers of complexity to existing business processes. These problems are compounded due to the lack of available skills[12].

The solution to these problems is being developed through integrated service management strategies discussed later in Part 3 of this book.

1.1.2 Pure vs. Partial E-Business [24]

Figure 3 characterizes e-business in three dimensions, each with two classes (physical and electronic) asper the classification suggested by Turban et al[24]:

- Products: include physical products, such as a furniture items, and electronic products such as music.
- Processes: include physical processes, such as physical delivery of furniture by truck or paper invoicing, and electronic processes, such as delivery and payment for music over the Internet.
- Agents: include physical human managers, and electronic software agents deployed extensively for various purposes over the Internet.

If there is at least one electronic dimension, we will consider the situation e-business, but not pure e-business. For example, buying a book from *Amazon.com* is not pure e-business, because the book is delivered by physical delivery channels. However, buying an e-book from *Amazon.com* or software from *Egghead.com* is pure e-business because the delivery, payment, and agent are all electronic. Pure physical organizations (corporations) are referred to as brick-and-mortar operations, whereas pure e-business organizations are referred to as virtual organizations[24]. An example of a virtual organisation is the transactions of shares over the net using services of an organisation, such as E-Trade.

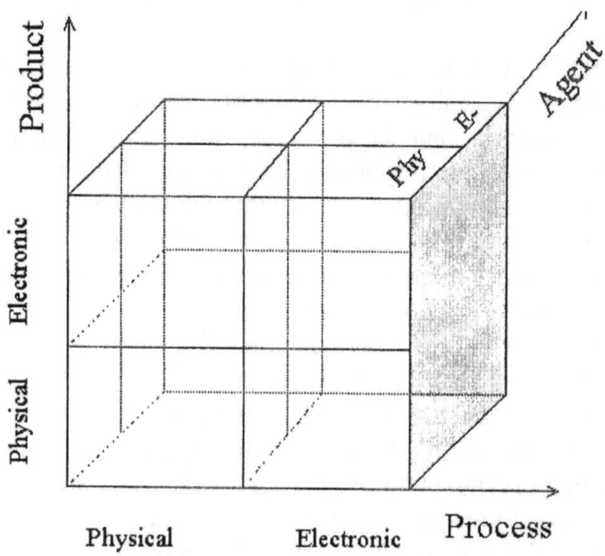

Figure 3. Three Dimensions of E-Business[24]

1.1.3 Virtual Enterprises

Businesses are moving so fast that it is impossible to predict the structure of a company or business division after five years. For example, the company may cease to exist, it may split, or it may merge with another company While the business environment is so volatile, the products and services need to be of high quality and low cost, and should be amenable to quick changes. Gone are the days when a business could plan a decade in advance. In other words, processes are required to bring out quality products and quality services but the life of these products and services may be very short and capital investment has to be paid off within that time. Of course, many new entrepreneurs do not wait to pay off the capital investment preferring to sell the venture at huge profit within two years of its inception. - This was the lure for starting dot companies in the recent past.

The companies or businesses of tomorrow will not be based on any individual company's business or individual company's people. They will be based on joint collaborative work amongst people from different companies at different geographical locations to achieve a particular business objective. A virtual corporation exists more in relationships, intellectual capital and information than in physical facilities. A virtual corporation is a flexible, nimble organizational structure that changes frequently in response to business needs, taps global talent and local markets around the world, and facilitates frequent outsourcing and new business alliances[24].

For example, in Australia four people started a virtual enterprise in investment banking. Typically, such a business is carried out by large banks and financial companies, but in this case, four people from different companies formed, and were responsible for running the entire corporation. They conducted company business entirely through the web, subcontracting out the different functions. The subcontractors specialized in different areas; brokers provided services related to the stock exchange work, bankers were available for on line banking services and so on.

Virtualization may be seen as the latest revolution in the world of technology as illustrated by the following time line [23].

- Industrialization (Steam to robots) 1750 onwards
- Mechanized Transportation (Railroads to luxury jets)- 1850-onwards
- Communication (Telegraph to cell phones)- 1850 – onwards
- Computerization (Mainframes to PCs)- 1950 onwards
- Virtualization (The Internet Economy)- 2000 onwards

While a virtual enterprise-based business model is quite efficient for operational and development purposes, it poses major challenges in the management of such an organization. Existing office-based management practices do not work. Also the success of such an organization is critically dependent on the effectiveness of the networked information infrastructure. But the network infrastructure based on Internet protocols is porous, i.e., there is no guarantee that the information will not get lost on the way. There is also no guarantee that the information will not be leaked to an unauthorized user. Hence network security systems are needed to protect the information at the source.

Since there are not many fixed assets, companies can be broken up or merged easily. The frequent change in telecommunication companies is a case in point. For example, in Australia, telecommunication services were provided until 1991 by a monopoly organization, called Telecom Australia (that became Telstra after deregulation). Thereafter deregulation took place ushering in companies, such as, Optus, Vodafone, AAPT, etc. Telstra then gradually started to privatize by dismantling some divisions into private companies. On the other hand, Telstra has bought the content rights of companies, which provide multimedia content and cable television, e.g., FoxTel. Eventually Telstra may become a virtual enterprise.

The last important advantage of virtual enterprises is the ability to access global talent from anywhere. This is particularly significant due to the worldwide boom in the IT industry causing a tremendous shortage of IT workers in almost all developed countries.

1.1.4 Internet-based E-Business Models

There have been a number of studies in evolving business models for Internet-based environments. It is important to link management solutions to these business models. It is not sufficient to develop technical management solutions solely based on network technology parameters, such as protocols, and software. Laudon and Laudon have classified Internet-based business models in their book, *Management Information Systems*[18], as shown in Table 1.

Table 1. Internet Business Models

No	CATEGORY	DESCRIPTION	EXAMPLES
1	Virtual Storefront	Sells physical goods or services online instead of a physical retail outlets	Amazon.com, Virtual vineyards
2	Marketplace Concentrator	Concentrates at a central point, information about products and services from multiple providers	DealerNet Industry.Net
3	Information Brokers	Provide product, pricing and availability information. Some facilitate transactions	PartNet, Travelocity, Auto-by-Tel
4	Transaction Brokers	Buyers can view rates and terms, and complete business transactions	Etrade, Discount Airtravels
5	Electronic Clearinghouses	Provide auction like settings where price and availability are constantly changing	Internet Liquidators OnSale
6	Delivery	Sells and delivers software, music and other multimedia products over the Internet	Cybersource, SonicNet, PhotoDisc
7	Content Provider	Creates revenue by providing content, earnings through customer pay-by-use or through advertisements	WallStreet Journal.Pathfinder, Catalog
8	Online Service Provider	Provide service and support to hardware and software users	Cyber Media, Tune Up.com

The first model is known as Virtual Storefront. This is a site that displays products and their specifications. A Virtual Storefront simulates the shop window over the web and provides all relevant information including prices, and discounts. *Amazon.com* is an example of a virtual storefront.

The second model is called Marketplace Concentrator. This basically provides concentrated information about a particular type of product, e.g., auto parts, or service, e.g., air travel, from multiple providers at a central point. Examples include DealerNet for auto spares and portals of car manufacturers.

The third model is the Information Broker, which basically makes a match between customers and suppliers. It could be a travel agent, for example, buying an airline ticket for a client on the web through *Travel Online*.

The fourth model is called a Transaction Broker and allows a business transaction to be performed over the web, e.g., buying an air ticket or company shares by paying for it over the net. It may be noted that information brokers are only for information and do not allow any transactions to be performed.

The fifth model is what is known as an Electronic Clearinghouse. This is a site that performs auctions of new and/or used goods, such as uBid.com. Items are on display and intending buyers are invited to submit the price they are prepared to pay within a stipulated time limit. After the expiry of the time limit the successful bidder is informed through the same web site.

The sixth type of e-business, the Distribution Model is commonly used for e-commerce these days. It supports the distribution of products and services over the web. Such products include software, company shares, music, small gifts etc., that can be delivered electronically.

The seventh model, the Content Provider, is concerned with the development and distribution of electronic content over the web. This includes music, electronic games, pictures, videos etc. In Japan, the success of a mobile e-business model called I-Mode is attributed to the effective channelization of content to customers. For example, I-Mode provides an efficient mechanism for large number of content providers to provide content, (e.g., news, tourist guides, timetables etc.) over the mobile wireless media.

The eighth model, the Online Service Provider, provides repair services for different types of equipment and automobiles. The user can furnish necessary information, and discuss simple problems with an online service provider over the Internet before booking a time for physical inspection. This saves substantial amounts of time resources for the user as well as a service provider.

The next section will present e-business concepts from the perspective of business strategies.

1.2 E-Business Strategies

A strategy is a broad-based formula for how a business is going to compete, what its goals should be, and what plans and policies will be needed to carry out those goals. According to Turban et al, *Strategy means a search for revolutionary actions that will significantly change the current position of a company, shaping its future*[24].

It is important that e-business management strategy should fit closely with the corporate business strategy of the firm. Similarly, the IT strategy of the firm is very closely linked to the e-business strategy. As a matter of fact the IT infrastructure forms the core of e-business structure. Hence we discuss in this section some of the business strategies that have direct relevance to e-business.

The two most important factors in determining a firm's strategy are survival and profit. Survival can never be overemphasized considering the failure of so many dot COM companies in the recent past. Therefore any IT solution must support these two major business objectives of a firm. The objectives of this section are:

- How to link business objectives with IT solutions? This question is answered through value chain analysis in Section 1.2.1
- How to define an appropriate service management strategy? Some of the factors are as follows:
  - Learn how and when to use service providers
  - Focus on applying production operation to e-business
  - Get involved in business planning, rebuild relationships with internal and external customers
  - Re-engineer infrastructure for centralized service delivery, remote management and comprehensive measurement of service levels

These factors are discussed in subsequent sections with a view to developing a service management strategy.

1.2.1 Competitive Strategies

A competitive strategy can be either offensive or defensive. An **offensive strategy** usually takes place in an established competitor's market location. Such a strategy is applicable where the market is stable with a few known competitors[24]:

The second type of competitive strategy, a **defensive strategy**, usually takes place in the firm's own current market position as a defense against possible attacks by a rival. According to Porter, defensive strategies aim to lower the probability of successful attack, divert attacks to less threatening avenues, or lessen the intensity of an attack[19]. Porter's competitive models are discussed next.

1.2.1.1 Porter's Competitive Forces Theory[19]

Michael Porter has identified two major models in the area of competitive environment of businesses. One is called the Competitive Forces Model and the second is called the Value Chain. This subsection discusses

Competitive Forces theory and the next subsection will discuss the Value Chain model.

The Competitive Forces theory (Figure 4) presents a conceptual model for the modern competitive business environment. For example, Figure 4 can be used to demonstrate parameters that affect business strategy for typical telecommunication solutions. A firm competing directly with traditional competitors will find the competitive environment is constantly being changed by a number of other factors, such as suppliers, new entrants, substitution products, and customers.

Let us first consider a new market entrant. For example, in Italy Telecom Italia was the monopoly service provider. Many European countries including Italy, UK, Germany and Spain, now allow unlimited competition in telecommunication services. To remain competitive Telecom Italia will have to take into account new market entrants, such as competitors Telefonica and WIND, and their strategies.

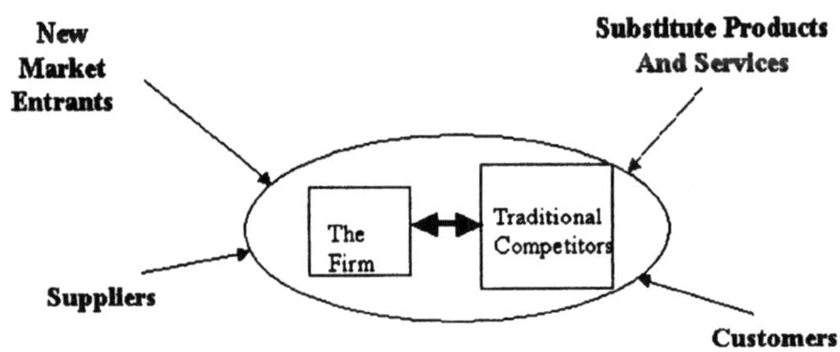

Figure 4. Porter's Competitive Forces Theory[18]

These new entrants usually offer many innovative services including mobile e-commerce, as well as traditional services, such as long distance telephony, data and fax services. They can have a devastating effect on traditional telecom carriers due to their strategy on product substitution.The different types of services may replace existing infrastructure requirements. For example, voice over IP is expected to revolutionize the voice telephony market. All telecommunication companies are now adopting voiceover IP as a major strategy. But consider user enterprises, which digitize voice on a PC and simply send it over the Internet through a server. The service may not be the best but the enterprise concerned often offers it as a substitute product at a very cheap rate. .

Another aspect to be considered is the customer. Customer can always go to the competitors. It is so easy these days to buy telecommunication services. For example, in Australia one can dial a 4-digit number and buy service from any telecom service provider. Customers can also always switch the primary telephone carrier.

Then there is the supplier, the equipment supplier and the service supplier. For example, an Internet service supplier buys the basic service from a telecom carrier. In the fast changing world of Internet services, the relationship between the carrier and the ISP is very important. Both the ISP and the carrier have the option to switch. The best way to safeguard your business is to erect barriers to make it difficult for people to change (change supplier, new entrant, etc.). For example, if the cost of entering the market is very high, new entrants will shy away. The General Motors' Just-In-Time (JIT) inventory system requires all suppliers to link to General Motors through networked computers. General Motors provides the suppliers with all the necessary facilities, software, telecom services, etc., which effectively ties the suppliers to the Company. To go elsewhere would mean high switching costs - having to replace expensive networking facilities that General Motors provides for free as part of the overall deal. Similarly, barriers can be erected for customers through package deals or incentives, such as fly-by points. For example, some telecom carriers give bundled broadband services through cable-telephony, Internet and cable TV.

Finally we must consider substitution services. Such services are very difficult to predict and therefore difficult to stop. One way to safeguard against substitution services is to broaden the communication channel between the firm, its customers, suppliers, and the external environment. This is the being achieved in modern e-business through the Internet and multimedia-based information. So suppliers can communicate with customers through multiple channels. Formerly communication between supplier and customer was restricted to the human-link medium of the sales. This communication channel is being enhanced through web-based links and many different multimedia approaches to connecting customers, suppliers and related organizations.

The next section discusses how the impact of IT is assessed on businesses through value chains.

1.2.1.2 Role of IT services in Value Chains

This section discusses the impact of Information Technology on businesses using a popular analytical technique called the Value Chain model proposed by the renowned management guru-Michael Porter. This model provides a mechanism to analyze the value of information systems and technology in a firm's chain of primary and support activities. Traditional management texts present this model in the context of a manufacturing business where primary activities are inbound logistics, operations, outbound logistics, sales/marketing, and services. The support activities are: administration, procurement, human resources, and R&D.

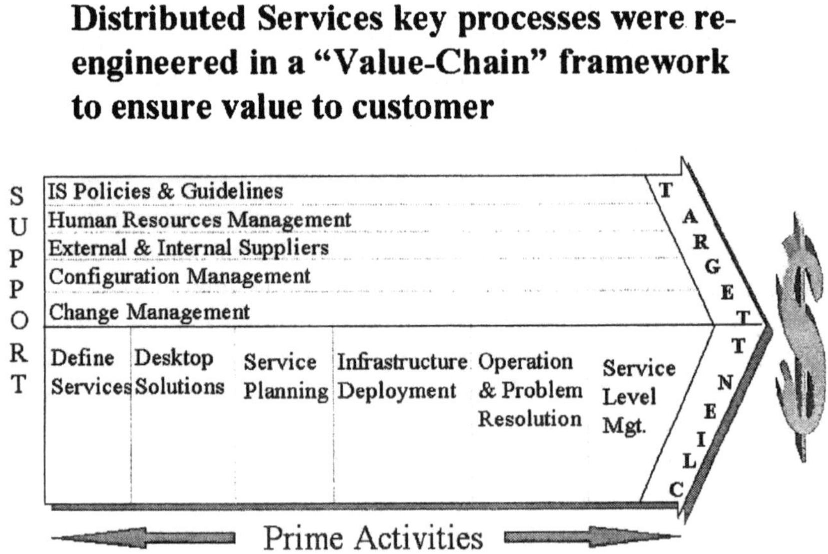

Figure 5. Value Chain Framework[20]

Figure 5 presents the chain of activities in the context of a service business. Here the primary activities are: define services, desktop solutions, service planning, infrastructure deployment, operation and problem resolution, and service level management. Support activities are IS policies, human resources, external and internal suppliers, change and configuration management. With this model it is possible to objectively assess the value of IT in each activity. This would help in the evaluation of IT contribution to the bottom line in a business[12].

For example, IT can be used for product differentiation, a competitive strategy for creating brand loyalty by developing new and unique products/services that cannot be easily duplicated by competitors. IT can also help in the identification of a differentiation scheme through data mining, that allows the analysis of large pools of data relating to customers and products to find patterns and rules that can be used to guide decision-making and predict future behavior.

1.2.2 Cooperative Strategies

There is a common saying in business *-If you can't fight them, join them.* The modern e-business environment offers great potential for collaboration within and across organizations. Cooperative Strategies are now very important for the success of e-business, as working with other firms helps gain a competitive advantage within an industry. A typical cooperative strategy involves a *strategic alliance* through joint venture or value-chain partnership. This may be done through consortia and e-marketplaces. A strategic alliance is a partnership of multiple corporations formed to achieve competitive advantages that are mutually beneficial. The major types of strategic alliance used in e-business are[24]:

Joint venture. A joint venture is a cooperative business activity formed by two or more separate organizations for strategic purposes that creates an independent business entity and allocates ownership, operational responsibilities and financial risks and rewards to each member, while preserving their separate identity/autonomy. Problems of joint ventures include loss of control, lower profits, probability of conflicts with partners, and the likely transfer of technological advantage to the partner. Some prominent examples include joint ventures between Telstra and other vendors (e.g., PCCW in Hongkong) in international telecommunications services.

Value-chain partnership. A value-chain partnership is a strong and close alliance in which a company forms a long-term arrangement with a key supplier or distributor for mutual advantage. An examples of such a partnership is between EDS and General Motors for IT services.

1.2.3 Role of Value Chain

Let us go back to the diagram of Value Chain Architecture (Figure 5). It suggests that any cost or service improvement needs to be justified on the basis of the value chain. So at every level of the value chain there should be value added to justify the feasibility of any management service.

It is possible that different parts are made or different functions carried out by different people or different organizations in a virtual environment. For example, an e-business company may only do the operations in house. The rest of the activities may be outsourced, with infrastructure deployment and logistics supported by different organizations. So management is reduced to the coordination of supplies by different parts of the virtual e-business organization (different companies cooperating through the Internet, and extranets). In this situation, the value chain becomes a supply chain.

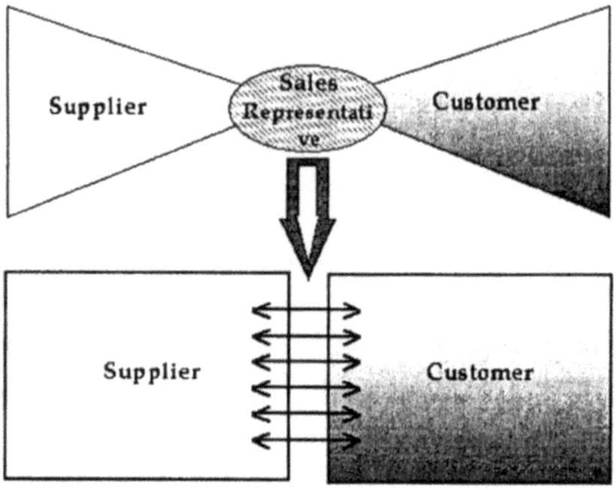

Figure 6. Impact of Internet on Broadening the Supplier-Customer Interface[13]

E-businesses over the Internet replace the traditional business models of buying and selling things on the market. According to the traditional business model a buyer goes to a supplier, or the supplier comes to a buyer, facilitating trust for the business operation. This trust is often created by a middleman or an agent. Management literature has emphasized the role of a sales person in building the trust between a customer and supplier. However, in a virtual environment, the buyer and the seller never meet, making it difficult to nurture the trust that comes through human contact. In e-business, intermediary web sites act as the middlemen.

This raises the question of how to build trust in an e-business environment? The world of e-commerce has developed the concept of a trusted third party. A trusted third party is an organization, e.g., a bank, which enjoys equal trust from both the buyer and the supplier. The sole job of the trusted third party is to provide identification and authentication to the two parties. Parties unknown to each other perform business transactions based on the trust created by the certifications from the trusted third party. The trusted thirds parties issue electronic certificates that address a number of concerns in the context of a business transaction, which include:

- The financial standing of the buyer and the seller
- Authentication of the buyer and the seller
- Authorization of credit card payments without compromising the privacy and confidentiality of credit card information

These issues are addressed in commercial e-business software through trusted third parties and network security features, such as encryption, authentication and authorization discussed in MIS and networking textbooks[7,18].

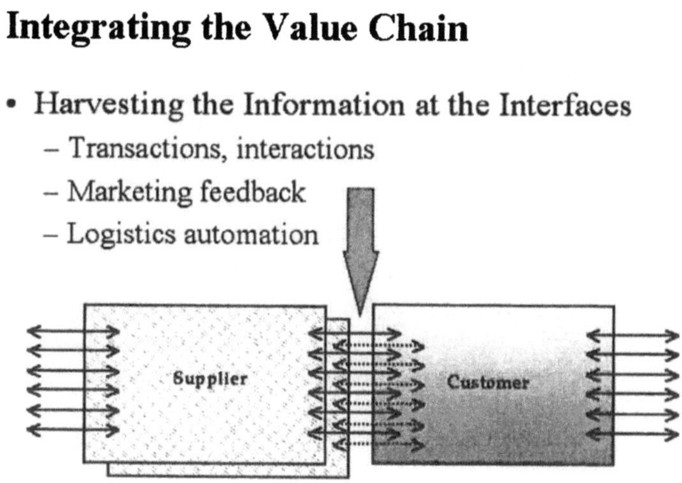

Figure 7. Integrating the Value Chain[13]

A supply chain is a collection of physical entities, such as manufacturing plants, distribution-centers, logistics, retail outlets, people, and information, which are linked together as processes supplying goods or services from source through consumption. The concept of a supply chain helps in the orchestration of strategies to put value chain analysis into practice. In this environment a firm can be seen as providing the most efficient and effective match between the primary producer and the end customer. In traditional businesses the sales representatives represent this bonding between suppliers and customers as shown in Figure 6. The Internet provides a much more effective means of doing that as shown in Figure 7, and obviates the need for any middlemen in a business. Section 1.3 will discuss the application of supply chain management in IT service management.

1.2.4 Changing Focus

Considering new capabilities and value chain analysis/supply chain management, it is imperative that the strategic focus of service businesses should move as shown in Figure 8. In order to implement the strategies shown in Figure 8, the following measures need to be implemented:

- Fact-based reporting on service quality and costs

- Provide utility-like services at high levels of reliability and predictable performance
- Define and report on Service-Level Agreements in business terms
- Participate in joint planning sessions

From		Toward
· Inward, technology-focus	→	Outward, customer and business-focus
· Infrastructure, operations management	→	Information and services management
· Intra-enterprise, back office automation	→	Inter-enterprise value chain integration
· Best effort, emerging technology service	→	Measured, accountable production service

Figure 8. Transition toward Service Managemen[t13]

The first point of fact-based reporting on service quality necessitates some standards and measures for service quality and costs. Service Level Agreements (SLA) are the instruments used for this purpose. Part 2 discusses the problem of the quantification of qualitative service parameters in a step-by-step manner.

The second point of utility-like services means that IT services should be as reliable and predictable as utilities like electric power supply and gas systems. The main problem in achieving this is the unpredictable nature of software performance. Software engineering has yet to achieve the reliability levels of other engineering systems like electric power grids. Standards for this are discussed in Part 4.

The third point is concerned with the definition of Service Level Agreements between service customers and service providers. The idea is to define SLAs in business terms. Since most of the networked service measures are technical, such as 'jitter' and 'throughput', it is necessary to link them to business-level terms. This is a crucial issue, and the whole of Part 3 is devoted to this problem.

Finally, part of software quality problems is due to the lack of clear specification and frequent changes during the course of development. Cooperative management, using Computer Supported Cooperative Work (CSCW) methods, can only solve this. This is discussed in detail in Part 5.

The next section analyzes the characteristics of e-business with a view to developing a framework for the management of e-business services.

1.3 Analyzing E-Business

The Gartner group has identified ten imperatives for the success of e-business. These are briefly discussed below[10].

- *Limit development plans to 24 months* - Due to rapid changes in the status of technology and business environments, it is inadvisable to plan e-business projects for durations of longer than 24 months.
- *Link e-business strategy to the full business strategy* - Many enterprises are handling e-business separately from the traditional business for the sake of speed. However, experience suggests that e-business strategies can be incorporated as part of traditional businesses fairly quickly, and it is the best way to go.
- *Separate strategies according to industry, geography and culture* - According to the basic tenets of management education, any business strategy, including e-business, must consider differences due to geography, culture and industry sector.
- *Give equal weight to internal and external processes* - While Business-to-Business (B2B) strategies give most consideration to the internal processes of large organizations, Business to Consumer (B2C) strategies are mostly based on external processes on the distribution channel. Basically these internal and external processes belong to the demand and supply side of the value chain.
- *Take a holistic approach to implementing e-business models* - Introducing e-business models in an existing business requires substantial time. Therefore, the time frames required and metrics used to measure progress should be estimated based on strategic objectives. Hence short-term metrics, such as quarterly earnings, should not be used as a measure of e-business project progress.
- *Consider alternatives to buy, spin off or transform business models* - The Internet offers many opportunities to transform a business model while adopting the e-business strategies, business process re-engineering. For example, one could buy a dot COM company for this purpose.
- *Adopt "new' rules of e-business* - In the recent past, dot COM companies have aggressively pursued market share without much consideration of operational profits. Accordingly the products have been priced low. Traditional businesses adopting traditional pricing strategies for e-business may fail. Hence they have to adopt the pricing strategy prevalent in e-business.

- *Enhance or destroy distribution channels based on their true power and value* - It is possible to plot distribution channels on a matrix with true power and value for the particular business. While channels showing low power and low value should be eliminated, channels with high power and high potential value must be pursued.
- *Establish new metrics that measure the true effectiveness of e-business* While traditional business measures, such as earnings per share may be adopted; e-business also needs new measures, such as "stickiness" to evaluate web-based businesses.
- *Speed and ruthless execution are everything* - Since e-businesses operate in ever shortening 'Internet time', it is important that an e-business project be implemented in the fastest possible time frame in order to beat any changes in the technology and competitive landscape.

The next sections discuss models to conceptualize the dynamics of e-business with a view to developing the right management strategy.

1.3.1 Umar's Multidimensional Model[26]

The definition of electronic business covers a broad spectrum of business processes involving interactions amongst producers, consumers, and intermediaries (of goods and services), and makes use of an array of technical solutions to support those processes. It is possible to identify several types of e-businesses depending on usage scenarios, parties involved, and a number of business related attributes. Each of these attributes can be given one of three discrete values - Low, Medium, High. The initial set of dimensions includes the following:[26].

- *Number of participants* involved in a single interaction and the *depth of delegation* in the case of supply chains. In a typical e-business environment the number of participants is less than ten, and the depth of delegation is 2/3 levels.
- *Number and Type* of boundaries is concerned with the different administrative domains/ organizational boundaries involved in a transaction. Typically, but not necessarily, boundaries are crossed at each delegation step in a supply chain.
- *Business Volume* is expressed as the typical number of transactions per unit of time. Depending on the types of parties involved, e-business transactions can be about ten transactions per day to tens of transactions per second.
- *Economic Value* of a transaction, e.g., credit card transfer, can also vary substantially. However, most merchants are not equipped to handle very low value (cents) transactions (micro-payments). Economic value also

has repercussions on the required trust level. For example, high valued transactions demand a high trust level.

- *Transaction Turnaround* (TT) is the time it takes for the delivery of electronic goods and services compared with the transfer time of corresponding data plus the overheads, negotiation messages etc. While conventional business TT increases with the increase in the levels of delegation, the number of delegations in the supply chain may not affect e-business TT. This is because of network-based operations. TT is also called Transaction Quality of Service (QoS).
- *Trust Lifetime* defines the time window for which trust must be ensured for an e-business transaction. Trust is implemented between a consumer and provider through various trust models, such as trusted third parties. Typically the cost of a transaction depends on the trust lifetime required for that type of transaction.
- *Level of Bonding* among business partners indicates the amount of information sharing that is necessary for a transaction to be successful. For example, systems using standard protocol or message format have a low level of bonding. But interactions requiring tight synchronization of data at the two ends of a transaction are said to have a high level of bonding. The level of bonding is also low if a transaction is temporary. More permanent transactions require a higher level of bonding.

  Figure 9 characterizes a typical e-commerce application with respect to the above parameters.

As shown in Figure 9, one can characterize an e-business application with the following qualitative parameters:

- Level of Delegation (Supply Chain Depth)- High
- Organizational Boundaries- Medium or High
- Transaction Volume- A range from Low to High
- Economic Value- Medium to High, however most current e-commerce transactions have only Medium value
- Trust Duration- Medium
- Bonding Level- High

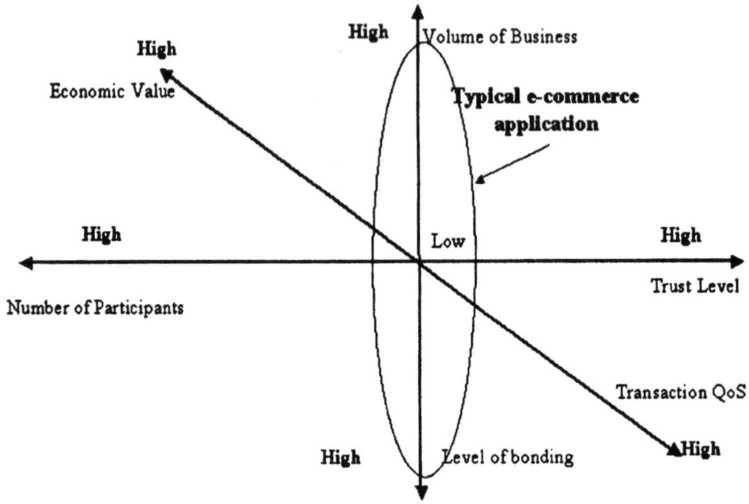

Figure 9. Multidimensional View of E-Business Applications[26]

We now discuss these six dimensions of e-business with respect to an example scenario of an invoicing and billing application:

1. Supply Chain Depth (number of partners) should support long chains with complicated billing as is now evident in many telecommunication services. This is likely to cause costly billing errors in e-business.
2. Organizational Boundaries are important to handle many disparate tax issues and discount structures put in place by different partners of the supply chain
3. Systems need to support high volume transactions in a billing/invoicing application. It is easy to underestimate the importance and volume of such a job.
4. E-businesses need to handle invoices of very low value
5. Usually trust duration for billing and invoicing applications are low in a modern e-commerce environment
6. Level of bonding is high in billing applications because various billing policies of different organizations in the supply chain must tie together to produce a consistent bill for the customer. This is very important because any flaws in this system are likely to cause irreparable damage to an e-business.

The next section presents taxonomy for various types of e-businesses.

1.3.2 Classification of E-Business[24]

A common way of classifying e-business is by the nature of the transaction. E-business may be classified as follows[24]:

- **Business-to-Business (B2B).** All of the participants in this type of e-business are businesses. B2B transactions include the Inter Organization Systems (IOS) transactions and e-market transactions between and among organizations[6].

- **Business-to-Consumer (B2C).** These transactions include retail transactions with individual shoppers. The typical shopper at *Amazon.com* is a consumer or customer. This business model is also called **e-tailing.**

- **Consumer-to-Consumer (C2C).** In this category consumers sell directly to other consumers. Examples include individuals buying and selling various things through ebay.com. Many individuals use personal web pages and portals as well as intranets to advertise items or services.

- **People-to-People (P2P).** This type of transaction is a special type of C2C where people exchange CDs, videos, software and other goods. A well-known organizer of P2P is Napster *(napster.com)*. Cash transactions are possible through Paypal.com.

- **Consumer-to-Business (C2B).** This category includes individuals who use the Internet to sell products or services to organizations, as well as individuals who seek sellers, interact with them, and conclude transactions online. *Priceline.com* is a well-known C2B organizer.

- **Intrabusiness (Organizational) EC.** This category includes all internal organizational activities usually performed on intranets or corporate portals, that involve the exchange of goods, services, or information among various units and individuals in that organization. Activities can range from selling corporate products to employees to online training and collaborative design efforts.

- **Business-to-Employees (B2E).** This is a subset of the intrabusiness category where the organization delivers services, information or products to individual employees

- **Nonbusiness e-business.** An increased number of nonbusiness institutions such as academic institutions, not-for-profit organizations, religious organizations, social organizations and government agencies are using various types of e-business to reduce their expenses or to improve their general operations and customer service. (Note that in the previous categories one can usually replace the word *business* with *organization.*)

- **Government-to-Citizens (G2C)** and to others. In this type of e-business, a government entity buys or sells goods, services or information to businesses or individual citizens.

Turban et al have also defined other classes , such as mobile commerce, collaborative commerce and Exchange-to-Exchange (E2E). It is interesting to note that e-business involves a collaborative relationship between various human and organizational entities. Hence Computer Supported Cooperative Work (CSCW) have a major role in the development and implementation of e-business applications as discussed in Part 5 of this book [21].

1.4 E-Business Infrastructure

Turban et al categorize e-business infrastructure as follows[24]:

1. Common business services infrastructure: security, smart cards/authentication electronic payments, directories/catalogues
2. Messaging and information distribution infrastructure: EDI, e-mail, Hyper Text Transfer Protocol, Chat Rooms
3. Multimedia content and network publishing infrastructure: HTML, JAVA, XML, VRML
4. Network infrastructure: Service (Telecom, cable TV, wireless, Internet), Network type (VAN, WAN, LAN, Intranet, Extranet) and Access (cell phones)
5. Interfacing infrastructure: with databases and business partners' applications.

This infrastructure spans different areas of computer science, information technology, multimedia and telecommunications. These are implemented using a variety of middleware that reside between the operating system and applications in a networked computing system. Middleware are of various types, depending on the e-business services involved, e.g., security, management, directory etc. It involves some of the ever-developing information technology concepts, such as newer protocols (SOAP), evolving definition languages (e.g., XML, WML) and distributed object technology (e.g., DCOM, CORBA, Java RMI etc.). Middleware for e-business management are discussed in Parts 3 and 4 of this book[24].

Two common major concerns of a middleware use are interoperability and integration.

- Interoperability problems occur because there are many different ways of implementing software solutions, and these different solutions may be incompatible depending on the types of formats, languages, and standards used. Software interoperability can be classified into: physical interoperability (depends on physical media, such as floppy, tape, etc.), data type interoperability (depends on data format used in a database), specification type interoperability (depends on interface specification e.g., in CORBA IDL), and semantic interoperability (depends on a variety of semantic interpretations based on context). The last one, semantic interoperability, offers the most challenges to the development of interoperable business solutions[4,22]. Various e-business frameworks such as ebXML, Rosettanet, and HL7 (in e-healthcare), are aimed at alleviating the problem of semantic interoperability.

- The next important issue is the need for the integration of various facets of e-business offered by different divisions of a company. For example, "A manufacturer discovered there were 175 different web pages on its website presenting information about an important industry trend. The pages, which had been developed by various business units from around the world, presented contradictory claims and projections"[14]. Section 1.1.2 discussed the fact that an e-business is likely to involve an electronic agent as opposed to a human agent (sales person) found in a traditional business. This phenomenon offers many benefits to e-business, e.g., reduced costs and better efficiency. However, an electronic agent may expose the integration problems within a company to outsiders. In a traditional business, such an anomaly may be effectively handled by a human agent or sales person. Therefore, commercial e-business solutions take special care to integrate enterprise-wide e-business infrastructure as discussed in Section 1.4.2 based on IBM's e-business framework.

The next section discusses the most important element of e-business infrastructure - intranets, extranets, and the Internet.

1.4.1 The Internet, Intranets and Extranets

The Internet refers to the global Internet that has the capability to offer untethered communication through computers in different parts of the world. For example, enterprises all over the world are now using the Internet for advertising and product promotions. Also the Internet protocols (e.g., TCP/IP) and services (such as email and web browsing) are now being used in different forms within and across organizations to implement intranets and extranets.

Hence business enterprises use intranets to share information within an organization and extranets to share information across organizations, e.g., suppliers, customers etc. A company intranet helps in the dissemination of information e.g., company policies, within the organization. An extranet allows some classified information, e.g., order execution status, to be shared with some specific external organizations, e.g., registered customers. Figure 10 shows a typical business enterprise using intranet, extranet and the Internet that provide the infrastructure for the e-business environment[13].

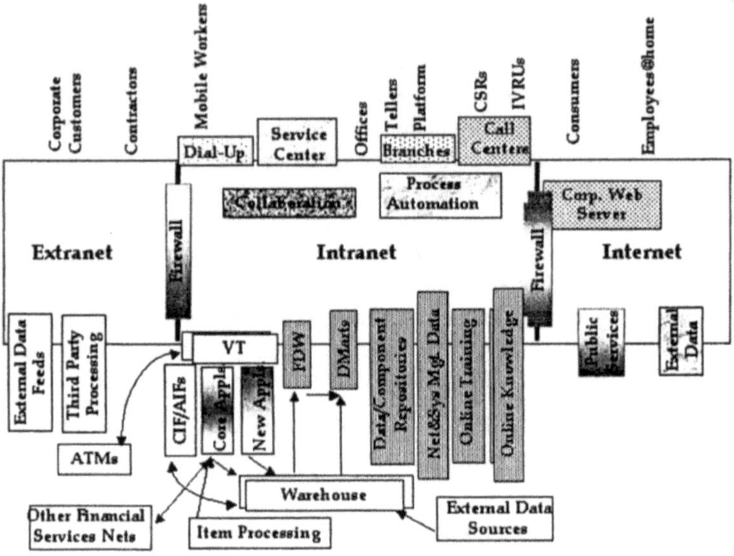

Figure 10. Intranets, Extranets and the Internet[13]

Information services are available on extranet in a restricted form to third party processing organizations or to business partner organizations including suppliers and customers. Extranets are implemented using firewalls that restrict the usage of company information by external organizations. Extranets are extremely important as they allow people from the outside to know about company business, products and services, without access to company private information.

1.4.2 Middleware for E-Business

E-businesses require more than just network applications like email and WWW. One needs to consider some services, such as, security and management that are common to many e-business applications.

Hence the world has seen the development of middleware, some network software that resides between the operating system and business processes, that facilitate the development of complex e-business applications. For example, the process of payment through the Internet involves important security considerations, such as confidentiality and privacy of credit card details. Recent commercial e-business products use a variety of middleware, such as directory, e.g., based on X.500, encryption, e.g., public key infrastructure), distributed objects, e.g., CORBA, Java beans, or DCOM, and management, (e.g., SNMP MIBs). A number of companies, e.g., Checkpoint firewalls, now specialize in different types of middleware that are eventually used in e-business applications.

Middleware could include various types of software that could support the development of e-business applications. Modern web-based information systems involve multimedia information being accessed from different locations on the globe. Hence there is a need to separate the information content and business logic from the infrastructure. This has led to a revolution in telecommunication services. In the previous generation voice telecom services, the service offerings depended on the type of telecom switch in place. The present day telecom switching and transmission separate service offerings from the switching and transmission fabric. Again the Internet based IP protocols are becoming the means of convergence between diverse software-based business services and largely hardware and firmware based network equipment.

Another major source of the popularity of e-business applications is that the web-browser provides a common user interface. That is perhaps, the biggest advantage that has come from Internet developments. In the past, different business applications had different looks and feels in user interfaces. Hence there used to be a learning curve, sometimes quite daunting, associated with any new application. Therefore the web browser has become the de-facto user interface for all service and planning solutions.

1.4.3 E-Business Patterns

Having seen the various examples of e-business middleware, the next question would be how to put together these middleware building blocks? The field of patterns is well known in the world of object-oriented software that involves mechanisms to allow the reuse of software, thereby improving the reliability, quality and cost effectiveness of a software solution. Patterns provide a flexible, business-level description mechanism for integrating middleware.

This section discusses evolving architecture for e-business using the pattern-based framework announced by IBM in 2001. Patterns for e-business are a group of reusable assets that can help speed the process of developing applications. According to a white paper from IBM, e-business patterns are discussed as follows:[15]

- Business patterns that identify the interaction between users and businesses.
- Application software building blocks/components that are driven by the customer's requirements.

- Product mappings to populate the solution. Products could be from IBM or other vendors
- Guidelines for the design, development, deployment and management of e-business applications.

1.4.4 Application framework for E-Business

E-business systems use a number of types of web technologies including Hyper Text Markup Language (HTML), Extensible Markup Language (XML), Extensible Stylesheet Language (XSL), Javascript, Structured Query Language (SQL), ActiveX Data Objects (ADO), Hyper Text Transfer Protocol (HTTP), VBScript, and Active Server Pages (ASP) [7,24].

Since e-businesses are developing so fast, one can not expect the availability of a Java programmer to put together a simple e-business application. Hence it is necessary to provide a simple "drag and drop" type user friendly development environment so that an e-business can be put together without any programming. Hence many software vendors have announced application frameworks for e-business system development, and these frameworks are now available in the e-business development environments.

The IBM Application Framework for e-business provides the framework, using open standards, to build platform independent applications for e-business. The Framework's architecture model is based on an n-tier distributed environment. Any numbers of tiers of application logic and business service are separated into components, and connected using industry-standard protocols, servers, and software connectors. The model identifies key elements for developing and deploying e-business applications. Each element is based on open, vendor-neutral standards, allowing the substitution of components from any vendor that supports those standards[15].

E-business application frameworks are now available from a number of leading vendors including Oracle, Microsoft, HP, Sun, and SAP and also from consulting organizations, such .as the Gartner group, Anderson Consulting, Price Water House Coopers, and SAA Consultants. We shall discuss the role of standards in next chapter and in Part 4 towards the integration of diverse e-business application and management frameworks.

1.5 Chapter Summary

This Chapter has provided a brief overview of an e-business environment and management issues.

The Chapter started with a discussion of the evolution of e-business models from the traditional business perspective. This was followed by a discussion of e-business strategies based on the traditional business strategies, such as Porter's competitive forces theory, and value chains, with particular reference to their relevance to emerging virtual enterprises.

Section 1.3 discussed ways of analyzing e-businesses based on certain academic and industry guidelines leading to the classification of e-businesses into a few categories, such as Business-to-Business, Business-to-Consumer, People-to-People, User-to-User, Business-to-Employee, Governemnt-to-Citizens etc.. There was then a discussion of e-business infrastructure including intranets/extranets, middleware and emerging e-business application frameworks and patterns.

The next Chapter will discuss the four dimensions involved in the deployment of e-business management systems; people, organization, process, and technology. This will be followed by discussions of architectural and standards perspectives in Parts 3 and 4 of the book. Part 5 will present an integrated view of integrated management at various levels; process level, architecture level, and standards/implementation level.

1.6 REFERENCES

1. Adams J., Koushik S., Vasudeva G. and Galambos G., *Patterns for E-business: A Strategy for Reuse*, IBM Press, 2001
2. Alexander S. and Kock J.D., "The World of the Future", *Insite Connect Innovations News Letter*, No. 48, Sydney Australia, Nov 2001, ISSN: 1441-0672
3. Amazon.com, http://www.amazon.com, 2001
4. Cameron H.T., et al; "Software Interoperability"; *Center of Integrated Facility Engineering*; Stanford University; 25/12/1996, http://www.dacs.dtic.mil/techs/interop/title.shtml
5. Comerford, R. "Keeping the Net Up", *IEEE Spectrum*, January 2001
6. Cunningham M. S., *B2B: How to Build a Profitable E-Commerce Strategy*, Cambridge: Perseus Publishers, 2001
7. Deitel H.M, Deitel P.J. and Steinbuhler K., *E-Business and E-Commerce for Managers*, Prentice Hall, 2001, ISBN:0-13-032364-0
8. Dev R., *Managing the Enterprise Network: Command and Control*, Cabletron Systems Inc., March 1993
9. Elmagarmaid and McIver W., "The Ongoing March Toward Digital Government", *Guest Editors' Introduction to the Cover Feature on E.Gov, IEEE Computer*, February 2001, pp. 32–39

10. Frick V. and Lill A., "Ten Imperatives for E-Business Success", *Gartner Group Commentary*, http://gartner11.gartnerweb.com/public, August 2000
11. Heard S., "The Good Electronic Health Record (GEHR) System", *Proceedings of the International Health Informatics Conference (HIC2000)*, Adelaide Australia, September 2000
12. Heiman V. and Pang A., "Evolving Challenges of Managing eBusiness", *An IDC White Paper*, IDC USA, June 2000
13. Herman J., "Achieving World Class IT Service Management", *HP-OpenView'98 presentation,* April 1998
14. Herman J., "The E-business Imperative for Enterprise Integration", *Business Communication Review*, pp 22-24, February 2001
15. IBM, "Navigating to a New Generation of E-Business Applications:Business Patterns", March 2001, http://www-106.ibm.com/developerworks/patterns/
16. Koehler D., "Service Level Monitoring", *HP-OpenView'98 presentation*, April 1998
17. Krammer M., Rozwell C., Reilly G., and Schulman J., "E-Business Dimension Model: Clarity Beyond the Hype", *Gartner Group Commentary*, USA November 2000, http://gartner11.gartnerweb.com/public
18. Laudon K.and Laudon J., *Management Information Systems: Organization and Technology*, Prentice Hall 1998
19. Porter, M. E., *Competitive Advantage: Creating and Sustaining Superior Performance*, New York: Free Press, 1985.
20. Raffoul W., "Pragmatic Approach for IT Service Management", *HP-OpenView'98 presentation,* April 1998
21. Ray P., *Cooperative Management of Enterprise Networks*, Kluwer Academic/ Plenum Publications, May 2000, ISBN:0-306-46276-1
22. Ray P. and B. Vargas, "Middleware for the Interoperability of Hospital Information Systems", submitted for publication, Nov 2001
23. Simke J., "Open Networks -Transforming to Networked Economy", Price Waterhouse Coopers, September 2000, http://www.pwcglobal.com/ca-presentations
24. Turban E., King D., Warkentin, M. and Chung H.M., *Electronic Commerce 2002: A Managerial Perspective*, Prentice Hall, (2nd Ed.), Chapter 1, pp 6-7, 2002
25. Umar A., *Object-Oriented Client/Server Internet Environments,* Prentice Hall, 1997
26. Umar A. and Missier P., "A Framework for Analyzing Virtual Enterprise Infrastructure", *Proceedings of the Ninth International Workshop on Research Issues in Data Engineering: Information Technology for*

Virtual Enterprises (RIDE-VE'99), Sydney, IEEE press, Los Alamitos, California, USA, March, 1999
27. Van Duk S., "Aust Vendors to Show case Online Government Model Overseas", *Computer World*, Australia, March 5, 2001, http://www.computerworld.com.au

Chapter 2. Management of E-Business

Chapter 1 presented e-business environments from the perspective of management theories and models, and infrastructure. This chapter presents e-business from the perspective of management and deployment of e-business. The discussion starts with the multidisciplinary nature of e-business. This is followed by the four key areas concerning the deployment and management of e-businesses, namely people, organization, processes and technology.

Because e-business is a new field, it is now developing its theoretical and scientific foundations. This field is based on several different disciplines. The major e-business disciplines and some samples of the issues with which they are concerned are marketing, computer sciences and software engineering, finance, economics, accounting and auditing, information systems[19]. For examples, e-business has revolutionalized the process of marketing management by changing the processes of market research (data collections analysis), segmentation, product development, sales and customer support operations. Similarly, taxation experts are grappling with the problem of developing uniform tax laws for e-business that cuts across the traditional boundaries of taxations (borders of countries). Information technology is playing and increasingly significant role in many of these problems as discussed in Chapter 1.

This book focusses on management issues relating to the e-business infrastructure (information systems, computing and information technology perspective). Many of these management problems are similar to those faced with the management of information technology infrastructure in a business enterprise. This chapter and the subsequent chapters will discuss management questions, such as:

1. How to specify the operational requirements of e-business management?
2. How to arrive at a common understanding of e-business operational management issues across organizational and national boundaries?
3. How to specify and design an automated management infrastructure?
4. How do Service Level Agreements map to underlying tools for network, systems and application management?
5. How to prioritize and tune networked IT services to meet the dynamic needs of an e-business?

Managerial issues in e-business come up quite late in the development cycle, during deployment and operations, often leading to ad-hoc solutions. Managerial issues concern a range of factors including performance, security, usability, maintainability etc.

There are many network and systems management products available in the market implementing standards, such as SNMP. However, there is a major difference between the requirements of network and systems management and e-business management. While network management and systems management solutions are designed for hardcore technical people, such as network engineers, and systems administrators, e-business management solutions must be easily understandable to non-technical people, such as entrepreneurs, business managers, marketing executives, accountants, and professional users from all walks of life. Therefore, it is necessary to approach this subject from a business management perspective, and the solutions must be designed in a top-down fashion. This chapter discusses e-business management issues with linkages to various other parts of this book wherever relevant.

2.1 E-Business Management Requirements

The significance of e-business management can be analyzed in terms of the business costs. Let us look at the telecommunication service costs over the past ten years vis-à-vis the cost of IT components. The costs of hardware and software have gone down exponentially but the costs of telephone services have gone down linearly during this period. The cost of management has gone up. Hence the management cost is the main factor determining the cost of e-business in telecommunication industry. Companies are now investing heavily in management technology because there is always some gain to be made through good management.

E-business amplifies the common problems of time to market, quality, and resource scarcity. According to a recent survey of business enterprises, companies are motivated to deploy e-business management solutions to achieve competitive advantage, optimize service levels, and provide users with business benefits and to deploy faster. The main challenges for e-business management are: dealing with rapidly evolving technology, lack of expertise, security, investment required, and the maturity of e-business management products. Since companies have been mostly busy with getting their infrastructures for e-business built, e-business management remains an unfulfilled customer need and vendor opportunity[6].

In view of these circumstances, enterprises take many different approaches to e-business management including specialized tools (37%), home grown solutions (13%), no management at all (13%), component managers (9%), and enterprise managers[11]. However, it is important to have a comprehensive integrated solution. The features required for e-business management are:

- *Service-Level Management-* concerned with delivering management information in business-terms. This issue is discussed in more detail in this chapter and in Part 3.
- *Cooperative management-* concerned with management solutions involving the collaboration of people within and across organizations, e.g., partners, vendors, and customers. It also involves methodologies to build, deploy, operate, and maintain management solutions[21]. This issue is discussed in more detail in Part 5.
- *Application management-* concerned with the management of diverse, complex e-business application software, and the hardware platforms they run on. This issue is discussed in more detail in Part 3.
- *Integration capabilities* – concerned with the integration of legacy and modern heterogeneous applications, using multiple application environments, and configuration management tools. This issue is discussed in more detail in Part 4.
- *Security-* an important factor inhibiting the growth of e-business is the lack of perceived security in the Internet environment. Organizations are fast adopting measures, such as Public Key Infrastructure (PKI) for this purpose. A discussion of this issue is beyond the scope of this book.
- *Scalability-* of paramount importance in e-business where the scale of operation multiplies within a short time to previously unpredictable proportions.

Investments in network and systems management have not had commensurate impact on the effectiveness of IT service management. That is because services are so closely related to business operations, and it involves a number of business related issues, hitherto not considered in network and systems management. A substantial amount of work still needs to be done in this area. IT service management requires collaboration amongst a number of groups of professionals with different types of expertise as shown in Figure 11. The key software systems used are network and systems management platforms and applications.

To increase the service effectiveness in an e-business system, it is necessary to equip people and the organization with the right concepts, processes and technology. People become part of the culture of an organization, and that culture is hard to change. Whereas with technology one can throw away equipment and bring something new, any cultural change requires a change in the mindset of people, and that takes time. Staff must be trained to understand the objectives of service management.

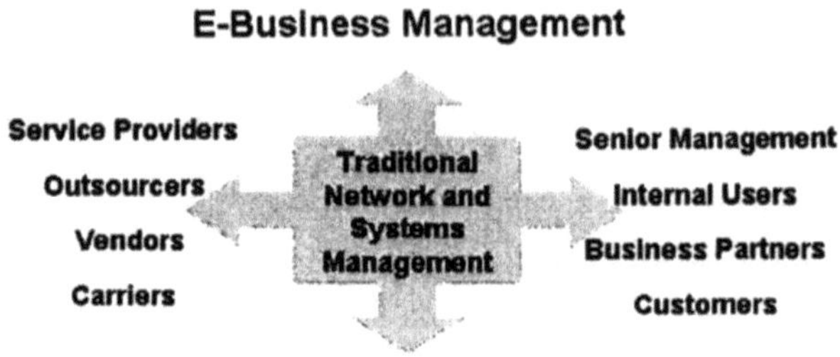

Figure 11. Expanding the Scope of a Management System[8]

There used to be a time when Telecom carriers, such as Telecom Italia, Telecom Australia, and Deutsche Telecom were monopolies. The managers in a user company in a particular country would be bound by the offerings of the monopoly telecom carrier. Options are now available for people to buy services from multiple service providers thanks to deregulation of telecom services Therefore telecom carriers and user organizations both now have to rely on IT-based service management techniques for the effective definition, deployment, and monitoring of services. The logical allocation of IT resources to different parts of the supply chain or value chain will depend on what is the valued being added in that part of the chain.

The deployment of e-business management needs to follow a set of practical guidelines:

- Define the services the business depends on and the service levels it needs and can afford. There is no need to define any theoretical measures that are too difficult to measure, or difficult to interpret.
- Make data-driven decisions on service provisioning, infrastructure upgrades and support process improvement, often intuitions can fail unlike in some other mature engineering disciplines.
- Report on IT service quality and costs in business terms; not technology terms-SLAs need to be simple to understand for all people involved in the business.

2.2 E-Business Management Framework

An e-business is much more than a corporate portal. The e-business field is a comprehensive one, involving many activities, organizational units, and technologies. There are dozens of e-business applications that include shopping in online stores and malls, buying stocks, finding a job, conducting an auction, collaborating electronically on research and development projects, and running global exchange[9]. To execute these applications, companies need the right information, infrastructure, and systems[21].

E-business management frameworks largely consist of four major factors:described as follows:

- **People** - with new skill sets for management of relationships with business partners, e.g., suppliers, outsourcers, and customers, over the network. Detailed discussions are available in Part 5.
- **Organization** - with new staff roles and re-centralization of analysis, report and support wherever feasible to save the cost of support and management services, as discussed in Parts 2 and 5.
- **Processes** - information driven, re-engineered, conforming to public policies. Network and Systems management policy frameworks may be extended to e-business management. Detailed discussions are available in Parts 2 and 3.
- **Technology** - incorporating management systems infrastructure including evolving protocols and standards as discussed in Part 4.

We now discuss each of these factors one by one. It may be noted that e-business management is in a stage of infancy right now. Hence this discussion borrows terminology and concepts from integrated management that consists of network, systems and service management.

2.3 Role of People in E-Business Management

As long as the systems and applications that they require are working, and required data is being passed to departments, users are unconcerned with the overall operation of the global IT infrastructure. This attitude is similar to a citizen's view of public utilities, such as water, electricity, telephone, and sewer services. Residents and businesses are dependent upon these services and expect them to be available and working well. The services require a sophisticated infrastructure, but if the infrastructure provides the required availability and performance, most citizens are not interested in the system's inner workings. The methods used to deliver the services are invisible to the consumers. If, for example, the electricity is shut off, the consumer's chief concern is when service will be restored, not whether it was due to a tree falling in their neighborhood or the failure of a transformer in a major substation.

On the other hand, the people at the electricity company must be very focused on the entire power grid and must be able to identify where problems start and how to fix them. However, they cannot focus upon the individual components to the point of losing sight of the fact that their objective is the delivery of electricity to the consumer. Their first concern must be with rerouting power around a failed component, if possible, before repairing that component. Likewise, IT's primary objective must be the delivery of services to the end user[11].

This involves a cultural change for many organizations that translates to more customer service focus and measured accountability. Staff need to understand the goals and objectives of the service management program. There is a need to cooperate with other service providers. No service business can provide everything on its own. There is a need to leverage other service providers. Going to the basics of value chain analysis, one needs to re-balance organization toward activities that add most unique value to the business.

The major contribution to management cost increases come from one factor- people. The quality of most services depends heavily on the quality and effectiveness of the people involved. Hence people costs consist of salaries, training and recruitment expenses, unpredictable absences, and the organizational costs of providing a productive environment for these people. Most of the support costs are factored in as a percentage of salaries of people. Hence there is the new ruthless campaign of reducing headcount (number of people) as a means of demonstrating efficiency. While headcount has gone down in traditional operations, there has been uncontrolled growth of headcount in some new technology areas due to the increasing size of support teams.

Thanks to the rapid strides made in global telecom services, it is now possible to access human talent on a global basis. For example, many multinational organizations, such as Intel, Siemens, HP and IBM have started their virtual service desk in Bangalore, India because of the availability of quality people at low cost in that part of the world. Companies are now able to provide a 24-hour service by routing the call to the appropriate part of the world. For example, when customers (world wide) call the company online service line, their enquiry may land at the desk of a technician in India, USA, Australia or Europe, all equally trained in the company products and services.

2.4 Organizational Perspective of E-Business Management

The success of deploying service management depends largely on how the organization adapts to rapid changes in the business environment. Although there is a tremendous amount of hype about technology, it is important to focus on service lines; not technology silos. It is necessary to establish service managers and process owners. There is this new reverence towards the internal customer. While decentralization gives flexibility, the pressures on margins will lead to greater centralization of operations and support. The key to success lies in seeking economies of scale, uniform measurement and appropriate automation.

There are three views of Information Technology and e-business[11]:

- Company Viewpoint
- User Viewpoint
- IT organization Viewpoint

A company focuses on the business goals that will lead to success in the marketplace, and sees IT as a provider of some of the infrastructure that is required to achieve those business goals. E-business involves many relationships with other organizations in a supply chain as discussed in the previous chapter.

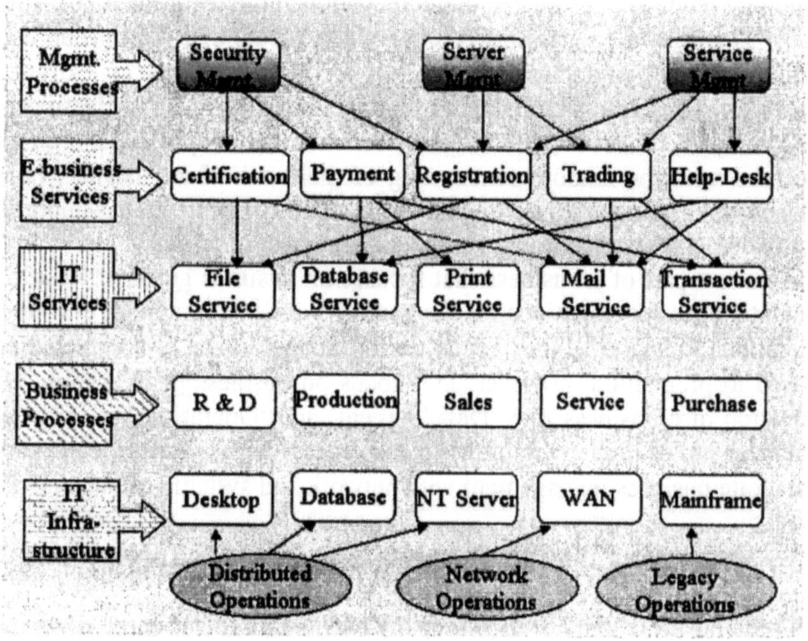

Figure 12. Islands of Management[11]

Executing the company's goals are business users, who need particular systems and applications to do their jobs. The users implement the e-business management policies of a company, using a myriad of IT tools and systems. There are a number of people issues, such as user training, and usability of IT, important for e-business as discussed in Section 2.3.

The IT organizational perspective of e-business management is concerned with the development better management of technology for the benefit of the company and users. This section presents the roles of an IT manager in this context.

As an e-business organization grows, individual groups are created with specific areas of responsibility. These groups focus on portions of Information Technology, or on one or two key business applications, and become 'Islands of Management' as shown in Figure 12. Each of these groups or islands has its own internal specialists who support the mission and goals of that group, but this is often to the exclusion of the needs of other departments. Management tools are deployed to assist each of the groups, which are usually very effective in their own environment, but are not designed for integration across the whole e-business environment.

As e-business organization grows and as islands of technology are integrated into more complex business systems, effective management of technology requires coordinated communication and integration across these groups. This results in attempts to integrate the tools that each group uses. Supporting this conglomeration of individual tools becomes extremely difficult for e-business organizations, and decreases the overall effectiveness of the company. Even outside IT, end-user department specialists are more concerned with the smooth functioning of their individual 'island', rather than how their applications integrate with other components in supporting corporate goals. This is the crux of the management problem.

There is a part of e-business that focuses on business goals, at least long enough to write specifications for the purchase or development of e-business applications to support those goals. Once the application is completed and released to production, however, IT's focus on business goals wanes. This bifurcation of e-business into 'Development' and 'Operations' is important to the problem of implementing Business Process Management- a term used to integrate business management with network and systems management.

2.4.1 Organizing the Development of E-Business Applications

As the business units of the company become more and more dependent upon IT to meet their goals, the tendency is for the IT developers that support a business unit to associate very closely with that unit, building the applications that their clients request. These 'stovepipes of development', result in business system architectures within the stovepipe that may not integrate well with the architectures of systems in other parts of the environment.

When designing the applications, the individual departments are primarily focused on including specific features and functions that will meet their own department's needs. This narrower view makes it more difficult to provide IT-based services across the entire enterprise. For example, if the

Customer Service Department wants automated information feeds from Marketing and Sales about new orders or new customers, the applications supporting the two departments have to be linked. This creates new combinations of not just applications, but also the e-business components upon which the applications operate.

This situation is compounded by the availability of off-the-shelf applications from vendors, which are typically applications that provide a common business function. In reality, these applications are even less integrated with a company's e-business management architecture. Therefore, the IT department ends up with many individually developed and implemented discrete components, which they are expected to seamlessly manage and service. Suddenly, Customer Service also wants to know when service problems arise with Marketing and Sales applications. Over time, this has become a very real problem, a manageability nightmare for the operations arm of the e-business organization[11].

2.4.2 Organizing E-Business Operations

The islands of management problem and the unmanageable application nightmare make it impossible for the e-business organization to manage the environment efficiently and effectively. The focus of IT, especially the segment of the organization that provides services to the end user, is to manage and report on discrete components. The end user is like the customer of the electric company; no matter how many of the components are currently operating at 100% availability, they still remember that their power was out last week, and are not happy about it.

The paradigm of islands of management and the unmanageable applications nightmare persist despite the frustration experienced. The first reason for this is inertia, where the momentum of past practice perpetuates itself in future practices. Small groups, major departments, and even entire companies are built on the islands of management described above, and continue to feed the proliferation of disjointed systems and applications. Business users and their development stovepipes perpetuate this situation because they are unconcerned with the interoperability of their applications, as long as the tools, data, and support they require are available.

The second reason is that IT focuses on ensuring that each individual component runs smoothly. Therefore, most IT management tools are oriented to managing individual pieces of technology. Even tools that are implemented company-wide, such as desktop management tools, are not necessarily designed to integrate with any other system in a corporation. A third reason, one that can begin to suggest a solution to the dilemma, is that the users of Information Technology have a different view than those who implement or support it. Communication between the disparate groups has never been sufficient to lead to a better way of conducting IT's business. In order to meet this challenge, it is imperative that companies adopt a new paradigm, Business Process Management.

Having gone through cycles of change in the business, such as efforts like Business Process Reengineering, companies now recognize that the key to success is a clear definition and thorough understanding of key business processes. Since e-business is so integral to the attainment of a company's business goals, it should play an important part in the execution of business strategy. Business Process Management (BPM) is a new and innovative management approach that dramatically increases the effectiveness of e-business organizations.

Beginning with business goals as the focus, e-business resources are viewed as an integrated system that supports these goals, rather than as discrete components that provide specific and distinct functions. That is, BPM is a business-centric approach to the management of the e-business environment, focusing on business objectives instead of components and technologies. According to a recent survey 65% of CIOs of top American companies believe their jobs are becoming more business-focused[11]. Using the BPM approach gives e-business the ability to focus on the business processes that it supports, the business functions that are implementing those processes, and ultimately, to support the success of their company in competitive marketplaces.

2.4.3 Dual Role of E-Business Service Manager

Traditionally IT service has been an internal service function in a corporate entity (a cost center). The new service management environment demand that the IT service management department be treated like an external service provider or a profit center. This transition presents some formidable organizational problems. For example, the head of MIS in a corporate entity is also the main expert in IT services for the organization. If his department is to be treated like other service providers, this expertise may cause some serious clashes of interests.

Therefore, the e-business organization within the company can be seen as playing two distinct roles:

1. IT as service provider to the business
2. IT as service manager for the business

The first role provides appropriate IT services to the business in partnership with various business functions. This role is charged with the responsibility of development, deployment, and maintenance of IT services for the business as per an agreed quality and cost level. It needs to carry out a measured fact-based value for cost analysis. Every item has to be systematically costed and charged. There is no leeway in this costing exercise unlike in many internal functions of an enterprise. At the same time, the IT organization has to play the crucial role of a partner in business-driven IT capability planning. The tasks of this role include systems planning, development and implementation, including software development.

The second role is charged with the responsibility of implementing the IT policies and projects of the organization using a mixture of internal and external service providers. This is more the role of a consultant. This role demands that IT organization devise standards and objective measures for professional, measured deployment and delivery of services. The tasks in this role include the development of enterprise-wide IT policies, standards, frameworks and architectures. One of the major tasks is to oversee the coordination of a number of internal and external service providers.

There are obvious clashes of interest in these roles. Therefore, many organizations are putting in measures to de-link these two roles. This problem is best described through a discussion of processes for e-business management as detailed in Section 2.5.

2.5 The Process Perspective

A business process is defined as "a collection of applications, workflows and associated e-business resources that are required to perform a set of related tasks that are of major importance to a business."[11] In today's corporate environment, business is increasingly empowered by a collection of applications and other resources. Business processes are based on those applications and are critical to the operations or profitability of a company. Adding to the mix is the proliferation of electronic commerce applications, which places the IT resource directly at the interface with key suppliers and corporate customers.

Most business processes require interaction between multiple applications. However, sometimes the umbrella of a major system, for example, SAP R/3, conceals the existence of these individual applications. Also, applications such as e-mail, that on the surface seem to only affect the internal processes of a company, may actually be a part of an automated workflow that is critical to certain key business processes. Traditionally, IT deals with individual applications, rather than groups of applications that are associated with a single business process.

Business workflow modeling software should allow users to assign business values to the components of the business process. This feature will provide e-business managers with the business impact of these processes. It also shows the business impact of outages, allowing for the proper prioritization of e-business tasks. In addition, IT can use these values to model the system cost of components, from a business perspective. BPM software should have simulation capabilities that allow business and IT managers to simulate 'what if' scenarios to assist in planning for the future. This feature will be invaluable in justifying proposed upgrades and the addition of new technology. In addition, it can help in determining if the availability of the current infrastructure is adequate to support business requirements.

2.5.1 Business Process Management (BPM)

Business Process Management takes a big picture view. It is the top-down management of the system of components in a business environment, rather than the management of discrete components. BPM is a holistic management approach, and consists not only of managing all the IT components of a system, but also of understanding and using the relationship between the components and the business process workflows for improvement of the business. Effective implementation of BPM includes the use of a comprehensive Service Level Management capability across the IT enterprise environment. It also includes the ability to identify and measure business transactions (Transaction Management). More importantly, BPM provides the ability to use the information gathered through these advanced management techniques to model and predict the impact of IT changes on the business and the impact of business process changes on the IT environment.

BPM must work in tandem with Service Level Management (SLM) software, in order to totally manage the provision of service to users. Therefore, the BPM software must be integrated with an SLM solution in order to compare the actual availability of the application to the service levels that are specified in the Service Level Agreement. In addition, BPM and SLM together, can analyze the effects of time to repair, as well as other important information related to the delivery of service. BPM software should perform business transaction management. This level of granularity is required in order to do an effective job of managing the business process from an end user's perspective.

Aggregations, which measure the average response time for a group of transactions, may be helpful. But if the BPM software can measure the response times of specific transaction types, this information is more valuable in monitoring specific segments of business processes. Risk management features, such as simulation capability, monitoring for minimum and normal requirements for critical resources, etc., should be included in the BPM software. The BPM graphical user interface (GUI) should be intuitive, user-friendly and easily navigable. The GUI should graphically display the relationships between the business process components, as well as real-time information about the status and health of the business process and its components. In addition, drill-down capability and relevant information must be provided in order to allow for quick diagnosis of a problem.

Ease-of-use is extremely important because the users of Business Process Management may include employees with diverse skill levels, including business users, management and IT staff. Once the right tool is selected and the implementation of it is planned, it is imperative that the e-business organization be organized in such a way that the BPM methodology is effective. This means that the 'islands of management' described earlier, be subsumed by an organization whose responsibility is to the business processes, organizations, and processes that are supported by BPM. This group must focus on how well e-business is functioning, not just on how well IT is functioning[11].

The IT environment of a company includes networks, databases, systems and applications. Software services like middleware and transaction monitors, policies for security, backup and recovery, shared data storage, etc. All have a part to play in the delivery of IT functionality to business. Each component is distinct from the others, yet together they comprise the whole business process[11].

2.5.1.1 Tools and Techniques for BPM

Beyond the broad scope of managing processes, BPM tools are beginning to emerge that enable the corporation to understand and measure specific business transactions – the components of processes. This allows a strong connection with business workflow modeling tools, allowing business planners to more effectively structure the company to meet its goals. This is significant because certain transactions within a company are more critical to the operations or profitability of the company. Companies that have the capability to monitor and measure these valuable transactions have a distinct business advantage over those that don't. The company that monitors specific business transactions will know when the response time for their critical transactions is not acceptable, and they can proactively correct the problem before it becomes a crisis. These companies can leverage the management of their IT infrastructure to proactively maximize their business opportunities and objectives, rather than 'firefighting' after the fact.

Even further, Business Process Management tools that can model the business processes of an enterprise, including the workflows and activities that are components of the business processes, are extremely useful tools for business managers and IT managers alike. BPM tools are especially valuable if they include the business value of each business process component. The business value provides a frame of reference from which IT and business managers can use to monitor and manage the business processes. If the business value of a particular business process is high, then IT must insure that the required IT services for that business process are consistent and reliable.

Whenever something is looked at from a business perspective, risk management must also be considered. BPM should be concerned about risk management in terms of minimizing the business risks that are associated with the IT infrastructure. A useful feature that BPM tools can provide to minimize the risk of the IT infrastructure is the ability to simulate business process models. This feature will allow IT and business managers to perform 'what if' analysis. For example, a simulation that looks at the possible effects of a database server processor upgrade on a critical business process could be used to justify the cost of the upgrade. IT managers finally have the tools to help them justify the costs of new IT technology or upgrades, and to analyze the business impact of service availability improvements that can be made to the IT infrastructure. The modeling and simulation features are valuable tools that can be used for IT's planning for the future.

Another feature that can help to minimize risk for the company is the capability to specify normal and minimum requirements for a business process. If the BPM tool can monitor critical IT resources for a business process by sending proactive warnings or alerts when the amount of resources falls below normal or has reached a minimum threshold, potential problems could be averted before they become crises. Proactive management reduces the risks to the company, while furthering the company's business goals[11].

In recent years, Service Level Management has come into focus as an important evolution in the management of the IT environment. Rather than merely managing sets of similar components proactively, as with IT's 'islands of management', meaningful service level management requires the measurement of performance from an end-user perspective. That is, it is necessary to look at performance on an end-to-end basis across all the domains involved in providing the service. Superior service level management tools measure response time and availability without respect to the business functions being performed. One can place the tools strategically to focus on key business functions, but the service management tools are not 'business process aware'.

Service Level Management and Business Process Management provide cross-sectional views of IT. The management of the business processes, including IT components that support the processes, become extremely effective when the corporation has an understanding of the performance expectations and the business impact of a business process, especially when the measurements of those processes can be obtained using the right combination of SLM metrics For example, SLM and BPM together allow IT to analyze the service expectations of critical business processes compared to the actual delivery of the service, and to also look at the business effects of IT exceeding or not meeting its guaranteed service levels for that particular business process[11].

2.5.1.2 Integrate IT with BPM for Business Success

The business-centric view afforded by a Business Process Management implementation is depicted in Figure 13. Components at various locations of a company are characterized by the functions that they provide to the business-critical system, in the context of an application, a key business process, or even the part of the organization that uses the system. Using a BPM approach, the specialist could review any of the major components in more detail to gain more specific data on the status of the component[11].

Using a BPM approach allows everyone to better monitor and manage the entire business system. An IT manager, business executive or end user is able to examine the health of the processes or services without having to specifically monitor individual components. For example, a manager may want to check the status of the corporate payroll system. Traditionally, this would have entailed looking separately at the intranet, LANs, servers, applications, and databases. From there, the next step would be to make the risky assumption that since each individual component has a high availability, that translates to a high availability for the payroll system. With BPM, a single overall view of the payroll system is presented, indicating its interoperability and overall functionality. A unique feature of BPM is that the business manager and IT manager, who are responsible for the payroll system, can use the same BPM view to monitor the health of the payroll system. Without BPM, the business manager does not have this information at his fingertips, but has to either coordinate efforts with different organizations within IT to assess the health of the payroll system, or wait until his employees complain about the payroll system.

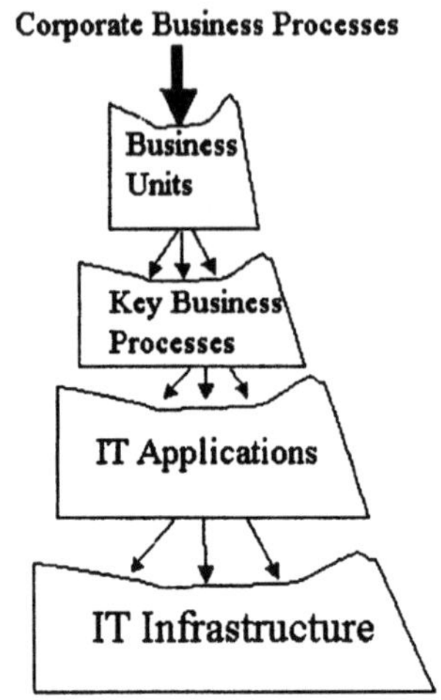

Figure 13. Integrated View of E-Business Management

As another example of how BPM benefits the company, consider the situation where the company's top troubleshooter is confronted with two outages at approximately the same time. The customer order database has crashed on Monday morning, just when customers are beginning to generate the week's orders through the EDI interface and through the company's web site. At the same time, a workflow system that supports the manufacturing department has developed a bottleneck, cutting the transaction rate by 75%. Without the business view, the troubleshooter might assume that the customer interface for orders is more critical, and attack that problem first. However, the BPM view shows that the temporary storage capability for orders on both the web site and the EDI interface is functioning well, but the 25% workflow rate in manufacturing has left 40 employees with no work to do. Letting the BPM tools monitor the temporary storage in case it fills up, the troubleshooter works on the problem for manufacturing first, knowing that the customer orders won't be lost and can be posted to the database as soon as it becomes available again. Knowing the business impact of IT services has helped to prioritize the management of those services[11].

The example above demonstrates the use of BPM to aid in troubleshooting. Even before the systems were deployed, however, the developers of the systems used the business process workflows, and modeling and simulation tools to better understand the customer order process. All of this preliminary work gives the IT troubleshooter confidence that the BPM approach can be trusted to help prioritize system recovery.

BPM is not a substitute for other views or tools used by IT for the management of the components. Ultimately, those views and tools are essential if any corrective action is to be taken to improve or restore service. BPM takes the 'big picture' view of the business process, while the existing management tools can be used to more closely examine the individual components.

2.5.1.3 Implementing Business Process Management

Implementation of Business Process Management is easily the most critical aspect for the effective use of IT (and e-business) management technology. Faulty implementation is the most common reason that the promise of technology is not achieved, so careful preparation and attention to detail is extremely important in a project of this nature.

A basic prerequisite to the implementation of Business Process Management is the existence of an underlying management infrastructure that feeds valuable business system information to the BPM software. Business Process Management gathers pertinent information from the specialized management systems and synthesizes that information, so the basic management components must be in place for a successful project. As noted earlier, one of the most critical capabilities is that of measuring service levels of IT components, which will be integrated closely with BPM.

Another prerequisite for Business Process Management is the ability to monitor and communicate with the applications in the business systems. Ideally, the applications have been instrumented for manageability; that is, the applications can provide data that is valuable for management purposes and respond to commands. Unfortunately, most applications today are not manageable, but even older applications that have no provision for manageability can be incorporated into BPM. Agents external to the application can extract some information about the application, through techniques such as log sniffing, but a much richer set of information is possible with applications that are appropriately designed for management. These techniques will be discussed in detail in Part 3 and Part 4.

The basic steps to effective implementation of BPM, along with the personnel involved in the task, are listed in Table 2. This is a guideline, and another methodology may work as well, but be sure the key points in this list are considered for the project[11].

Table 2. Business Process Management Implementation Chart[11]

TASK IMPLEMENTATION	RESPONSIBILITY
Analyze the IT organization's state of readiness for BPM: prerequisites management support, willingness to change, availability of business process workflows, and workflow modeling tools	IT Systems Management Architects

TASK IMPLEMENTATION	RESPONSIBILITY
Select Implementation Team Members. This will include management and staff from IT and from the business planners in the company. Be sure to obtain clear support from Executive sponsors on both sides of the business.	IT Management, Business Planning Management
Identify a critical business system to implement first. Consider the priority to the business, the potential for benefit with BPM, and likelihood of a successful first implementation with that system.	Implementation Team
Develop requirements for BPM products to be selected (IT and non-IT requirements)	Implementation Team
Conduct industry search and select BPM tools	IT Members and Implementation Team
Determine the appropriate organizational structure for IT to be able to effectively use BPM, and begin the changes necessary to achieve that structure	IT Management and IT Systems Management Architect
Create a well-documented phased plan for BPM implementation	Implementation Team
Model and document the selected business system. This includes looking at components, dependencies, relationships etc.	IT members and Implementation Team
Document the business process workflow, identify business models and simulations used to create and modify the workflow, identify key linkages between models and BPM tools	Line-of-Business members of Implementation Team
Conduct a pilot implementation of BPM and use it to validate model accuracy	Implementation Team
Create a repeatable process to define and provide business system component information to the BPM software (instrumentation)	Selected IT technical staff

In theory, BPM can be implemented without the acquisition or use of any new management tools, but in most environments the only practical way to implement Business Process Management is with the aid of additional software. A crucial step in the implementation of BPM is the selection of the tools that will make it possible. The following features should be considered when selecting a product for Business Process Management: A key component of any BPM implementation is the definition of the potentially complex system model. Constructing the model can be simplified, expedited and made more accurate using a modeling tool to assist in this function. This model will easily interface with the product selected to monitor the systems. The model should include the workflows, activities and transactions.

Another useful feature of BPM software is the ability to assist in the instrumentation of the applications and the other components of the business process. The deployment of BPM will be simplified by using an implementation tool, allowing an employee without programmer-level skills to use and maintain a configuration of a business process. Business Process

Management software must have the capability to automatically detect any changes to managed business systems. This capability is similar in function to auto-discovery found in some network management tools. Not only should the software be able to detect changes when they occur, but it should also dynamically update the BPM topology to reflect those changes.

The BPM software must to be able to determine the status of each component in the business system model on a real-time basis. This status can be determined either indirectly from other management software, or directly by querying the individual components.

The BPM software should not only allow for system monitoring, but also facilitate taking corrective action. IT personnel should be able to fix any problems identified from within the BPM tool, as well as generate a trouble-ticket to alert the Help Desk to the presence and business impact of a problem.

The BPM software must be able to import data or templates from other existing standard business workflow models. This will provide for interoperability, which is always desired by users and makes sense from an industry standpoint.

2.5.2 BPM in Multi-Enterprise E-BusinessContext

It is best to start the discussion of modern IT service environments with the supply chain model discussed in Chapter 1. This shows that the service manager role of an IT service organization has a direct interface with the user(s). Hence this is the most important role from a business perspective. The in-house service provider and external service providers are expected to compete for the role of a service provider. They in-turn would sub-contract part of the tasks to systems integrators, application developers and public service providers. These roles would again procure software and services from suppliers of specialized services/software, platforms and equipment. Obviously, the job becomes more and more technical and specialized as one traverses down the supply chain. However, the service manager has the ultimate responsibility of integrating services from the perspective of the user.

The service manager role processes implement the following functions:

- Negotiate Service-Level Agreements with service providers
- Use similar metrics for internal and external service providers to compare their service levels
- Link into service reporting systems of service providers
- Integrate internal and external support processes to achieve overall service quality and cost requirements

These processes are best considered from the perspective of supply chain introduced in Chapter 1.

2.5.2.1 Supply Chain Management

A supply chain highlights the complexities in maintaining service levels in a service that involves a chain of suppliers. Different suppliers have different internal processes, and the overall quality of service depends on the aggregate of interactions of all these internal processes. Therefore it is necessary to translate the original service level agreement between customer and main service provider into so many associated service level agreements for each member in the supply chain as shown in Figure 14.

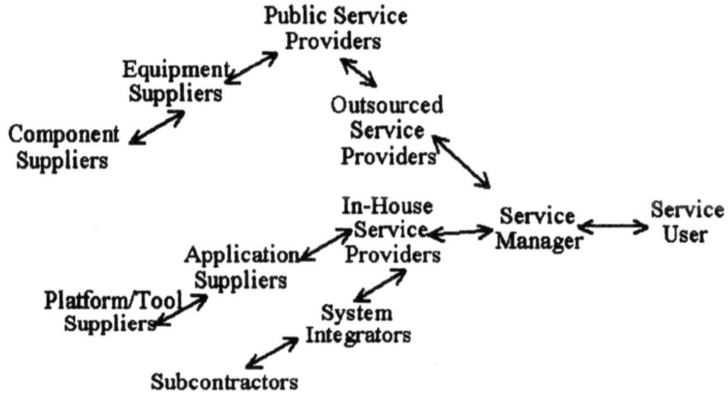

Figure 14. Managing the Service Delivery Chain[8]

As far as the user is concerned, the service manager is responsible for providing the service. But the service manager is also dependant on such a huge chain. There could be a host of service providers within the organization. These days there are also applications service providers. Systems integrators, like service providers, often get their systems developed by other companies. Those systems contribute to the overall service levels that the service manager is responsible for. Similarly, system integrators, and sub-contractors too develop software modules, as do applications suppliers and platform input suppliers. And then there are sub contractors at lower levels. Any problem anywhere in the chain is going to affect the service levels. Because of the chain of suppliers involved in this process, the implementation of the SLA is not easy. It is difficult to map high-level customer SLAs to SLAs between any two entities in the supply chain. Even if one can subjectively assess service levels, the problem is how to measure, monitor and track services objectively in an e-business environment? The hard measures are important for charging purposes.

2.5.2.2 Customer Relationship Management (CRM)

In today's e-business environment, competitive barriers are gradually being pulled down thanks to the proliferation of the Internet and applications running over the Internet. Hence it is extremely important to acquire and retain customers. According to the Boston Consulting Group, the cost of acquiring a new online customer is approximately thirty-four dollars, while using the online channel to market to a current customer costs around seven dollars[20]. Many readers may have seen promotional schemes by telephone and Internet service providers offering incentives for switching to a competitive service provider.

Customer Relationship Management (CRM) focuses on providing and maintaining quality of service for customers by delivering products, services, information and solutions to address customer problems, wants and needs. CRM can include customer call handling, sales and delivery tracking, and technology for conducting customer support transactions over the web[3,21].

2.5.3 E-business Service Management Lifecycle

Typically an e-business service lifecycle consists of the following four main stages[18]:

- Service Creation
- Service Deployment
- User access / Information Transfer
- Withdrawal

Each of these stages needs to be managed using a service management lifecycle shown in Figure 15.

The overall architecture has been defined here. In this process, one starts with a higher-level service requirement defined in a service level agreement, and designs the process parameters based on that service level agreement. So if the process is right, getting the right SLA will basically boil down to attaining certain values in measurable parameters that govern a service level. The whole concept is based on data generated through research on service provisioning infrastructure, including service parameters, and their relationships to network and systems parameters. So the whole process takes into consideration the provisioning of present as well as future improvements.

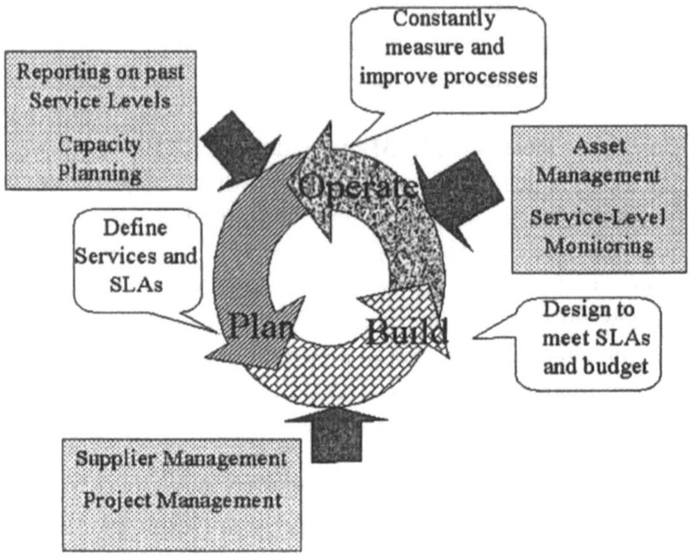

Figure 15. E-business management Life Cycle[8]

The service management lifecycle defined in Figure 15 has three distinct phases:

1. The Planning phase involves the definition of services through service level agreements, and related parameters. This phase uses data from past service level monitoring, and capacity planning
2. The Building phase involves the development of software and systems to implement and monitor service level agreements. Business level systems implement service levels within stipulated budgets. These systems may depend on network and systems management applications to be discussed in Part 3. However, the high-level service level parameters are all business-oriented, and their monitoring involves supplier and project management tools.
3. The Operations phase involves the data collection and reporting on service levels. Some of this data is generated through periodic surveys of subjective parameters, such as user satisfaction. Other data is generated through automated network and systems management tools described in Part 3.

So the objective of the service provider is to provide services at that level of service agreements or better. But this is very difficult to achieve. First, service levels are not easy to quantify all the time. Second, even if one can quantify at the service levels through parameters, such as availability, it is very hard to translate that into low-level physical monitoring requirements. There are often various, ambiguous ways of defining the service level. Let us say the objective is to provide the availability of Internet service at 99.99%. Does it mean that there should be no packet losses 99.99% of the time? Or does it mean that the system uptime should be 99.99%? Standards are evolving in this are to resolve such ambiguities as discussed in Part 3.

2.5.4 E-Business Management Approaches

There are three ways of attacking the problem. The first one is known as the *systems-oriented* approach, which basically uses a systems theory, or reliability theory based approach. This involves the mathematical modeling of the service as a whole and the tracking down of the service requirements of each component[2]. So the aggregate requirements will be as defined in the SLA. This approach is quite popular with management science professionals. The main problem of this approach is the non-availability of definitive mathematical models of real-life management environment and processes.

The second approach, known as the *architecture-oriented* approach, also called the building-block approach in that systems are designed using commercially available, general-purpose, building blocks with some specialized components and interfaces. The ISO standard OSI 7 layer communication model defines communication services as a hierarchy of layers where each layer provides service to a higher level, using the services of a lower layer. If the infrastructure is very reliable, the enabled services can be reliable. For example, if one develops a network environment based on optical fiber where the error rates are very low; achieving 99.99% availability is not a problem. Communication engineers and IT professionals have traditionally used this approach[15]. Proponents of this approach would suggest that e-business management can be achieved by gradually building superstructures using proven reliable building blocks of software and hardware. However, it is difficult to articulate various complex relationships amongst various building blocks and their components, particularly in view of the interdisciplinary nature of e-business management.

There is a third approach, known as *methodology-oriented* approach, is perhaps most appropriate for our discussion. It is based on a combination of both the above two approaches. For example, in a typical cable-based network, e.g., based on optical fibers, the availability problem can be approached from an architectural (building-block) approach where the availability of a communication system can be projected based on the performance figures of optical fiber media (relatively stable performance). On the other hand, the performance of wireless communication depends on various atmospheric parameters that are unpredictable. In that case top down mathematical analysis (systems-oriented approach) is more useful to derive the wireless system design from the service requirements. In this case the same components may deliver different performances based on environmental factors. This methodology-based approach involves a series of guidelines on how to design a service using whatever knowledge is available at the infrastructure level.

This book adopts the methodology-based approach because e-business design involves various environmental factors (needing systems approach), while e-business implementation uses many commercially available software and middleware components (architecture-oriented). The beauty of the methodology-based approach is that it can be very flexible and it can encompass solutions at different levels as follows[7]:

- Business Level- This level is concerned with the service at the business level
- Application level- This level is concerned the service realization in the form of software/hardware applications and their management
- Data Level- This level is concerned with the service related data, and its distribution, and their management
- Network Level- This level is concerned with the underlying network and its management
- Technology Level- This level is concerned with the real technology, and products used to realize the above requirements.

In the methodology-based approach, one can combine available technological standards with some top down analysis. A number of industry groups, such as the Telemanagement Forum (earlier the Network Management Forum), have adopted this approach. But at the same time a number of standards organizations, like DMTF, and ITU-T, are approaching the problem from an architecture-oriented perspective.

It is important to present all requirements in business terms. Another important aspect here is the measurement of service levels from the end-user point of view. Engineers understand and know how to measure jitter, resolution or response time. But consider the point of view of a doctor using a telemedicine service between Europe and Australia to diagnose patients remotely. It is not possible for a doctor to specify service levels using jitter, resolution or throughput. In this case the specification of the quality of service requirements is a major problem. Engineers may like to include measurable parameters, such as response time, throughput and jitter in SLAs. These parameters may be easy to measure, but they cannot be easily translated to service or business level non-technical parameters. The answer is to use cooperative information systems methodologies (involving the user right from the design stage) for service management as discussed in Part 5[1].

The Total Quality Management (TQM) approach believes quality is decided by the process used in developing and building a product. Hence product quality will improve if the process of development and delivery is enhanced. The focus of any service design effort, including e-business services, will be on defining parameters which can in turn define and measure different aspects of a service design and management process as discussed in Part 2[15].

2.6 Technology

The Internet community is responding to the technological requirements of e-business infrastructure in two ways:

- Outsourced Management Service Providers (MSP) that provide management services over the Internet[8].
- In-house management solutions implemented in various ways as discussed next.

Management technology for networks and systems has developed very rapidly over the last decade. These include management protocols, frameworks, architectures, and standards to be discussed in Parts 3 and 4. E-business management solutions are being developed in three ways.

1. Custom-built with vendor partnerships, e.g., Telecom carriers like AT&T, Telstra, using a service management methodology as discussed in Part 2
2. Enhancement of Network and Systems management products, e.g., Tivoli, CA, HP OpenView, as discussed in Part 3
3. Standards based approaches, e.g., TOG ARM & AIC, DMTF SES & CIM, TMF TOM etc., as discussed in Part 4.

This section discusses the major technological challenges of e-business management through separate subsections as follows::

- Identification and development of common management building blocks
- Illustration of the process in one business sector, such as telecommunications
- Mapping some major middleware technologies to these building blocks
- Integration Techniques

2.6.1 Building Blocks for E-Business Management Solutions

As discussed in Section 2.5.3, there are four stages of an e-business service lifecycle. Here are the management mechanisms required at these four stages:

- Discovery/Registration facilities required during service creation and deployment

- Configuration/Monitoring facilities are required during service deployment and user access
- Diagnostics and Correction of problems required during user access/ information transfer.

Figure 16 shows the technological realization of the processes in the service management lifecycle. It shows a number of software building blocks needed to implement such an interface. The caption at the top of the diagram 'internal customer' means the entity at the higher level in the supply chain and the caption at the bottom of the diagram 'external systems' means an entity at the lower level of the supply chain. The building blocks shown in Figure 16 belong to two categories. Existing functions on the right show the various IT service management blocks already in existence. The building blocks on the left show the new functions that are designed to support e-business. These building blocks will be discussed in more detail in Part 3 as part of IT Service Management architecture.

One of the major considerations of a service manager is to provide the integration of management information from different entities of a supply chain. The integration problem is tackled with one or more of the following tools and techniques:

Management data integration across different levels, subsystems and interfaces, using object-oriented platforms (discussed in Part 3) involves:

- Management data models and adapters –using standards, such as SNMP, CMIP and DMI, (discussed in Part 4)
- Scalable, distributed data aggregation and analysis-using management applications from different vendors, such as CA, Compuware, and Tivoli
- Models that capture relationships of business processes with infrastructure elements, e.g., event correlation software launched from trouble ticketing
- Service management reports and analysis- from management applications (discussed in Part 3).

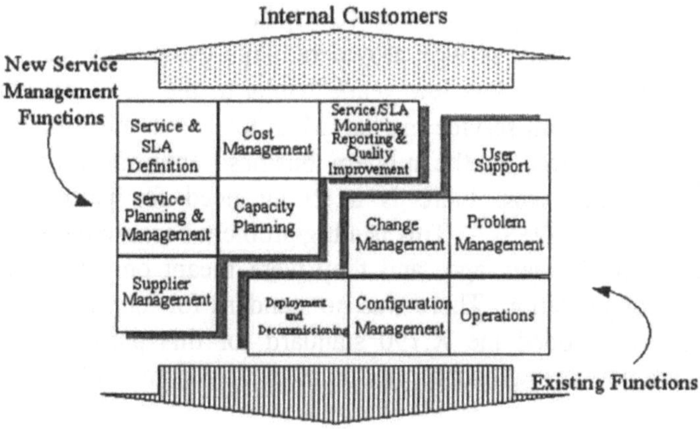

Figure 16. Service Management Disciplines[8]

2.6.2 E-Service Management in Telecommunication Industry

In the operations phase of the service management lifecycle, it is necessary to define and implement a framework for the monitoring, reporting and control of SLAs. This is a part of the operations environment. Help desk is a business model, which helps us in putting service management processes into operation. The e-business management operations environment includes a number of integrated management functions, such as remote monitoring, centralized service desk, automated software distribution system, asset management, and configuration management. Figure 16 shows some of these building blocks, which are being defined and marketed as standard products by some vendors.

The major challenge is to come up with strategies that will help assemble solutions that can also be dismantled very easily. As shown in Figure 17, the best way is to define service operations environments around the global Internet and intranets. This would help retain many of the advantages of virtual organizations. In future supply chain oriented service management; many external organizations will have to share large amounts of information with each other. This underlines the motivation for standards. For example, when telecom companies merge, they have to interoperate/integrate voice services and data services.

The Operations Support Systems (OSS) has been the service operations environment in telecom service providers. This technology has undergone many changes over the last few years thanks to the rapid growth in new entrants to the telecom service market. Most telecommunication companies rely heavily on OSSs. In the modern business environment of mergers, break-ups and alliances, there is a strong need for partners to share information through OSSs[12]. This is a big problem because most OSSs were designed 10 to 20 years ago, and they were meant only for the original company or organization. There was no standard for interoperation. ITU-T has recently developed the X.790 standard for this purpose. These new standards are now being incorporated in the next generation OSSs.

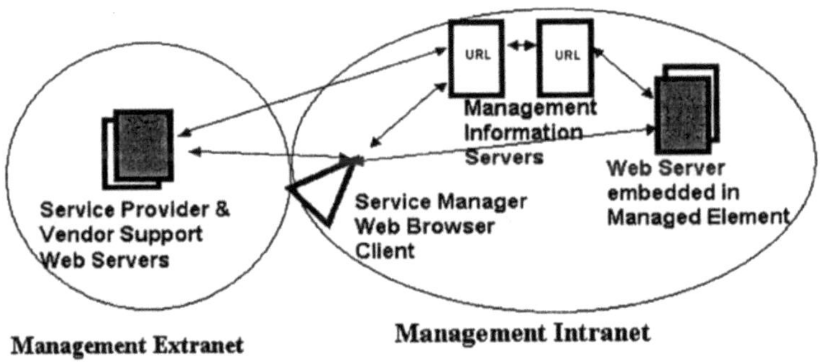

Figure 17. Web-based Service Management Architecture[8]

The modern world of e-business supports virtual enterprises, which means decentralization. However, it has been established that efficient management demands that management information is centralized for the sake of consistency and effective analysis. It has been estimated that the cost of support of a PC (bought at approx $3000) is approx $30000 over five years. It is extremely difficult to keep the management costs of PCs under control without centralization of management.

The question of how to obtain data from different systems on the common semantic level from different sub systems interfaces is addressed through different standards for integrated management as discussed in Parts 3 and 4. For example, Distributed Management Task Force (DMTF) CIM (Common Information Model) helps in modeling data across different systems. Also using XML helps to integrate the transport and presentation of management information in a standard format. Web-Based Enterprise Management (WBEM) standards allow the centralization of management servers, and access to management information over protected intranets by management technicians in remote locations. Figure 17 shows evolving web-based service management architecture. This topic will be discussed in more detail in Part 4.

2.6.3 Middleware for E-business management

Modern e-business management has seen some major developments in the framework for enterprise level IT service management[21].

Process Management – "A process is a representation of knowledge organized into the design of an action whose results will meet a goal"[21]. Process knowledge can be categorized into the following classes:

- Task knowledge, relating to the specification, design and performance of a task
- Context knowledge, relating to the rest of process knowledge concerning the goal, its motivation and the environment/context

Process management - Primarily concerned with the integration of task and context knowledge in an application. Processes vary from place to place and organization to organization. There is a growing realization that management applications should be designed around key work processes. For example, trouble ticketing automates the process of problem management. Future management systems are expected to incorporate process management that enable the operations staff to shift its focus from managing equipment to managing processes. Management will become a distributed, cooperative problem solving activity.

Policy Management - Management policies provide a flexible framework for the definition of management objectives, independent of underlying implementation mechanisms. Policies are the link between the two disciplines of Corporate Management and Technical Management of networks, systems, and applications. From the corporate management point of view, policies achieve certain sets of goals within the corporate operating environment with human elements. On the other hand policies have been successfully used in configuring and controlling communications environments, such as for routers[21].

Knowledge Technologies - Traditionally rule-based expert systems have been considered as auxiliary tools for network management. Over forty such systems have been used in Regional Bell Operating Companies (RBOCs) in the USA for diagnosing faults in telephones outside plants. Network management researchers are now experimenting with a number of Artificial Intelligence (AI) techniques, such as expert systems, case-based reasoning, fuzzy logic and intelligent agents for integrated management. This can range from re-routing circuits in case of failure, to alerting operations personnel of the impending failure of a network element. Providers of network and systems management systems have also incorporated into management systems various other paradigms of AI including intelligent agents, model-based reasoning, case-based reasoning and fuzzy logic. All these techniques are now being incorporated in the IT service operations/management environment through the help desk process.

In addition to these, attention is now being paid to evolving management solutions to meet a wide range of problems including configuration and change management, intellectual property licensing, value chain performance monitoring, and converged communications management. Some of these issues will be discussed in Part 3.

Before we conclude this discussion on the technological factors, it is necessary to present a brief discussion on the role of middleware technologies in modern e-business operation and management. All of the above mentioned functionalities are supported as part of management middleware that we shall discuss in greater detail in Part 3.

Umar [24] has classified middleware as follows:

- *XML/EDI and format translators*- required for interchange of electronic business information across organizations. These developments started with international standards for Electronic Data Interchange (EDI), such as ISO EDIFACT and ANSI X.12. All these have given way to the all-encompassing XML and related standards from the World Wide Web Consortium (WWWC) that is defining a series of standards for the management of multimedia electronic content, its presentation, and interchange over the Internet. The XML standards are working towards supporting all the six dimensions of e-business through, measures, such as multiple translations (multiple levels of supply chain), scalable implementation (to support high transaction volume), distributed transaction processing (to support higher economic values, necessary trust levels), and standard based stateless processing (to support all functions at low level of bonding).
- *Directories, catalogues and data warehouses* - Needed to consolidate information relating to a large number of different entities. The IETF standard on Directory Enabled Networks and the Microsoft support for active directory systems have far reaching consequences in the middleware configurations for e-business. The implications of multiple dimensions of e-business are as follows: there is a need for data warehouses to consolidate large number of catalogues (to support high numbers of partners in the supply chain); new interoperability mechanisms are needed to support heterogeneous data sources (to

support multiple organizations); long-lived trust duration is needed to facilitate free access to and exchange catalogues and catalogue security may become an issue for high valued economic transactions.

- *Remote Operations Middleware, e.g. RPCs*, - Needed to invoke remote services through CORBA or Message Oriented Middleware (MOM). Asynchronous MOM enables safe communication amongst large supply chains. It requires standard interfaces for the interoperability of message formats across organizations. High volumes of transactions affect the performance requirements of CORBA and MOM services. The level of bonding depends on the ways used to support transparent access to remote services.
- *Remote Data Access (RDA) middleware* - Needed to support diverse databases through ODBC/JDBC calls. In this case the support of many partners requires access to data warehouses. Unified schema and standard drivers support multiple organizations. But RDA performance is adversely affected by firewalls and politics. Transaction volumes are affected by any bottlenecks in access gateways. High economic value can be supported through higher gateway security. Access control mechanisms need to be in place to support long trust durations.
- *Workflow Management systems* - Now essential components of any e-business systems in managing the flow of work between business partners. Multiple partners can be handled through delegation mechanisms to handle complexity. Inter organization workflow is required to coordinate work across boundaries. High volumes of transactions need a more robust workflow engine. Access control policies decide the duration of trust in transactions. The workflow management coalition has defined standards to facilitate integrated workflows between bonding partners.

2.6.4 Integrated Management of E-Business

One of the major problems of integration lies in relating service management parameters to network and systems management parameters. Some of the problems in integration are as follows:

- Negotiate SLA with service providers. The problem is to make sure all concerned understand the different parameters in the SLA.
- Translate original SLA to sub SLAs for different entities down the supply chain. Use similar metrics for internal and external suppliers to compare. The question is whether it is possible to keep internal and external service providers at par in real terms.
- There is no point having SLAs at different places and having different implementation characteristics at different points in the supply chain.

There is a need for a single integrated service management facility to track the SLAs online. This is not easy because different entities in the supply chain typically use incompatible management platforms.

- Integration of management information across organizations is a difficult problem because it is very difficult to map those service agreements and then give them the same semantic definitions. This is discussed in Part 3 in relation to an HP labs research project.

From a general business perspective, the term 'service' raises many daily commercial scenarios, such as airline services, restaurant services, banking and health services. While a marketing management professional is likely to look at the common characteristics of any service design and management problem, a technical/operational professional would say that these are entirely different types of services, and need different solutions. A service design and management methodology that starts with a common high-level service independent model and then recommends techniques for the design of IT services is described in Part 2. This will help in integrating the viewpoints of management schools with that of IT services.

2.7 Chapter Summary

This chapter has provided a brief overview of the range of issues involved in the management of e-business systems. The chapter began with a discussion of the interdisciplinary nature of the area of e-business management.

This was followed by a discussion of the four dimensions involved in the deployment of e-business management systems; people, organization, process, and technology. While the discussion of people issues was based on the need for bringing together the existing "islands of management", the discussion of organizational issues focused on Business Process Management (BPM). Appendix 1 supplements the discussion in this chapter with a case study on Business Process Management. While processes are considered the important issue of the management supply chain, the discussion of technology centers on e-business middleware.

This chapter has completed Part 1 of the book. The next part will start a top-down discussion of integrated management from an e-business perspective. We shall use a methodology-based approach to encompass various issues from a process perspective. This will be followed by discussions of architectural and standards perspectives in Parts 3 and 4. Part 5 will wind up the discussion with an integrated view of integrated management at various levels; process level, architecture level and standards/implementation level.

2.8 REFERENCES

1. Avison D., and Fitzgerald G., *Information Systems Development: Methodologies, Techniques and Tools*, (2nd Ed.), McGraw-Hill, Berkshire, UK, 1995
2. Bhattacharjee S., Ramesh R. and Zionts S., "A Design Framework for e-Business Infrastructure Integration and Resource Management", *IEEE Transactions on Systems, man and Cybernetics*, Vol. 31, No. 3, August 2001
3. Deitel H.M, Deitel P.J. and Steinbuhler K., *E-Business and E-Commerce for Managers*, Prentice Hall, 2001, ISBN:0-13-032364-0
4. Dev, R., "Managing the Enterprise Network: Command and Control", *White paper from Cabletron Systems Inc.*, (March 1993)
5. Drake J., "An HP IT Service Management Reference Model", *HP White Paper*, July 1997
6. Durante A., Bell D. and Goldstein L., "E-Business Management-The Customer View", *HP White paper version 2b*, September 2000
7. Goldman J.E. and Rawles P.T., *Applied Data Communications*, (3rd Ed.), John Wiley & Sons, 2001
8. Herman. J., "Achieving World Class IT Service Management", *HP-OpenView'98 presentation*, April 1998
9. Huff S.L. et al. *Cases in Electronic Commerce*. Chicago: Irwin Professional Pub. 1999
10. IBM, "Navigating to a New Generation of e-Business Applications: Business Patterns", *IBM White paper*, March 2001, http://www-106.ibm.com/developerworks/patterns/
11. Intelligent Communication Software (ICS), "Business Process Management: Managing IT to Empower Business", *ICS White Paper,* Germany, http://www.ics.de, accessed April 2002Kavanagh D., "Establishing an End-to-End Integrated Management Platform by Combining Network and Service Management with Operational Support Systems (OSS's), Forge Australia White Paper, www.forge.com.au/products/Papers, December 1999Lucent Technologies NetworkCare, "Business Technology Management", *A VitalSoft White Paper*, USA August 2000
14. Management Insight Technologies, "E-Business Management-The Customer View", *White paper version 2b*, September 2000
15. Manolessos Y., Prezerakos G., Meliones A. and Theologou E., "A TQM-based Approach to QoS Management", *Journal of Network and Systems management,* Vol 8 No. 2, June 2000
16. Ray P., *Cooperative Management of Enterprise Networks*, Kluwer Academic/ Plenum Publications, May 2000, ISBN:0-306-46276-1

17. Rosen A., *The E-Commerce Q and A Book: A Survival Guide for Business Managers*, New York: AMACOM. 1999
18. Sahai A., Machiraju V., and Wurster K., "Next Generation E-Services", *HP Labs Report*, HPL-2000-120, September 2000
19. Shaw M.J. et al. *Handbook on Electronic Commerce*, Berlin: Springer-Verlag. 2000
20. Thompson B., "Keeping Customers is Smart and Profitable", *Business Week Special Advertising Section*, July 2000
21. Turban E., King D., Warkentin, M. and Chung H.M., *Electronic Commerce 2002: A Managerial Perspective*, Prentice Hall, (2nd Ed.), Chapter 1, pp 6-7, 2002
22. Umar A., *Object-Oriented Client/Server Internet Environments*, Prentice Hall, 1997
23. Useem J., "Dot-coms: What Have We Learned", *Fortune*, 30 October 2000
24. Zwass V., "Electronic Commerce: Structures and Issues", *International Journal of Electronic Commerce*, Fall, 1996

PART-2

METHODOLOGY AND PROCESS VIEWPOINT

Chapter 3. E-Business Management Methodologies

"Trying to assess the true importance and function of the Net now is like asking the Wright brothers at Kitty Hawk if they were aware of the potential of American Airlines Advantage Miles", Bran Ferren, Chief Imagineer, Walt Disney Company. [23] Any discussion on e-business services and their models presents a similar level of uncertainty.

E-business now covers a variety of business sectors including telecommunications, healthcare, manufacturing, finance and entertainment industries. E-businesses are being implemented over different IT platforms using different set of standards. Hence it is necessary to discuss e-business management irrespective of the business sector, and type of IT platforms. Businesses are bewildered by such a wide range of issues. It is therefore important to understand the issues, and present the knowledge with respect to a taxonomy that is easy to understand. Many IT consultants are tackling the range of issues by using methodologies and guidelines for e-business. This chapter presents a methodology-oriented viewpoint of e-business management.

"The most important thing to understand about e-business is that it is first and foremost about business, not technology. Technology, while important, is not the hard part. The hard part is managing the changes in institutional processes that must take place for the enterprise to take advantage of e-business, or to avoid losing out to others who do. E-business starts with the CEO, not the CIO"[20].

This Chapter introduces the methodology-based approach to the development of e-business management systems. We address questions, such as:

- What are the constituents of a methodology?
- What are some existing methodologies for e-business?
- What are the major issues in the devlopment of a methodology for e-business management?

We begin with a discussion of the major dimensions of e-business, namely e-marketplace, e-communities, e-processes, e-infrastructure, e-content and e-services with particular reference to management issues. This is followed by a discussion of the components of a methodology. We then analyze some business process models and notations. The chapter concludes with a discussion of types of high-level methodologies for e-business management.

3.1 E-Business Services and Analysis

The recent impetus in e-business has come from the exciting prospects of Business-to-Business (B2B) e-commerce. Researchers all over the world are now studying the structure, development, operations, and management processes and models for B2B activities that can be broadly classified as portals, buy-side marketplaces, sell-side marketplaces and exchanges[23]:

In view of the fast-growing vocabulary of terminology in this area, it is important for us to assign some taxonomy to be able to develop management strategies and communicate them effectively. We use in this Chapter the following taxonomy defined by Turban et al based on the work by Delphi Group in the context of B2B e-business management[23].

- E-Markets
- E-Processes
- E-Communities
- E-Content
- E-Services
- E-Infrastructure

We have already discussed e-infrastructure and its management issues in Part 1. The next subsections describe four of these dimensions that have strong management implications.

3.1.1 E-Markets

As discussed in Part 1, E-business technologies, such as data mining and intelligent agents have brought about some significant changes in marketing strategies for business-to-business marketing, sales and advertising. For example, data mining is being used to answer questions, such as who are the customers? What do they need? Call centers, help-desks, and intelligent agents have drastically increased the efficiency and effectiveness of customer support. Multimedia content technology assists with a more effective marketing and presentation of many existing and new innovative products for markets, such as real estate, and financial markets.

Here are some of the relevant management issues[23]:

- Acceptable standards for response in customer service must be set. For example, customers want acknowledgment of their query within 24 to 48 hours. Most companies want to provide this response time and do it at a minimum cost. The investment in technology may be offset by a reduction in the number of customer service representatives needed and, more importantly, in savings resulting from customer retention.

- Market research and service are done online. E-business strategies must be integrated with the evolving Customer Relationship Management (CRM) to achieve synergy and avoid any conflicts.
- There is a need for measuring customers' satisfaction from a web site. Thanks to free software in cyberspace, this important e-business need can now be met in many ways.

E-business management schemes need to support the above requirements.

3.1.2 E-Processes

The process of the development and management of e-business consists of the following steps[23]:

1. *E-business strategy formulation* is concerned with formulation of e-business goals and linkage with information system design.
2. *E-business application design* is concerned with the logical and physical design of software for e-business in front-end and back-end levels. Examples of e-business applications include payment and financial applications and logistics, and supply chain handling.
3. *Building (or buying) e-business applications* is concerned with building and hosting e-business services through in-house and outsourced vendors.
4. *Operations and Maintenance of e-business* is concerned with the testing, validation, and operation of e-business.

Most e-business management tasks are designed around the objectives of Step 4 of this process. However, it is important to build in management functions right from Step 1 of this process for effective e-business management system design. An eight-stage e-business service design and management plan will be discussed in the next chapter.

3.1.3 E-Content

The success of many e-business products (e.g., entertainment, and music) is heavily dependent on content and its delivery to large number of consumers. For example, the phenomenal success of I-mode based mobile e-commerce services is largely due to an effective conduit provided by NTT DoCoMo from a large number of content providers to consumers.

Management of content for e-business involves content generation (knowledge creation), syndication (distribution of content through many delivery companies), delivery and management. E-content is complex due to the need for frequent updates on content from a variety of sources and formats. For example, content could involve multimedia format, location sensitive, and multilingual material. Hence e-content management involves the following issues[23]:

- Content Delivery Networks (CDN) help companies update content, increase consistency, control content, and reduce time needed for creating and maintaining a content site.
- Content management involves cataloging content by collecting, standardizing, classifying, hosting, and continually updating catalogue data.
- The deliveries of multimedia information, such as animation, video clips, music, and flash media need streaming transport with high network bandwidth that may not be available on a wireless media, such as for I-mode services in Japan.

This area of e-business management is very important because we need more potent tools to extract relevant information from the web. The World Wide Web Consortium is working towards the framework for the semantic web. On the other hand, researchers in information management are working on frameworks for ontology definitions that would help the e-business become smarter[25].

3.1.4 E-Services

E-services are the common services provided to e-business to support e-markets, e-processes, and various types of e-infrastructure facilities, including application development and content management. E-services could be of different types and different levels of complexities. Here are some of the prominent e-services now available as middleware in the modern e-business environment:

- Directory Services, Search Engines, and their integration with applications.
- Call Centers and Help-desk facilities for Customer Relationship Management (CRM).
- Partner Relationship Management (PRM) extends CRM for the management of facilities to corporate business partners. For example, customers may need to access the suppliers' inventory to know what items can be delivered fast.
- Integration and hypermediation services help manufacturers communicate directly to end customers without middlemen.
- Other B2B services include trust and payment services, trademark and domain name registration, e-business rating, encryption services, and web research services.

Having discussed the various aspects of e-business complexities, we now turn our attention to an effective approach to the management of e-business using a methodology-based approach. The next chapter discusses a methodology for the development and management of e-services. The next sections present the problem from an e-business methodology perspective.

3.2 Methodologies for E-Business Management

"The corporation as we know it, which is now 120 years old, is unlikely to survive the next 25 years. Legally and financially yes, but not structurally and economically." Peter Drucker, August 22, 2000.

E-business is a complex combination of models, processes, and techniques. While much of the models, and processes are specific to the business domain, most of the techniques are in the form of information systems and software. Hence it is worthwhile to borrow knowledge from the information systems, and software engineering industry to tackle the complexity of e-business. While information systems and software engineering methodologies concentrate mainly on issues relating to software development, e-business methodologies need to incorporate service design and management methodologies from a business perspective.

3.2.1 Why Methodologies?

The objective of a methodology is to provide a guideline for the development of quality systems within cost constraints for complex business

There have been a number of methodologies for the development of e-business by IT consultancy organizations, such as Gartner Group, Price Waterhouse Coopers Lybrand, and Arthur Anderson etc. Similarly there are a number of development methodologies for object-oriented software. Generally, methodologies are a combination of concepts and models, processes and guidelines, formalisms and tools, which may include graphical and textual notations, documentation standards and possibly CASE tools [2]. The aim of a methodology is to provide a process of developing better systems, i.e., more complete, more effective, correct, robust, economical, maintainable, flexible and understandable.

Methodologies are most often applied when a system's complexity, or size, gets to a point where it is no longer possible for a single person or small team to comprehend the system design fully, or where effective communication is lost between those requiring the system and those designing the system. For example, a large system design requires effective communication between different groups, possibly separated in time and space, concerning the details of a problem[21].

3.2.2 Constituents of a Methodology

Typically a methodology consists of the following elements:

- Model
- Process
- Techniques and Notations
- Tools

A model could be described as a conceptual framework describing the relationships between various conceptual elements in a system. The system could include a social system, a business/economic system, an information system, or a healthcare system. Modeling could include constructs from a range of management theories discussed in the beginning of Chapter 1. These models may be described in verbal, mathematical, graphical, or any other form of expression. Some of the popular models include business process engineering for business task modeling, data modeling used for database designs, object-oriented modeling of software, formal methods for software engineering, and participatory designs for computer supported cooperative work. Emerging Internet-based e-business models have been discussed in Chapter 1. Management models will be described in terms of integrated management of e-businesses with underlying applications, networks and systems.

A process is a sequence of steps that needs to perform a business, economic, or social task. For example, information systems development processes are described by the waterfall model, the fountain model, or the spiral mode[15,16].

Techniques and notations are graphical, or language-based constructs (or programs) used to automate various parts of a complex process in a system. These constructs help in clarifying requirements, facilitate inputs from multiple groups of people, and allow consistent execution of the requirements that are expressed in a form that is understood by all concerned. Examples of techniques or notations include various types of matrices (QFD matrices described in Chapter 4), Data Flow Diagrams (DFDs) and Entity Relationship Diagrams (ERD) used for information systems development, Use-cases and class diagrams used for object-oriented software development, a number of programming languages (e.g., VB, Java) and scripting languages (e.g., PERL), and workflows to express the dynamics of business interactions.

Tools help in automating the usage of techniques on a computer based interactive system. These tools are extremely important in assisting information systems professionals for the specification, design and documentation of information systems. They include Computer Aided Software Engineering (CASE) tools that automate the task of program coding from their graphical specifications, repositories for knowledge management, data dictionaries for database developments, and project management tools to keep track of resources in a project.

All these constituents form a methodology. Methodologies have been defined for many areas of complex systems developments, such as military systems, information systems, semiconductor systems, social and economic systems, ergonomic systems, aviation systems, healthcare systems, and information systems. Some of the well-known methodologies include Structured Systems development methodologies (e.g., STRADIS, YSM), Soft Systems Methodologies (e.g., SSM and ETHICS), Workflow Methodologies (e.g., Action workflow), and service design methodologies, discussed in the next chapter.

3.3 E-Business Management Models and Processes[13]

We have already discussed some e-business management issues and models in Chapter 2. We have also discussed some Internet-based business models in Chapter 1. These models are applicable to the evolving field of e-business management. However, it is important to understand some basic business processes that are applicable to e-business.

Understanding insights that come from world-class businesses requires a point of view, called a process view. This viewpoint reveals similarities between businesses because, at some level, all companies perform the same processes. As a result, they can learn from one another. This section presents a discussion of some evolving business process models with a view to deriving the e-business management processes.

The MIT E-business Process Repository currently holds over 5000 process entries. Many of these entries are indexed via the e-business links on the directory page. In addition to the framework and content of e-businesses, the Repository includes selected case examples and models from a variety of other areas of business[13]:

The repository includes several process models that cover all (or most) of what goes on in a business:

- European Foundation for Quality Management (EFQM) model[5]. This view was developed to assess an organization's progress along a path to excellence. The model is split into four 'enablers' (leadership, people management, policy and strategy, resources and processes) and four 'results' (people satisfaction, customer satisfaction, impact on society and business results). This process structure is described in Section 3.3.1.
- Supply Chain Operations Reference (SCOR) model[21]. The Supply Chain Council, a trade association of over 400 companies interested in supply chain management, developed this model. The SCOR model contains

standard process definitions, standard terminology, standard metrics, supply-chain best practices, and references to enabling information technology as discussed briefly in Section 3.3.2.

- International Benchmarking Clearinghouse Process Classification Framework[1]. This model was developed by the International Benchmarking Clearinghouse - part of the American Productivity and Quality Center, and by Arthur Andersen. This model has about 280 activities defined through key processes and sub-processes that every business performs as discussed in Section 3.3.3.

The following subsections briefly describe the above three process models.

3.3.1 European Foundation for Quality Management (EFQM) model (EFQM)[5]

The European Foundation for Quality Management (EFQM) is a membership-based not-for-profit organization, created in 1988 by fourteen leading European businesses, with a mission to be the driving force for sustainable excellence in Europe and a vision of a world in which European organizations excel. By January 1999, membership had grown to over 750 members from most European countries and most sectors of activity.

To help guide organizations to improve their performance, the EFQM launched, in 1991, the EFQM Excellence Model. This Model, which is the application of the fundamental concepts reflected in a structured management system, is now being used by tens of thousands of organizations across Europe and beyond. Companies, schools, healthcare organizations, police services, utilities and government offices all use it. The Model additionally provides these organizations with a common management language and tool, thus facilitating the sharing of 'good practice' across different sectors throughout Europe.

These fundamentals concepts are expressed as EFQM eight essentials for excellence of management: [5]

- Results Orientation
- Leadership and Constancy of Purpose
- Customer Focus
- Management by Processes and Facts
- Continuous Learning, Innovation and Improvement
- People Development and Involvement
- Partnership Development
- Public Responsibility

The achievement of excellence requires total management commitment and acceptance of these concepts. The following subsections describe these eight essential factors[5].

- Results Orientation: Excellence is dependent upon balancing and satisfying the needs of all relevant stakeholders, which includes employees, customers, suppliers and society in general as well as those with financial interests in the organization. This dimension of management yields relevant measures, including leading indicators in place for all stakeholders
- Leadership and Constancy of Purpose: The behavior of an organization's leaders creates a clarity and unity of purpose within the organization and an environment in which the organization and its people can excel. This leads to maximized people commitment and effectiveness, a clear sense of direction, and market place respect
- Customer Focus: The customer is the final arbiter of product and service quality. Customer loyalty, retention and market share gain are best optimized through a clear focus on the needs of current and potential customers. This dimension of excellence provides maximized participation, positive attitude and morale, positive company recruitment and retention, and effective sharing of knowledge
- Management by Processes and Facts: Organizations perform more effectively when all inter-related activities are understood and systematically managed and decisions concerning current operations and planned improvements are made using reliable information that includes stakeholder perceptions. This approach helps to focus on desired outcomes, maximization of use of people and resources, and fact-based management for setting realistic goals
- Continuous Learning, Innovation and Improvement: Organizational performance is maximized when it is based on the management and sharing of knowledge within a culture of continuous learning, innovation and improvement. This would lead to organizational agility, cost reduction, opportunity identification, and performance optimization
- Partnership Development: An organization works more effectively when it has mutually beneficial relationships, built on trust, sharing of knowledge and integration, with its Partners. The expected benefits are the ability to create value for both parties, competitive advantage through relationships that endure, and synergy in terms of resources and costs
- Public Responsibility: The long-term interest of the organization and its people are best served by adopting an ethical approach and exceeding the expectations and regulations of the community at large. The expected benefits are credibility, performance and organization. Value is enhanced by public awareness, safety, trust and confidence.

This high-level perspective of business management is embedded in many e-business infrastructures and applications.

3.3.2 Supply Chain Operations Reference (SCOR) Model[21]

The Supply Chain Operations Reference-model (SCOR) was developed by the Supply Chain Council. It is intended to be a cross-industry standard for supply chain management. The model includes: all customer interactions from order entry through paid invoice; all material transactions from the organization's suppliers' supplier to customer's customer; all market interactions from understanding aggregate demand to fulfillment of each order.

The model excludes: sales administration and infrastructure; technology development; product and process design and development; post-delivery customer support; links to these excluded processes. SCOR defines a number of process activities categorized as "source", "make", and "deliver". These processes map to the Porter's value chain processes. For example, *Source* processes are concerned with inbound logistics activities, such as obtaining, inspection and issue of source material. *Make* processes are concerned with manufacturing and testing activities. *Deliver* processes are concerned with outbound logistics including warehouse and transportation management.

These processes are now extensively used for the management of supply chains, an important aspect of e-business management. However, the next section discusses a process structure that will be of direct relevance to e-business management

3.3.3 International Benchmarking Clearinghouse Process Classification Framework[1]

Benchmarking is a well-known mechanism for the identification of strengths and weaknesses of a business, by comparing with external and internal competition. The measures include qualitative parameters like company image and quantitative parameters, such as revenues from different geographical areas. They help uncover gaps in business performance. While quantitative benchmarks show what sort of business performance is possible, qualitative benchmarks show how to improve performance. We use a variation of this benchmarking concept in our collaborative management methodology calleed CoMEN that will be described in Chapter 10.

Just as doctors systematically monitor a patient's vital signs such as heart rate, pulse rate, and blood pressure to track improvement in a patient's health condition, companies monitor performance measures to track business process improvement. These business measures translate subjective judgments into precise quantitative metrics. For example, instead of saying that the sales system is "good", a performance measure may report that the number of error-free invoices produced is 100%. By providing reliable, quantifiable data to evaluate business processes, performance measures allow companies to offer employees concrete feedback about current performance and to set goals for future improvement. For example, "increase inventory turnover by 30%" is a business-oriented performance goal. Finally, when monitored consistently, performance measures help a company identify process problems as they occur, often well before the problems adversely affect profitability. The Chapter 4 will present a methodology that helps quantify many service management parametrs that are qualitative in nature.

International Benchmarking Clearinghouse Process Classification Framework defines benchmarks and business performance measures by analyzing business processes into the following classes[1]:

- Operating Processes, and
- Management Processes

As the names suggest, operating processes are concerned with the direct operational activities of the business, whereas the management processes help with the monitoring, control, and resource management of the business.

We are more interested in management processes, which are described next.

The management processes (defined in the Porter's value chain as support processes in Part 1) consist of the following processes that can be performed concurrently[1]:

1. Develop and Manage Human Resources
2. Manage Information Resources and Technology
3. Manage Financial and Physical Resources
4. Execute Environmental, health and safety management program
5. Manage External Relationships
6. Manage Improvement and Change

Although all these management processes are important, sub-processes # 2, 5 and 6 are of particularly important for e-business management, and hence they are analyzed further in the following subsections.

3.3.3.1 Manage Information Resources and Technology

This process consists of the following sub-processes[1]:

- Manage Information Resources
- Manage Information Technology

Management of information resources is becoming a more and more important aspect of modern e-business environment. It involves leverage of organizational knowledge, protection of intellectual property, and the management of relevant records and documents.

Management of information technology involves the following major activities: Acquire, develop, deploy, and support technology solutions

- Manage technical environment
- Manage security
- Ensure continuity of systems (backward and forward compatibility)

Chapters 3 and 4 will discuss an architecture-oriented view of this aspect of management.

3.3.3.2 Manage External Relationships

This is a process of high importance in any business. For example, the government decision to deregulate the telecommunication service has caused a massive increase in the number and types of telecommunication services being offered on the market. The business scenario changes completely with mergers, such as the merger of AOL and Time Warner, and with Netscape, which has created major competition for Microsoft in the Internet service sector.

Outsourcing is heavily used in e-businesses. The development of relationships, facilitated by the above processes, amongst business partners is an important aspect of e-business management. We shall discuss in Part 5 and in Appendix 3, the application of a collaborative management methodology called CoMEN for e-business management.

3.3.3.3 Manage Improvement and Change

Since the barrier for entry into the e-business market is low, it is not difficult for any start-up company to challenge established players. Hence it is important for all e-business companies to improve and change continuously. It has been observed that most management problems and breakdowns occur during or after a change. Therefore it is extremely important to formalize change management processes listed below:

- Measure organizational performance
- Conduct quality assessments
- Benchmark performance
- Apply best practices
- Implement Total Quality Management (TQM)

Measuring organizational performance involves the creation of measurement systems for measuring costs, cost of quality, cycle time, productivity, and service quality.

Measuring quality assessment based on external and internal criteria.

Benchmarking performance involves the development of benchmarking capabilities of organizational processes including competitive benchmarking.

Applying best practices seems to be a significant activity in the management of e-businesses, evidenced by the release of best practices by major consultants on different aspects of e-business. The sub-processes are:

- Create commitment for improvement
- Implement continuous process improvement
- Reengineer business processes and systems
- Manage transition to change

The field of TQM has generated a number of interesting techniques for the design and management of services, through the eight-stage service design and management methodology, as discussed in the next chapter. Since change management is a significant aspect of cooperative management, we shall discuss in Part 5 the application of a collaborative management methodology called CoMEN in a change management scenario.

3.4 E-Business Management Methodology Notations

There is no comprehensive standard notation for e-business systems. However, literature suggests a proliferation of graphical representation techniques, as illustrated below. Many of these are based on the mathematics of graph theory[4]. E-business Management Methodology could use a number of notations, such as rich pictures, activity maps, tables, and matrices as we shall see in the next chapter. This chapter briefly describes some of these notations.

3.4.1 Rich Picture

A rich picture is an informal macro-level view of a real-world cooperative work situation. It shows the characters (roles), working context, internal and external environment, using cartoon characters and various pictorial annotation techniques. This presents a holistic view of a cooperative work environment. This is used to get an overall picture in the requirement gathering stage of the project.

3.4.2 Enterprise Analysis

This technique is based on IBM's Business Systems Analysis that presents a holistic view of an organization in terms of organizational units, functions, processes, and data elements. This notation involves the development of matrices of organization/processes and processes/data based on interviews with people involved in the organization.

For example, Table 3 shows the involvement of various human roles in an organization with respect to certain processes related to a new product development and marketing.

Table 3. E-Business Organization Roles

Processes	Marketing Manager	Finance Manager	Operations Manager	Customers	R & D Manager
Specifying a Product	M	S	S	M	M
Developing a Product	M	S	S	S	M
Launching in Market	M	S	S	M	S
Delivering a Product	S	S	M	M	S

M= Major Involvement, S= Some Involvement

Table 4 shows a matrix of the roles of various information repositories in these organizational processes. Requirements of processes with respect to information repositories have been classified as R= Read Access, W= Write Access, and N= No Access.

Table 4. Role-Function Matrix

Processes	Customer Information	Product Information	Market Analysis	Development Tools
Specifying a Product	R	R/W	R	R
Developing a Product	R	R/W	R	R/W
Launching in Market	R/W	R	R/W	N
Delivering a Product	R/W	R	N	N

Enterprise Analysis provides a formal methodology to carry out the first few stages of SSM. These matrices can be used to capture and analyze various types of organization-wide information. The next chapter will present some matrices called "House of Quality" matrices for e-business service management.

3.4.3 Process Diagrams

This technique is based on human computer interaction studies, called Activity Analysis[16]. In this case, an e-business activity is graphically modeled in terms of human roles and their interactions. While ellipses represent human roles, directed arrows represent interactions.

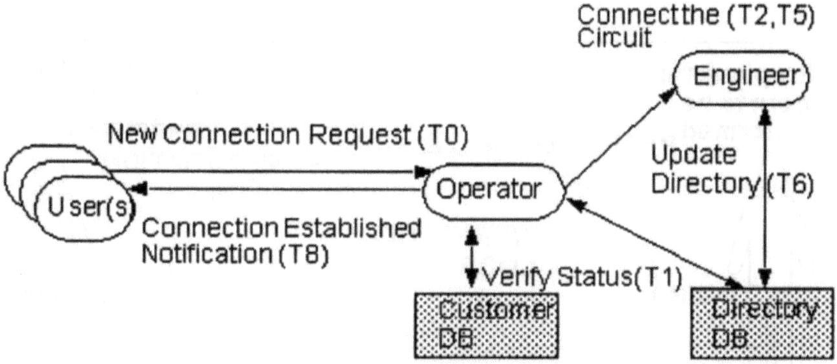

Figure 18. Activity based Process Diagram

Figure 18 illustrates the use of activity-based process diagram notation for a part of the new connection provision process in a telecommunication system. This process is composed of several human roles (users, operator and engineer), and their interactions. The notation provides a simple representation for e-business processes but the process diagrams do not capture process objectives such as customer satisfaction. Therefore, an e-business management methodology uses some matrix notations/tables for the analysis of cooperation. These notations are illustrated in the next chapter and in Part 5.

3.4.4 Action Workflow Diagrams

This representation stems from Winograd and Flores "Conversion for Action Model"[24]. This methodology assumes that the objective of business process re-engineering is to improve customer satisfaction. It reduces every action in a workflow to four phases based on communication between a Customer and a Performer (Figure 19).

- *Preparation*: The customer prepares to ask for something and the performer offers to do some work for the customer.
- *Negotiation*: The two entities agree on the work to be done and clarify the terms.
- *Performance*: Work is done to produce and deliver agreed results.
- *Acceptance*: The customer reports satisfaction or dissatisfaction with the work.

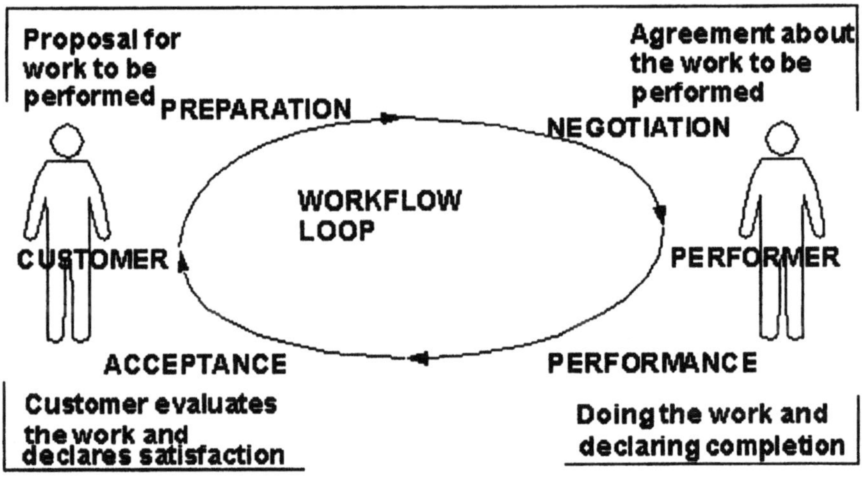

Figure 19. Action Workflow Diagram

Each workflow loop between a customer and performer can be joined with other workflow loops to complete a business process. The performer in one workflow loop can be a customer in another workflow loop. The resulting business process reveals the social network in which a group of people, filling various roles, fulfils a business process. Harris and associates[6] have provided an understanding of Action Workflow notation from the perspective of participation and coordination.

Figure 20 illustrates a business process for procuring materials. The main Workflow loop (procure materials) requires several secondary workflow loops during the performance phase (verify status, get bids, place order). A buyer in the procurement office acts as the customer in the secondary loop. The loop Verify Status allows the buyer to verify the stock status of the item from the stores. The buyer then gets bids from suppliers before finally placing an order. The workflow is completed when the buyer reports to the user that the materials have been procured.

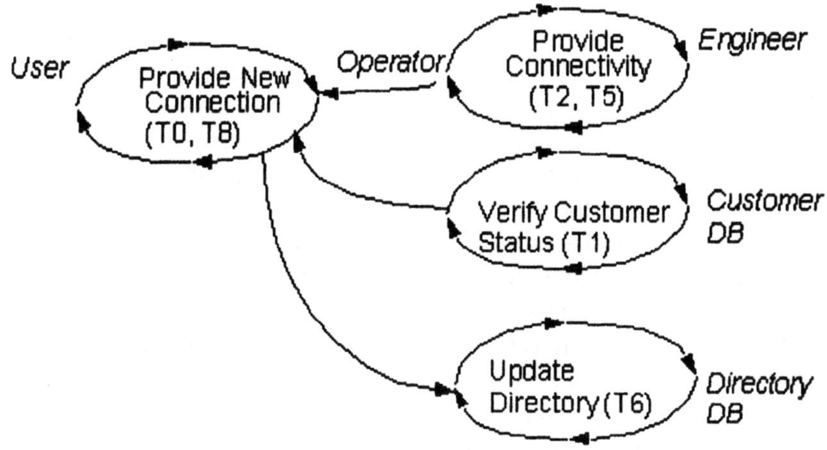

Figure 20. E-procurement modeled with Action Workflow

It may be noted that workflow specification based on this Action Workflow methodology does not indicate which activities can occur in parallel or if there are conditional or alternative actions. The communication-based and activity-based workflow models can be combined when process re-engineering objectives are compatible with both models. The use of these notations is shown in further detail in the next chapter and in Part 5.

3.5 Development of an E-Business Management Methodology

As discussed above, we have considered a number of business level models and processes for a variety of businesses including manufacturing, aviation, financial services, healthcare and telecommunications. We have also seen some management processes in Section 3.3.3. Many of these processes are applicable to e-business.

As discussed in Section 3.2, a methodology consists of business models, processes, and techniques and notations. We discuss e-business models in Chapter 1. We discuss business processes in Section 3.3. We will discuss techniques and notations as part of an integrated service design and management methodology in the next chapter.

This section presents a discussion of various types of information systems methodologies that may be adapted for e-business management.

3.5.1 Information Systems Methodologies

E-business systems are developed by multiple vendors and users located at different geographical locations. These systems are fairly complex and difficult. Designers of such systems have traditionally adopted methodologies for software engineering (e.g. Computer-Aided Software Engineering-CASE tools). However, CASE tools are usually closely dependent on a methodology. In other words, a CASE tool is an implementation mechanism for a methodology. Before discussing management methodology for e-business, it is necessary to examine the characteristics of e-business problem domains.

The first characteristic is the evolving nature of Internet business models, architectures, and protocols (constantly updated by IT vendors), which, as discussed in Chapters 3 and 4, suggest that all e-business problems can be solved by the appropriate Internet protocols, and software components. While a lot of research is being carried out in the software components area (e.g., Java beans, ActiveX) and programming languages (e.g., Java), there is less attention given to developing unified mechanisms to integrate these e-business applications to business models due to their diversity. As discussed in Part 2 – Part 5, workflows and agents are increasingly being used for the integration of businesses with object-oriented Client-server Internet environments.

The second characteristic is the scarcity of skills for the efficient management of enterprise networks. This shortage is caused by the increasing complexity, and rapid changes in such systems. There is a growing need for tools that not only support the automation of e-business tasks, but also allow free cooperation amongst all concerned, such as retailers, suppliers, distributors, service providers, and customers.

The third characteristic is the existence of a variety of competing protocols (e.g., SNMP), models (manager-agent), standards (e.g., DMTF CIM, ITU-T TMN), platforms (e.g., HP OpenView™, Aprisma Spectrum™, Tivoli TME™ etc.), and applications (e.g., trouble ticketing, help-desk) that are now extensively used for the management of networks and systems. Many people think that these platforms can solve the problem of e-business management. However, it may be noted that most of these tools are designed for managing specific tasks, such as measuring network throughput, and network inventory. Some vendors are in the process developing service management capabilities into their products as discussed in Part 3.

The fourth characteristic is the multidisciplinary nature of e-business systems. E-business strategies can be applied gainfully to a range of businesses, (e.g., airlines, retailing, banking, healthcare etc.). We need to develop a methodology that can be applied to all these different business sectors.

The fifth and last characteristic relates to the difficulty in the evaluation of e-business systems. While there has been some work on the performance evaluation of e-business applications and platforms, there is no standard methodology for the evaluation of integrated e-business systems from a business perspective.

3.5.2 Types of E-Business Methodologies

The first classification is based on the three schools of management theories discussed in Part 1. For example,

- Methodologies based on the Technical Rational School of management- TQM methodologies (e.g., Ramaswamy's model discussed in the next chapter) belong to this category. Also some information systems development methodologies (e.g., SSADM), that are oriented towards the codification of existing office procedures, also belong to this school.
- Methodologies based on the Behavioral School of management- Cooperative information systems development methodologies (e.g., Soft Systems Methodologies and ETHICS) belong to this category. Part 5 discusses some of these concepts in more detail.
- Methodologies based on the Knowledge Organization School of management- Researchers in management and information science have been concentrating on this area with a view to identify and automate creative management processes, such as the evaluation of most promising e-business ideas [5]. The object-oriented software development methodologies (e.g., UML), and knowledge-based systems development methodologies (e.g., KADS) belong to this category[2].

We can also classify methodologies based on their purpose. For example,

- Some methodologies help in the identification and evaluation of business ideas as required in the modern world of e-services[5,21]
- Some methodologies help in the quantification of qualitative requirements as required in modern competitive business strategies[17]
- There are well-established methodologies for the systems analysis and design as used in any information systems development[2, 9, 15]
- There are some evolving methodologies for the development of networks and their management systems[12,21]
- Methodologies for the development of service management systems are now evolving[11]
- Similarly there are methodologies for the development of databases using Entity-Relationship (ER) diagrams

Part 3 discusses the IT Service Management framework to support the entire lifecycle of e-business services including deployment and operations.

It may be noted that the success of businesses in modern knowledge-oriented economies depends on the adoption of the right methodologies in explicit or implicit forms. Such methodologies are often called best practices. The large management consultancy houses (e.g., Anderson Consulting, Price-Waterhouse Coopers, KPMG, Gartner Group, and Deloitte Touche) have been working on these best practices and their applications in different business sectors[1,5,8,20,21].

The next section presents an analysis of business processes with a view to develop a generic service design and management methodology.

3.6 Chapter Summary

This chapter has presented a process and methodology perspective of e-business management, which is so important for dealing with the complexities of managing knowledge in this dynamic field.

The chapter began with an analysis of e-business with respect to six dimensions, namely e-marketplace, e-communities, e-processes, e-infrastructure, e-content and e-services. This was followed by a discussion of the constituents of a methodology. There was then a discussion of various types of business processes and notations with a view to developing a generic methodology for service design and management, independent of business type.

This chapter concluded with a discussion of various types of information systems methodologies that might be adapted to e-business management. The next chapter will illustrate all components of a methodology by developing a methodology for e-business from the perspective of a service business.

3.7 REFERENCES

1. Arthur Andersen, *Global Best Practices*, http://www.globalbestpractices.com/resources-bench.html, May 2000
2. Avison D. and Fitzgerald G., *Information Systems Development: Methodologies, Techniques and Tools*, (2nd Ed.) McGraw-Hill, 1995
3. R. J. Butler R.J; Friel D.F.; Richard D. Lang R.D.; Park G.; Santello S.A., "Healthcare Provider-Sponsored Virtual Communities: The Benefits of the Electronic Village", J. Foreman (editor), *Journal of Healthcare Information Management*, Jossey Bass, A Wiley Company, http://www.josseybass.com/JBJournals/him.html

4. Daneshgar D. and Ray P., "Awareness Modeling and its Application in Cooperative Network Management", *Proceedings of the 7th International Conference on Parallel and Distributed Systems* (ICPADS2000)", Iwate, Japan, July IEEE Press, 2000.
5. European Foundation for Quality Management (EFQM), *EFQM Excellence Model*, http://www.efqm.org, created in Dec 2001
6. Harris G., and Taylor S., "Creating a New Process Model to Support Participation and Improve Coordination", *Center for Quality Management* Journal 6(3) (Winter 1997)
7. Internet Engineering Task Force (IETF), *Internet RFCs*, http://www.ietf.org, last accessed Dec 2001
8. Krammer M., Rozwell C., Reilly G. and Schulman J., "E-Business Dimension Model: Clarity Beyond the Hype", *Gartner Group Commentary*, USA November 2000, http://gartner11.gartnerweb.com/public
9. C. Larman, *Applying UML and Patterns: An Introduction to Object-Oriented Analysis and Design*, Prentice Hall, 1998, ISBN:0-13-748880-7
10. Laudon Kand Laudon J., *Management Information Systems: Organization and Technology*, Prentice Hall, 1998
11. Lewis, D., "A Review of Approaches to Developing Service Management Systems", *Journal of Network and Systems Management* (JNSM), Vol. 8 No 2 (pp 141-156), June 2000
12. Lucent Technologies, "Standardized Design Deliverables in the Enterprise", *Lucent White paper on NetKnowledge*, March 2001, http://www.lucentservices.com/knowledge/whitepapers
13. MIT, "E-Business Process Repository", http://process.mit.edu, Dec 2001
14. Management Service Provider Association, http://mspassociation.org, Dec 2001
15. Olle T.W., Hagelstein J., Macdonald I.G., Rolland C., Sol H.G., Assche F.V. and Verrijn-Stuart A.A., *Information Systems Methodologies: A Framework for Understanding*, IFIP, Addison Wesley, 1991, pp. 26–42, ISBN:0-201-54443-1.
16. Preece J., Rogers Y., Sharp H., Benyon D., Holland S. and Carey T., *Human-Computer Interaction*, Addison Wesley, 1994, ISBN 0-201-62769-8.
17. Ramaswamy R., *Design and Management of Service Processes*, Addison Wesley, AT&T Engineering Process Improvement Series edited by J.W.Wesner, 1996.
18. Ray P., *Cooperative Management of Enterprise Networks*, Kluwer Academic/ Plenum Publications, May 2000, ISBN:0-306-46276-1

19. Simke J., "Open Networks -Transforming to Networked Economy", Price Waterhouse Coopers, September 2000, http://www.pwcglobal.com/ca-presentations
20. Stewart T.R., "The E-Business Tidal Wave", *Deloitte and Touche White paper*, September, 1999
21. Supply Chain Council, *Supply Chain Operations Reference (SCOR) Model*, http://www.supply-chain.org, Dec 2001
22. Tao L., "Shifting Paradigms with the Application Service Provider Model", *IEEE Computer*, Vol. 34, No. 10, October 2001
23. Turban E., King D., Warkentin M. and Chung H.M., *Electronic Commerce 2002: A Managerial Perspective*, (2nd Ed.), Chapter 12, Prentice Hall, 2002
24. Winograd T. and Flores F., *Understanding Computers and Cognition: A new foundation for Design*, Addison-Wesley, New York, 1987
25. World-Wide Web Consortium (WWWC), http://www.org, Dec 2001

Chapter 4. E-Business: A Service-Oriented View

Part 1 of this book discussed e-business models, and management issues from a generic business perspective. We started with management theories, and then described and analyzed e-business models. This was followed by a discussion of e-business management issues and evolving techniques for e-business management solutions. Most examples were given from the e-business domain in general, and from the telecommunication sector in particular. We highlighted the fact that a business service had to be defined and measured through business level parameters. Although we discussed the framework based on Service Level Agreements (SLA), it was not clear how qualitative service parameters could be quantified and measured to track a business service performance. Therefore, some of the questions may be formulated as:

- How to define e-business management specifications irrespective of the type of e-business (e.g., book publishing, travel service, e-commerce, e-healthcare, or e-government)?
- How can an e-business management solution be designed from scratch?
- How are qualitative business service parameters translated to measurable, quantitative parameters?
- How do we breakdown the complexity of such a design and deployment process?

This chapter addresses the above questions through a top-down discussion of e-business from a service perspective. The term "service", now extensively used in the domain of e-business, defines e-business from operational and management viewpoints. Parts 3 and 4 illustrate how e-business software specifications are derived from service requirements. This definition of e-business services emanates from the world of service-oriented businesses, such as banking and tourism. Hence many e-businesses can be specified by parameters used for measuring services, such as cost, reliability, availability, and satisfaction. Therefore, a generic methodology for the development and management of services should be applicable for e-business management as illustrated in this chapter.

We discuss a methodology for the design and management of a generic service (from restaurants to airlines). The concepts are illustrated using examples from the e-healthcare sector This methodology shows how a qualitatively defined service can be assessed, measured and monitored using the quantification of qualitative parameters. This is done systematically in eight stages. Most of the concepts have been borrowed from the Technical-Rational Management School.

This chapter starts with the definition of a service in generic form. We conclude with some examples of e-business in the healthcare domain. Sections 4.2 to 4.10 illustrate the Total Quality Management (TQM) based Eight-Stage Methodology for Service Design and Management from a generic service business standpoint. All through the discussions e-business perspectives are highlighted wherever appropriate. Section 4.11 identifies the need for a more focused methodology for e-business management. This is illustrated by presenting a now popular architecture-oriented methodology.

The next section discusses the basic concepts of a service.

4.1 Business Concepts of a Service

This section discusses and compares some qualitative business concepts relating to a service. At this stage we do not distinguish between an IT service and a restaurant service. Later these concepts will be used to define a methodology for the design and management of services. Such high-level methodologies need to be illustrated with some real service examples. Our examples in this chapter are taken from the e-healthcare domain.

4.1.1 Service Based Competitive Strategy

We start with a Tale of Two Companies:

- Company A maintains a competitive edge by bringing out new products regularly, and beats competition by product technical features
- Company B copies technical features of a new product from a competitor, and beats competition by better service strategy (e.g., longer service warranty, free replacement of defective products etc.).

Firstly, let us compare these two companies. Company A, by bringing out new products regularly – beats competition by product features. Company B, which copies the features of a product from a competitor – beats competition by better service standard e.g., longer service warranty. Which strategy is better from a business service perspective?

Company A accepts service as a product – which is the case for many new service providers. They have to survive and make profit in the market place. They cannot lag behind the competition. Let us consider the competitive market for telecommunication service in Italy whereTelecom Italia is the incumbent carrier and had all the market before deregulation. After deregulation of the telecommunication industry in Italy, other competitors, such as WIND came into existence. WIND and other new carriers had to come up with new product strategies, and competitive strategies to survive in the market. Company A's strategy may be suitable in this case because the investment on a new product is affordable.

On the other hand, a company dealing with high investment manufacturing, such as automobiles, cars, televisions or computers, requires high investments and lead times for new product development. In such cases, perhaps CompanyB's strategy is better. Two Views of a Service

Service may be viewed from two different perspectives:

1. As a support offered with a tangible product e.g., service of cars, televisions, and computers. We call this *support service.* In this case service is important for the success of the product business
2. As a product on its own e.g., airline travel, banking, Internet Service. We call this *primary service.*

In the case of a support service (e.g., in automobiles, TVs etc.,), service design is different from product design, though they may depend on technicalities of manufacture and support mechanisms. Essentially service management processes are independent of product development and manufacturing processes. Similar service management processes could be used for a range of different businesses, such as automobiles, televisions or bicycles.

Unlike the above services, which are mainly for support, several other services are emerging as products in a big way in the modern, service-based economy. Examples include telecommunications, banking, and tourism. In this case service management is tightly coupled to the type of business. For example, the technical features of the service design and management in banking would be quite different from that of telecommunication or health care.

In this chapter we discuss situations where service itself is a product (primary service). We now define service management from a global perspective. Service management is concerned with the specification, design, implementation and evaluation of services as integrated processes. Design and management go very much hand in hand for services, particularly for businesses where service is a product. However, it is important to understand the key common principles of service design and management that do not depend on the type of business. The next section discusses some of these key principles.

4.1.2 Key Principles of Service Design and Management

In the case of a primary service, irrespective of the type of business, the following principles need to be considered for design and management processes[17]:

- Involve the customer in all stages of a service process that consistently and reliably meet customer expectations
- Derive the specifications of the design from the customers, not only from previous designs
- Derive the technical aspects of the design from above customer specifications. In other words technology should NOT dictate the design
- Design and evaluate the service as a cooperative work between people from all relevant organizations
- Provide service at a cost that keeps the company profitable

One needs to know what customers want, and should be able to express customer needs in a quantitative form.

It is necessary to derive design specifications from the primary customer, and not only from previous designs, as is commonly done for many manufactured products, such as cars, computers and bicycles. Deriving specifications from the primary customer differentiates service design from the design of manufactured products.

It is necessary to segregate customer specifications from product design. In other words, technology should not dictate the design. This exposes some of the weaknesses in the IT industry. One cannot impress the customer by talking only about technology. It is important to be able to deliver the service based on the customer's requirement. Evaluation and design involve the cooperation of people from all relevant departments within and across all concerned organizations, e.g., the customer, the supplier, and outsourcers.

All the above considerations are true for e-business services offered electronically over the Internet, such as share transactions, travel bookings, online shopping etc.

This chapter presents e-business management from a service industry perspective. There are various types of service-oriented e-businesses, including travel, finance, telecommunications, etc. E-healthcare is perhaps now the most significant area of service-oriented e-business in the world as discussed in the next section.

4.1.3 E-Healthcare: An E-Business of Major Significance[5]

The healthcare market worldwide is worth more than a trillion dollars, and it is easily the largest industry worldwide. In most countries governments solely control healthcare. Hence the increasing cost of healthcare is a major concern for most governments. Governments are bringing in private investments in healthcare through private healthcare funds. These funds have, in the past, passed on all cost increases to subscribers. That is not possible any longer. Hence healthcare insurance agencies are forced to develop more and more efficient processes for healthcare services[13].

This has given rise to a tremendous growth in the area of healthcare information technology. Many service features concerned with telecommunication are relevant here. For example, e-healthcare needs, high-resolution graphics for X-rays and scans; videoconferencing facilities for consultation amongst specialists located at distant locations, and it also requires object-oriented software technology for storage and retrieval of patient record systems.

For example, if an overseas visitor has an accident in Italy, the local doctor would not have his/her medical history. Hence it would be difficult for that doctor to treat the condition. For example, this person could be allergic to penicillin. Systems have now been developed where people can have access to their Electronic Patient Record (EPR) on the web. They could provide an authorized doctor any where in the world with access to their EPR especially in cases of emergency. An EPR could be linked to a person's passport, though there are major privacy issues that prevent governments from implementing such a system. EPR is the key to the success of e-healthcare and. telecommunication and computing technologies can be useful in enabling an effective EPR system. In the UK and in other developed countries (e.g., Australia), there is now a major initiative towards sharing health-care records over the Internet. Grimson and associates have presented the outcome of projects (Synapses and SynEx) for sharing fragmented medical information over the web[6].

In the US, the Internet2 (Next Generation Internet) initiatives are focusing on healthcare as one of the sectors that need enhancements in Internet based services. Healthcare is a new service, and it is likely to be a major business area for many network service providers. In this chapter all illustrations of this management model are based on healthcare IT services. Table 5 summarizes a comparative picture of the functional requirements of healthcare IT[20]. 1=minimal importance 4=great importance.

Table 5. Technical Demands of E-Healthcare

Application	Bandwidth	Latency	Availability	Security	Ubiquity
Clinical Care	4	3	4	4	2
Biomedical Research	4	3	2	2	2
Professional Education	3	2	2	1	3
Consumer Health	2	1	2	4	4
Public Health	1	1	3	3	3

The next section presents a few case studies in Healthcare IT taken from leading publications (referenced with the section heading) in the e-healthcare domain. This should serve to familiarize readers with the characteristics of e-healthcare from the perspective of e-business.

4.1.3.1 Military Launches Big Internet Initiative[4]

The U.S. Department of Defense Military Health Services needed an e-healthcare system to link illnesses, such as Gulf War Syndrome, to paper and electronic medical records after the Gulf War. The Department recently awarded a multi-year, $20 million contract to build an Internet portal designed to give patients, physicians and the Department easier access to a range of health care information.

The portal will enable patients, physicians and military hospitals to build Web sites, hosted on the portal. Patients will be able to use the Internet portal to create a personal/family medical history and populate it with their official medical records, access medical information content and send electronic mail to their physician to request appointments, drug refills and other information.

The portal will enable physicians to access patient records residing anywhere in the military health system. It will enable a wide range of transactions, including laboratory/radiology orders and results, pharmacy orders, claims submission, insurance eligibility inquiries/responses, claims status, patient referrals and electronic consultations. Physicians will have electronic access to patient records, a library and clinical guidelines.

This system will enable physicians to use e-mail to send preventive medicine messages or treatment reminders to patients. Physicians will also be able to disseminate additional information to patients by posting it on their Web sites, hosted on the portal. The portal will give the Department a single entry point for collecting and analyzing data.

4.1.3.2 Medical Center Takes Data Tracking to Heart[1]

The San Fransisco Heart Institute is a pioneer in the use of information technology for cardiac care. This northern California cardiovascular center mines its 20-year database of 25000 patients to analyze and improve the quality of care. The vast, historical database is the springboard for initiatives that range from decreasing patient length-of-stay after heart surgery to avoiding clinical complications arising from cardiac catheterization.

The benefits of data collection and outcomes analysis at the Heart Institute extend beyond the clinical arena. For example, decreasing length-of-stay by making changes to practice patterns based on outcomes research, has led to savings of $500,000 annually in care provision costs. Further, the institute's track record for high-quality cardiac care has helped it obtain valuable managed-care contracts, pushing it into the ranks of the top 100 cardiovascular centers in the country.

A multidisciplinary team that includes physicians, clinical nurses, technicians and data coders, collects the data upon which these and other assessments are based. The data points collected during a patient's hospitalization include demographics, history, risk factors, medications and clinical lab values; lesion size (both pre- and post-op); treatment outcomes and complications; physicians involved in the patient's care; procedure utilization and cost; and patient function and satisfaction after discharge. This data is entered into the Heartbase database in a number of ways: keyboard data entry, scanning and through electronic interfaces with other information systems. Some data is coded through chart abstracting and some is collected during procedures.

In addition to constantly mining its data to track performance and chart quality improvement, the San Francisco Heart Institute also uses technology and outcomes data to help nurture a better understanding of coronary artery disease in the global cardiology community.

4.1.3.3 Internet-based Managed Care Transactions [5]

When a patient comes in for treatment, it's the responsibility of administration staff (as per managed care processes) to confirm basic but crucial information before a clinical encounter. Eligibility, treatment authorization, pre-certification and referral status, for example, must be confirmed before health services are provided. If such information is not confirmed, provider organizations face the daunting task of tracking down information for denied claims and navigating the lengthy haggling process with managed care organizations to determine how, why and if a doctor is going to get paid.

The lack of communication between many payer and provider organizations is acute. Hence payer organizations (e.g., healthcare insurance providers) and health care information technology vendors are rolling out e-healthcare systems designed to provide quick and easy answers to eligibility, referral and authorization questions, among many other managed care transactions. However, this is not easy due to complex procedures involving many different organizations providing various types of services, such as pathological tests, imaging, consultations, hospital operations etc. Many payer organizations operate legacy databases and mainframe systems that are often difficult to integrate with Internet-based systems. This has led to the development of a number of interoperability standards, such as. HL7, DICOM, IEEE MIB etc.[3]

In addition, a number of health care I.T. vendors are marketing Internet-based transactions services that enable providers to perform managed care transactions with multiple payers through a single Web site. Standard transaction formats mandated by the Health Insurance Portability and Accountability Act (HIPAA) are expected to speed up efforts to move managed care transactions and other health care transactions to the Internet.

4.1.4 The Eight-Stage Service Design and Management Methodology

We now discuss a methodology that captures and illustrates some of the important processes in the development and management of services, including e-business services.

The suggested strategy in this case is to use an Eight-Stage Service Design and Management model. This is an integrated model based on quality management discussed by Rohit Ramaswamy[17]. This model has evolved in the AT and T's service development over the last decade or so and is very useful in the formulation of qualitative service management requirements, and their top-down quantification.

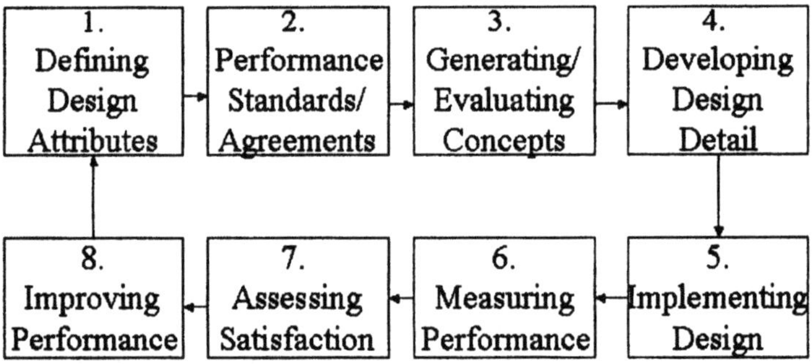

Figure 21. Eight-Stage Service Design and Management Model[17]

The first stage of this model defines service needs based on customer requirements. In the second stage designers and customers come together to finalize some kind of performance benchmark for service. This benchmark is then incorporated into Service Level Agreements (SLAs). The third stage involves the generation of concepts for design purposes. This helps in developing the design framework. The next stage is to develop the design in more detail. Of course at every level one needs to be as quantitative as possible. Stage 6 involves implementation of the design. Stage 7 entails the measurement of design performance, and assessment of customer satisfaction in relation to the initial requirements. Finally, in Stage 8, one can go ahead with improving performance, based on the satisfaction level measured in Stage 7. So the Eight-Stage model is an iterative loop of 8 stages (Figure 21), which help us design and refine a service and work out management strategies.

Stages 1-4 of this methodology are primarily design steps. Stages 5-8 are primarily the management of service. Thus this model provides a way of integrating design and management functions of any service. The beauty of this model is that it is generic and can be used for any type of service, including airline service, banking service, restaurant service, health care or telecommunication services. It is applicable to a wide variety of e-business management situations. This methodology uses Total quality Management (TQM) techniques discussed next.

4.1.5 Total Quality Management (TQM)

The objectives of Total Quality Management (TQM) of Technical-Rational management theory may be summarized as follows:

- Increased User satisfaction
- Decreased Errors
- Enhanced products and services
- Shorten Time to market
- Reduce Prices

These objectives are addressed with the following sets of techniques[14]:

- The ISO 9001 standard establishes a common language between customers and service providers, and helps define the agreed quality levels (and processes and systems to achieve them). This provides an overall framework for management
- The Structured Analysis and Design Technique (SADT) helps break-up a complex process into sub-activities to delineate the authorities and responsibilities of multiple human roles involved. We'll use a variation of this in CoMENS methodology in Part 5.
- Quality Function Deployment (QFD) matrices are used to design attributes of a product or service over its entire lifecycle. This technique will be used extensively in this Chapter
- Analytic Hierarchy Protocol (AHP) is a decision support technique for evaluation and prioritizing alternative solutions. We'll use variations of this technique (e.g., Pugh's method) in this chapter.
- Statistical Process Control (SPC) provides a quantitative measure of the statistical behavior of a system. Network management platforms provide such measures as discussed in Parts 3 and 4.

- Dynamic Scaling Services (DSS) provides a control technique for dynamically adjusting network parameters based on service requirements. Such techniques (not used in this book) are used for the management of Quality of Service of electronic services, such as videoconference.

As discussed, we use QFD and AHP techniques in different stages of the Eight Stage Service Design and Management Methodology. Now we look at the different stages with relevant illustrations from a telemedicine service that enables a clinical healthcare service from remote geographical locations.

4.2 Stage-1- Customer Needs Assessment

The first stage of the model shown in Figure 21 is related to the assessment of customer needs.

4.2.1 Stage-1 Operation

The process at this stage (assessment of customer needs) involves the following.

- Identify the key customers and their service needs
- Prioritize the needs in order of importance
- Specify the design attributes required by a service that meets these needs
- Create quantitative measures for attributes
- Establish the relationship between needs and attributes
- Determine the most important attributes

The key issue here is cost relationship between metrics of requirements vis-à-vis what is on offer. There is a metric for user needs, in the order of importance and the right technical attributes required to meet the needs. For example, in the case of a television service, like video conferencing, the technical attributes could be picture resolution and response time. One can correlate user needs according to the quantitative measures of these technical attributes.

4.2.2 Stage-1 Illustration: E-Healthcare

Here are the major points related to customer need assessment in an e-healthcare business, involving patient treatment by groups of healthcare professionals (including doctors, nurses, radiologists, pathologists etc.) in community and hospital environments.

- Hospitals with networked computing environments and staff willing to use them

- Needs: Online diagnoses with scan images, pathology test results, patient records, and communication amongst medical staff.
- Attributes: Picture quality, response time, ease of use.
- Relationship: Online diagnosis requires right picture quality, right response time

Now let us see how these concepts apply in this e-healthcare service. The major customers are nurses, doctors and other healthcare workers. The service is patient care (including on line diagnosis with scan images, customer queries, patient records and communication with medical staff) from a distance using Internet connections. Stage 1 in this case needs to clarify the customer requirements, which include x-rays, scans, pathological tests etc, and to specify a service that satisfies these needs. Now the communication media could be fax, Internet email, or face-to-face conversation.

This requirement is first expressed from the point of view of a doctor or from the point of view of a hospital administrator. They do not need to know the technology at all at this stage. When the design is actually implemented, the technological attributes come to the fore. So we will say picture quality, and response time (there could be many more such parameters) are the attributes that specify a telemedicine service from the point of view of the IT service provider.

Step 1 must correlate the business level service specification (user needs) with the technical level service design. On line diagnosis requires right picture quality and right response time. The problem is that it is not easy to translate user needs to technical design parameters, even with the help of the doctor (user). For example, the doctor may not know what a picture resolution of 1000*1000 means in relation to the quality of the scan required to effectively diagnose a medical condition. Hence it is necessary to deploy some quality management techniques to derive quantified values from various service parameters.

4.2.3 Quality Function Deployment (QFD) Matrices

Quality Function Deployment (QFD) is a systematic matrix-based visual approach for designing quality products and services. QFD is based on the Total Quality Management (TQM) philosophy that high-quality products and services distinguish themselves by adhering to quality standards in all activities throughout their life cycle[17].

The best-known matrix is the first in the QFD hierarchy. This matrix, referred to as the House of Quality (HOQ), is used to translate customer needs into service design characteristics. The term was made popular by

Hauser and Clausing (1988) in their seminal *Harvard Business Review* paper of the same name. HOQ has eight compartments (Rooms).[7]

4.3 House of Quality Matrices

In order to translate the vague terms like "right" or "good" to quantitative values, it is necessary to use some kind of systematic modeling tactics. For this purpose, we use by way of example the quality function deployment matrix or QFD matrices, which have been used extensively in the area of Total Quality Management (TQM). These matrices help resolve issues in the quantitative formulation of design and management specifications from the qualitative attributes that we saw in Section 4.2. There is a wide range of matrices used for this purpose, the most common being the House Of Quality (HoQ) matrix (see Figure 22). HoQ will be used extensively in this methodology.

House of Quality conceptualizes the process of arriving at user needs, and service specifications, from a set of visual rules. The rules are as follows:

The process of specifications is:- talk to the customer in Room #1 (away from technical designers). Then take the designers or the implementers of the systems (technical people) into another room, Room #2, and talk to them separately about the competing services available for that purpose. If the two groups are brought together it is quite possible that the user group may feel inhibited due to the lack of technological knowledge, and not spell out the requirement clearly. Similarly, a less than optimal technological solution, specified by some users, may inhibit the technical design group. One can combine the data generated from the consultations with the customer and technical people and using some simple calculations, to be specified later, arrive at the requirements. The visual paradigm of HoQ is organized in eight compartments of thinking (rooms). This compartmentalization and subsequent systematic correlation helps in deriving the specification in an unattached, objective manner.

The next step, in Room #3, is to rank the needs according to their levels of importance. Let us say that most important for this diagnosis, is the x-ray or the scans, or the pathology test. One can assign some kind of a notional value, or a ranking factor to each of these needs. Relationship matrices are defined with design characteristics as rows, and needs as columns. This is followed by deliberations in Room #4 (with customers) on the extent to which the already ranked needs are satisfied by competing services (e.g., fax and Internet).

Once that is done, move into Room #5 where one needs to ask the viewpoints of the designers. This is followed by deliberations in Room #6 where designers are asked to define the alternatives against some criteria for comparison.

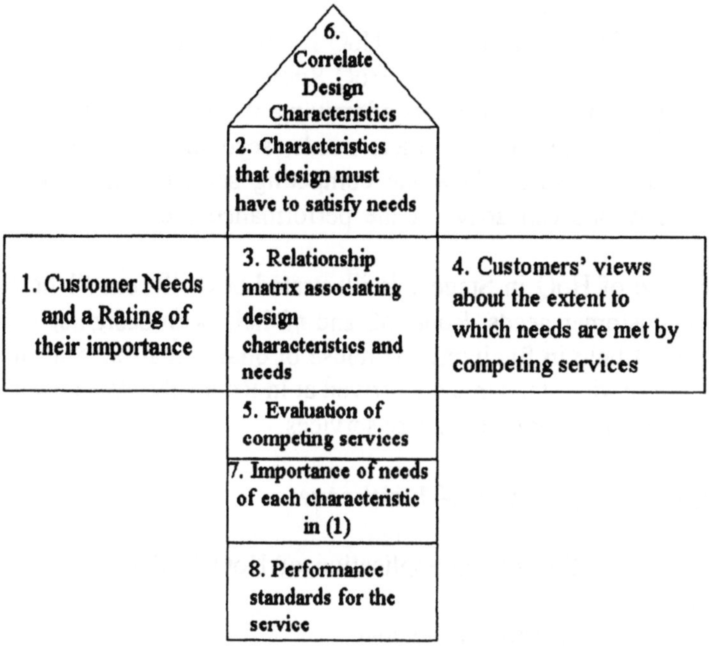

Figure 22. House of Quality (HoQ) Matrix

Customers then view the matrix in Room #7 to check on the extent to which needs are met by the competing services. Finally, in Room #8 quantitative benchmarks are specified for the management of the service under consideration.

Therefore, QFD matrices (as shown with HoQ), provide the following benefits:

- A structured method for defining quality standards early in the design process
- A system for incorporating quality standards in the service design methodology
- A technique for the propagation of the quality throughout the service lifecycle
- Establishment of quality relationships at different levels of service parameters

HoQ matrices can be used in different stages of the Eight-Stage Service Management model. The next section illustrates the application of HoQ in Stage 1 of the model.

4.3.1 HOQ in Stage-1

Application of HoQ in Stage 1 involves:

- Understanding Customer Needs - HoQ Room #1
- Generating Design Characteristics - HoQ Rooms# 2 and #3
- Determining Important Attributes - HoQ Rooms# 6 and #7

HoQ helps us perform the process of arriving at service specifications in several steps: firstly identify customers needs; secondly identify designer attributes; and thirdly assess how the competing services meet customer needs, and finally one can arrive at the performance specification of that service.

The relevance of HoQ in Stage 1 is illustrated next. Room #1 helps in understanding customer needs. Room #2 and #3 help with design specifics. Rooms #6 and #7 help in finalizing the house of quality matrix. And finally the e-healthcare service standards are arrived at in Room #8. We now detail how Stage 1 is handled for e-healthcare services.

4.3.2 HOQ in Stage-1 for E-Healthcare

Here is an illustration of the application of HoQ in Stage 1 in our e-healthcare scenario.

- Room #1: Voice of Customer (doctor)
- Room #2: Design Attributes
- Room #3, #6 and #7: Relationship between 1 and 2

In Room #1 one hears the voice of the customer (the doctor). He says, "I want to see the patient's scan and pathology result". Room #1 considers the request from the technical perspective of an IT person. The issues may include technical parameters, such as resolution, response time, and data formats. For example, multimedia data storage is required because patient record has to be linked to Patient history, and also any interviews the patient has had with other doctors. This must all be put together in common hyperlinks from the patient's id. Then Rooms #3, #6 and #7 show the relationship between #1 and #2 in terms of the attribute importance. Figure 23 shows the results of this analysis.

Room #1 is where the user (e.g. a doctor) states the requirements in the order of importance (1-4 in ascending order of importance). As shown in Figure 23, patient history is most important (importance level 4), next important is the test reports (importance level 3), followed by the scans (level 2). From the designer's point of view, these are two very important attributes (picture resolution and multimedia record access). There could be more attributes like this. However, we show the analysis process using these two variables as examples.

- Room 1: Voice of Customer (doctor): "I want to see patient Case History and any scan/pathology test results"
- Room 2: Design Attributes: Resolution of scanned images, multimedia data storage and retrieval
- Room 3,6 &7: Relationship between 1 & 2, Attribute Importance:

User Needs	***Picture Resolution***	***Multimedia Record***
Patient History (4)	Moderate (2)	Strong (4)
Test Reports (3)	Weak (1)	Moderate (2)
X-Ray Scans (2)	Strong (4)	Strong (4)
Attribute	4*2+3*1+2*4=19	4*4+3*2+2*4=30
Importance	38%	62%

Figure 23. Stage-1 Illustration in E-Healthcare

The next step is to rate the importance of two technical parameters with respect to each of the user needs. For the case history the multimedia report is important (4) and the picture resolution is not that important (2). For x-rays and scans picture resolution and the multimedia report are both important. Next question is what is the relative importance of picture resolution and multimedia record access? The answer is arrived at by performing a weighted addition across all needs for each of the design parameters. So the weighted sum for picture resolution is 4 x 2+ 3 x 1+2 x 4 = 19. Similarly, the weighted sum for multimedia access parameter is 4 x 4+3x2 + 2x4 = 30. After normalization the relative importance of these two technical parameters are: 38 per cent for picture resolution, and 62 per cent for multimedia record. We have grossly over-simplified the calculation with only two technical variables and only three user-need parameters. However, it is possible to carry out similar analyses in relation to a large number of technical parameters in the design of a service, using a computer program that follows the above algorithm.

Similar analysis processes can be used to define services qualitatively for any business sector, and arrive at the relative quantitative importance of design parameters for any other application domain. It is worthwhile to point out that such simple calculations are often useful in the design of multidisciplinary services.

It is important to ascertain customer needs. The scenario here corresponds to B2C type of e-business. However, many of the e-businesses operate on B2B basis, and hence it is important to clearly define customer, as opposed to a B2C environment. Also it is desirable to use graphical techniques as discussed later in Section 4.8. QFD matrices complement these techniques.

Now based on the quantitative measures of the attributes, one can correlate the user needs consequent to specifications of the technical attributes.

4.4 Stage-2: Specifying Performance Standards

Having specified the user needs with respect to service design parameters (and their relative importance levels), the next job is to specify the performance standards. For example, the analysis in the previous section does not tell us the specifications for any particular attribute. What is the picture resolution - whether it should be thousand by thousand, 400 by thousand, or any other value? Similarly what are the specifications for response time? Are there other attributes needed to design the system?

- Identify the customers' desired performance level for each attribute
- Analyze the performance of competitors
- Determine the Relationship between performance and satisfaction
- Specify design performance Standards/Agreements for each attribute

Next we talk about the importance of competitors. In the design of an engineering product, technical design issues are considered most important. However, in the design of a service (which is so closely related to business issues like cost and competition), competitive solutions must be compared before designing a new service.

Therefore a service design needs to start from a business perspective. The business perspective is often understood by looking at the offerings from competitors - the competitors of that company for the same product and existing solutions to the specified problem, say for example, in the case of telemedicine, the existing solutions include fax and Internet.

It is necessary to arrive at the relationship between performance and satisfaction. In order to be able to arrive at the quantitative specifications of the design attributes, it is necessary to derive the relationship between performance and satisfaction of all the competitive solutions. In the case of telemedicine, the options include, the Internet, face-to-face meeting, and fax. As shown in Figure 24, it is possible to plot the different competitive solutions (e.g., fax versus Internet) against any measure of performance (e.g., picture quality). Then the user satisfaction level curve is superimposed on this plot. That gives the relative satisfaction/performance of different competitive solutions.

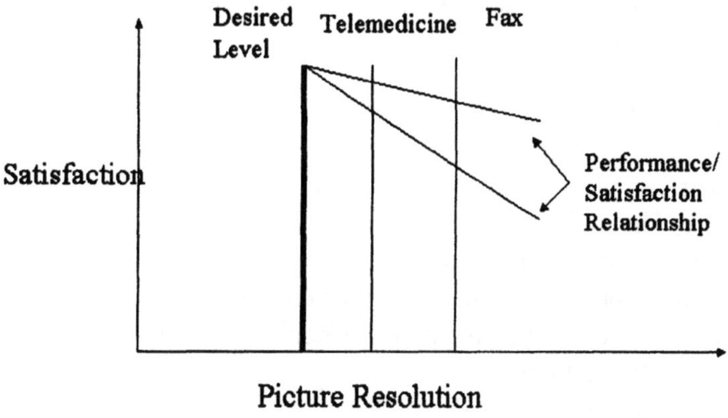

Figure 24. Specifying Performance

4.4.1 Stage-2 Illustration: E-Healthcare

The application of Stage 2 in e-healthcare business creates the necessity to consider the following major points:

- Online diagnosis requires response time less than 30 sec
- How does e-healthcare perform in comparison with face to face consultations
- Even though the doctor can diagnose remotely, patient needs a doctor's healing touch
- To fire a screen, user key strokes<n

On line diagnosis requires a response time of less than 30 seconds. The question is how does e-healthcare perform in comparison with face-to-face consultation. A face-to-face service is better, despite the fact that the doctor can do the same thing remotely because a patient needs the doctors "healing touch"- a psychological advantage. But when one considers the waiting time, the travel time for physical consultation, and the cost, e-healthcare offers a great solution. Similarly, one can relate satisfaction levels with some physical parameters. For example, the number of keystrokes for a job is a quantitative indicator of performance that relates easily to the satisfaction level of a keyboard user. The higher the number of keystrokes, the less satisfying the service.

Thus Stage 2 helps in the quantification of some qualitative design parameters for a service.

While many of the service performance parameters are based on easy-to-understand real-life parameters, some aspects, such as cooperation cannot be easily measured, and hence abstract parameters, such as awareness levels are required, as described in Part 5 of this book.

4.4.2 Relevance of HOQ in Stage-2

The HoQ matrices play an important role in Stage 2, leading to the definition of SLAs. The major points are:

- Performance Standards (Defining SLAs)
- Measuring desired performance level (Implementing SLAs)
- Customer and Technical Benchmarks (HoQ Rooms 4 and 5)
- Performance/Satisfaction Function
- Setting performance goals (HoQ Room 8)
- Estimating performance/satisfaction relationship

Unlike engineering products, the ultimate effectiveness of a service can only be measured by the satisfaction level of customers. Since this is a qualitative parameter, various techniques are used in this methodology to relate satisfaction level to some quantitative parameters (performance standards). These parameters and their benchmarks are included in SLAs.

At the end of Stage 2, we offer some quantitative figures for service performance standards. One can monitor and manage service performance levels by implementing service level agreements.

4.4.3 HOQ in Stage-2 for E-Healthcare

In this case the users (doctors) are asked to rate (on a scale of 1-5, in ascending level of importance) different competing solutions for remote diagnosis. As we saw in the previous sections, there were three options. One is face-to-face doctor-patient consultation with the hard-copy x-ray reports, hard copy scans, and hard-copy pathology reports. The second option is based on fax. Reports and scans are faxed to the doctor, and the doctor faxes the treatment. The third option is to use e-healthcare, which allows the use of the Internet for scans, reports and consultations.

As shown in Figure 25, the e-healthcare remote diagnostics service is based on two major parameters- test reports and scans. It is now necessary to fix benchmarks for both of these in order to define service levels as part of an SLA. The process involves conjoint analysis, described as follows.

The user (doctor) is asked to rank the importance of the two service parameters (test reports and scans) on a scale of 1-5 with ascending order of importance. In this case both parameters are equally important (value 4). Then the user is asked to rank the satisfaction level on a scale of 1-5 with ascending order of satisfaction, for each parameter of the existing competing services, i.e., fax and hardcopy. In this case hardcopy has the highest satisfaction level for both parameters (5,5). Now the service performance parameters (e.g. picture quality) values are generated for the case with highest satisfaction level, which in this case is hardcopy. The value for picture quality for scans is 1000x1000, and for test reports it is 640x400. Similar parameters could be used for other technical design variables, such as the response time, and jitter.

- Room 4: Customer evaluation of 2 services competing with telemedicine (hardcopy & fax) in scale 1-5
- Room 5: Technical measure of an important attribute Picture resolution in both cases:

	Doctor Importance	Picture Resolution	Hardcopy Service	Fax Service
Test Reports	4	1000*1000	5	4
Scan Images	4	640*400	5	2

Figure 25. Stage-2 Illustration

Then rank attributes, in order of a decreasing slope of performance, satisfaction functions, so the attributes of picture resolution will be based on the decreasing slope of performance satisfaction. We have two strings of ranks. One rank is for the various performance levels versus satisfaction. The second rank is for the various attributes. The attributes could be response time, throughput, picture resolution and so on. Each of them will have a slope curve, as shown in Figure 24. Just like picture resolution, one can use a similar graph for 10 other variables.

One can also derive a single index of satisfaction level for each competing service solution by taking a weighted sum of satisfaction levels for each service solution. For example, the value for hardcopy service will be 5x4+5x4=40, and the value for the fax service will be 4x4+2x4=24. So the question remains as to what should be the benchmark for picture quality? Obviously, the e-healthcare minimum acceptable satisfaction level should be 40 (the same as hardcopy in this case). This can be expanded and applied to a larger number of service parameters. However, the problem is more difficult if actual customer satisfaction does not match the desired level, and there are a large number of performance parameters. In this case, the most practicable way of quantifying the quality of service parameters is to use an iterative computer-based algorithm. The process starts with a few important performance parameters, we drop the less important ones. We fix their benchmarks and then extend the calculation to a larger number of variables.

Although we have used a very simple case for illustration, the same algorithm can be followed in a much more complex situation with many service parameters (e.g. scans), and many performance parameters (e.g.,picture quality). The same method of analysis could be used for any other type of service, such as banking, restaurant, or travel. This method is also quite suitable for any non-technical user.

4.4.4 HOQ Room 8: Setting Performance Goals

This is the last and most important process of Stage-2 using HoQ matrices. The steps are:

- Specify minimum acceptable satisfaction threshold
- Rank attributes in order of decreasing slope of performance/satisfaction function
- Rank attributes in order of importance
- Set design performance levels for each attribute
- Predict the overall satisfaction of attribute performance levels set in previous step
- Determine whether the predicted satisfaction is higher than the minimum acceptable threshold
- If not, tighten the performance of some attributes, or drop some less important ones.

We have seen in the previous section how competing services are compared with respect to service parameters, and how that is translated to corresponding values of performance parameters. The question is then what should be the performance goals, or standards? We look at Figure 24 again to establish the relationship between satisfaction and performance. The principle is based on sensitivity, i.e., the slope of satisfaction vs. performance curve in Figure 24. If the sensitivity is not high, one can choose a design standard that is most practicable or cost effective for the service. Otherwise the performance goal should be close to the desired level. If we look at Figures 24 and 25, the sensitivity being high, the values for hardcopy (e.g. picture quality=1000x1000 for scan) become the benchmark for the new service of Internet based on e-healthcare. The idea is to present to customers a number of options and plot the satisfaction levels with respect to various competing options. If the sensitivity is not high, one has some flexibility in defining the standard (considering other business parameters like cost); otherwise the best option is to accept the most desirable solution from the existing comparison. So we started with something vague and totally qualitative and arrive at a thousand by thousand picture resolution for the e-healthcare objective.

As discussed earlier, a service can be defined at a number of levels in a top-down fashion. For example, one can start with a service level specification, and then drill down to system level, subsystem level, and finally to component level. Once the process has been completed for one of the highest levels, it is possible for the other levels as well. Let us say the top level is multimedia applications, according to the doctor's requirements, the second level could be communication level with four major characteristics, namely throughput, jitter, response time and delay This is done using a hierarchy of QFD matrices, discussed next.

4.4.5 Hierarchy of QFD Matrices

After Stage 1 and 2 one should be able to obtain the targets for all the different layers of the system. If the levels are service level, application level and software component level, one can drill down from service level, to application level, and then to system, and subsystem levels. As shown in Figure 26, the same HoQ matrices can be used to derive the performance standards at each level. So this is a hierarchical multiple-level technique used to arrive at the quantitative design parameters for a service situation. The performance standard of one level becomes the user needs for the next level of design.

The beauty of this whole process is that it can be applied to any type of service. It does not have to be for e-healthcare or telecommunication services only. It can be for an airline service or restaurant service also. Rohit Ramaswamy describes the application of this methodology to various service scenarios in different domains of businesses[17].

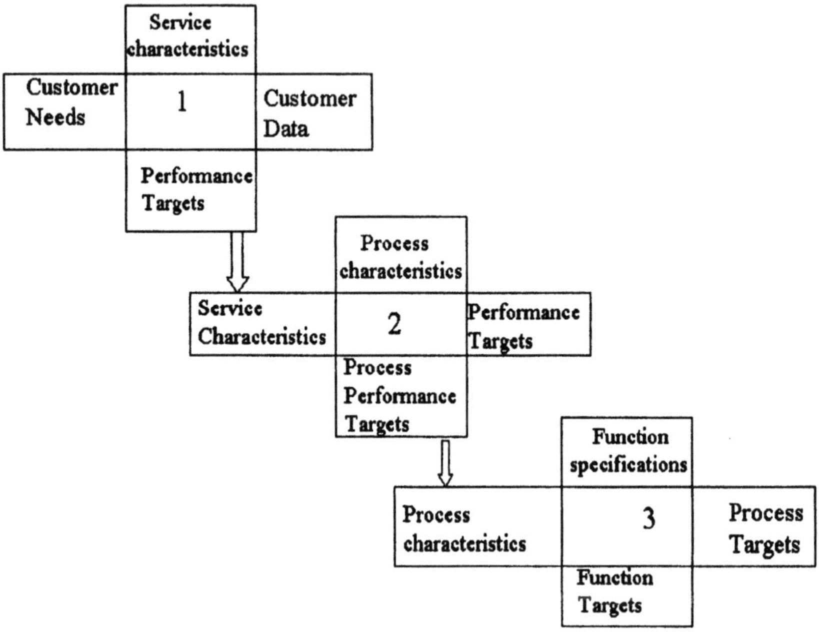

Figure 26. Hierarchy of House of Quality (HoQ) Matrices

4.5 Stage-3: Generating and Evaluating Concepts

This stage involves the following sub-processes:

- Define the key functions needed to provide the service
- Assemble these functions into processes
- Document these processes using a graphical notation
- Create alternate design concepts for service
- Evaluate and select a concept for design

Having covered Stage 2, Specifications, we are now at Stage 3, Design Selection for generating and evaluating the concepts. Here we must evaluate and select the best strategy for design solutions. Firstly, we define the key functions needed to provide this service. Then assemble these functions into processes, document these processes using graphical notation, and create design concepts for service.

Initially the key functions have to be created in some graphical notation. Then alternative strategies for implementing these functions are examined and the best strategy is selected.

4.5.1 Stage-3 Illustration: E-Healthcare Service

Stage 3 can be illustrated through e-healthcare services as follows:

- Updating patient records, storage and retrieval of images based on an index
- Involves both human and machine actions; data entry by receptionist, followed by timed update of remote files
- In-house information system versus outsourced service
- Cost-benefit analysis (payback period)

In the case of e-healthcare services, the application design considerations could include updating EPRs, i.e., how to update multimedia patient records and their storage/retrieval images, based on some index. The choice here could be whether to use the in-house application or whether to outsource. One has to use cost-benefit analysis to arrive at the best option.

4.5.2 Pugh Method for Evaluating and Selecting Concepts

The Pugh method described below helps in the evaluation and selection of a strategy from a number of options.

- List Concepts as evaluation matrix columns
- Select Criteria for evaluation and list as matrix rows
- Select Baseline concept
- Evaluate Concepts against Baseline
- Total the +, -, and S ratings for each concept
- Identify Opportunities to remove negatives
- Identify opportunities to accentuate positives
- Create improved concepts
- Remove weak concepts from matrix
- Rerun matrix with new concepts and a new baseline

Specifications from Stages 1 and 2 are translated to the process level to establish the performance requirements of each process. This involves the generation and evaluation of requirements for each process, which is followed by the selection of the alternative that satisfies performance standards.

This method of evaluation starts after a brain storming exercise that gives a number of possible solutions. The process of selection involves a systematic rejection of less relevant options. Consequently, the options under consideration reduce gradually until the best possible option is found. The idea is to list the alternative design concepts in the columns of an evaluation matrix. Then the criteria for evaluation need is listed in the rows

One of the concepts will be for the reference column, or baseline column, and the other concepts will be evaluated one by one by comparison with the baseline. The other columns would be either same, better or worse compared to the baseline. We use S for same, + for better and – for worse. Next one needs to identify the total of +s and –s. The negative options need to be gradually removed. The options that are most negative should be removed at this stage. After removing the most negative, the baseline may be readjusted in the positive direction, and then carry out the same process repetitively until the best option is found. This method was devised by Stuart Pugh as part of the process of Total Design[16].

As shown in Figure 27, evaluation criteria for our service are based on attributes, such as picture resolution, cost and timeliness. The concepts are (1) based on hard copy (2) telemedicine and (3) fax. We take the fax as the baseline and compare this baseline with the other two options for each attribute. For example, the picture resolution in the case of hard copy is better (+) than fax. Costs of hard copy are cheaper (-) than that of fax. Timeliness for hard copy is worse (-) than fax, take more time. Adding the positives and negatives, in the case of hard copy there are 2 negatives, whereas for fax there is only one negative. So obviously the hardcopy option would be eliminated. If more options are available, the same process can be repeated by shifting the baseline closer to a level higher than that of fax. However, there are only 3 options here, therefore telemedicine is the best option. This is one method or technique to select the best alternative out of a number of choices. Again this methodology is applicable to restaurant services, airline services, telecommunication services, or any other service.

Evaluation Criteria	***Concept1: Hardcopy***	***Concept2: Telemedicine***	***Concept3: Fax***
Picture Resolution	+	+	Baseline
Cost	-	S	"
Timeliness	-	S	"
Sum of positives +	1	1	"
Sum of negatives -	2	0	"
Sum of sames (S)	0	2	"

Figure 27. Illustration of Pugh Method for Evaluating Health Informatics Options

4.6 Stage-4: Developing Design Details

Once the design concepts or strategies are finalized, one needs to develop the design in detail as follows:

- Partition concepts into process-level design components
- Generate design alternatives for each component
- Predict performance of each alternative
- Evaluate and select alternatives for each component
- Evaluate and select design for implementation
- Test performance of overall service design
- Make any necessary modifications to the design
- Specify detailed functional requirements

Stage 4 develops the design detail. The objective is to select the design alternative that delivers the highest level of performance at an acceptable cost. It is important to note that the performance may be sensitive to service operating characteristics. Hence it is necessary to select a design that is stable over a range of operating conditions. The robustness test for this purpose may be carried out using simulations.

This is where the design requirements and the design will be different for different types of services. In this case, it will involve looking at the general design of each component, evaluating and selecting alternatives for each component, evaluating and designing for implementation. Concepts have to be partitioned. When designing for picture resolution, there could be different types of concepts. And these concepts could be broken up into process design parameters, such as how to achieve best picture quality? One can apply the Pugh's method for selecting the best option at any level. The same process can be repeated for other technical parameters.

Obviously, this detailed design stage can be more technical than the previous one. Therefore, the decisions involve more technical knowledge relating to the service implementation, in this case the IT environment.

4.6.1 Stage-4 Illustration: E-Healthcare Service

This section illustrates Stage 4, using our e-healthcare service. Here are the salient points:

- Image storage and retrieval process could use different types of databases and client-server designs
- Simulate the performance of each design alternative for different traffic conditions
- Select Oracle7-based design over Internet
- Tune database configuration and access protocols to suit the performance needs

Since this e-healthcare service environment uses IT infrastructure, the considerations could be networking design and database design. Therefore, the design considerations may include the choice of the type of communication protocols (e.g., TCP/IP vs., Novell SPX/IPX), or type of database (Access vs. Oracle).

Obviously, this detailed design stage can be more technical than the previous one. Therefore, the decisions involve more technical knowledge relating to the service implementation, in this case the IT environment.

This stage needs to be expanded into a number of levels, as suggested in the CoMENS methodology in Part 5.

4.6.2 Stage-4 Tools and Techniques

Stage 4 in e-business management involves the design of workflows, and software to implement the workflows, using a variety of distributed information systems methodologies, such as:

- Unified Modeling Language (UML) for the design of distributed object based software[9]
- International Standards Organization (ISO) standard Reference Model for Open Distributed Processing (RM-ODP). View points discussed in Part 4
- Action Workflows discussed in Part 5

Workflows help to graphically model the flow of work within and across organizational entities. This is perhaps one of the most potent tools in the integration of business processes with technical IT systems.

Since the design of the service is based on IT tools and techniques, we use software engineering methodologies, including dataflow diagrams, ER diagrams etc., at this stage to diagrammatically model software and information systems. Also one could use diagrams for modeling the relationship between data entities for a database design (ER diagrams). Since these systems are distributed in nature, one could use Open Distributed Processing (ODP) viewpoints, and/or methodologies for object-oriented software, such as Unified Modeling Language (UML)[21]. So we started the first case with business level requirements and went to the service level details that are at an abstract level, then arrived at quantitative parameters for application design. We then arrived at the specification of applications using software tools.

Computer Supported Cooperative Work (CSCW) techniques, including workflows, are discussed in Part 5 of this book.

4.7 Stage-5: Implementing the Design

In this section we present a project management view of design implementation that is applicable to any type of business service. Chapters 3 and 4 will discuss architectural issues related to the implementation of the software for e-business service management. A project management based implementation process consists of the following steps:

- Develop Implementation project plan (people, project time frames)
- Develop service construction plan (software development, procurement of hardware, documentation, and training)
- Develop a pilot testing plan (deployment at various locations)
- Develop a communication plan (communicate to all concerned of necessary changes)
- Develop a rollout and transition plan
- Develop a service management plan (plan for service monitoring)
- Implement all plans

The final stage is the actual implementation of the design. As in any project plan, this stage is concerned with the sequence of different parts of the work, each characterized by start and end dates, costs, and other resources. In some cases the deployment of a newly developed service may replace an existing service, which would require a transition plan from the existing to the new service. There are many temporary fixes applied at this stage, and these fixes must be recorded. It must be noted that these fixes cannot be easily dismantled.

4.7.1 Stage-5 Illustration: E-Healthcare Application

Application of Stage 5 processes to e-healthcare involves the following:

- Implementation timeframes
- Establishing hardware, software and procedures for the service
- Making arrangements for operations to continue in case of failures
- Communication with all related people
- Service management plan foresees troubles and solutions during operation In the case of e-healthcare services, implementation time has to be selected, establishing the hardware and software, and procedures for the service, making arrangements for operations to continue in case of failures. This is a critical phase for a healthcare environment because any lapses can cause danger to human lives. A healthcare environment has people from different disciplines with different viewpoints; hence one needs to have a very elaborate plan by this stage. Stage 5 needs to be combined with ITSM stages, and many architectural attributes/standards as discussed in Parts 3 and 4.

4.8 Stage-6: Measuring Performance

Just as doctors systematically monitor a patient's vital signs such as heart rate, pulse rate, and blood pressure to track improvement in a patient's health condition, companies monitor performance measures to track business process improvement.

One of the main advantages of using performance measures is that they enable companies to express the results of a business process in quantitative, not qualitative, terms. Instead of using subjective words like "good", "fast" or "low cost" to report the results of a business process, performance measures translate subjective judgments into precise metrics, which companies can then record and analyze just like any numeric data. If, for example, the accounts payable process is being analyzed:

- Instead of saying that the accounts payable process is "good", a company reports that the percentage of invoices processed without error per month is 100 percent.
- Instead of saying that the accounts payable process is "fast", a company reports that the average number of days to edit and review an invoice is two.
- Instead of saying that the accounts payable process is "low cost", a company reports that the total cost to finance accounts payable as a percentage of total revenue is 5 percent.

By providing reliable, quantifiable data to evaluate business processes, performance measures allow companies to offer employees concrete feedback about current performance and to set goals for future improvement. For example, by using performance measures at annual performance reviews, not only can managers tell employees what activities they hope to improve but also how much improvement they expect to see. They find that employees often understand performance goals better when expressed in quantitative terms such as "reduce cycle time by 50 percent" or "increase inventory turnover by 30 percent".

Moreover, business people everywhere have long acknowledged, "what gets measured gets done". The practice of simply measuring a task or activity focuses powerful attention on it and, as a result, people will naturally strive to improve it.

Finally, when monitored consistently, performance measures help a company identify process problems as they occur, often well before the problems adversely affect profitability. In fact, to ensure that they receive constant feedback throughout the business process, companies often take a two-pronged approach by monitoring two different types of performance measures: outcome measures and activity measures.

Outcome measures report the results of a process and let companies know how well they are performing in a particular area of their business. The outcome measures are usually chosen based on the company's overall business goals and are intended to demonstrate the impact of a process on the company's finances, efficacy, and efficiency. Senior management analyzes outcome measures to keep score on company performance and to help control and allocate resources for improvements.

For example, even though the responsibilities of the senior managers of a company (such as the CFO) extend beyond processing accounts payable, they may choose to analyze the outcome measures relevant to that process, including:

- The average days in accounts payable
- The total cost to finance accounts payable as a percentage of revenue
- The number of accounts payable staff per $1 million in sales

By analyzing the relevant outcome measures, senior managers can trace the impact of the accounts payable process on the company's overall cash flow and revenue stream. In fact, regular examination of outcome measures helps senior managers determine how efficiencies in a particular business process contribute to the overall health and wealth of the company.

While outcome measures look at the results of a process, activity measures detail the journey toward those results by tracking improvements in process-specific activities over time. Where outcome measures address issues of importance to the company as a whole, activity measures address issues of concern to those charged with carrying out process-specific activities.

For example, the midlevel managers of a company, who are directly responsible for processing accounts payable, would monitor activity measures such as:

- The average number of days to edit and review an invoice
- The average number of errors on payments
- The average percentage of invoices paid on time

By monitoring specific activity measures rigorously, midlevel managers identify problems in a business process as soon as they occur. Such timely alerts create opportunities for managers to take immediate action to solve problems before they affect the company's overall growth. Midlevel managers also use activity measures as a motivational tool by showing employees how constructive changes in the way they perform activities directly improve the results of activity measures and how such improvements often lead to better outcome measures as well.

Companies today, regardless of the industry or geography, share three common business goals: to deliver products and services of the highest quality, at the lowest cost, and in the shortest amount of time. Hence, in addition to looking at activity versus outcome measures, companies need to choose performance measures that reflect cost, quality, and time concerns.

In fact, cost-based, quality-based, and time-based performance measures function as a unit to provide a comprehensive evaluation of business performance:

- **Cost-based measures** cover the financial side of performance; for example, measures such as "cost to finance accounts payable" reflect the impact that a business process has on the company's bottom line.
- **Quality-based measures** assess how well a company's products or services meet customer needs; for example, measures such as "average number of days to resolve payer's requests and inquiries" offer reliable information about the quality of service provided by the company.
- **Time-based measures** focus on the efficiency of the process; for example, measures such as "the average days in accounts payable" track the cycle time of a process.

Companies are said to earn a balanced scorecard – that is, across-the-board excellence – on their performance measures when they deliver both value and service to customers. Customers recognize value in high-quality products that are made available to them at a low cost; furthermore, they recognize service when those same high-quality, low-cost products are also delivered to them at a fast rate. Therefore, for those companies that wish to achieve a balanced scorecard, it is vitally important that they choose performance measures that reflect an optimum balance of cost, quality and time.

The process at Stage 6 can be summarized as:

- Select key attributes to be analyzed
- Measure performance attributes relative to standards/agreements (effectiveness measure)
- Measure capability of attributes (variability measure)
- Measure efficiency of key processes (operating costs and resource utilization)
- Develop reporting and analysis procedures
- Identify attributes whose performance does not meet standards/agreements
- Analyze root cause of poor performance
- Perform any corrective action, if necessary

Now having implemented this process, the next phase is measuring performance. This necessitates the development and use of measuring parameters. The first consideration is the selection of key attributes that can be analyzed against certain standards and agreements. This is the most important part of a management solution. Typically Service Level Agreements (SLAs) are used at this stage.

The service management plan must be in place before the deployment of a service. Management of a design prototype – measuring a prototype would be quite different from managing in a production service environment.

Service performance metrics are of three types:

1. Effectiveness Metrics to measure the performance of the service relative to SLAs and indicators of the effectiveness of service
2. Capability Metrics are the averages of standard deviations of performance of key internal process activities. Increase in variability provides early warning of future problems
3. Efficiency Metrics, such as operating costs and resource utilization levels

It is important to point out that service process performance may deteriorate over time due to inefficient implementation, inadequate training, negligence, boredom, or unexpected changes in process inputs.

In the measurement phase, the first step is in the management of a service. Now there are two objectives of management. One is to track performance, make sure that performance is to set standards or set agreements. And secondly, if performance is not up to set standards and agreements, analyze the root causes of the poor performance. By the time the service is designed, the customer's requirements may have changed. This could be due to various reasons. For example, a new service product may have come on to the market.

In an e-business environment, measurement of services presents some challenges due to the need for mapping service attributes to related network and system level technical parameters. This will be discussed in detail in Parts 3 and 4 of this book.

4.8.1 Stage-6 Illustration: E-Healthcare Service

The following is an illustration of Stage 6 for an e-healthcare service:

- Key attributes: Picture quality, response time
- Service Level Agreements based on these attribute values
- Increased variability of picture quality causes alarm
- Measure operating costs and resource utilization levels
- Problem could be because of network traffic increase

In the case of e-healthcare, most service monitoring can be done electronically, and through periodic surveys of user satisfaction. While effectiveness can be measured by user responses, and some related parameters (e.g., picture quality, response time), variability can be tracked on a daily basis, especially during the peak loads. Efficiency can be tracked automatically through SLA parameters.

4.8.2 Stage-6 Tools and Techniques

Stage 6 is extremely important for e-business management. We shall discuss various architectural schemes, and standards for this purpose in Chapters 3 and 4. Some examples are given below:

- Management Platforms
- Performance Management Applications
- Network Management Tools
- Systems Management Tools
- Integration of Network, Systems and Service Management

Recently there have been some major developments in the monitoring of IT service management. There are commercially available management platforms, such as HP OpenView, CA TNG, Tivoli and Aprisma Spectrum, that help in the monitoring and correlation of service parameters with those for underlying network and systems. These are called network and service management tools[21]. These issues will be discussed in much greater detail in Part 3.

There are two objectives of e-business and service management. One is to track the service performance, i.e., to measure performance relative to standards and or agreements (e.g. SLAs). The objective is to analyze the root cause of less than expected performance. Again the less than expected performance may come about for two reasons. Firstly, it could be because of a malfunction in the system or bad system design. Secondly, it could be because of the change in customer requirements in response to the dynamic service business environment. This in turn could be for various reasons. For example, a new product may have come on to the market. The next stages help us address this problem of management in a systematic manner.

4.9 Stage-7: Assessing Satisfaction

This is another very important stage involving the evaluation of e-business management products and services, which is discussed in detail under COMENS methodology in Part 5. Some of the main activities at this stage are:

- Measure Customers' Satisfaction with Performance of Service
- Measure Satisfaction relative to Customers' Expectations
- Measure Satisfaction relative to the Competition
- Validate these Results against those from Stage 2

Stage 2 establishes the performance level of attributes that would meet customer satisfaction. Hence the design and implementation should meet customer expectations. However, in reality this may not be the case for various reasons. For example, competitors may have developed a better service. There are three approaches to measuring customer satisfaction:

- On an Absolute Scale (1-6)
- Relative to Expectation (e.g., better than expected
- Relative to Competition (e.g., better than competitor x)

Results of the measure may point to a correction in design, and a correction in implementation.

4.9.1 Stage-7 Illustration: E-Healthcare Service

The Stage 7 concepts may be applied to e-healthcare services as follows:

- Measure satisfaction levels of various interactions in a process
- Measure satisfaction relative to face-to-face situation
- Measure satisfaction relative to other service providers
- Compare with original expectations

In this stage, e-healthcare service satisfaction is measured using a standard set of surveys and interviews as described in the next section.

4.9.2 Stage-7 Tools and Techniques

Following are some standard tools and techniques used to assess customer satisfaction in any businesses:

- Surveys and Market Research
- Group Interviews
- Personal Interviews
- Observation
- Contextual Interviews

There are a number of means of assessing satisfaction. While surveys can be done for a large number of respondents, interviews can be done for a few people. Contextual interviews allow interviews to be done while displaying some new tools, software relevant to the context.

There are some interesting developments in the area of the evaluation of Commercial Off –the-Shelf (COTS) software. CoMENS incorporates some of these concepts to develop a fully-fledged evaluation methodology as discussed in Part 5.

4.10 Stage-8: Improving Process Performance

Process performance improvement is a major goal of TQM. The process involves the following steps:

1. Estimate relationship between financial objectives and overall satisfaction
2. Set Strategic Satisfaction Targets
3. Estimate Relationship between satisfaction and attribute performance
4. Select one or more attributes for improvement, and set targets
5. Estimate Relationship between service-level and process-level attributes
6. Select process-level improvement alternatives

7. Select and Implement process improvement initiatives
   Improvement choices during a service lifetime are as follows:
- Reactive- to align processes more closely with customer service requirements
- Strategic-focusing on enhancing the firm's competitive edge through exceptional service quality

The activities at Stage 8 of the service design and management model involve the development of:
- Relationships between strategic financial objectives (e.g. market share) and overall satisfaction
- Relationships between overall satisfaction and service-level and process-level performance

These are then evaluated on the basis of the firm's cost-benefit expectations.

An e-business management methodology needs to incorporate the latest developments in the area of software engineering for process improvement. The Capability Maturity Model (CMM) of the Software Engineering Institute (SEI) illustrates these development[14].

4.10.1 Stage-8 Illustration: E-Healthcare Service

Here are some points regarding the application of Stage 8 in an e-healthcare environment:
- More satisfied a medical staff, less cost of providing manual records
- Complete online patient record system
- Relationship between satisfaction level and attributes, (e.g., picture quality)
- Quality of Service parameters can be categorized into different hierarchical levels
- Improvement may involve providing an ATM communication infrastructure to hospitals

E-healthcare is changing rapidly, and hence offers a lot of scope for improvement in light of the Internet2 initiatives, as discussed in the case studies in this chapter. This author has been involved in a project on the improvement of network services for e-healthcare in a hospital environment in Australia as discussed in [18].

4.11 implications on e-business

The Eight Stage model is applicable for any type of service (restaurant, airline or IT). But it is too generic from an e-business perspective. It does not consider issues related to IT application development, and some of the very important collaborative aspects of e-business management. All e-businesses are implemented using software. Hence there is a need to establish strong links between methodologies for e-business management and information systems/software engineering methodologies.

4.11.1 Information Systems Methodology Viewpoint

Let us now discuss Ramaswamy's Eight Stage Service Design and Management methodology from the perspective of an IS/IT perspective of e-business in terms of the major constituents of a methodology:

- Model
- Process
- Techniques and Notations
- Tools

Ramaswamy's methodology uses different models for the quantification of qualitative variables at different stages. In the case of e-business, these models do help in quantifying many business parameters that are qualitative in nature, as discussed with e-healthcare illustrations. However, the implementation of e-business needs the development of appropriate information systems/software. Ramaswamy's methodology does not provide any insights for this purpose. For example, the e-business system development may adopt one of the following approaches:

- Full In-house software development from scratch
- Application software package based development
- End-User Development using 4GL tools
- Outsourcing

The process involves the steps, phases or activities required to construct a system. It would normally include a life-cycle model for information systems. There are a number of information systems life cycle processes, such as the waterfall model, the spiral model and the fountain model. However, the traditional Systems Development Life Cycle (SDLC) based on the waterfall model is the most extensively used[15]. While the Eight Stage process of Ramaswamy's methodology considers the entire e-business life cycle, information systems development is concerned only with the information system aspect of the business. It would be desirable to incorporate information systems analysis and design in the overall e-business lifecycle.

A notation may be textual, graphical or a combination of both. It is a means of expressing the model. Typically, most techniques use graphical and numeric (matrices) as seen in the Ramaswamy's model. There are a number of graphical and numerical techniques used in the development of information systems, such as ER diagrams, dataflow diagrams, class diagrams, business systems planning etc.[9,15,21]

There are software project management tools, such as MS project manager, and various graphical charts that can be automatically developed using these tools for any business development, including e-businesses. However, Computer Aided Software Engineering (CASE), such as Rational Rose, are now being used extensively for the design and documentation of software and information systems[9].

An e-business management methodology can gain substantially by using CASE tools, repositories, and evolving knowledge tools, such as expert systems, and knowledge bases.

4.11.2 Methodology for E-Business Architecture

Koontz suggested a six-step process for developing an e-business architecture[11]. The steps are[21]:

1. *Define the e-business strategy.* The e-business strategy of an enterprise is formulated by fusing the corporate business strategy directions and information technology possibilities. The e-business strategy has implications on corporate marketing strategy and IT strategy. The outcomes include application portfolio, guidelines (and methodologies), and a resource allocation plan. This is perhaps the most important stage of an e-business management methodology. While it is not expensive to correct errors at this stage, any errors that go uncorrected at this stage may become more and more expensive at later stages[13]. The other management problem at this stage is how to convert qualitative and vague business parameters to more precise quantitative parameters (as discussed in this chapter).
2. *Define the information architecture.* In this step one defines the information necessary to fulfill the objectives and build the e-business applications. One should examine each strategic objective, identify the information available and determine if any of the information is digitized. HP IT Service Management (ITSM) architecture (discussed in Part 3) and Microsoft's Distributed Internet Architecture (DNA) are examples of such architectural frameworks for e-business. Chapter 5 shows how users may be involved in the development of an e-business and its management strategy. This step is carried out on a high level of abstraction.
3. *Define data architecture.* Once the e-business application processes are known, one needs to determine exactly what data and information is needed from customers. Of special interest is the investigation of all information that flows within the organization and to and from business

partners. Techniques, such as Business Systems Planning (BSP) are used at this stage[21]. This involves an analysis of the data, understanding its use and examining the need for new data. All this needs to be done with an eye toward security and privacy. If large amounts of data are used, tools such as Microsoft Transaction Server, Tuxedo, and data mining tools should be considered. Part 5 of this book will discuss some data architectures for cooperative management.

4. *Define the application architecture.* This step considers some information requirements, such as security, scalability, and reliability. This can be achieved (in modern software component-oriented design) with components or modules of the application that will interface with the required data defined in Step 3. This step builds the conceptual framework of the application, but not the infrastructure, as discussed in Part 1, that will support it. Many vendors including IBM, Oracle, and Microsoft offer sophisticated e-business application platforms that can significantly reduce the amount of code programmers need to write. Other factors that must be considered are scalability, security, the number and size of servers, and the networks. The need to interface with legacy systems and read real-time data is also important. In addition, interfacing with sales, ERP, accounting, and human resources data must be considered. Parts 3 and 4 present service architectures for integrated management of e-businesses.
5. *Define the e-business technical architecture.* During the previous steps, the designers informally considered the technical requirements. In this step, one must formally examine the specific hardware and software required to support the analysis in the previous steps. An inventory of the existing information resources is made and an evaluation of the necessary upgrades and acquisition is performed. At this stage, developers must examine the middleware needed for the application. E-business applications require a considerable amount of transaction processing software. Again, many vendors, ranging from IBM to TIBCO, have products to offer. The more there is a requirement for scalability and availability, the more one needs to invest in additional application servers and other hardware and software. When selecting a programming language, Java, Visual Basic, C, CGI, and even COBOL may be considered, depending on the application. Also in this step, the operating systems, transaction processors, and networking devices that are required to support the applications must be decided upon. Part 4 of this book presents the manager-agent technical architecture for integrated management.
6. *Define the organization architecture.* An organizational architecture deals with the human resources and procedures required by Steps 1–5. At

this time, the legal, administrative, and financial constraints should be examined. Partial outsourcing may be a useful way to deal with some of the deficiencies. In the worst-case scenario, the entire job can be outsourced, but the architecture can be given to the vendor as a starting point. Also, vendor selection can be improved if an architecture is defined. The electronic Telecommunication Operations Map (e-TOM) from Tele Management Forum (TMF) presents such an architecture for e-business management in the telecommunications industry, as discussed in Part 4 and in Appendix 2.

This architecture-oriented approach is perhaps most popular in the e-business and IT industry today. Parts 3 and 4 of this book discuss management standards and architectural frameworks for e-business with a view to adapting this architecture-oriented approach for e-business management solution development.

4.11.3 CoMENS Methodology

An e-business management methodology needs to incorporate the following features:

1. Solid grounding on a theoretical base like many information systems methodologies that are based on coordination theory, object-oriented software, or ethnography
2. Standard notations are required for the analysis and design of e-business services
3. Some formal methods need to be used to translate analysis to design
4. Need a formal evaluation methodology or templates
5. Analysis and design mechanisms to support cooperation within and across organizations - so important for modern e-businesses.

There have been substantial developments in the arena of information systems development methodologies (e.g., SSM, and Multi-view) that can be used to adapt a more generic model (e.g., Ramaswamy's Eight Stage model) to e-business management. We shall discuss a holistic approach, encompassing human, organizational and technical factors for the development of management solutions for e-business in Part 5 of this book[7,21].

The above factors are considered in the development of a new Cooperative management Methodology for Enterprise Networks and Services (CoMENS), an adaptation of this author's methodology called CoMEN[21] discussed in Chapter 5.

Before discussing CoMENS, readers need to appreciate some of the technical characteristics of e-business management, discussed in Chapters 3 and 4.

4.12 Chapter Summary

This chapter has presented a generic TQM based Eight-Stage methodology for the design and management of any business service from a top-down customer-oriented perspective. The eight stages of this methodology were illustrated with e-healthcare scenarios. This was followed by a discussion of the components of an information systems methodology (models, processes, and techniques) with a view to develop a methodology more appropriate for e-business management. Finally, this chapter presented a discussion of features missing in the above methodologies based on the technical-rational approach. We concluded with the need for a new holistic e-business management methodology encompassing organizational, human and technical factors for e-business management. Part 5 of this book will present the Cooperative management Methodology for E-business Networks and Services (CoMENS), which overcomes the above weaknesses.

The next two chapters will discuss the architectures for integrated management from e-business perspective.

4.13 REFERENCES

1. Avison D. and Fitzgerald G., Information Systems Development: Methodologies, Techniques and Tools, 2nd ed., McGraw-Hill, 1995
2. Dakins D.R., "Center Takes Data Tracking to Heart", Health Data Management online article, January, 2001, http://healthdatamanagement.com/html/current/index.cfm
3. Ganguly P. and Ray P., "Telemedicine over Enterprise-wide Networks: A Case Study", IEEE Global Telecommunications Conference (GLOBECOM98), Sydney, November 1998
4. Goedert J., "Military Launches Big Internet Initiative", Health Data Management online article, February, 2001, http://healthdatamanagement.com/html/current/index.cfm
5. Gillespie G., "Payer organizations and health care information technology vendors help move the industry toward Internet-based managed care transactions", Health Data Management online article, March, 2001, http://healthdatamanagement.com/html/current/index.cfm
6. Grimson J., Stephens G., Jung B., Grimson W., Berry D. and Pardon S., "Sharing Health-care records over the Internet", IEEE Internet Computing, May-June 2001
7. Harris G., and Taylor S., "Creating a New Process Model to support Participation and improve Coordination", Center for Quality in Management Journal, Vol. 6, No. 3, Winter 1997

8. Hauser J. and Clausing D., "The House of Quality", Harvard Business Review, 66 (3) (May-June), pp63-73, 1988
9. ISO 10746, X Reference Model for Open Distributed Processing (RM-ODP) Parts 1,2, 3 and 4, 1995
10. Kelly B., "Intranets Succumb to Irresistible Pull of e-health", Health Data Management online article, January, 2001, http://healthdatamanagement.com/html/current/index.cfm
11. Koontz, C. "Develop a Solid E-Commerce Architecture," E-Business Advisor (January 2000)
12. Larman C., Applying UML and Patterns: An Introduction to Object-Oriented Analysis and Design, Prentice-Hall, 1998, ISBN:0-13-748880-7
13. Laudon K. and Laudon J., Management Information Systems: Organization and Technology, Prentice Hall, 1998
14. Manolessos Y., Prezerakos G., Meliones A. and Theologou E., "A TQM-based Approach to QoS Managemen", Journal of Network and Systems Management, Vol. 8 No. 2, June 2000
15. Olle T.W., Hagelstein J., Macdonald I.G., Rolland C., Sol H.G., Assche F.V. and Verrijn-Stuart A.A., Information Systems Methodologies: A Framework for Understanding, IFIP, Addison Wesley, 1991, pp. 26–42, ISBN:0-201-54443-1
16. Pugh S., Total Design: Integrated Methods for Successful Product Engineering, Addison-Wesley Publishing Company, Reding MA, 1991
17. Ramaswamy R., Design and Management of Service Processes, Addison Wesley, ATandT Engineering Process Improvement Series edited by J.W.Wesner, 1996.
18. Ray P. and Weerrakkody G., "Cooperative Service Management over Enterprise Networks A Case Study in Healthcare Environments", IEEE Global Telecommunications Conference (GLOBECOM99), Rio de Janeiro, Brazil, Dec 1999
19. Ray P., Cooperative Management of Enterprise Networks, Kluwer Academic/ Plenum Publications, May 2000, ISBN:0-306-46276-1
20. Shortliffe H., "Networking Health: Prescriptions for the Internet", discussion in IEEE Spectrum January 2001, pp109-110
21. Telemedicine Information Exchange (TIE), "TIE News", February, 2001, http://tie.telemed.org/news/default.asp#item416
22. E. Turban, D. King, M. Warkentin and H.M. Chung, Electronic Commerce 2002: A Managerial Perspective, Prentice Hall, (2nd Ed.), Chapter 12, 2002

PART-3

ARCHITECTURAL VIEWPOINT

Chapter 5. Anatomy of E-Business Management

As business becomes increasingly 'e-focused', there will be increasing expectations on IT to deliver dramatically higher levels of performance, availability, and security. Hence the management of e-businesses is so heavily dependent on IT management.

Moving to an Internet-based e-business effectively invites company customers and business partners into the heart of the e-business infrastructure. While this situation facilitates business over the Internet, it exposes businesses to the vagaries of some customer moods and fickleness. As a recent Gartner Group report indicates, the e-customer comes with a demanding set of expectations for quality of service. From the time an end user lands on a website [12]:

- They'll wait an average of just 20 seconds to see something on the page
- You have a maximum of 40 seconds to complete the home page display
- Within 6 seconds the customer has decided to stay or leave the site
- The customer will use a maximum of 6 mouse clicks to find the desired information
- The maximum amount of time spent on a site is, on average, 12 minutes

In Part 2 we discussed the methodology-oriented view of service management - the generic lifecycle of services including specification, design, implementation, deployment, monitoring and evaluation. It was essentially a top-down business-oriented perspective of services in general. The lifecycle, characterized by an eight-stage model consisted of two major parts: design and management.

In this book we are mainly interested in the management aspect. The management phase consists of four stages of the eight-stage model described in Part 2. These stages are: deployment, service measurement/monitoring, assessing satisfaction, and improvements. In an e-business environment, services are delivered through an Information Technology (IT) infrastructure. Hence the architecture of the infrastructure and the service delivery mechanism assumes tremendous importance for e-business services. This chapter will discuss these stages from an architecture-oriented perspective.

In the case of an architecture-oriented approach, one needs to first define some generic (and reusable) building blocks (also called e-services as discussed in Chapter 4), and then build services around those architectural building blocks. This book uses the terms e-services and e-business services almost synonymously. There is a range of hardware/software building blocks defined for different types of business environments, such as telecommunications. This chapter presents the architectural-perspective for service management in e-business. We also demonstrate how the 4-stage generic service management model from Chapter 4 can be adapted to an e-business environment with respect to various emerging frameworks, and techniques. The discussion is organized into three main high-level architectural features of e-business management, namely

- E-Business Process Management
- Service Level Management
- E-Business Transaction Management

We start with the landscape of e-business, followed by a discussion of the key requirements of e-business management. Then we discuss the different aspects of the anatomy of e-business management, namely e-service management, e-business transaction management, and the implications of the management of the underlying network and systems. The discussion will include an e-service management architectural model, called IT Service Management Model (ITSM). This model succinctly illustrates how e-service management can be defined with the help of certain major common software building blocks. We demonstrate how it is applicable to almost all types of IT and telecommunication services. We discuss the process of e-service level management and the use of Service Level Agreements (SLAs) for this purpose. This discussion is best performed at the e-business transaction level. Hence we look at the management issues of e-business transactions.

5.1 E-Business Services and their Management

E-businesses will deploy the next generation of modular internet-based applications that communicate with one another over the Internet, thereby bringing in more automation, federation and dynamism. E-businesses reduce the amount of human interaction needed to exchange and transfer information, by allowing applications to automatically interact with other applications within and across organizations (e.g., by using intelligent agents as e-business components). Service providers outsource non-strategic parts of their e-businesses to external service providers - an example of federation. Instead of statically binding a set of applications, it is possible to dynamically discover and negotiate new e-business services with desired sets of features (e.g., through broker agents).

A typical e-business scenario consists of:

- Consumers who consume e-business services (possibly create new ones)
- Service providers which create and offer e-business services by using their own application and services from suppliers For example, the provider of a book selling e-service may create new e-services (for

exploring, selecting, and buying books) by composing (statically or dynamically) e-services from suppliers who may be offering component e-services for purposes, such as billing, shipping and payment [22].

5.1.1 E-Business Service Landscape

The evolving e-business service landscape transforms the paradigms of e-commerce by replacing the assumptions of B2C and point-to-point B2B connections with a many-to-many B2B model. It transforms the paradigm of isolated storefront by allowing the storefront to buy and sell to other e-business services as peers. It transforms the application-hosting paradigm by allowing an e-business service to dynamically discover and connect to e-business services hosted by other providers. It transforms the outsourcing paradigms by automating the process for connecting heterogeneous e-business services electronically over the network. Transactions and workflows can potentially span across a number of physically separated cooperative applications.

E-business technology seems to be a natural extension of the web technology. However, there are some significant differences between an ordinary web-based application and the realization of the above e-business paradigm. This landscape presents a number of challenges, such as:[18]

- Technical requirements (e.g., secure transactions, highly available servers)
- Support for uniform discovery mechanisms
- Common vocabulary and semantics to combine multiple e-business services
- Coordinating heterogeneous business processes

Patricia Seybold identifies five factors differentiating tomorrow's e-business services from today's web-based applications. These factors are listed below with quotes from Seybold in italics[25]:

1. ***Discovery, Invocation, Communication (DIC)***- *An application running in any device-on or off the Net- can request an e-service. Once the request is received, the appropriate e-services will kick into action. This translates to two requirements.* Firstly, an application needs to have a way of discovering the e-service (discovery mechanism and protocol). Secondly, applications running on heterogeneous platforms and devices need to have a common means of communication (e-communication), such as DCOM or CORBA.
2. ***E- Services as Modular Resources (EMR)*** - *E-business services are self-contained, modular, mix-and-match applications. They act as resources to other applications. E-business services can be performed, initiated, scheduled, and/or committed by software with or without human*

intervention. This factor implies the three interoperability needs of an e-business service. Firstly, e-business services must have means of invocation (e.g., API calls) for integrated with other applications. Secondly, interaction of e-business services requires some standard means of exchanging information. Thirdly, in order that e-business services can be "initiated, scheduled, performed and committed" without human intervention, some mechanisms/protocols required that would allow heterogeneous e-business services in a potentially insecure environment to interoperate with managed risk.

3. ***Self –Describing Applications (SDA)*** - *E-business services are self-describing applications. Each e-business service knows what functions it is capable of performing, what inputs it requires, what output it produces, and what its attributes are (e.g., security, location, cost).* This implies that e-business service providers must agree on some definitions of minimum sets of self-descriptive information that e-business service providers must provide to each other for different contexts.
4. ***Instrumenting for Manageability and Visibility (IMV)*** - *E-business services need to be highly visible and manageable. They are instrumented so that they can be monitored by external application management and workflow systems.* From the point of view of e-business owners, an e-service may be running on a system they do not own or control, running on an operating system they know nothing about, or written in a programming language they are not familiar with. An e-business owner should be able to detect and manage the state of the e-business service application and the status of its outcome. This factor implies some sensitive trade-offs related to security and openness. For example, an e-business service needs to expose all information related to its usage by other potentially unknown e-business applications. On the other hand, it should not expose information that competitors might exploit.
5. ***E-Service Marketplace (ESM)***- *E-business services can be brokered and auctioned. Once a request is received by an e-service broker or directory service, different e-business services applications may vie for opportunity to perform the requested functions, based on their attributes and their current state (available or busy, highly secure or less secure, price per transaction and volume of transactions that can be handled within a time frame, and so on).* This factor implies three requirements.

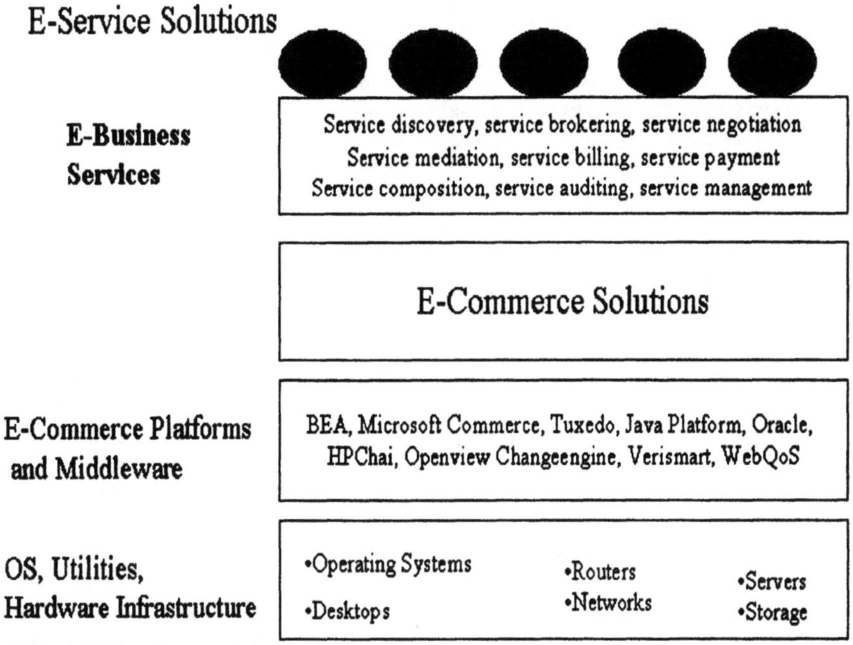

Figure 28. E-business Landscape[18]

Firstly, a market place must exist to allow acts of brokering and auctions. It is unclear how far this needs to automate capital market activities (information, order routing, execution, clearing and settlement phases). Secondly, in order for e-business services to be brokered without human intervention, it must be possible to construct connections between e-business services dynamically. Thirdly, the e-business services must have some means of being represented in an auction in loosely coupled interactions.

Out of the above factors, the first four read as distributed computing/enterprise-computing requirements. The last one is at a higher level concerned with the establishment and operation of an e-business service market. Figure 28 shows the software stack to realize this e-business service paradigm.

Kuno has analyzed the e-business software offered by major companies in Table 6 against the five Seybold factors described above [18].

Table 6. Comparison of E-business Software[18]

Vendor	DIC	EMR	SDA	IMV	ESM	Other
HP	E-speak, Chai-server, Jet-send	E-speak, Speak-easy, Chai-server	E-speak, Speak-easy, Chai-server	E-Speak, Chai-server, OpenView, Smart Internet Usage	Broker-in-a-box, Speak-Easy	HP has partnered with i2 for a supply-chain e-business framework
Microsoft	UPP, Biztalk, SOAP, Babylon	Babylon	UPP, XML, SOAP	MS AppCenter Server, UPP		Babylon, XML/SOAP, AppCenter Server/Shiloh as part of DNA2000
Sun	Jini	Jini, iPlanet (with Netscape)	Jini			Allied with Netscape to build rental applications based on Jini
IBM	T-Space, San Francisco	San Francisco	Aglets		Alphaworks, such as Intermediary development kit for Java, DIPLOMAT and Common Rules	IBM T-Spaces white board system being dropped
Lucent	Inferno's Styx protocol	Inferno				Inferno customers building inferno based web telephony systems
Hitachi	Tradelink	TradeLink				Trade link is aimed at SupplyChain

5.1.2 E-Business Infrastructure

Shim et al present a comparison of the most popular B2B e-commerce frameworks. Many of them use EDI (standard from ISO and ANSI) and XML (a standard from WWW Consortium). These frameworks are[26]:

- Open Buying on the Internet (OBI) standard, promoted by several Fortune 500 companies. Envisions a dynamic, interoperable trading web. It complements EDI using CGI and HTTP
- ECo framework from CommerceNet, a consortium of 35 companies primarily sponsored buy CommerceOne, Viewing interoperability in a set of levels, eCo uses XML to allow businesses to define, publish and exchange metadata descriptions.
- RosettaNet consortium develops XML-based business standards for supply chain management in IT and component industries. It streamlines business processes through guidelines for supply chain trading partners, called Partner Interface Processes (PIPs).
- Commerce XML (cXML), a joint effort by 40 companies led by Ariba, is an open Internet-based standard to facilitate easy exchange of catalog content and transaction information between trading partners using some lightweight XML DTDs.
- Microsoft Biztalk serves as a platform based on XML and existing standards to facilitate efficient e-business.

The comparison is based on the following metrics (Table 7):Industry target, Security, Communication protocol, Message format, Ontology, Query Mechanism, Scalability, and Repositories.

Table 7. Comparison of B2B E-commerce Frameworks[26]

Feature	ECo	Biztalk	OBI	CXML	RosettaNet
Industry Target	Unspecified	Unspecified	Materials MRO, supplies	MRO, office supplies, books etc	IT electronic components
Security	Optional	Existing Standards	SSL with HTTP, digital signatures	Authentication in message Header	SSL v HTTP, dig certificates signatures
Communication Protocol	HTTP	Wide variety; HTTP/MSMQ	HTTP	HTTP, URL form encoding	HTTP/CGI
Service Discovery	Extensive Support	Supported	Not addressed	Not addressed	Not address
Repositories	Locally maintained	Centralized repository	Owner's responsibility	Not addresses	Not address
Message Format	XML documents	Biztalk documents based on Biztags	Encapsulated EDI documents	XML documents	Valid X documents
Query Mechanism	URL-based	Not addressed	Not applicable	Not addressed	Not address
Scalability	Sufficient	Centralized repositories may limit	One-to-one framework does not	Scalable based on XML DTDs	Allows extension implementat

	ECo	Biztalk	OBI	CXML	RosettaNet
			impact scalability		guidelines
y	Common Business Library	Collection of Biztags	EDI X.12 data dictionary	Collection of XML tags	Technical and business dictionaries

Throughout March 2000, Lucent Technologies conducted a web-based industry survey, which was completed by 102 network professionals, on the issues of building and maintaining an e-business architecture and infrastructure. This survey yields valuable insight into the current and future e-business network architecture/infrastructure strategies of network professionals. It also identifies the barriers, and challenges that network professionals expect to encounter as they plan and implement network architectures to support e-business. These results will assist networking organizations to assess their individual progress as compared to the industry, and identify opportunities for improvement[21].

For this survey, e-business is defined as business activities performed over a network using Internet-enabled technologies to communicate data, voice, fax, or video. E-business activities can be between an enterprise and a consumer (business-to-consumer, or B2C), between two enterprises (business-to-business, or B2B), or completely within an enterprise. An e-business network architecture consists of local-area networks (LANs) and wide-area networks (WANs) that support these e-business activities, along with the tools and services required to manage these networks. The e-business network architecture encompasses both the network infrastructure (layers 1-4) and application services (layers 5-7) of the OSI network architectural mode[1].

- Seventy-two percent of respondents believe that it is very important to implement/improve their network architecture for e-business within the next six months.
- Over the next two years, 45% of respondents plan to make significant changes in their network architecture for e-business, while 23% plan a complete overhaul.
- Fifty-four percent of respondents needed help in development of their e-business strategy, while not understanding e-business payback opportunities is a major issue for 43% of respondents.
- More than half of respondents stated that organizational issues, including processes and procedures, are their biggest challenge to evaluating, implementing, or enhancing the e-business network architecture.
- Ninety-five percent of respondents considered improving network security important to the success of their e-business strategy.

- Forty-four percent were likely to outsource/out-task security penetration analysis and testing, and another 30% are likely to outsource/out-task remote security monitoring.
- Large companies were more likely than smaller companies to have a network architecture capable of supporting a full e-business strategy, but are also more likely to need help in evaluating/enhancing the network operations and implementation phases of their e-business network architecture development.

By a wide margin, lack of experienced staff is the most frequent barrier to improving a company's e-business network architecture.

This survey shows some linkages between e-business management and the management of underlying networks[1].

5.1.3 E-Business Service Management

The problem of e-business management is to maintain the e-business service in a desired state by monitoring and controlling its operations and use of resources. Poor performance, lack of availability, crossing certain thresholds, and contract violation are some of the ways in which e-business services can deviate from the desired state of operation. Such deviations could occur for various reasons including errors in application or service logic, failures in networks and systems that host these services, improper configuration parameters and unauthorized intrusion. An integrated e-business management system either detects or corrects problems in real-time, or it observes trends in order to predict and rectify the situation before problems occur. E-business management systems can also perform historical analysis of the services they manage and help in planning activities. In addition they can be integrated into more powerful business management systems to assess the impact of the services on the overall business.

Managed services are important in three areas of an e-business. These are

- E-business processes including Service Level Management
- E-business transactions and interactions
- E-business infrastructure

Management has a key role to play in all stages of an e-business service, i.e., business planning, design, development and deployment, and operations. The management of e-businesses at a process level is discussed in detail in Section 5.2.

E-business involves some complex processes to allow many-to-many B2B transactions as stated in Patricia Seybold's factor #5 (Section 5.1.1). Hence a simple facility (e.g., viewing web response at http level) can not uncover the dynamics that underlie an e-business transaction. The complete set of transactions that users face - browsing and/or searching an e-catalog, filling a shopping cart etc.- and the underlying processes need to be modeled in order to get meaningful information for transaction management (e.g., bottlenecks, response-time lags). This is discussed in Section 5.3.3.

As discussed in Section 5.1.2, e-business infrastructure is composed of Internet-based networks, networked desktops and storage (systems), and e-business applications and middleware to support security, scalability, and flexibility. The management of this area is known as Integrated Management (combination of networks, systems and application management), which has seen some major developments over last decade. These standards and frameworks of integrated management will be discussed in Part 4 of this book.

5.1.4 E-Business Management Requirements

A well-managed e-business service exposes sufficient information, measurements, and control points (with appropriate instrumentation) for use by the management system. A good e-service management uses this information effectively to monitor the state of the service, to analyze and diagnose problems that occur within the service, to control its behavior, and to expose some or all the metrics and control points for use by other services, management systems with appropriate management platforms and management applications. This section is based on the work done by V. Machiraju, M. Dekhil, M. Griss, and K. Wurster of HP Labs as reported in[22].

E-business management space can be viewed in three dimensions [22].

- Tasks, such as monitoring, analysis, diagnostics, planning, and control
- Metrics, such as performance, availability, contracts, and negotiations
- Time frame, such as historical, current, and future (estimates)

This space can be applied as a top-down service stack consisting of five levels; business, service, application, system and network. As discussed earlier, architecture-driven e-business management needs to use two approaches; the top-down approach, and a bottom-up approach.

Adopting a top-down view, we have the overall business of the provider at the top level. The next level consists of a number of services. In order to manage these services, one needs to manage elements that influence the e-service (applications, systems and networks at the lower levels). So service level objectives drive application level objectives and so on. Therefore, an e-business management system should facilitate drill-down across the layers of the stack in order to identify the root cause of the problem. For example, if a service fails, the e-business management system should be able to drill-down through the application, system, and network layers to identify the exact cause of the service failure. This approach is used in our discussions of e-business management.

In the bottom-up approach a network management system collects all the measurements necessary to manage the network irrespective of system, application and service goals. Similarly, an application management system selects a set of network and system metrics that it needs and manages the application layer without consideration to higher service level objectives.

Irrespective of a top-down or bottom-up approach, an e-business service management system should be able to perform the following two tasks:

- *Roll-up*: Events, measurements, and metrics collected at lower levels should be rolled-up to higher levels in the service stack. For example, network parameters should be rolled up into system, application and overall service performance.
- *Drill-down*: There should be facilities to drill-down through the layers of the service stack in order to identify the root cause of a problem. For example, when a service fails due to a network problem, the e-business management should be able to drill down through application, system, and network layers to identify the exact cause of service failure.

In order for a management system to fulfill these requirements, the managed e-service should provide the following information:

- *Models*: A set of models representing the structure and configuration of the e-service, state transitions within the e-service, and workflow of supported transactions.
- *Measurements*: Real-time measurements whenever transactions are started and stopped at service and sub-service boundaries, availability heartbeats, contract and offer details, lifecycle state change, etc.
- *Events*: Events whenever errors occur within an e-service
- *Control points*: Interfaces to change the lifecycle state of the e-service (start, stop, suspend), to increase the availability (load balancing, replication) etc.

In order to achieve these objectives in a heterogeneous environment, standard interfaces, and protocols need to be defined as discussed in Part 4.

5.2 Management of E-Businesses at the Process Level

For decades, service management was seen as an extension of development, more of a necessary evil than a valuable element in automation. In recent years it has been characterized by a turnaround, supported not least by Gartner publications, which show that around 70-80% of the life cycle costs of an information system are incurred in the exploitation phase. This shows that the exploitation phase is a rewarding area of activity when it comes to cost control. This is further supported by the discovery that developers spend around 60% of their time on maintenance. All in all, the organization of e-service management is a field to which very careful attention should be paid. Especially in a world which is characterized by a landslide of technological developments and increasing demands on the time-to-market, flexibility and performance of information systems[27].

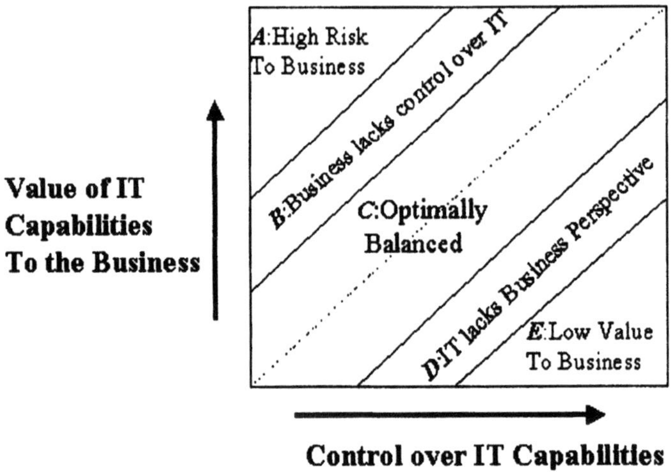

Figure 29. Impact of Manageability on E-Business[8]

Figure 29 shows the impact of manageability on e-business. The picture is divided into five regions - A to E. Regions E and D have low value to business. They are typically applicable to established traditional information systems applications, such as payroll. These applications are not normally e-business targets; hence we are interested in them. Region C is ideal from the manageability perspective of e-business. Regions A and B both have high value to business, and modern e-business applications belong to this category. The objective of e-business management strategies is to make regions A and B like region C. There are two ways to achieve this. Firstly, e-business management processes need to be standardized, as discussed in Section 5.2.1. Secondly, there is a need to adopt Service Level Management (SLM) as discussed in Section 5.2.2.

5.2.1 E-Business Process Management

There are many definitions, of which the following is perhaps the most appropriate: 'E-service Management is a set of processes that co-operate to ensure the quality of live e-services, according to the levels of service agreed with the customer'. It is superposed to management domains such as systems management, network management, systems development and to many process domains, like change management, asset management and problem management[3]. E-Service Management and IT Service Management are analogous for our discussion.

The importance of E-Service Management is becoming increasingly widely recognized. Whereas in the Sixties and Seventies interest was still focused mainly on the improvement of hardware, and whereas the development of software was the major concern until well into the Eighties, the Nineties was the decade, which saw the rise of service management. E-Service Management provides an overall framework within which to operate individual activities such as the Customer Service Desk and the implementation of Service Level Agreements (SLAs). The principal objectives of E-service Management are[3]:

- providing customer focused e-services
- aligning e-services with the organization's objectives
- the implementation and management of cost-effective SLAs

E-Service Management is based on industry best practice, embracing public and private e-service providers.

IT process and service management covers a whole range of interdependent disciplines. Let us consider the following scenario that gives some insight into impacting factors (relevant e-service management building block is shown in italics)[8].

1. A user calls the *service desk* to register problems with the response time of an online service.
2. *Incident Management* looks for the root cause, prioritizes the trouble-tickets and deals with the fault.
3. *Problem Management* analyses the underlying cause and involves Capacity Management in eliminating it. SLM is alarmed because an SLA has been violated.
4. A *change management* request is triggered. The request for change asks for an upgrade to the server hardware.
5. *IT financial management* analyses the economic implications of the hardware upgrade.
6. The *IT Service Continuity* process is now involved to ensure that the changed configuration still meets the requirements for availability, redundancy and data security.
7. *Release Management* carries out the improvement by exchanging the hardware and software, and reinstalling it. It ensures that *Configuration Management* gets the latest release and version data.
8. *Availability Management* checks the new components to see they meet the availability and reliability requirements.

9. *Configuration Management* must ensure that all relevant data is updated in the configuration database.

This section discusses the standardization of this variety of e-business service processes, as shown in Figure 30.

The ITSM reference model gives us a top-down view of the overall service management framework and then within the four sectors of this framework, we define the different building blocks which will constitute the various types of processes and software to implement this kind of a scheme.

Figure 30 shows the high level process linkages, and the building blocks in each of these four major phases[6].

- Business-IT Alignment
- Design and Management
- Development and Deployment
- Operation

There are two core functions which are common to all these phases. One is change management, which is in the middle, and the other is configuration management, which is also in the middle of Figure 30.

5.2.1.1 Business-IT Alignment

As shown in Figure 30, the quadrant on Business IT alignment has three major building blocks that incorporate sub processes;

- the business assessment
- customer management
- IT strategy development

The *Business assessment* building block assesses business strategy and defines requirements for e-business services to the value chain. The sub-processes are value chain analysis, ascertaining business goals and definition of IT requirements as discussed in Part 1.

The building block on *Customer management* anticipates new requirements, communicates service value, keeps a pulse on customer satisfaction levels and engages in joint problem solving. The sub-processes are customer satisfaction review, customer liaison, strategic business reporting, identification of new service needs and definition of customer support requirements. Most of these processes were discussed in Part 2.

The building block on *IT strategy development* optimizes the IT contribution to business objectives. The sub-processes consist of the definition of policies and standards, determination of IT capability, definition of technical architecture, definition of IT process models, and definition of IT organization models. Some of these will be discussed later in Part 4 and in Part 5.

5.2.1.2 Design and Management

The second quadrant, which consists of design and management, has got five building blocks

- Service Planning,
- Service Level Management
- Availability and Continuity Management
- Capacity Management
- Cost Management

The Service Planning building block defines service requirements; service plans, and identifies gaps in current e-service capabilities. The sub-processes consist of the definition of service requirements, definition of new services, financial planning, define and model service data, benchmarking and gap analysis.

The Service Level Management building block establishes and manages Service Level Agreements (SLAs) and Operational Level Agreements (OLAs) to provide reliable, cost-effective services based on IT strategy, customer requirements, and IT capabilities. The sub-processes maintain service catalogs, establish service level requirements, negotiate and document service levels. Most importantly, this building block takes care of service level monitoring and reporting. There are also three building blocks that support Service Level Management, namely Availability and Continuity Management, Capacity Management and Cost Management.

The Availability and Continuity Management building block defines, tracks and controls IT resource availability to customers, and determines plans and tactics for service continuity, contingencies, and physical and data security. The sub-processes are risk analysis/management, security design, supplier relationship management, and ongoing management for service reliability and serviceability.

The Capacity Management building block tracks and controls e-business service capacities to ensure that infrastructure improvements are ready to meet demands of customers. The sub-processes consist of performance analysis, demand management, workload management, application sizing and capacity planning.

The Cost Management building block defines, tracks, and controls service cost structures to ensure e-service cost recovery. The related sub-processes include service costing, service value management, definition of accounting policies, cost recovery, financial asset management, and Total Cost of Ownership (TCO) computation.

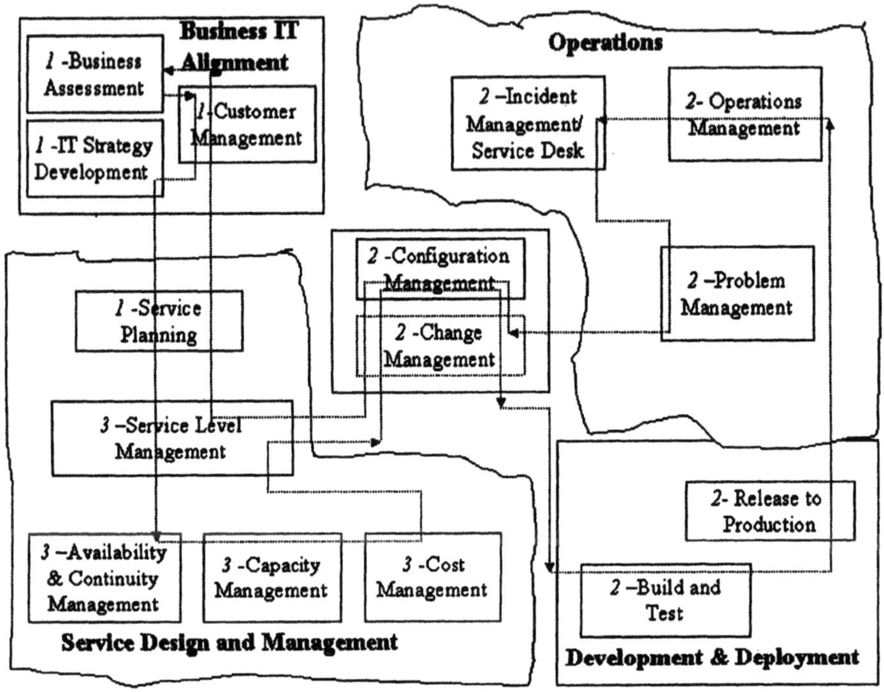

Figure 30. IT Service Management (ITSM) Model

5.2.1.3 Development and Deployment

The 3rd quadrant (clockwise) has two building-blocks:

- Build and Test
- Release to Production

The Build and Test building block develops and tests services, infrastructure (process, people and technology) and related applications specified in the service design. The sub-processes are development project management, risk management, development of infrastructure, functional testing, training and recovery planning, hardware and software staging, application development, and development of support mechanisms.

The Release to Production building block manages the introduction of products and services into the e-business environment, as specified in the service design. The sub-processes are building, test and integration, hardware and software control/distribution, and implementation of training and service for operation.

5.2.1.4 Operations

The fourth and last (clockwise) quadrant of Figure 30 is concerned with the operations of e-business services. The objective is to proactively collect resource status data, filters for potential problems, and to provide notifications of incidents. This area also deals with the day-to-day change administration.

The major building blocks are

- Operations Management
- Incident Management / Service Desk
- Problem management

The sub-processes consist of client-server administration, LAN/WAN administration, IP administration, and database administration. They also deal with output management, backup management, store management, production scheduling and processing, performance monitoring and tuning, security access and control, environment data collection and filtering, event detection and notification, preventive maintenance, voice-infrastructure management, and transmission-related activities.

The incident management/Service Desk building block handles all events, problems, customer requests and queries. It also escalates unsolved incidents to problem management process. The sub-processes are customer interface, incident classification, impact and urgency assessment, call and event tracking/routing, business operations support, escalation and incident resolution/closure. The next chapter discusses the environment for incident management in a multi provider environment.

The problem management building block determines the root cause of recurring, critical, and/or escalated incidents, and analyzes the environment to prevent problems. The sub-processes are incident root cause analysis, problem tracking, concurrent problem resolution, and problem prevention. It uses a number of Artificial Intelligence techniques including model based reasoning, expert systems, and case-based reasoning integrated with help-desk for this purpose.

This demonstrates how one can integrate the overall process of business to service definition, service definition to service design, design to management, and management to deployment. That is, the life cycle of the service. This is most obvious in building blocks which are common, typically in an IT and telecommunication environment. The next most important, aspect is the realization of the e-service cycle based on software framework, which brings us to the lower level details of implementing the service in a cooperative environment. Such a cooperative-system environment involves a networked platform and a set of tools to assist the design, implementation and testing of an e-service system.

5.2.1.5 Change and Configuration Management

With SLAs in place, ITSM Service Level Manager provides the monitoring and measuring necessary to ensure service levels are met and automatically escalates procedures in the event of an SLA violation.

Many corporate enterprises have now adopted a very serious approach to configuration and change management, which is basically the core of the entire management system.

ITSM Service Level Manager is designed with these core design approaches:

- Change management
- Configuration Management

Change management is the process of rapidly controlling and implementing authorized changes to an IT infrastructure. By carefully managing changes, IT organizations can offer better support for the ever-changing business needs and expectations of business users, while minimizing the impact of change to the existing quality of IT service to the business.

Change Management has the following sub-processes:

- Initiation, which initiates the change
- Tracking, which tracks the changes and information throughout the lifecycle
- Authorization, which schedules change advisory board meetings and sets up approval cycles
- Risk and impact assessment, which identifies the impact of the change to the overall e-service provision
- Scheduling, which schedules change time frames with minimum impact on overall e-service provision
- Building, which identifies a backup plan any dependencies on the change, and so forth
- Coordination, which coordinates the work related to changes
- Verification, which verifies if the change was implemented as planned
- Review, which runs reports and aggregates information for decision support

Configuration Management is a discipline that gives IT management precise control over IT assets by allowing them to:

- Specify the versions of configuration items in use in the IT infrastructure
- Provide information on the status of configuration items, for example, "scheduled for live use," "in live use," "scheduled for upgrade," and so forth
- Determine who owns each item (the individual with primary responsibility for it)

- Determine the relationships between items (components, connections, and so on)
- Control changes to the configuration items by making sure changes are made only with the agreement of the appropriate authorities
- Audit the IT infrastructure to make sure it contains the authorized configuration items and only those configuration items

Figure 30 shows the linkages between these building blocks using dotted lines. Arrows show the lifecycle of the process.

5.2.1.6 Implementation Strategy for IT Service Management

Although the ITSM Model shows fifteen architectural building blocks for e-business service management, and their relationships, it is not possible to implement all of them at once. Hence it is important for an enterprise management to know which building blocks need to be implemented and when? Hence we categorize them into three strategic classes as follows:[6]

- Long-term Strategic Goals
- Short-term Tactical Goals
- Medium term Tactical Goals

The ITSM building blocks related to long term strategic goals, shown with number prefix "1" in Figure 30, focus on developing strategic e-business service management processes. Building blocks in this category include all the three in Business-IT Alignment area (Business assessment, Customer Management, IT Strategy Development), and Service Planning in Service Design and Management area. These building blocks concern the people, organization and process aspects of e-business service management.

The ITSM building blocks related to short-term tactical goals, shown with number prefix "2" in Figure 30, are concerned with processes for the development, integration, deployment, and ongoing monitoring and maintenance of service processes and their infrastructure components. They ensure that e-business services will be measurable, and controllable, which means that such services can be improved on an ongoing basis.

These building blocks, usually implemented after the customer needs are known, are most important in terms of the short-term realization of value for e-business service management. Hence most enterprises have been focusing on facilities to implement these building blocks that include all three in the Operations area (Incident Management, Operations Management and Problem management), both in the Development and Deployment area (Build and Test and Release to Production), and the two common key building blocks (Configuration and Change Management). This part of the book and Part 4 are devoted to the understanding of models, architectures and standards for the implementation of these building blocks. Many vendors of network, systems and application management offer products in this area, as discussed in Part 4.

The ITSM building blocks related to Medium Term tactical goals, shown with number prefix "3" in Figure 30, are concerned with taking e-service management to the next higher level of sophistication once the short-term tactical goals are achieved. There are four building blocks in this category, all from the Design and Management area, namely Service Level Management, Availability and Continuity Management, Capacity Management, and Cost Management. These features are now increasingly being supported, in some form, in many commercial network, systems and application management products, such as ICS Continuity, HP OpenView, CA TNG, Tivoli etc.

5.2.2 Service Level Management

Service Level Management (SLM) benefits business enterprises by promoting proactive, structured working practices along with two-way communication and agreement among the stakeholders in the business process. Direct business benefits are improved services and reduction in costs. Additional and ongoing benefits of SLM are[2]:

- Better ongoing communication between the business owner and the IT department
- Better understanding on the part of IT of the requirements, concerns and needs of the entire business process, rather than just the technology services
- Clear definitions of agreed-upon levels of IT service, for agreed-upon costs
- Increased business value for current and future IT costs
- Increased satisfaction with IT service quality
- Improved IT staff morale through clearly defined goals, clear processes and clear expectations

A business process is not just the application software. The business process may, for example, consist of multiple purchased e-business and business-to-business applications as well as internally developed custom applications. SLM for the business process must address the entire business process at the level of the business owner and the CIO, as well as deal with the underlying technology layers that support the business process.

To meet the needs of the business and to provide SLM, service providers must first understand and then meet the availability and performance expectations of business owners and end users who are engaged in the business process. Although the business unit and the IT team must share responsibility for setting service expectations, judging how well these expectations are being met should be measured from the end users' perspective. And to ensure service to end users, all of the technology layers supporting the application must be managed in concert.

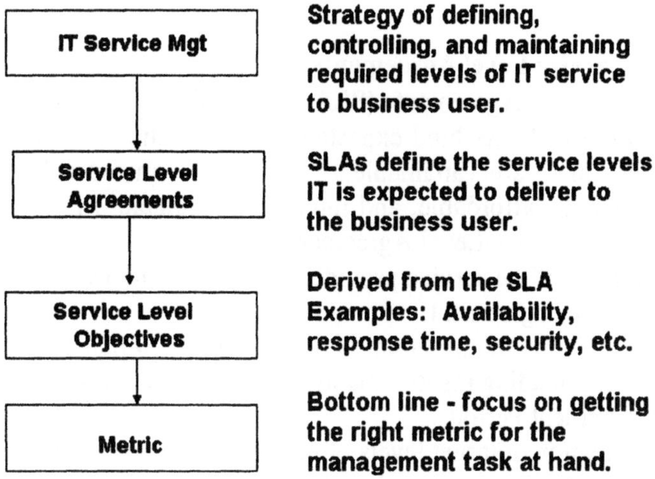

Figure 31. Service Level Management Process[16]

SLM is a proactive, disciplined methodology for establishing and managing acceptable levels of service in keeping with the business process and costs. The SLM model reflects the continuous process of defining, measuring, managing, reporting and *improving* IT service quality for the business process with the goal of managing end-to-end performance from the user's perspective. Given this new era of e-business and IT's changing role in business organizations, it is important to keep in mind the important and valuable outcomes of effective SLM as it relates to the business.

One of the basic problems is the variation of user perception of e-business service quality based on varying factors, such as user knowledge and experience, network infrastructure, and business needs. Defining Quality of Service (QoS) for e-business services is very much a research topic[4].

Specifically, Service Level Manager helps IT organizations to:

- Understand which components in the IT infrastructure are involved in delivering crucial e-services to the business
- Identify the desired IT infrastructure
- Design and define e-services
- Define business impact levels
- Track service level agreements (SLAs) to agreed-upon costs, service hours, availability, and performance.

The best way to manage services for e-business can be called "Service Level Management". The idea is to define a set of metrics for measurement that relate to the measurable and important attributes of the service, and then mechanisms should be in place to monitor these metrics. The process is defined in Figure 31[11].

5.2.2.1 Service Level Agreements (SLAs)

Service Level Agreements (SLAs) define the expectations of a service in business terms. SLAs bind expectations to realistic levels by incorporating measures that are attainable, meaningful, measurable, controllable, understandable, affordable, and mutually acceptable[27]. Here are the salient features of a Service Level Agreement (SLA):

- Definition of the service provided, the parties involved, and the effective dates of the agreement.
- Specifications of the hours and days during which the service will be offered, including testing, maintenance and upgrades. This is the Service Measurement Period.
- Specification of target levels of service quality, including:
  - Expected Service Level during service period
  - Minimum Service Level during service period
  - Annual Adjustments to these levels
  - Performance Forfeits for not achieving the service level.
  - Earn Back measurement Period
  - Earn Back Process

Figure 32 gives an example of a real SLA. As stated earlier, the end user does not care how the service is configured. For example, the underlying network may have a large number of switches and routers located all over the world. The management of this network itself is a huge problem. But that is not a direct consideration of service management, which is concerned with the end-to-end delivery of the service as seen by a user or a user organization. The user is concerned with the service but not with the network application infrastructure of the service. For example, the user is interested in the delivery status of an email, but the location and status of a mail server is of no interest.

SLA - Total LAN Segment Availability Percentage (TLSAP)
Definition - TLSAP = [1 - fls / tls] x 100%
where fls = failed lan seg = # of lan seg with LSAP < 98.5%
tls = total no. of lan segments being managed

LSAP = [1 - (Unscheduled Down Time / Scheduled Up Time)]x 100%

Expected Service Level - TLSAP = 99.5%
Minimum Service Level - TLSAP = 98.5%
Performance Forfeit = $ 50,000.00
EarnBack Period = 3 months following forfeit

Figure 32. A sample SLA in Telecommunication Network Environment[21]

Another problem that arises is due to the deregulated nature of today's network and telecommunication environment, where the customer is connected to a chain of service providers. In the case of an end-to-end guarantee, the customer does not care which service provider provides the service. An overall guarantee of the performance is imperative. For example, two competitive carriers, such as Telecom Italia and WIND may have to cooperate to meet the SLA guarantee for a large customer, such as Pirrelli. Because of the competitive pressures, on one hand telecom service providers (e.g., Telecom Italia and WIND in Italy) may be at loggerheads, but they have to join hands to collaborate and satisfy the end customer.

Typically network services are organized into a number of levels of computational and management architecture, often expressed as physical, logical and virtual network services. For example, telecom service providers are concerned with the management of switches, transmission systems, and other network elements that support a variety of telecom service consumers (individuals, corporate users, other service providers etc.). Internet Service Providers (the users of telecom services) are concerned with the management of their own service infrastructure (that supports various types of customers) consisting of routers, and various types of servers (DNS servers, mail servers, web servers etc.). Finally, end-users are mainly interested in the management of services being used by them (e.g., mail services, web services, etc.). The Service Level Management has to be designed accordingly.

For example, a telecom service provider would need to know a substantial amount of information, such as how the service maps to network, system and down the line infrastructure. But the customer need not know these details. If there is fault somewhere in the telecom service provider's switching or transmission infrastructure, the customers need to know how that might affect various end services (e.g., email, web services).

The second objective here is that SLA should be relevant to the business. There is no point including a large number of variables for an SLA. One should only pick up a few relevant variables. Most importantly, SLA must be based on measurable parameters. For example, there is no point in stating that the "quality service will be high". If quality of service is to be included in the SLA, it must be measurable and quantifiable. Thus SLAs form the integrating concept of service management.

The next important objective is that SLAs should be used as a means for improving the quality of a service. That would mean motivating people to set higher and higher levels of quality targets, often requiring aggressive SLAs. Hence SLAs are of two types: contractual and advisory. While the contractual SLAs may be conservative to avoid any contractual problems, advisory SLAs (with some incentives) are great for improving the service quality in an organization. This requires the involvement of people concerned with different aspects of the service. Part 5 discusses a methodology for the development of service management in the context of collaboration of different groups of people within and across organizations.

There are penalties for not meeting the specified SLAs. But the penalty is applied based on service performance over a predetermined period (e.g, one year). Also the service provider can earn back the penalty by providing a higher level of service during the subsequent period. This illustrates the kind of incentives implemented through SLA, for improving the quality of service. The other aspect of SLA development is to recognize the fact that the business environment is dynamic and hence SLAs need to be adjusted annually. This in turn, affects penalty levels, and the earn back mechanism.

Therefore, a typical SLA needs to incorporate the following:[27]

- Parties of the Agreement (Customer, Service Provider)
- Term (e.g., a period of 2 years)
- Scope (services covered by the agreement in terms user applications)
- Limitations (service provider's caveats, e.g., highest volume of transactions)
- Service Level Objectives
- Service Level Indicators (operational parameters)
- Non-performance (penalties)
- Optional Services (options, e.g., weekend support levels)
- Exclusions (needing explicit statements about service types exclusions)
- Reporting (formats, frequency of reports to monitor SLAs)
- Reviews and Revisions (periodic adjustments based on changing business needs)
- Approvals (process of acceptance of change in SLAs)

Now having defined the SLA from the point of view of the customer, the next task is to define the Service Level Objectives in terms of measurable parameters (e.g., response time, delay etc.), and operational parameters (e.g., maximum time for back up of systems, and quantifiable levels of security). These are discussed in the next section.

5.2.2.2 Service Level Objectives

As discussed earlier, the formulation of Service Level Objectives is guided by the overall positive strategy of improving the service quality. Some such objectives are given below. Each of these Service Level Objectives needs to translate to corresponding Operational Level Objectives that form the Operational Level Agreements (OLAs). A bullet states the service level objectives, and the list within each bullet states the corresponding operational level parameters:

☐ Define availability over established time periods

- Maximum outages/durations over a period of time
- Maximum time to initiate backup systems

☐ Establish course of action for plan deviation

- Establish responsiveness and throughput
- Set system and application response time thresholds

☐ Quantifiable levels of security

- Applications and systems must have mechanisms in place to ensure confidentiality

☐ Set accuracy and recovery levels

- Application and system accuracy levels must be set
- Recovery plans and time frames must be in place

It is important to define all the objects, and operational parameters from an e-business perspective. Firstly, availability must be defined appropriately; otherwise its measures would be insignificant. For example, in one network service SLA, the availability was set at 100%, and availability was defined as the percentage of time there was some traffic over the network. This target was usually met (and was probably good for the earnings of the service provider), but it was of no consequence to the e-business service. Therefore, Service Level Objectives need to be derived in a top-down manner (from business/service needs), though it may be easier to instrument SLAs in a bottom-up fashion.

Definition of SLA parameters can be quite complex, and service management platforms support various types of computations defined for this purpose. For example, The Tele-Management Forum (TMF) has defined availability for a telecom service provider business as[28]:

$$UA\% = 100\% * \sum[SAP - Weight * \sum(SAP - Outage - Interval * SDF)] / \sum(SAP - Weight * SAP\_Activity - Time)$$

Where:

- Service access Point (SAP) is a logical element located on the interface between customer's domain and the service provider's domain representing the point at which the service is delivered. A SAP group represents a group of SAPs against which service availability must be reported by Performance Reporting.
- SAP-Weight represents a value or relative priority attached to each SAP, and influences the relative significance placed on that SAP by the service provider (and eventually the customer). It is defined independently for each SAP within the associated SLA.
- SAP-Outage-Interval represents the time interval of a specific outage period within the defined reporting period. An outage period is a period of service unavailability (say, due to fault) which occurs during an SAP Activity interval for a given SAP, and which is not due to causes excluded by the associated SLA (e.g., force major). It must be measured for each outage period of each SAP within a SAP group.
- SAP Activity-Time represents the total time of all SAP activity of a specific SAP within the defined reporting period.
- Service Degradation Factor (SDF) defines the factor by which the service can be described as a fraction of its full performance level.

The above example of the definition of availability in a telecom service provider environment helps us illustrate some of the complexity in defining and measuring Service Level Objectives. An e-business environment is more complex because of the need to support a variety of businesses, and infrastructures that play a role in deciding service levels. This requires a hierarchy of levels of service level management.

5.2.2.3 Operations Level Agreements (OLAs)

It is important to define SLA parameters in terms of underlying network and systems management parameters, in order to implement SLAs in an operational environment. SLAs are then implemented through Operations Level Agreements (OLAs)

The idea is to define these service level objectives using QFD matrices defined in Part 2. Business and Service level parameters can map to the technical metrics and cost requirements. For example, it is possible to do the costing for different layers of the infrastructure (e.g., the network and systems) and see how it contributes to the service. Figure 33 shows an example of how different types of IT services and transactions can be translated to corresponding operational, hardware and software parameters. For example, the cost of a business transaction consists of three main items:

- Cost of software
- Cost of hiring programmers
- Cost of help-desk

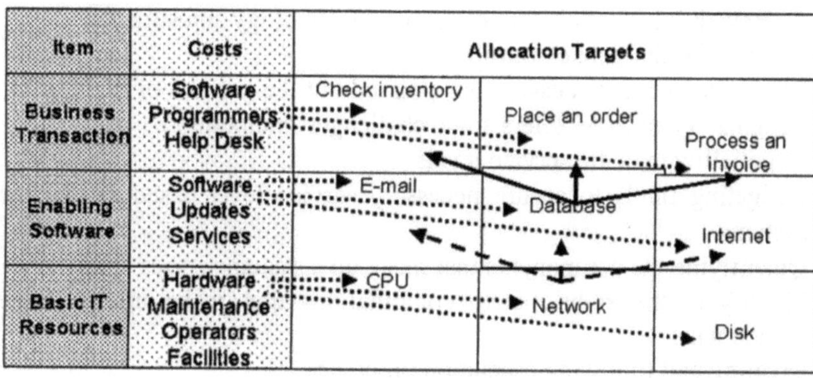

Figure 33. Mapping of Service Objectives to Operational Level parameters[5]

Each transaction (e.g., check inventory) will have these costs. In addition, a transaction will incur costs related to information infrastructure (e.g., Database). Each infrastructure cost in turn will depend on the underlying network and hardware costs. Therefore, it is not easy to apportion the cost of downtime to the myriad of services, and devices in an e-business environment.

The process of service level management can be summarized as:

- Inventory IT Resources by system of application (involving CPU, memory, disk, bandwidth, etc.)
- Baseline the critical metrics on each system (Look at the big picture - Graphical displays are best)
- Define existing levels of service
  - Pre-existing knowledge of the system is important
  - End-user interviews can be used to quantify existing levels

- Identify critical end user needs and wants
  - Define needs and wants based on business metrics
  - Both needs and wants are important to end user satisfaction
- Quantify service levels
  - Define service levels by system
  - Map business needs/wants to technical support metrics
  - Cost by system for needs and wants
- Establish service level targets (particularly critical applications and important systems)
- Write formal SLAs (include background, terms, time limits, system limits, etc.)
- Review SLAs
  - Identify trends and compliance
  - Revisit business objectives & make technology adjustments
  - Set new chargeback rates

While the above discussion has pointed out the process of SLM, it must be recognized that SLM offers some challenges, including:

- Negotiating realistic service levels
- Budgeting funds to secure necessary service level based management systems
- Quantifying the components that make up a system service level
- Identifying the right metric combinations that make up the system components
- Creating and following escalation processes
- Maintaining well trained support staff

A number of standards bodies and international organizations, such as TeleManagement Forum (TMF), Distributed Management Task Force (DMTF), IT Service Management Forum (ITSMF) and International Telecommunication Union (ITU) are working towards defining guidelines to overcome these problems. These efforts lead to best practices for SLAs and Operational Level Agreements (OLAs). These standards will be discussed in Part 4.

SLAs and OLAs are defined for:

- Business unit end users see seamless level of service
- Uniform support across geographical boundaries
- Escalation processes are defined for change management and problem resolution
- Operational support demarcations are well defined
- Process + Tools + People = uniform service levels

These factors are taken into consideration in the design of systems for the management of modern end-to-end multi-provider telecommunication services[7]. As a matter of fact, multi-provider telecommunication services (e-telco) can be seen as an excellent illustration of e-business management as discussed in Chapter 8.

5.3 E-Business Transaction Management

Section 5.1.3 discusses e-service management requirements in terms of tasks, metrics, time, models, measurements, events, and controls. The discussion is presented from top-down and bottom-up perspectives. This section presents the discussion based on end-to-end transactions and their sub-transactions across consumers, service providers, and suppliers. The discussion is based on the Vitalsoft (part of Lucent Technologies) white paper[21].

Every transaction, initiated by a service consumer, follows a particular set of steps (a workflow) before being fulfilled. In particular it starts in the consumer applications, flows through the Internet (Internet service provided by ISP), executes through the business applications of the provider, and may even flow into the applications of the external suppliers. In each of these stages, the transaction can flow through e-service middleware that provides mechanisms for secure cross-enterprise communication. An end-to-end management system should tap into all the possible sources of information through this workflow in order to monitor, diagnose, and fix problems. In particular, there are three types of sources from which transactional and other measurements or metrics can be taken[22]:

- *Consumers*: Metrics collected here would help in understanding the consumer's perspective of the e-service quality.
- *E-Service Provider*: The business logic in the provider's e-business service is implemented using complex applications that are distributed across provider's intranet/extranet (e.g, web servers, databases, application servers, etc.). Measurements collected from each of these elements need to be put together to understand any problems in the e-service provided.
- *External Suppliers*: Since some of the components of the e-service are outsourced to other providers (suppliers), it is important to collect measurements from the outsourced e-services as well. The examples include the ability to track transactions through a courier company, such as FedEx and UPS in the USA. The external manageability is sometimes a differentiating factor between two competitive e-services.

The metrics collected from the participants of an e-service transaction can be used to complete the end-to-end picture of that transaction's workflow.

Many of the modern distributed e-business systems use distributed transaction management systems that are designed to implement the

Atomicity, Consistency, Isolation and Durability (ACID) properties of an electronic transaction. These are implemented using commercial products, such as BEA Tuxedo, Microsoft Transaction Server (MTS), IBM MQ etc. They are based on standards, such as OMG CORBA, DCOM etc.[24]

Transaction management is the backbone of most networked business application operations. This topic is usually discussed in detail in the context of distributed databases, and distributed systems[21]. Relevant standards are briefly discussed in Section 5.4.

5.3.1 Business Transaction Performance[21]

This shift toward "business transaction monitoring" changes the way IT organizations are measured and evaluated. In the past, IT's performance was typically judged against resource-specific (e.g., network or server) availability goals; if the goal (say 99 percent availability) was achieved, the organization was considered successful.

Today, however, the yardstick is no longer resource availability but the more complex and elusive issue of "business transaction performance" - the overall, end-to-end availability and performance of applications that support the organization's critical internal and e-business business processes. This new method of measurement requires aligning IT performance with business metrics, bridging the gap by translating e-services into business terms that are meaningful to the user[21].

5.3.2 Support for Critical Business Processes

Today's enterprise networks exist to support the applications that run the business. Users don't care what's behind the walls or inside the PC - platforms, protocols, objects, databases, etc. The business user cares about the application's availability as a means of performing a specific task, whether it's a day trader placing an online stock order, a home-based business owner accessing his credit line, or a channel partner visiting a website searching for product update news. In this scenario, what matters most is that the transaction is completed quickly, efficiently and reliably, regardless of the myriad "behind the scenes" activities required to complete the task. To business users, the transaction is a single activity that is absolutely critical to perform their jobs.

Clearly, as businesses grow more dependent on the network, it becomes increasingly important to monitor the performance and availability of these transactions from the perspective of those who are affected most - the users themselves. The driving force behind this requirement is much more than financial; the high costs associated with downtime means businesses that operate online can't afford delays and bottlenecks, let alone catastrophic failures. The more integral the IT technology is to the business, the greater the cost of downtime, whether it's lost employee productivity or loss of a valued customer.

It is important to measure business transaction performance because any organization striving to increase its chances for success must first improve the underlying business processes that support the operation. Improving business processes first requires the ability to *measure* those processes.

5.3.3 Client/Server and Web-based Transactions

A transaction can be defined as a user-initiated sequence of data exchange between the client and a server. A monitoring solution that looks at transactions from the user's perspective can provide a valuable and insightful view of e-business application performance. In many instances, however, it is even more valuable to determine *what specific transaction is occurring* and report performance at that level. This is achieved by identifying sub transactions.

A sub transaction, or verb-level transaction, is defined as the *action performed in any given transaction.* For example, a database SELECT statement is distinguishable from a database INSERT statement at a granular sub transaction level. Certain common networked applications perform sub transactions that can be recognized via specialized packet analysis. For example, POP3 and SMTP e-mail traffic is recognizable. Once recognized, the application can be monitored at the sub transaction level.

This granular analysis is quite valuable to the network administrator or the application manager concerned with quality of service for his or her particular application. However, as IT aligns more closely with the e-business processes it supports, and as business managers become more interested in the performance of the technology as it relates to the business, a new level of visibility is required - visibility into the actual *business transaction*[21].

A business transaction is a collection of client activity and network traffic that accomplishes a specific, *meaningful* unit of work for the end user.

5.3.4 Anatomy of E-Business Transaction Management

As an extension of application performance management, business transaction management solutions must share a number of attributes that are indispensable to application performance management solutions. These include reporting performance with three critical characteristics[21]:

- **End-user perspective:** The business transaction management solution must monitor performance from the desktop, as experienced by the end-user. After all, a business transaction is ultimately all about what the end user needs. By using an agent at the client desktop, it is possible to measure performance as experienced by the end user because the agent can provide a complete end-to-end view of any e-business transaction from the time of its inception at the client until the application completes the request. Through TCP/IP packet analysis, the agent can also demarcate how much transaction time was spent in the client, the network or the server.

- **Historical analysis:** Business transaction management solutions must report on e-business network and application performance over days, weeks and months to provide a broad historical overview. This historical perspective is critical in order to give the network manager a reference point to determine how performance is evolving - is it improving or is it declining? Using this information, the network manager can then improve the technology infrastructure in order to support future e-business demands. A historical view enables analysis of the data to understand the changing nature of demands on the network and changes in the quality of services related to those demands. In many cases, Service Level Agreement (SLA) thresholds have been established to baseline acceptable performance standards. An effective and powerful analysis tool will provide a display that includes all components within the network, showing SLA violations at a glance.

- **Real-time:** In addition to providing a historical summary, the business transaction management solution must also report alarms and faults in a real-time, help-desk environment to enable rapid event troubleshooting and resolution.

Another area where business transaction management capabilities must exceed typical application performance management solutions is in the ability to monitor and manage different types of applications. Because e-business applications are so complex and varied, visibility into all types of networked applications within an organization is absolutely critical. These include:

- **Custom Applications:** Typically, an organization that has invested in developing custom software has tailored it to support very specific, high profile business needs. For example, consider a large retail bank that is enabling its services over the web so its customers can access their accounts and conduct various on-line transactions.

A complete performance management solution must track the unique application activities that comprise this business transaction.

- **Packaged Applications:** Often, companies rely on packaged software to support critical business functions for everything from human resources and financials to supply chain integration with other organizations. A complete performance management solution must monitor these applications at a meaningful, business transaction level.

- **Browser-based Applications:** The future of application development is the web. Distributed applications, the Internet, intranets and extranets all use browsers to interface with the end user. A complete performance management solution must monitor critical business transactions as they are redefined for a web environment.

5.3.5 The Changing Face of Network Performance Metrics

Business transaction management has the potential to change the way IT professionals perform their jobs. In the past, relatively simple SLA and performance data about the infrastructure - technology-centric metrics such as device availability, packet loss, round-trip-time, etc., was sufficient. As business processes become more intertwined with technology, however, IT is challenged with providing executives and other non-technical personnel with performance data in the form of business-centric metrics - i.e., how well is the network supporting the business?

Consider, for example, a claims processor who is experiencing problems with a business application. While a network manager may analyze performance data and see problems in the application servers, the claims manager may analyze the same data, presented in the form of business transactions, and see that a specific transaction - *look up policy* - is where claims handlers are experiencing delays. By presenting the information as a business metric, it becomes possible to understand where and how poor network and application performance affects actual *business processes* - and determine how to improve that performance.

With the right performance management solutions, IT can continue to monitor and manage technology-centric metrics while providing executives and others with the business-level equivalents. The right solution can present network and application performance statistics, including information about SLA violations, availability and demarcation of infrastructure problems (client, network, or server). The next chapter discusses some practical implementation frameworks for e-business management.

5.4 Evolving Standards in E-Business Management

We can classify standards at the business level according to generic e-business dimensions:

- Process Management standards at the business management level are in the form of best practices to manage the process of e-business, as discussed in Chapters 2 and 3. We illustrate that through ITSMF/ ITIL standards accepted by British Standards Institute. These standards are now owned by CCTA, the Govt. of UK, and this standard is now being adopted by many organizations all over the world[15].
- Transaction Management evolved from the world of databases and transaction processing so important for any production-level, large-scale e-business service. These have evolved from database and transaction processing technologies[24].
- The Infrastructure Management standards at this level deal with knowledge management and exchange within and across organizations, developed jointly by Desktop Management Task Force (DMTF) and Customer Support Consortium (CSC). These standards and lower level network and systems management standards are discussed in Chapter 6 and in Part 4 of this book.

5.4.1 Process Management Standards

There are two major international efforts towards the development and standardization of the management of e-business services.

- IT Infrastructure Library (ITIL)
- IT Service Management (ITSM)

The Information Technology Infrastructure Library (ITIL) was initially developed by the Central Computer and Telecommunications Agency (CCTA) in the United Kingdom. ITIL (now owned by UK Govt. agency OGC) is a systematic and practical method to optimize the management of the IT environment/infrastructure[17]. This methodology covers: People, Processes & Infrastructure Experiences of suppliers, consultants and users of information technology, as discussed in Section 5.2.1.

The IT Service Management (ITSM) Reference Model is built on ITIL. While ITIL suggests what to do, ITSM provides the know-how. In particular, ITSM: encompasses the IT supply chain, adds the technology component, specifies process linkages, and thoroughly incorporates the U.S.

experience. Some leading vendors of service management products, including HP have adopted this model[6].

The IT service management forum, which consists of about 400 global organizations and members, spans a wide variety of industries, including communications, energy and chemicals, financial services, government, healthcare, retailing and travel and transportation. The ITSM is the user organizer for the IT Infrastructure Library or ITIL which has been developed by the Central Telecommunications Agency of UK (now called OGC). ITIL is the only comprehensive library of publicly available IT service management best practices guidelines. The library consists of ten well-documented modules including service level management[17].

ITIL provides a

- •Comprehensive, consistent, coherent *Best Practices*
- •Promotes business effectiveness in the use of Information Systems
- •Drawn from industry experts, consultants and service management practitioners - worldwide
- ITIL goals are:
- •Clarify the business goals and objectives for IT Service Organizations
- •Align IT services with business objectives
- •Identify performance measures and recommend improvements
- •Formalize and document process and procedures
- •Implement and manage cost-effective SLAs ITIL consists of a number of publications. Some may be more relevant to specific audiences within an organization or all publications may be relevant, depending on a range of factors. The important point is that they do complement each other and together they form a coherent set. ITIL modules can be classified in two broad categories:

- Service Delivery
- Service Support

ITIL Service Delivery modules include the following:

- Service Level Management
- Capacity Management
- Cost Management
- Contingency Management
- Availability Management

ITIL Service Support Modules include the following:

- Configuration Management
- Change Management
- Software Control and Distribution
- Help Desk
- Problem Management

It may be noted that most of these modules are discussed as part of the ITSM architectural model based on ITIL in Chapter 3.

ITIL has been included in the British Standards Institute (BSI) recommendations.

The formal specification (BS15000) defines what organizations need to achieve, the Code of Practice is effectively a high-level management overview of the subject area, with the individual volumes of ITIL containing detailed guidance on people and process issues. The self-assessment workbooks are to assist organizations in understanding where they currently stand.

It is the intention that the BSI standard will subsequently become an ISO standard. A formal certification scheme, with *it*SMF as the accreditation body, is under development and there will be a number of supplementary publications for auditors and those preparing for an audit[15].

5.4.2 Transaction Management Standards

Transaction management has evolved as an essential part of the production environment of modern information systems. This is discussed in great detail in advanced database and distributed processing texts[24]. We provide a brief overview in this section because the transaction management standards may affect an e-business management strategy. A Transaction Processing Monitor (TP Monitor) in a production e-business environment consists of:

- Transaction Manager TM- manages transactions from origin to termination
- Services include monitoring, load balancing, process restarts, priority re-scheduling. E.g. IBM's CICS, Tuxedo, Encina
- TM facilities in RDBMS, Network Operating Systems, Comms. Managers

TP Monitor tasks are:

- Process Management (starting server processes, funneling work to them, monitoring execution, load balancing)Transaction Management (guarantees ACID properties for all programs that run under a TP Monitor)
- Client/Server Communication Manager (allows clients to invoke an application component through mechanisms including request-response, conversations, queues, publish-subscribe and broadcast)Transaction

processing can be classified as:

- TP-Less - do not use any transaction management
- TP-Lite - use database procedures to handle updates

- TP-Heavy - use a distributed transaction manager to handle updates - concurrency, update synchronization, data integrity.Standards are needed

for:

- interoperability of two TMs from different vendors, egg Tuxedo, Encina, CICS
- interoperability with database managers for a vendor X TM to operate with a DBMS from vendors Y and Z. egg CICS with Sybase.

X/Open defines interfaces XA and XA+ for this purpose. ISO Transaction Processing Standard (OSI TP) is used to provide global transaction control. More details are available in[24].

With the proliferation of the object web (object-oriented client-server Internet environments), distributed transaction processing standards subsume some standards in distributed objects (e.g., CORBA, DCOM, RMI) and web technology standards, such as Extended Markup Language (XML), Directory Enabled Networks (DEN), and Enterprise Java Beans (EJB). Many of these standards bodies, such as OMG have announced separate interest groups and supplements for standards to support transaction processing. Vendors, such as BEA, IBM and TIBCO have developed products around these standards[27].

5.4.3 Infrastructure Management Standards

E-business infrastructure is heavily dependent on Internet standards and protocols for networking. This aspect is managed by network management. Also all implementations use client-server systems based on PCs, workstations, and servers. This aspect is managed by systems management. Finally, multi-vendor software applications implement the features of e-business. This aspect is managed by application management tools and processes. All these constitute infrastructure management discussed in Part 4 of this book.

We also discuss standards at the knowledge infrastructure level. This is a matter of critical importance in the modern knowledge-based system design that requires diverse products to work together. Customers increasingly require and expect products and the companies supporting them to work together to provide a total solution to their needs. These trends have created a demand in many industries for support providers to access a support information structure. Customer support is a fast growing e-business service.

5.5 Chapter Summary

This chapter has discussed a top-down architectural perspective of e-business management services. We started with a discussion of e-business services in the context of the evolving middleware technologies. This was followed by a discussion of the management requirements of e-business services. We categorized e-business management into three dimensions, namely management of e-business processes, management of e-business transactions, and the management of e-business infrastructure (integrated management of networks, systems and applications).

The process perspective of e-business management has assumed maximum importance in the context of the integration of e-business management with the management of e-business infrastructure. This has led to the development of best practices and guidelines, such as the ITIL recommendations from CCTA (OGC) of the UK, and the E-TOM guidelines from the Tele-Management Forum. These guidelines focus on the processes and sub-processes of e-business management from the perspective of business sectors, such as telecommunications. While the process perspective provides a holistic view of e-business management, the transaction perspective provides a more practical view of e-business management as discussed in this chapter. Hence transaction management standards (extensively used in the database world) assume new importance in e-business management.

Although transaction management captures some of the practical insights of e-business management, it is important to consider some new concepts used to link e-business process management to e-business infrastructure management. Service Level Management (SLM) has emerged as the best way of achieving this objective. The next chapter and Appendix 4 will present SLM in detail with some practical illustrations based on existing commercial products.

5.6 References

1. Blum R., "E-Business Network Architecture/ Infrastructure", *Network Industry Survey, Lucent Technologies* NetworkCare, www.lucent-networkcare.com/surveys, accessed on April 2001
2. BMC Software, "Best Practices in Service Level Management", *BMC White paper*, http://www.bmc.com/products/whitepaper.html, March 2001
3. Bon J. von (ed), *World Class IT Service Management Guide*, Den Haag, ten Hagen & Stam, The Netherlands, ISBN: 90-76383-46-4, 2000
4. Bouch A., Kuchinsky A. and Bhatti N., "Quality is in the Eye of the Beholder: Meeting Users' Requirements for Internet Quality of Service", *HP Labs Technical Report HPL-2000-4*, January 2000, Palo Alto USACook P., "Information Technology Financial Management*HP-OpenView'98 presentation*, April 1998

6. Drake J., "An HP IT Service Management Reference Model", *HP White Paper*, July 1997
7. Dragan, D., Gringel T., Hall J., Rosa, E., Tschichholz, M., "Trouble Management for Multimedia Services in Multi-Provider Environments", *Journal of Network and Systems Management* (JNSM), Vol. 8 No. 1, March 2000
8. Fuss A., "Understanding and Improving IT-Service-Provisioning", *White paper from Intelligent Communication Software (ICS)*, Germany, March 2001, http://www.ics.de
9. Ghetie I.G., *Networks and Systems Management: Platforms Analysis and Evaluation*, Kluwer Academic Publishers, 1997
10. Hegering H., Abeck S. and Wies R., *Integrated Management of Networks and Systems*, Morgan-Kaufman Publishers, 2001.
11. Herman J., "Integrated Management for the Networked Milleneum", *IFIP/IEEE International Symposium Integrated Management (IM'99)*, Boston, May 1999
12. HP OpenView Group, "hp openview e-services management", "itsm service level manager information library http://www.openview.hp.com/library/misc/literature/Literature_HTML-2.asp, March 2001
13. Hurwitz Group, "Beyond e-Intelligence: The Intelligent Enterprise", *Hurwitz Group White paper written for Computer Associates International*, USA, April 2000
14. Intelligent Communication Software (ICS), "Service Level Management with Continuity", *ICS White paper*, http://www.ics.de, 2000
15. IT Service Management Forum, "*What is IT Service Management*" http://www.itsmf.com/
16. Koehler D., "Service Level Monitoring", *HP-OpenView'98 Presentation*, April 1998
17. Kostick R., Williams J., and Arnold M., "Service Level Management", in *The World Class IT Service Management Guide*, ISBN 9076383464
18. Kuno H., "Surveying the E-Services Technical Landscape", *HP Labs Technical Report HPL-2000-22*, February 2000, Palo Alto USA
19. Laudon K. and Laudon J., *Management Information Systems: Organization and Technology*, Prentice Hall, 1998
20. Lewis L. and Ray P., "On the Migration from Enterprise Management to Integrated Service Level Management", *IEEE Network*, January 2002
21. Lucent Technologies, "Business Transaction Management", *A Vitalsoft White Paper*, August 2000, http://www.lucentservices.com/knowledge/whitepapers/index.asp#e,

22. Machiraju V., Dekhil M., Griss M., and Wurster K., "E-Services Management Requirements", *HP Laboratories Technical Report HPL-2000-60*, Palo Alto, USA, May 2000
23. Ramaswamy R., *Design and Management of Service Processes*, Adison Wesley, AT&T Engineering Process Improvement Series edited by J.W.Wesner, 1996
24. Ray P., *Cooperative Management of Enterprise Networks*, Kluwer Academic/ Plenum Publications, May 2000, ISBN:0-306-46276-1
25. Seybold P., "Preparing for the E-Services Revolution", http://www.hp.cpm/e-services/pdfs/seybold.pdf, Feb 2000
26. Shim S.Y., Pendyala V., Sundaram M. and Gao J., "Business-to-Business E-Commerce Frameworks", *IEEE Computer*, October 2000
27. Sturm R., Morris W. and Jander M., *Foundations of Service Level Management*, Sams Publishing, Indiana, USA, 2000
28. TeleManagement Forum (TMF), "Performance Reporting Definitions Document", NMF701, April 1997
29. Tele-Management Forum (TMF), "Telecom Operations Map (TOM)", http://www.tmforum.org, October 2000
30. Umar A., *Object-Oriented Client/Server Internet Environments*, Prentice Hall, 1997

Chapter 6. Operation and Implementation of E-Business Management

Chapter 5 discussed the architectural framework of e-business management in terms of the three viewpoints: Process Viewpoint, Transaction Viewpoint, and the Infrastructure Viewpoint. Implementation of e-business management is complex due to the interplay of a range of associated factors, such as network management, systems management, and application management. It is important to integrate management process models, such as help desk with platforms for integrated management. Hence the discussion of the operation and implementation of e-business management may be broken into the following categories to facilitate understanding:

- Realization of the service perspective of e-business management as discussed in this chapter
- Realization of the infrastructure perspective (including network and systems management) as discussed in Part 4 (Chapter 7) of this book

We discussed some guidelines and best practices for e-business management in Parts 1 and 2. As stated in the previous chapters, it is important to present e-business management parameters and their values in business terms. Hence the operation and e-business management may be viewed as a service as discussed in Part 2. Therefore, e-business management is best implemented with tools and techniques called "Service Level Management" (SLM) in technological parlance. E-business may be viewed as a collection of a number of generic e-services each of which can be managed with SLM.

This chapter begins with a discussion of the operational level building blocks for e-business management. This is followed by the definitions of some important parameters for e-business management at service level. We then discuss the implementation strategy of e-business management based on Service Level Management (SLM). The operational framework is discussed with respect to the help-desk business model and evolving knowledge management tools. Finally, we discuss some evolving standards for the interoperability of SLM across organizations.

6.1 E-business Management Architecture

The advent of e-business presents unique management problems for today's leading edge companies. Management of existing Information Technology (IT) infrastructure has never been more important, but at the same time controls must be placed around the combination of internal and external systems that form the basis of the e-business model. Intranet e-business applications provide broader employee access to internal business information, potentially straining the existing e-business infrastructure with new traffic (e.g., web browsing). Internet e-business applications, such as e-commerce, provide business partners and customers access to business information, creating more traffic for the e-business infrastructure and introducing more stringent security, reliability and availability requirements.

Service Level Management (SLM) tools manage e-business applications and the underlying infrastructure as a single entity. For intranet environments, *Enterprise Systems Management* integrates the management aspects of e-business applications to provide a consolidated view of an enterprise's business solutions, the applications they use and the underlying e-business infrastructure which consists of three layers: network, system, and application. Managing e-business applications requires effective management of each of these layers. To achieve this, each layer supports a broad set of management functions that adhere to enterprise defined policies and procedures. The management functions include deployment, availability, operations and administration, and security.

The e-business infrastructure management architecture defines the structure and services to integrate the management functions across the layers of the application stack. The architecture is composed of the following key elements[7]:

- *Management agents* that monitor and control the resources used by an e-business application. These agents run on the same machine as the resource they manage, respond to specific requests from management applications and collect management information for the resources. Managed resources and their agents exist at each layer of the application stack.
- *A management framework* that supports communication between management agents and management applications, provides a storage mechanism for collected management information, and supports a mechanism to apply policies and procedures to the management environment.
- *Management applications* that analyze data collected from agents and initiate commands to agents for problem resolution. Management applications may focus on a particular function, such as a software distribution application, or they may focus on the management aspects of a particular resource, such as a database management application.
- *A management console* that provides a consolidated, central view of resources and management applications.

The elements of this framework and related standards will be discussed in Part 4. The remainder of this section will describe the e-business infrastructure management architecture in more detail. First, the supported management functions will be described within the context of an e-business application lifecycle.

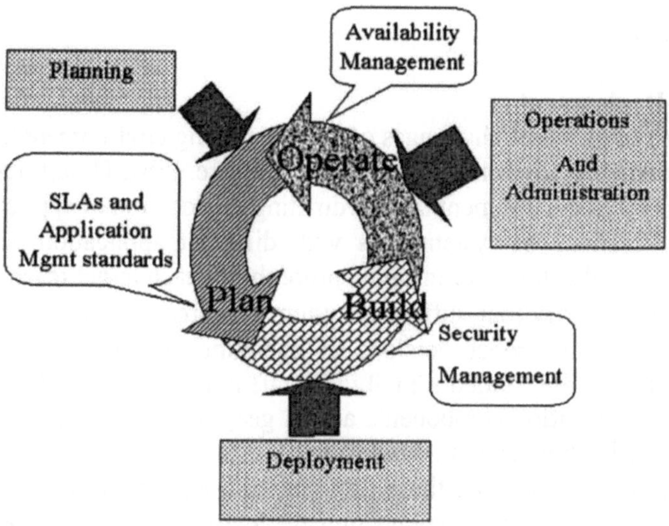

Figure 34. The Management Dimensions in E-Business[8]

6.1.1 Management Functions

The complete lifecycle of software (Figure 34) is fundamental to the management of e-business applications - from initial development and distribution to operation and subsequent upgrades. The e-business infrastructure management services supported by the Framework[8]:

- Efficiently deploy software to the right users, on the right platform at the right time,
- Monitor the availability and performance of hardware and software,
- Control access to and usage of e-business applications and their resources,
- Support management operations for e-business applications and their resources.

The Framework provides a flexible, policy-based management platform that allows administrators to apply management functions to individual resources or to collections of resources. For example, updates to an e-business application may be applied concurrently to an entire group of

machines or the update may be applied to individual machines on an "as needed" basis. The subsequent sections discuss the major dimension of e-business management[8].
- Deployment
- Availability
- Security
- Administration and
- Operations

6.1.1.1 Deployment

One of the greatest challenges of any computing environment is ensuring the successful deployment of application software. First, IT staff must set-up the deployment environment by coordinating the location of application files and modifications of system files with different application versions to ensure that applications are installed properly for each target machine. Then, IT staff must verify that sufficient system resources, such as memory, are available and the proper versions of operating systems and middleware configurations are installed. Finally, IT staff must be able to *flip the switch* on all the application components across geographically dispersed systems without overloading network bandwidth.

In many environments, these first and last deployment steps, discussed above, apply primarily to application deployment on one or more server machines. The Framework supports a server-managed deployment model in which applications and application components are installed and configured on a server and dynamically downloaded on-demand to requesting client machines. As a result, applications are not deployed on individual client machines thereby reducing the costs of client management significantly[8].

To address these deployment requirements, the Framework promotes the Tivoli-lead industry supported Application Management Specification (AMS) as the way to capture the details necessary to effectively deploy e-business applications. Tools are provided to build AMS files that describe an e-business application.

6.1.1.2 Availability

Now more than ever, the availability and performance of mission-critical applications is crucial to business transactions, regardless of where the components reside. Businesses can suffer unrecoverable loss of profit and productivity when customers, suppliers, and employees lack access to critical applications. For this reason, management agents must provide availability and performance characteristics of e-business applications and their resources.

The management agents monitor the various resources used by an application and send event messages to one or more management applications. Agents adhere to enterprise-defined policies and procedures, which can, for example, define performance thresholds as well as dictate which management system should receive which messages. The Open Group standard Application Response Measurement (ARM) APIs can be used by management agents to measure e-business application response time.

6.1.1.3 Security

Mission critical e-business applications must be deployed in an environment that provides authentication, access control and auditing capabilities to ensure the integrity and privacy of business critical information. Although the Framework promotes the use of public key infrastructures that use X509v3 certificates and SSL, many of the applications and data in business systems today use proprietary mechanisms or private key infrastructures. In fact, different security systems may be utilized at each layer of the application stack.

To support these environments, the Framework defines the tools and services that allow administrators to manage different security schemes in an integrated fashion. Once a user is authenticated to use an e-business application then all security needs of lower layers are automatically handled by the system. This is sometimes referred to as single sign on. In addition, system management services provide a flexible, role-based security model to assign the appropriate rights to users of the various e-business application components[8].

6.1.1.4 Administration and Operations

Mission critical e-business applications must be able to adapt to changes in their environment, such as location of temporary storage, and recover from problems encountered during usage, such as data that is out of date. To perform these functions, e-business applications must issue event messages when problems are encountered and provide access (e.g., via command line interfaces) to features and functions so that changes can be made or problems fixed.

The Framework supports a rules-based event monitoring system that enables administrators to invoke application management operations, such as backup and restore, in response to specific events or at scheduled intervals. The Framework supports a number of event formats including SNMP.

For the Internet environment, *Cross-Enterprise E-Business Infrastructure Management* supports a collaborative management approach that extends management functions to environments beyond company boundaries[8].

6.1.2 Evolution of Integrated Management of E-Business

The lowest level management situation is unmanaged or reboot (Figure 35).

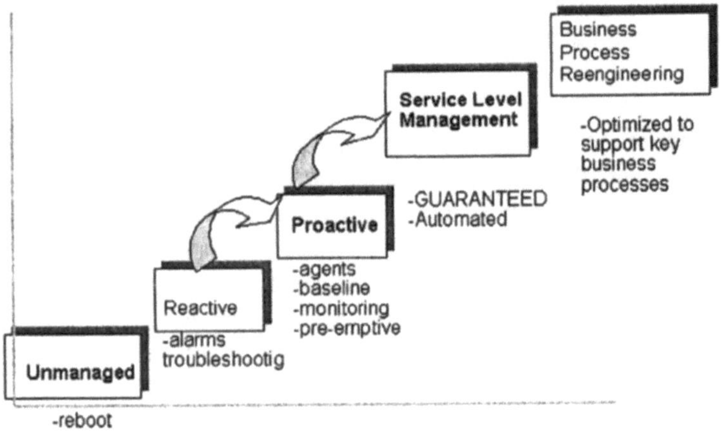

Figure 35. Evolution of Integrated Management[16]

The next level is reactive; the most common in network and systems management world. In this case, the management system reacts to events or alarms in the system. For example, the management system starts investigations after the occurrence of an alarm. In many situations this is too late. One should be able to find out before the fault happens, so action can be taken to avoid the fault. The solution approach is known as pro-active management. Many commercially available management products now support this feature.

And finally we come to intelligent management. This is basically a system where the management task is delegated to agent(s) to perform specific aspects. It may consist of two levels as with platforms like Aprisma SPECTRUMTM, and CA TNG™.

Service Level Management is the next level of network service management. There must be guaranteed service and automatic ways of monitoring service levels with respect to the lower levels parameters. Most importantly, the business level SLA parameters have to be linked to underlying network and systems management objects. There are commercial products to support SLM.

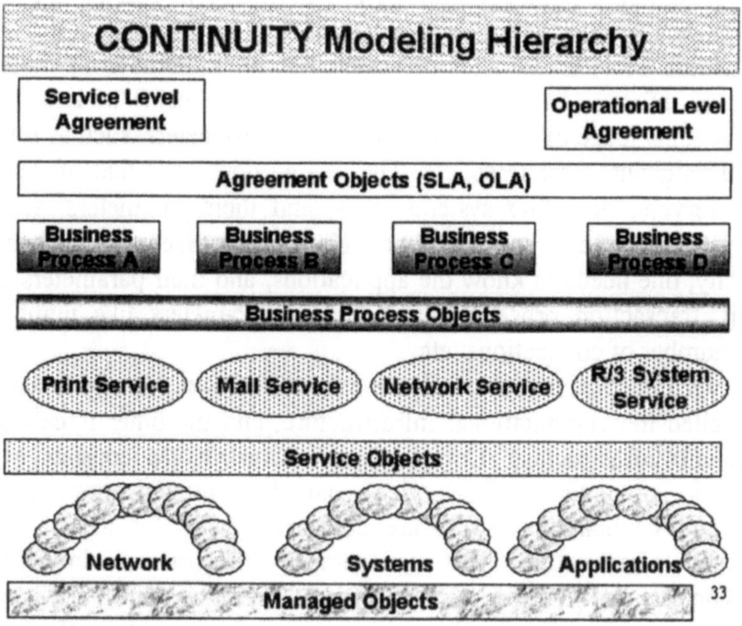

Figure 36. Mapping of SLAs and OLAs to Network, Systems and App. Mgmt[9]

Figure 36 shows how SLM is implemented in a commercial product - Continuity™ from Intelligent Communication Software (ICS) of Germany. This scheme conceptualizes the integration through three levels of objects[9]:

- Agreement Objects- encapsulate the SLA parameters defined in Section 6.2.2
- Business Processes -encapsulate data and workflows associated with e-business processes as discussed in Chapter 5
- Service Objects- encapsulate management information related to networked services, such as mail service, print service etc.
- Managed Objects- define management information related to networks, systems, and applications.

The highest level of integrated management involves business process re-engineering that involves the complete reengineering of management processes to exploit the latest technological developments. For example, it may be possible in future to deploy mobile agents in Directory Enabled Networks to collect and correlate management information from remote nodes, obviating the need for a management platform.

6.1.3 Integrated Management of E-Business Infrastructure

E-business service management spans across a number of different domains of information infrastructure – different domains of knowledge. One is the knowledge of networks, and network parameters, such as routers, delays, throughput, error rates, etc. The second domain is that of systems, such as servers, operating systems, PCs, and their parameters, such as memory utilization, disk space, software distribution, licensing mechanisms etc. Finally, one needs to know the applications, and their parameters, such as email, transaction processing and related parameters like number of threads, number of connections, etc.

Today's information infrastructure consists of two symmetric aspects. One is called the computational infrastructure, and the other is called the management infrastructure. Computational infrastructure consists of the three major components of e-services, namely communication network, systems and applications. Users are concerned with this aspect of the information infrastructure. The management infrastructure, invisible to users, consists of network management, systems and applications management building blocks. Management operators are typical users of such an infrastructure. So communication and network systems are managed by network management tools/techniques, and systems are managed by system management tools. The applications are managed by application management systems. Relevant standards are discussed in Part 4.

Figure 37 shows different aspects of computational and management infrastructure, and their relationships as three levels. While the upper half represents the computational aspects, the lower half represents the corresponding management infrastructure. A computing user interacts with the systems through applications and services (e.g., email), which are supported by systems (e.g., operating systems, file systems), and communication systems (e.g., modems, multiplexers, etc.). Similarly, the management operators and other staff are concerned with the availability of the services and their management.

While network management is mainly concerned with the management of the communications infrastructure (e.g., links, protocols), systems management deals with other distributed facilities such as software distribution, print services and file services. Systems management is concerned with the management of desktops components, like PCs, file systems, servers etc. Systems management also deals with mechanisms, such as software distribution, licensing, etc. Traditionally this area has evolved from the management software in mainframe systems where systems management utilities were used for the management of input/output, peripherals, memory and processors. The importance and the difficulty of this task have grown substantially with the rapid growth of networked PCs in client-server systems. PC networks were initially used for file and resource sharing. Now they are being used more and more for mission-critical applications, such as transaction processing. Systems management is a very important aspect of managing Internet based e-businesses.

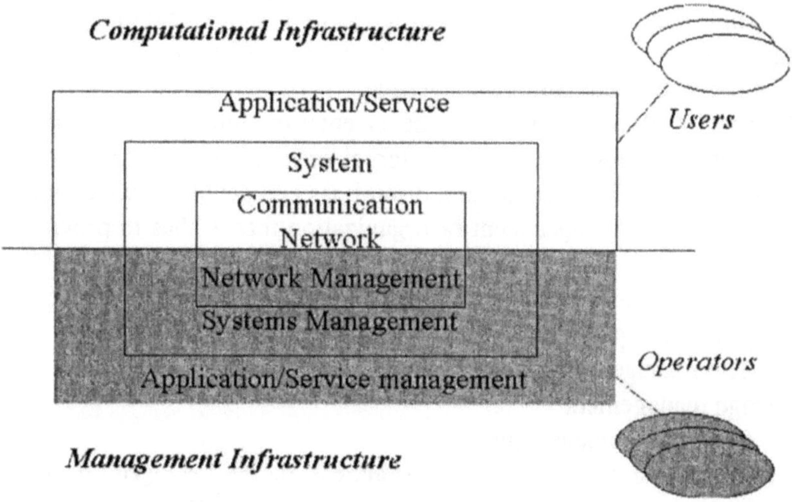

Figure 37. Integrated Management of E-Business Infrastructure[3]

Applications/Service management provides a higher-level view with respect to end-user applications such as electronic mail and video conferencing. These services are now distributed. It is necessary to have integrated management encompassing network management, systems management and service management. For example, a stockbroker may perform calculations using a financial service located at a remote application server (not known to the user). This application could use network services, such as directory services implemented over TCP/IP protocols. Any failure in the network will appear as a calculation service failure to the stockbroker, or as a problem with the stockbroker's local system.

Therefore, it is difficult to separate service management problems from underlying network or systems management problems. On the other hand, a different set of people could be assigned to solving problems in these different areas. For example, from the stockbroker's perspective, the networked service over the Internet would be provided by the Internet service provider (e.g., CompuServe). The network connection to home would perhaps be the responsibility of the local telecom service provider (e.g., Bell Atlantic), and the local PC might be under service with a local PC shop. This necessitates integrated management.

Earlier generations of network switches in the 1980s were used in the telecommunication domain, with 90 per cent of the software devoted to management. Only 10 per cent used for features. In the case of PC LANS, at that time, 90 per cent of the software was devoted to features and only 10 per cent was devoted to management - An example of two different domains with two completely different viewpoints on management. But over the last 5 years, there has been tremendous progress in this area, and today systems management in the PC domain and network management from telecommunication domain are converging.

Service Level Management is the science of delivering controlled IT functionality to a customer, either external or internal, in terms of quality, quantity and cost. There are several disciplines and activities, which must be addressed by any IT department or organization that wishes to provide true and effective service level management. These processes are as follows[9]:

- Availability management
- Capacity management
- Problem management
- Change management
- Configuration management

Depending on the business environment to be managed, it may be necessary to cover other disciplines in addition to those listed above, for example:

- Business process management (especially for mission critical applications)
- Business Continuity Management (especially in government or financial institutions)
- Security management (defense organizations, or to protect long-term strategy and planning

In order to provide efficient IT services, it is necessary to understand the relationships between service level management and other supporting processes within the structure of an IT organization. Figure 38 illustrates the different aspects of service level management and their relationships to these processes.

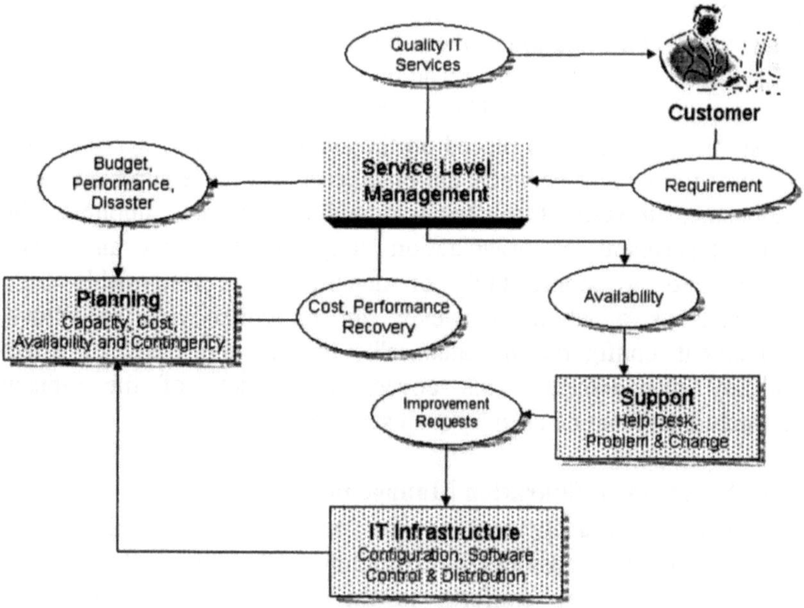

Figure 38. SLM in the Context of E-Business Management[9]

Network and systems management vendors, together with the various standards bodies have responded to the needs for SLM-based e-business management by developing several large-scale management systems designed to support the following six management disciplines[9]:

- Deployment
- Operations management
- Problem management
- Configuration management
- Change management and
- User support

6.1.3.1 What is Availability Management?

Availability management is the process of optimizing the availability of components in the e-business infrastructure to the extent that the requirements of the enterprise's business processes are being consistently maintained. There are a number of factors which influence the availability of IT services including:

- Complexity of the systems
- Reliability of the systems
- The maintenance provided by the equipment suppliers

- The policies of the IT service organization
- The overall configuration of the E-business infrastructure

IT services may be provided by an internal department or organization, in which case the enterprise itself owns the IT systems and infrastructure. In this case, the requirements placed on the availability of IT services may be drawn up in contracts between the enterprise and the equipment supplier. The e-business infrastructure itself is provided by several suppliers. The IT services department or organization supports the users and business processes and no single body or department is responsible for the environment as a whole. However, an enterprise-wide repository or "Management configuration database" provides the basis of effective availability management. This covers all aspects of the e-business infrastructure and can be used by each service department.

6.1.3.2 What is Configuration Management?

Configuration Management is the process of controlling all the components of the e-business infrastructure and defining their modes of operation so that they conform to the specifications of a particular environment. In configuration management terminology, IT components, or configuration items are models of the managed objects, i.e., hardware devices and software applications. Configuration items can be formed into logical groups or managed on an individual basis depending on the degree of control that is to be exercised upon them. Figure 39 illustrates this concept.

System A consists of sub-systems A1, A2, A3 and A4 and sub-system A3 can be further broken down into components A3.1, A3.2 and A3.3. Each component is a configuration item including System A itself, which is known as the "parent object". All configuration information is recorded and maintained in the Configuration Management DataBase (CMDB). Most large organizations make use of multiple configuration management databases, which tend to be distributed across the enterprise. For practical purposes, an object-oriented configuration management database, as opposed to a relational type, is more readily applicable to the process of modeling e-business infrastructures. The main purposes of maintaining such a database are:

- Grouping components into logical models either manually or through the process of auto-discovery
- Automating fault correlation and alarm control
- Providing inventory information for configuration items
  Identifying all equipment located at any particular site.

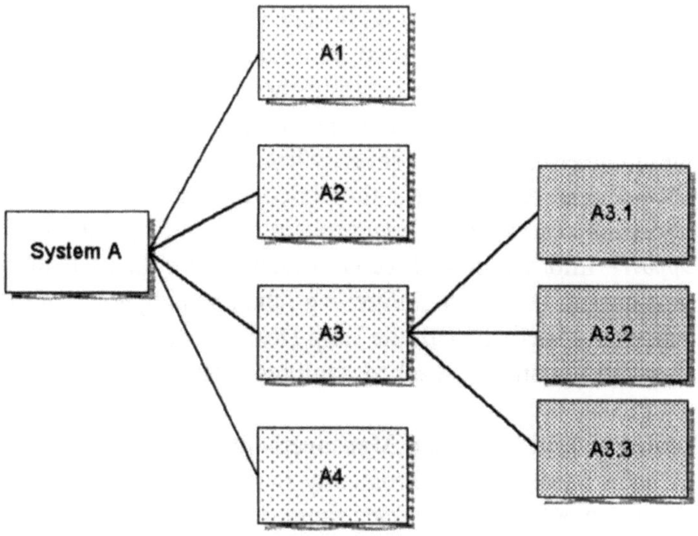

Figure 39. Configuration-Management[9]

6.1.3.3 Service Level Agreements

A Service Level Agreement is a written agreement between an IT service provider and the customer that documents pre-agreed service levels for any specific IT service. Service Level Agreements can be broken down into three separate parts. Firstly there is the textual form of the agreement followed then by a definition of the level which the service is required to maintain and finally, a mechanism for guaranteeing and measuring response and reaction times when the service fails.

The following synopsis of an SLA is included to clarify the above definition. It includes the levels of functionality and the severity levels that need to be implemented in the management system. *It is not complete and must not be regarded as definitive for any specific operation or organization*:

- ***SLA Text*** - the actual written agreement containing the SLA.
- ***Service Description*** - The names of the participating parties, duration of the agreement, special considerations for holidays, etc.
- ***Service Availability*** – The minimum percentage availability during normal service hours for any user of the service - e.g., **96%.** The average percentage availability for all users is e.g., **98%.**
- ***Service Breaks*** – The maximum number of service disruptions that can occur during a defined "rolling period".

- ***Service Hours*** – The periods of guaranteed service availability, e.g., Monday – Thursday: 08:00 – 18:00 Friday: 08:00 – 16:30
- ***Service Reliability*** – The pre-agreed minimum level of functionality that the service is required to meet during the rolling period. The service functionality also includes definitions of the severity levels and the maximum number of errors per severity level during the rolling period.
- ***Repair Time*** – The repair time is the period of time, which has elapsed before a disrupted service has been brought back into operation.
- ***User Support*** – Information and recommendations for the users in the case of support queries or service failure: e.g., the manning hours of the Help Desk, who should actually call the Help Desk, procedures to be followed if the Help Desk cannot be reached, fault resolution times, etc.

6.1.3.4 Real-time and Historical Measurement

Without some system of electronically managing them, Service Level Agreements are worthless. This electronic management functionality is essential for monitoring both service availability, service performance and for ensuring that pre-defined service levels have been met. Measuring and monitoring the quality of a service is a complex process and is the key to providing proactive Service Level Management. Most current methods of measuring service levels revolve around evaluating polled historical data. The measurement frequency is usually a period of a week or a month and is based on historical data, which makes the Service Level Management retrospective in nature. In addition, the evaluation is generally performed by the operative personnel and not by an automated tool. In contrast, a proactive approach involves automating the measuring procedure and reducing the measurement frequency to intervals of minutes. In effect, the measurement frequency is then equal to the monitoring frequency and allows us to trap exception conditions immediately. By adding event processing, we ensure that the monitoring procedure occurs in real-time. The infrastructure for such measurements is provided through the underlying network, systems and application management, as discussed in Part 4 of this book.

The major benefit of this approach is an enormous reduction in the time taken in fault detection and diagnosis. Due to the maximum possible degree of automation, faults can be identified and assigned to the appropriate operative immediately. The repair procedure can be initiated automatically (e.g., using either an email procedure triggered by an alarm or a trouble ticket), and it can then be tracked through all its separate stages using standard problem management techniques until it has been satisfactorily resolved. This process is now extensively used in the operation of SLM, as described in Section 6.3.

6.2 Implementation of E-Business Management

The current management focus needs to be thought over and re-applied in such a way that it covers methods of managing IT Services *from the user's point of view*. Some examples of such services are Email, WWW services and all-in-one financial applications. Considering the sheer importance of modern data-processing, it becomes increasingly apparent that without endorsing the concept of service-oriented management, the business processes of the enterprise are at risk. Instead, it must be prepared to take a conceptually new approach to the management challenge by shifting the focus away from pure technology monitoring, towards the idea of managing IT *services* and *business processes* and providing support for Service Level Management (SLM).

6.2.1 Planning SLM

An efficient service level management strategy can only be realized by adopting a systematic approach to the planning, design, implementation and operation of the e-business infrastructure. The systematic approach in turn, can only be realized by implementing and adhering to an e-business infrastructure planning model.

The e-business infrastructure consists of the hardware components as well as the software and communications technologies that together make up the IT services an organization provides:

- Hardware
- Software – distribution, development and applications
- Configuration and management
- Networks

Management issues that pertain directly to the E-business infrastructure are:

- Capacity planning
- Cost benefit analysis
- Administration
- Test and evaluation.

Here are the problems of E-business infrastructure management:

- Component and software incompatibility
- Changing technologies
- Restrictive corporate policies
- Security
- Fragmented IT ownership

Since the e-business infrastructure represents the means by which IT services are constructed and operated, it makes sense that the scope, scale and architecture of that infrastructure should be carefully and strategically planned based on the levels of service which are to be provided. Planning the e-business infrastructure is a discipline that should not be pursued in a haphazard or piecemeal manner but according to the perspective of the corporate IT strategy as a whole. Technical benefits of designing a good infrastructure include:

- Ability to expand and adapt
- Increased control
- Documentation
- Calculable quality-of-service
- Effective support
- Adherence to standards

Thus the primary purpose of the e-business infrastructure is that of achieving the corporation's business objectives through efficient deployment and use of its IT services. Since business objectives depend on IT services, which in turn are composed of various technologies, it is necessary to relate these technologies to business needs.

6.2.2 Mapping SLM to Infrastructure Management

We now discuss the mapping of SLM to network, systems and application level management.

Firstly, we consider mapping to network management. Many service management problems boil down to network management problems. Such problems could be due to faults or congestion in network, or due to lack of capacity. These problems can be identified by various types of network performance monitoring tools, such as RMON probes, sniffers, packet analyzers, and facilities available at management platforms. Standards in these areas will be discussed in Part 4. The following formula helps in conceptualizing availability management.

Availability Management=Performance Management + Configuration Management+ Fault Management.

The next consideration is mapping to systems management. There are two major problems in systems management in client-server environments. The first has to do with the proliferation of PCs and PC-based systems as clients. While PC buying may be cheap, supporting PCs is very expensive. This is particularly so if a person has to be dispatched to the site to support the PC. The second has to do with the management of the servers (web servers, new servers, proxy servers, main servers, etc.). This is one of the main problems of systems management. Here management is concerned with the utilization and availability of the servers, considering that so many invisible clients need to be served by a server simultaneously in the modern e-business environment.

The mapping to application management is perhaps most important and complex in view of the many dimensions of application management problems including performance, security, and configuration management issues. Application management is concerned with the development, testing, deployment, and troubleshooting of networked applications. At this stage, it is necessary to distinguish between networked applications and networked services. Application covers the source code as well as the executables for that particular application whereas, typically, a service is concerned with the application in operation (run-time code) and the context of the application.

6.2.3 Mapping SLM to Applications Management[21]

Two trends are propelling and complicating the need for performance management. First, the near ubiquity of the Internet Protocol and the declining cost of network throughput make application outsourcing more feasible than ever. Second, many critical applications are distributed across multiple architectural tiers and independently controlled networks.

The implications of these trends warrant examination. Companies may choose to turn over components of their applications to application service providers, management service providers, or some other sort of service company.

One of the most commonly desired requirements for applications is a short and predictable response time. A few ISPs are willing to include latency in their SLAs, though they generally restrict the circumstances to such an extent that the guarantee has little value. Most commonly, only traffic that remains on the ISP's network is guaranteed. In addition, it is common practice to average latency measures over periods as long as a month, which, like the gross availability measure, may correlate imperfectly with real-time user experiences. Useful response-time measures should be taken as they occur and should be reported immediately, as well as averaged over longer periods.

Application users have a number of other service level measures that provide a closer tie to their actual experiences than gross uptime or delay. For example, the percentage of transactions that run to completion may be more important than minor delays. It may be important to know percentages of customers that fill out complete forms and then abandon the transaction. The measurements that matter to a user in a real-time videoconference would not be geared so much to discrete transactions as to the details of factors such as latency and jitter. In many cases, some of the most interesting performance metrics are specific to a particular application. Not only are commonly guaranteed network performance specifications irrelevant to users, but generic application-layer performance specs may also fail to indicate acceptable performance.

While the increasing demand for detailed SLAs calls for client-centric management, the demand for end-to-end management requires insight into network elements and servers that may not be instrumented for performance measurement. New n-tier application architectures aren't necessarily rolled out with integrated management capabilities. Application servers that process the business logic of an application, database servers that feed data to the application server, load-balancing devices, firewalls, and virtual private network processors may all contribute to application degradation. Ideally, these devices should have granular performance-management capabilities. The situation is further complicated for critical applications because many of these architectural components may be duplicated (or triplicated) for redundant operation. This is very true for organizations, such as stock exchanges.

Successful end-to-end performance management isn't the end of the struggle. Typically, transactions and other application events are only interesting as part of a business process. For example, taking an order from a customer is part inventory management, shipping and accounts receivable. The aim isn't to manage a technical operation with servers, disk arrays, routers, and so forth, but to make business processes efficient and pleasant for customers, suppliers, partners, and employees.

Application performance management vendors have traditionally addressed three management techniques:[21]

1. In this case, programmers insert markers or break points within applications. The performance statistics are written to a file or communicated to another program at each crucial step to be monitored. This is a well-known method used for application debugging.
2. This involves acquiring all or selected parts of the traffic on the network, correlating requests with replies, and inferring application performance based on packet analysis.
3. This technique installs a sort of parasitic agent alongside each client or perhaps on the same LAN segment as a group of clients. The agent looks at events, such as opening windows and on-screen form submissions, and is either told or can infer what to measure.

The advantage of the programmed break point is that the original programmers know precisely what the right events for accurate and comprehensive instrumentation are, and there should be no doubt that the measurement is correct. Furthermore, the measurement can be as granular as needed.

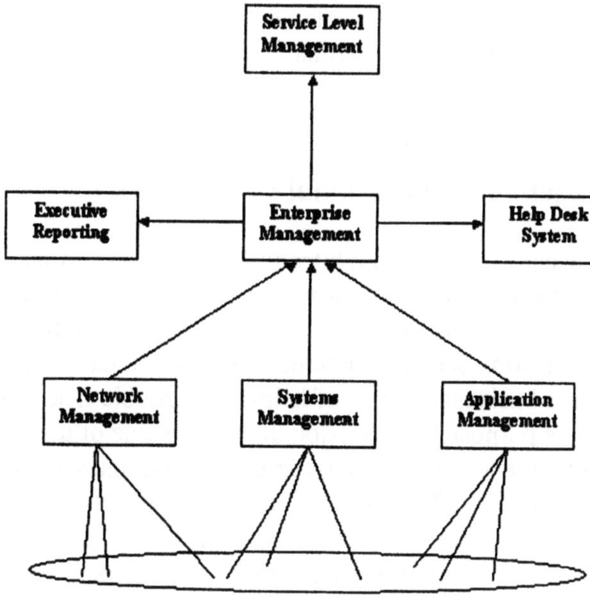

Figure 40. Integrated Service Level Management Architecture[13]

6.2.4 A Practical Framework for Service Level Management

As stated earlier, the infrastructure management consists of network management, systems management and applications management. Figure 40 shows the architectural block diagram to implement service level management and its mapping to application, network and systems management. As we shall see in detail in Part 4, present day service level management has the following important building blocks[20]:

1. An Enterprise Management Platform, such as Aprisma Spectrum, Tivoli TME, HP Open View, and CA TNG
2. Network Management Components, including RMON probes, Specialized monitoring agents, SNMP MIBs, and SNMP agents
3. Systems Management components, including DMTF MIFs, DMTF service providers, storage and printer management systems
4. Application Management components, including mail and directory MIBs, DMTF WBEM based Application Management applications, application response monitoring agents, and APIs
5. Help-desk (trouble-ticketing) based operational management system Executive reporting system to implement and monitor SLAs.

Appendix 4 describes a multi-vendor implementation framework of SLM based on CONTINUITY™ from ICS Germany and SPECTRUM™ from Aprisma USA.

Lundy Lewis provides some practical case studies of SLM in his book[14].

6.3 Service Management Operational Framework

We have already discussed various architectural frameworks to manage e-business services. However, it was not clear how such schemes would be integrated in a practical operations system. The service management world, particularly telecommunication service providers, has traditionally adopted the easily understandable business process of help-desk (trouble-ticketing in telecom industry) for this purpose. This section discusses some of the issues related to incorporating the evolving management technologies in an e-business operational framework. This discussion has been presented from the perspective of a generic enterprise. The telecommunication industry has traditionally used Operations Support Systems (OSS) for this purpose. The Tele-Management Forum (TMF) has developed a set of recommendations, as part of Fulfillment, Assurance and Billing (FAB) processes for e-business in the telecom industry[24]. This will be discussed in Appendix 2.

The operational framework for SLM depends on a number of factors:

- Level of business dependence of the application being managed can be assessed from the amount of revenue generation, and the tolerance for downtime of that application.
- The return on investment on SLM can be calculated from cost to payback ratio and the increase in end-user productivity.

Based on the above analysis one can determine hours of coverage and the measures for SLM, such as:

- Event Management for Availability
- Performance Monitoring for Availability and Response Time

6.3.1 Help-Desk based Service Management Environment

Help-desk is the model used for the operation of service management systems for e-business. In telecommunications this model is known as trouble-ticketing. SLM tools, such as event management, performance monitoring, and a number of emerging Artificial Intelligence (AI) mechanisms (e.g., expert systems) are now becoming available to enhance the capabilities of a help-desk system. Each problem is linked to a service or support call through a unique call number or a trouble-ticket similar to hospital patient bedside records. The objective is to enable less trained people to perform the job of e-business support.

Help-desk resolves an e-business operational problem by routing the call to appropriate people, and a well-defined escalation process based on time spent on the call. For example, the help-desk operator would receive a call, and try to solve the problem using the automated tools, in the service management environment. If unsuccessful within a stipulated time limit, the call would be referred to a technician who (if unable to resolve the problem) in turn would escalate the call to a technical expert. If the local expert can not solve the problem, it would be escalated to an international expert. The process continues until the problem is solved. The more technical expertise needed, the higher the cost of handling a call.

Hence the strategy of reducing the cost of service operations is to resolve as many calls as possible at the no-touch or first call levels. The trouble-ticketing system and the intelligence provided by software tools help in solving this problem.

Here are the definitions of these escalation levels:

- Dispatch--desk side visit by a technician
- First Call Resolution--could be transferred, but call is resolved
- No touch--automated, self help

Here are some cost estimates of help-desk depending on how a call is resolved[18]:

- Dispatch call ~$100
- First Call Resolution~$25
- No touch ~$10

Hence the objective of help-desk based SLM operations should be to move more calls from dispatch to first call and no touch buckets. Figure 41 shows the phased improvement of the help desk process to achieve this objective. It is possible to achieve dramatic operating cost reductions, but substantial initial expenses are required for tools (including intelligent agents) and implementation. ROI for tools depends on the area of IT operations it impacts.

The help-desk based service monitoring system requires different levels of metrics to be incorporated in the service management system depending on the situation as illustrated below:

- Normal health and service compliance would need to monitor (1-10) metrics/system
- Second Tier Problem Resolution would need to monitor up to 40 metrics/system
- Detailed Troubleshooting and modeling would need to monitor as many metrics as needed

The larger the number of metrics to be monitored, the more the overheads for management. Hence normal operations would need the monitoring of less metrics. This would be most efficient in terms of the operational overheads and the cost would be minimal.

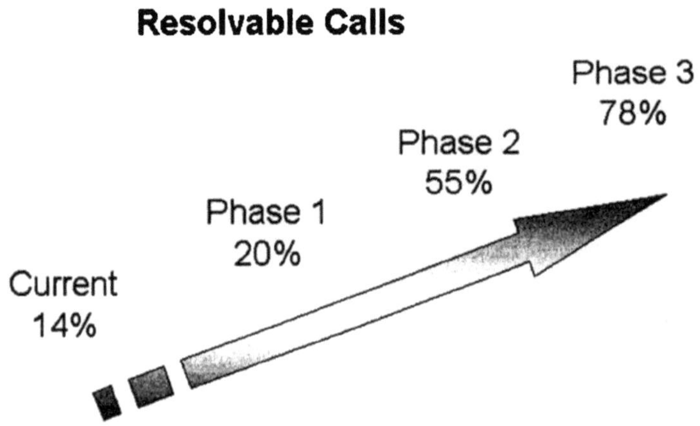

Figure 41. Quality Improvement through Improvements in Help-Desk Process[18]

The Second tier problem resolution will need more investment and more operational overheads, requiring more metrics. The process would involve the following:

- Capture metrics for trouble shooting
- Drill down from a yellow or Red alert
- 80/20 Rule -- Capture enough metrics to fix 80% of the problems
- Support high level trending analysis
- 5 minute sample intervals typical
- Store data for 30 day intervals

Detailed troubleshooting would require fairly sophisticated monitoring facilities with expensive tools and a substantial amount of overhead. The process may be summarized as follows:

- Monitor as many metrics as needed
  - Default mode most commonly used today
  - Very time consuming
- 30 second sample interval or less typical -- live feeds
- Support detailed problem resolution or capacity analysis.It is impractical to monitor all metrics because:

1. A substantial amount of network bandwidth is required to get the information and
2. A substantial amount of processing overhead is needed to process all these metrics

Hence the best strategy is to look at the most important variables of the problem and whatever metrics need to be captured. For example, for high level trending analysis, 5 minute intervals may have been difficult in the past, but this is one of the practicable figures used in the help desk environment today.

Part 4 of this book will look at the infrastructure technologies for performance monitoring. We now discuss the issues involved in the implementation and operation of a practical SLM-based e-business management system that spans across multiple organizations.

6.3.2 SLM in a Cooperative Environment

Management of e-businesses needs to deal with the fact that many e-business partners could be competitors too. Hence the sharing of management information needs to be planned very carefully, and the decision to share various blocks of management information may be altered dynamically based on business situations. This leads to two fundamental requirements of Service Level Management in a cooperative e-business environment [1]:

- 1. Cooperative service management and diagnosis require the knowledge and view of the end-to-end service. This means that management information has to flow across administrative domain boundaries of organizations involved in an e-business transaction.
- 2. Business requirements restrict information sharing across domains because the details of the service implementation and much of the customer information are considered proprietary by each business. Thus business policies restrict the sharing of details about components and infrastructure used in delivering the service. These policies are particularly stringent if customer data needs to be shared across e-business partners.

6.3.2.1 Cooperative SLM in E-Business

Meeting these objectives requires that service management systems need to:

- Selectively share information about the components of the overall service only to the extent necessary to ensure overall operation of the service.
- Hide the details of the system components by abstracting information.
- Provide SLAs to ensure that service level obligations provided by an e-business to its customers and partners are being met. These SLAs contain (along with other legal obligations) details of information that is shared and service level guarantees that are offered by the provider.

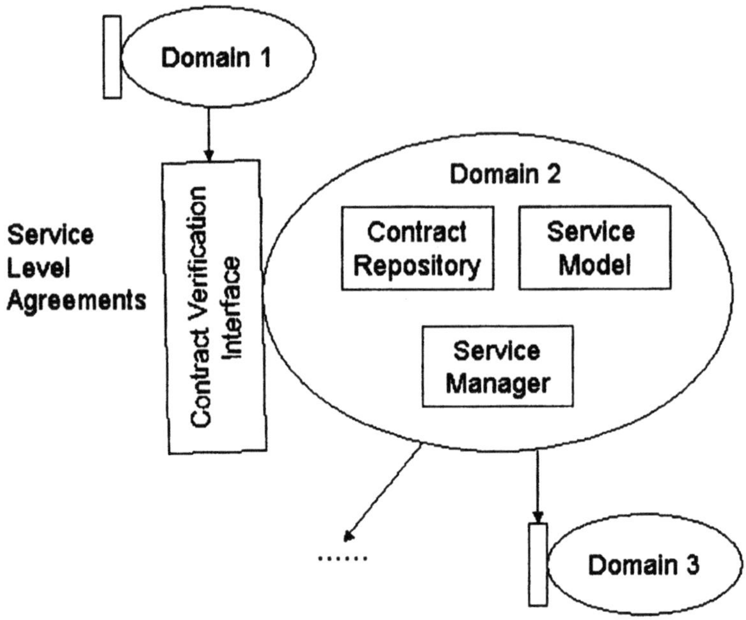

Figure 42. Cooperative Service Management in E-Business[1]

Bhoj and associates have developed an architecture to allow SLA monitoring and sharing of selective management information across administrative domain boundaries in a secure way using verifiable and consistent contracts as shown in Figure 42[1]. In this diagram each administrative domain of management is shown with an oval.

Each admonstrative domain has the following building blocks for management:

- A Contract Repository
- A Contract Verification Interface shown with a rectangle adjacent to oval
- A Service Model
- A Service Manager

A *contract* is a specification (derived from the SLA) of the service attributes that are meaningful and automatically measurable for correct service behavior. The contract specification contains both the attributes and the bounds within which the attributes must stay in order for the service to behave in a desired manner. Attributes have to be both quantifiable and measurable to be included in a contract. The *contract repository* contains a set of contracts, which this domain has with its providers and customers. It contains information on how to validate an incoming contract verification request and places constraints on what data may be accessed from outside the domain as well as how that data is computed.

Different domains are likely to contain heterogeneous systems, it is thus important that there be agreement on how contracts will be invoked and how the systems will communicate. All external interactions to a given domain happen through one or more *Contract Verification Interfaces* provided by the domain. Service Level Agreements offered by the domain define the nature of information provided at the interface and the security parameters needed for the interaction. The architecture provides a recursive and hierarchical model for communication in a cooperative e-business environment.

The *service model* includes a description of the service that this administration is managing[1]. It also

- Identifies the various components that enable a service. For example, if the top level service being managed is electronic mail, the service model would list the components as the email server host, the networks connecting the email host to the internet, the email application itself, the name server used to resolve hostnames to internet addresses, etc.
- Expresses interdependencies that exist among the different elements of the service. From the above email example, all components identified in the service model should function properly for the email service to work.
- Identifies the measurements that are available from each component. Thus, the email server could identify the number of email transactions, and active measurements could be used to get an estimate of the response time seen by email clients.

The *service manager* is the engine responsible for directing the verification task. It has the knowledge of how to evaluate an incoming contract verification request. This would involve interfacing with the contract repository to get the details of the contract, and interfacing with the local resources and local system and service management modules to collect information needed to verify the contract.

6.3.2.2 Cooperative SLM Contracts

This section presents the formal model proposed by Bhoj and associates[1].

Formally, a contract C is defined by the triple (P, M, A), where P is the set of *properties* associated with the contract, A is the set of *assertions* agreed upon by the parties, and M is the set of *methods* (or operations) available on the contract. *Properties* define information needed for contract verification and do not necessarily relate directly to the specific service that is the subject of the contract.

Examples of items in P are

P = {authentication mechanism, access control, invocation methodology,}

Assertions contain service-related agreements or guarantees. The assertion set *A* consists of *A* = {(v)} where *v* is a vector of variables that reflect some aspect of the service and (v) is a relationship that constrains those variables according to contract agreements. At any given time, (v) takes on the values TRUE or FALSE depending on whether the constraint described in the relationship is being met or not. Examples of assertions in *A* may be :

A = {availability > 99.9%, packet loss < 2% □round trip delay < 150 ms, ... }

Methods describe the operations available on the contract at the contract verification interface. They permit the invoker to query the truthfulness of the assertions in the contract, identify assertions that are FALSE, and retrieve the values of associated variables in the assertions. For example, *M* may consist of

M = {verify contract, query variable values, register constraint, notify event, ...} Contracts are described by a *Contract Definition Language* (CDL) which gives a formal declaration of the assertions in the contract, and allows the service manager to associate the contract with a number of *handlers*, which hide the details of the service and the means of verification.

It is necessary to share some common standards for the syntax and semantics of SLM across organizations as discussed next. We shall discuss some of these issues as "cooperative management" in more detail in Part 5 with respect to Computer Supported Cooperative Work (CSCW) techniques. The next section discusses some evolving standards in cooperative service management.

6.3.3 Standards for Cooperative SLM

In Part 2 we discusssed the two views of a service, namely service as a product and service as a support. We have so far focused on service as a product. Although there are architectural similarities with service as a support, there are differences between these two views at the business level. Therefore standards for cooperative SLM have evolved from a number of different sources. For example, telecommunication service providers have developed the Electronic Telecom Operations Map (e-TOM) from TeleManagement Forum, as discussed in Chapter 5. Similarly ITU-T X.790 standards have evolved from the need to share telecom billing information across service providers. Customer Support Consortium (CSC) has developed Problem Resolution Standards (PRS) from the perspective of providing cooperative support service by multiple organizations. These standards are discussed in this section.

6.3.3.1 Customer Support Consortium (CSC) PRS[4]

In the past decade, there has been exponential growth in both the complexity and interdependence of products in the computing industry. This is due to rapid advances and growth of technology as well as the increased openness between products. There are a number of problems with trouble-ticketing. For example, they are based on end-user "opinions". The tickets need to be hand entered by support personnel, and stored in proprietary formats. There are no standard processes defined. Hence the results may be inaccurate, some times key information is lost or not conveyed, and it may be difficult to share escalation.

Several factors are driving the support industry to adopt a standard method for exchanging Service Incidents. These factors stem from the multi-vendor nature of the computer and software industry. Many different companies create the computer components, peripherals, operating systems, and application software that comprise the personal computer market. Successfully providing customer support in today's multi-vendor environment requires high levels of cooperation between support organizations. Providing such support has created efficiency and cost challenges to support providers and product vendors. Standardized incident exchange provides a mechanism for support organizations to share incident information effectively and ultimately reduce the cost of supporting computers, thus reducing the total cost of ownership to customers.

To solve the above problems the following efforts are required:

- Agreement on Data Model
  - Common abstraction of problem
- Agreement on Format
  - How do we format data for exchange?
- Agreement on Transport
  - How do we actually exchange data?

Before describing the solution, it is necessary to analyze the workflow of a support transaction that consists of:

1. Requesting and entitling service involving the following workflow
2. Support Service Consumer requests service
3. Support Service Provider responds with entitlements
4. Problem and Resolution exchange involves the following workflow
5. Support Service Consumer submits problem
6. Support Service Provider accepts problem
7. Support Service Provider submits resolution
8. Support Service Consumer accepts resolution

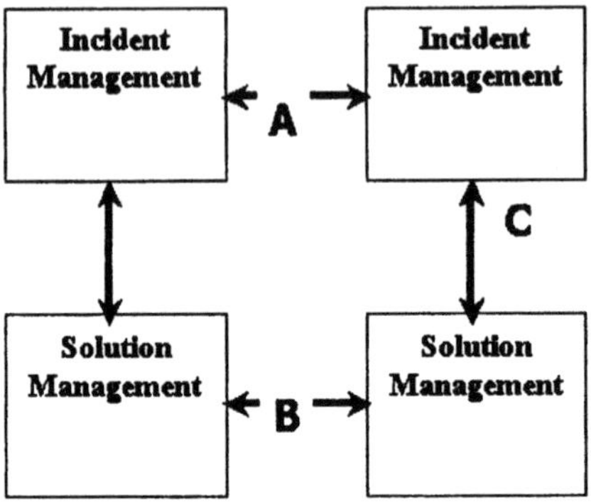

Figure 43. Requirements for Help-Desk Process Management[13]

This sequence is handled through an incident and solution management system, such as trouble-ticketing. The secondary workflows involve

- Submission of Supplements, and
- Administrative tasks

Figure 43 shows the requirements of standards to support incidents, and their solutions cooperatively across service provider organizations. At this abstract level one can define three interfaces as follows:

A. Incident management systems sharing: data and incidents in an automated fashion
B. Solution management systems and search engines sharing data in a standard fashion
C. Solution and incident management systems sharing data in a standard fashion.

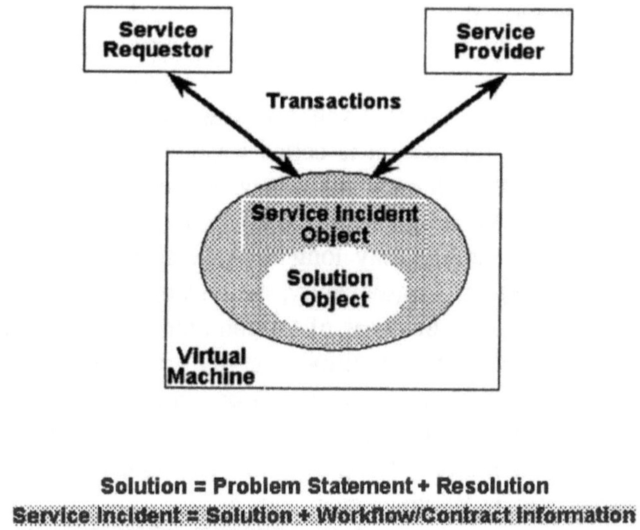

Figure 44. Requirements of Process Management Standards[2]

Distributed Management Task Force (DMTF) and Customer Support Consortium (CSC) have joined hands to develop standards for this purpose. These standards are called Problem Resolution Standards (PRS) and consist of two major standards:

- Solution Exchange Standard (SES)
- Service Incident Exchange Standard (SIS)

The Solution Exchange Standard (SES) allows multiple organizations to share the knowledge generated from operations through trouble-ticketing systems while SIS allows multiple organizations to share incidents related to support (e.g., trouble-tickets). The features of SES/SIS are:

- Standardized data model
- Multiple levels of encoding
- Standardized exchange language (e.g., XML)
- More accurate information distributionContent encoded by *Producer*,understood by *Consumer*,preserved during transfer.SES benefits are:
- Supports increased complexity and interdependence of problem space
- Facilitates knowledge distribution

Figure 44 shows the conceptual model for the implementation SES and SIS. Service providers, such as Telstra and Optus in Australia, can share the management knowledge for service incidents and solutions. The same model can be used for a variety of e-business services.

6.3.3.2 ITU-T X.790

A few years ago, the US opened up its local telecom market to competition. Previously, the long distance market was open to competition but the local market was protected. The existing company providing service is called an Incumbent Local Exchange Carrier (ILEC) and the new company coming into the market is called a Competitive Local Exchange Carrier (CELEC). A telecommunication service user now has the choice of obtaining some services (e.g., local calls) from one from one service provider and another service (say long distance telephony) from another different service provider. Consequently, a standard ILEC/CLEC interface became imperative .for the business of telecommunication to work because most services now required multiple service providers to cooperate. Unfortunately, most existing telecom carriers had been managing their businesses (in US and other countries before deregulation of telecom market) through Operations Support Systems (OSS) with proprietary interfaces. The ITU-T X.790 standard is designed for multiple service providers to share service and billing information across proprietary OSS, using a common model as shown in Figure 45.

This brings up the concept of trouble management function. There are two service providers – they have completely different systems. It is quite possible that the end user has trouble and reports the problem to the service provider 1. This service provider 1 finds the problem in the domain of service provider 2. They are working together and therefore the problem is reported to service provider 2. Hence two service providers need clear communication and sharing of information. The International Telecommunication Union (ITU-T) standard called X.790 has defined the trouble-management function that provides an abstract common model for trouble ticketing (help-desk based management) across service providers.

The two service providers, SP1 and SP2 each have their own internal proprietary trouble-ticketing system. However, they can share support and billing information across the two different trouble-ticketing (TT) systems using the common trouble-management function defined by the ITU X.790 standards that specifies models and formats for:

- Reporting of troubles on services or resources on a managed network or system;
- Tracking the progress of trouble to resolution;
- Clearing and closure of trouble.
- Recognizes proprietary TT system with individual telecommunication service providers
- Specifies Generic TT model for Information Interchange between different organizations As stated earlier, service management standards for e-business will keep evolving for some time.

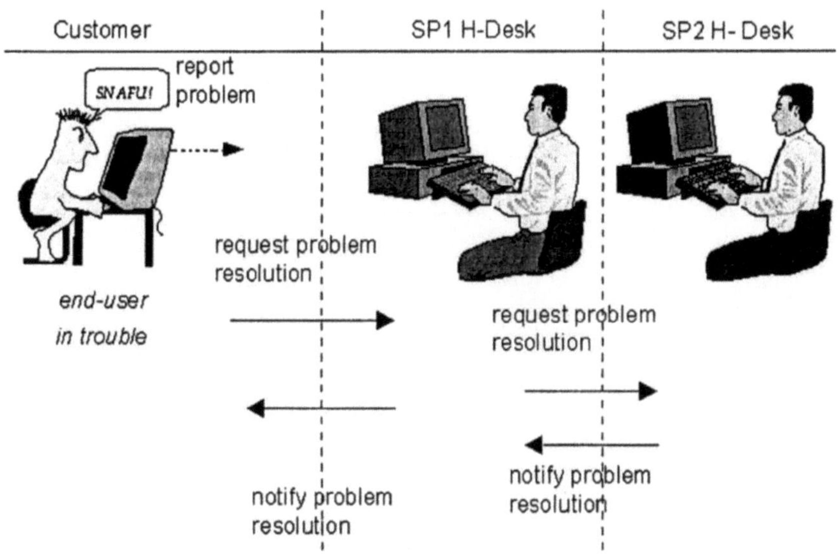

Figure 45. **ITU-T X.790 Trouble-Management Function**

6.3.3.3 A Unified View of Service Management Standards

As seen in this part of the book, there are a number of standards bodies including OGC, ITSMF, TMF, IT-T, DMTF-CSC, which are working on the development of service management standards for e-business. Figure 46 presents a unified architectural view of these standards from the perspective of practical implementation of e-business management[11]. This figure shows the ITIL standard building blocks and their interactions in the context of e-business management as discussed in Part 3. The diagram also shows the linkages to e-business infrastructure management, such as network management to be discussed in Part 4 of this book.

Figure 46 shows e-business management building-blocks of four types:

1. Shaded building-blocks related to customers shown on the right half of the picture. Interfaces for these building-blocks have been standardoized.
2. White building-blocks used by management users shown mostly on the left half of the picture. A number of DMTF Working Groups (WGs) are now working on interfaces for some of these building-blocks, such as[26]
   - Service Desk to Help Desk
   - Application Management to Configuration Management
   - Change Management to Release Management
3. Half-shaded building-blocks that are part of the management and security infrastructure

Shared building-blocks at the centre of the picture shared by management users and customers.

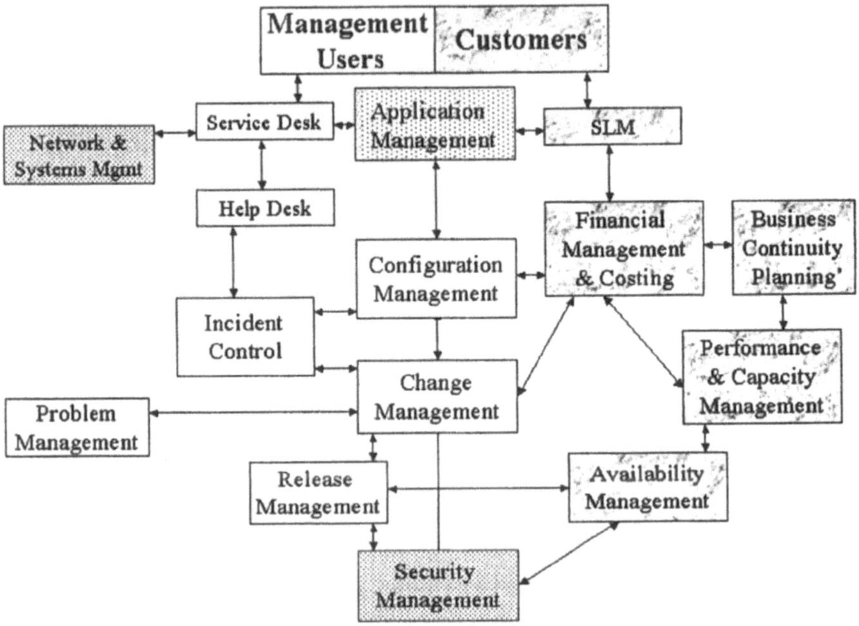

Figure 46. A Unified View of E-Business Service Management Standards[11]

6.4 Chapter Summary

This chapter has discussed a practical perspective for the operation and implementation of e-business management. Service Level Management (SLM) and help-desk business model together play a very important role in this process. We presented some evolving standards for the interoperability of service management incidents and solutions across different service provider organizations. Finally, we presented a unified architectural perspective of e-business service management with respect to standards from a number of different bodies, such as ITSMF, CSC, ITU and TMF. Appendix 2 illustrates some of these concepts through a discussion of the Telecom Operations Map (TOM) from TeleManagement Forum (TMF).

SLM is now being supported by a number of commercial products in the market, such as HP Open View™, TIVOLI TME™, ICS CONTINUITY™, CA TNG™, BMC PATROL™ etc. However, no single product can achieve all objectives of a process-oriented SLM. The trend is towards combining a number of complementary products from different vendors as discussed in Appendix 4.

Having discussed the architectural viewpoint of e-business management, we shall discuss the technological viewpoint and relevant standards in the next two chapters (Part 4) of the book.

6.5 References

1. Bhoj P., Singhal S., and Chutani S., "SLA Management in Federated Environments", *The 6th International Symposium on Integrated Network Management (IM'99)*, Boston, USA, 1999Chmaj J. and Callahan S., "*Support Exchange Standards*", DMTF Developers Conference, May 1999, USA
3. Dev R., *Managing the Enterprise Network: Command and Control*, Cabletron Systems Inc., March 1993
4. DMTF, *DMTF-CSC Support Standards*, http://www.dmtf.org/spec/stan.html, March 2001
5. DMTF, *DMI Standards*, http://www.dmtf.org/spec/dmis.html, March 2001
6. Eurescom, "E-commerce Impacts on Service and Network Operations and Management", Project P1106, http://www.eurescom.de/public/projects/P1100-series/P1106/p1106.htm
7. Ghetie I.G., *Networks and Systems Management: Platforms Analysis and Evaluation*, Kluwer Academic Publishers, 1997
8. IBM, "An Open e-Business Foundation", *E-Business White Paper*, 1997
9. Intelligent Communication Software (ICS), "A Definition of Service Level Management", *ICS White paper*, November 2000, http://www.ics.de
10. Internet Engineering Task Force (IETF), "Application MIB", 1998, www.ietf.org
11. IT Service Management Forum (ITSMF), "*ITSMF-DMTF Alliance*", DMTF Developers Conference, June 2000, USA
12. ITU-T Recommendation X.790 (11/95) - *Trouble Management function for ITU-T applications*, http://www.itu.int/plweb-cgi/fastweb?getdoc+view1+itudoc+5727+1++X.790
13. Lawrence D.G., "Service Incident and Knowledge Exchange", *DMTF Developers Conference*, June 2000, USA
14. Lewis L., *Managing Business and Service Networks*, Kluwer Academic/ Plenumb Publishers, 2001, ISBN:0-306-46559-0
15. Lewis L. and Ray P., "On the Migration from Enterprise Management to Integrated Service Level Management", *IEEE Network*, January 2002

16. Mahon C., "Network Services Management: A Practical Approach", *HP-OpenView'98 presentation,* April 1998
17. Organization of Government Commerce (OGC formerly CCTA), "ITIL and BSI Code of Practice on IT Service Management", *IT Service Management Forum (ITSMF)* web site in UK, http://www.itsmf.com/itsmf/i2.htm, April 2001
18. Pritchard D., "ENTEX Information Services", *DMTF Developers Conference,* May 1999, USA
19. Ray P., *Cooperative Management of Enterprise Networks*, Kluwer Academic/Plenum Publications, May 2000, ISBN:0-306-46276-1
20. Sahai A., Machiraju V., and Wurster K., "Managing Next Generation E-Services", *HP Laboratories Technical Report HPL-2000-120,* September 2000, Palo Alto USA
21. Steinke S., "The Well-Mannered Application", *Information Week,* USA, http://www.informationweek.com/, January 29, 2001
22. Tele Management Forum (TMF), *A Service Management Business Process Model*, 1995
23. TeleManagement Forum (TMF), "Performance Reporting Definitions Document", *NMF701*, April 1997
24. TeleManagement Forum, *Smart TMN Technology Integration Map*, GB909 issue 1.1, October 1998, http://www.tmforum.org/Umar A., *Object-Oriented Client/Server Internet Environments*, Prentice Hall, 1997
26. Williams R., "DMTF Technical Roadmap for Enterprise Management for e-business in the 21st Century", *DMTF Developers Conference*, June 2000, USA

PART-4

TECHNOLOGY AND STANDARDS VIEWPOINT

Chapter 7. E-Business Infrastructure Management

Part 3 of this book discussed the architectural view of e-business management, which could be defined as strategies for managing processes, managing transactions, and managing infrastructures. Part 4, containing Chapters 7 and 8, discusses the technological viewpoint of e-business infrastructure management. We discuss the technologies used by e-business infrastructure management to facilitate the interoperability of heterogeneous management elements. The question is why this heterogeneity?

It would be nice if all e-business implementations had a single architectural framework with the same protocols and component structures. However, this is not the reality. Today's e-business infrastructure uses many types of communication technologies (mobile, multimedia), many types of hosts (PCs, workstations, and Internet appliances) with different hardware (microprocessors, intelligent controllers) and operating systems (windows, linux). An e-business infrastructure uses many types of software components (ActiveX, Java), a variety of software tools, and languages (Java, visual Basic, C). Hence one of the major challenges for e-business management is to define standards so that heterogeneous e-business systems can be managed in a uniform manner. The task of standardization is complex due to the existence of a variety of mechanisms at different levels of e-business architecture. This chapter presents an analysis of the various evolving standards that are relevant to e-business infrastructure management.

We start with some abstract concepts and an integrated management framework for e-business infrastructure. This is followed by a discussion of technologies and standards for the three aspects of e-business management architecture that follow:

- Network Management
- Systems Management
- Applications Management

It may be noted that most of the material presented in this chapter is already available in the books, standards documents, white papers of vendors and journals of network and systems management. We have tried to present the information in the context of integrated e-business management.

7.1 Integrated Management Concepts and Framework

During the 1970s and 1980s, the world saw a proliferation of proprietary management solutions from different vendors for their own systems, such as multiplexers, switches, hubs and transmission systems. There were also different systems for managing networks and computer systems. These management solutions were only applicable to the specific systems for which they were designed. It is well known that the success of an enterprise-wide networking and computing system depends very much on the successful integration of the subsystems. The failure of one subsystem may affect the operation of other subsystems. Hence, users need an integrated management view of their overall enterprise-wide facilities that may include, for example, transmission system from one vendor, multiplexers from another vendor, and computers from a third vendor.

This requires a seamless integration of business, applications, systems, and network management, which in general involves:

- using multi-vendor distributed management applications for managing heterogeneous client-server environment,
- handling multimedia, multi-session, and multipoint communications, and
- interfacing business processes/practices with integrated management.

7.1.1 Integrated Management Concepts

This section provides a brief overview of the concepts and technologies used in integrated management, and it is based on the contents of Kluwer Academic/Plenum book by Ray[17].

7.1.1.1 Management Model

Today's enterprise networks and services use heterogeneous components from different vendors spread over distant geographical locations. Hence, it is necessary to collect and analyze management information from different devices and systems distributed over the enterprise network. Many networked organizations such as telecommunications service providers, electricity network operators, and railroad operators use a central control location (also called management center) for this purpose. This is the location of the centralized management station. A management solution involves transferring of management information from all network elements to this management station. International Standards Organization (ISO) and the Internet Engineering Task Force (IETF) have defined management standards for this purpose.

Both these standards embrace the manager-agent model consisting of a manager at the management station and an agent at the remote managed element, as shown in Figure 47. Manager and agent are data communication software entities that communicate through a management communication protocol. Managers and agents may have one-to-many and many-to-one relationships. While ISO OSI Management uses the Common Management

Information Protocol (CMIP) on the OSI 7-layer communication protocol stack, Internet Management uses the Simple Network Management Protocol (SNMP) on the Internet UDP/IP protocol stack as the management communication protocol between the manager and the agent. In both of these protocols, the manager uses "get" commands to retrieve information from, and "set" commands to modify management information at remote managed elements (hardware or software) through an agent[10,9].

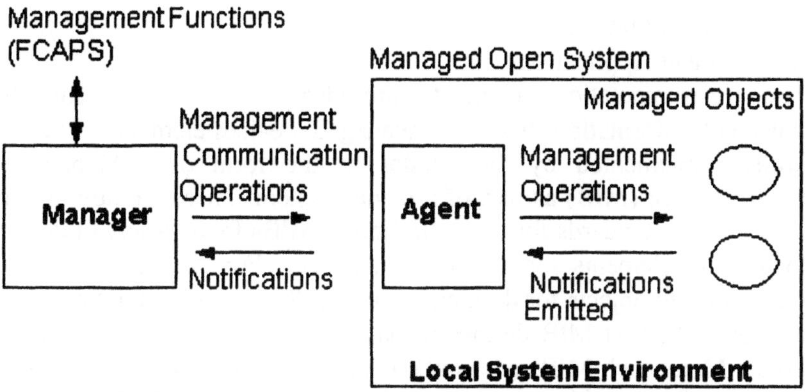

Figure 47. The Conceptual Management Model

A typical enterprise network consists of hardware and software of diverse types from different vendors. Managed Objects (MOs) provide a standardized format to represent the resources/elements that need to be managed. The Management Information Base (MIB) is a collection of MOs. These are defined using the ISO standard language Abstract Syntax Notation 1 (ASN.1), or its subset.

A manager (management station) performs the management (monitoring and control) function by accessing information from various elements. ISO has defined five basic management functions: Fault management (identification and rectification of faults), Configuration management (changes in configuration, e.g., software versions), Accounting management (tracking and charging for resource usage), Performance management (analysis of system performance), and Security management (mechanisms for authentication, access control of resources), in short FCAPS[10].

7.1.1.2 Integrated Management Framework

As discussed earlier, organizations in the 1970s and 1980s had different management solutions for their different subsystems, such as communication systems, computers, and some applications. Once organizations realized the importance of the integration of the management of enterprise-wide networks, they started demanding a common framework for the management of heterogeneous, multi-vendor facilities. This provided a motivation for all concerned to develop management solutions that integrate to provide a common enterprise-wide view. Figure 48 shows the resulting framework for adopting integrated network management in the deployment of integrated management today. It consists of the following elements:

1. Instrumentation
2. Management Platform
3. Management Applications

The instrumentation element provides "hooks" for collecting management information from the managed devices/elements. They are generally implemented by the vendor in the form of a Management Information Base (MIB) as part of a device/system. There are now Internet and ISO/ITU-T standards for the definition of MIBs for a variety of devices, protocols and elements for enterprise networks. For example, Host MIB defines managed objects for desktop systems (CPU, memory utilization, and printer) and Ethernet MIB defines managed objects for Ethernet local area networks. Many such MIBs are now commercially available from a number of vendors of networking products. Although ISO and SNMP MIBs are defined in the ISO standard platform independent language called Abstract Syntax Notation (ASN.1), DMTF DMI allows the information models to be defined in simple ASCII format called Management Information Format (MIF).

A management platform provides a common distributed computing platform for the management of heterogeneous devices/systems using multiple communication protocols, Application Programming Interfaces (APIs), a common user interface and a set of generic management services based on client-server architecture. While the management user/application is the client, the platform provides the server functions required for network management (e.g., naming and addressing, management communication, object management, and a common database). Presently there are a number of commercially available integrated management platforms, such as HP OpenView™, Aprisma Spectrum™, Tivoli TME/NetView™, and CA TNG™ [6].

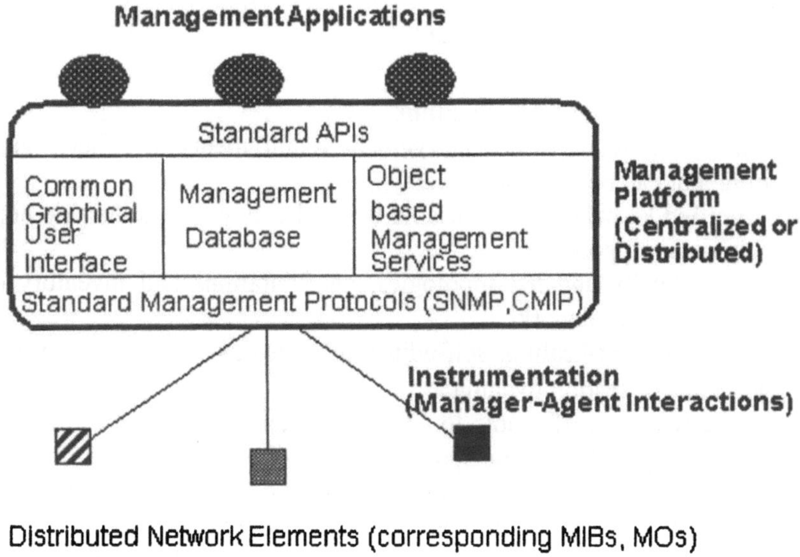

Figure 48. Integrated Management Framework

It is necessary to use a common distributed object model at platform level to hide the differences in management protocols (e.g., CMIP and SNMP), and information models (e.g., OSI and Internet) in heterogeneous managed elements. Although many platform vendors provide proprietary object models, it is felt that standard object models, such as Object Management Group's (OMG) Common Object Request Broker Architecture (CORBA) and Microsoft Distributed Common Object Model (DCOM) would provide a basis for this interoperability[23]. Some commercial organizations have developed platforms using Java Remote Method Invocation (RMI) technology.

Management applications (e.g., trouble-ticketing, and inventory) have been traditionally developed by system vendors, user organizations and telecommunication carriers. Their requirements vary from organization to organization. Hence, management solutions vary widely. For example, the network management center of a large telecommunication organization may have more than fifty different types of software for solving different management problems. Some of these incorporate sophisticated computational techniques, such as Expert Systems, Model-Based Reasoning and Intelligent Agents. It is not possible for one organization to provide all sorts of management solutions. It is possible to achieve a substantial amount of productivity gains by sharing software amongst different applications. This necessitates a distributed-object-based framework (e.g., CORBA) for the interoperability of management applications developed by multiple groups of people. ISO /ITU-T TMN, ISO- ODP, DMTF -WBEM, and TINA are efforts in this direction[8,11,27].

7.1.1.3 Management Applications

The emerging network management requirements in a heterogeneous environment can be summarized as:

- A unified knowledge-base usable by moderately knowledgeable network help-desk support staff
- Automatically updated topologies, configurations and inventory of all devices in the network
- Intelligent, self-healing, self-adjusting networks that know how to ease periodic congestion dynamically
- Predictive "what-if" tools to analyze trends, simulate new traffic loads and plan upgrades for transport network and access facilities
- A secure network management framework capable of managing security support like access control, encryption and key distribution.

Two key technologies are now being investigated to reduce operator workload, improve service levels and reduce operating costs in complex multivariable management systems. These are:

- Distributed Object-based Management Systems, such as OMG CORBA-based management. These systems enhance management software productivity (reduce development and maintenance costs, better quality) through reuse and encapsulation, using object-oriented software. Much of these are now supported as middleware in e-business environments.
- Intelligent and adaptive techniques, such as Expert Systems, Intelligent Agents and Data Mining. They provide help in correlating multiple MOs to solve management problems.

Figure 49 shows the Integrated Management Framework with some real commercially available components in a hierarchy of layers.

As expected the lowest layer shows the real managed elements, such as networks, databases, workstations, PCs and applications. The instrumentation (SNMP/OSI/DMI) provides management information to the platforms from these managed elements.

The next level shows basic functionality of a management platform, such as event correlation (identifying the source of problems from certain manifestations of management events), remote control access (remote manager), and reporting software (e.g., historical event listing).

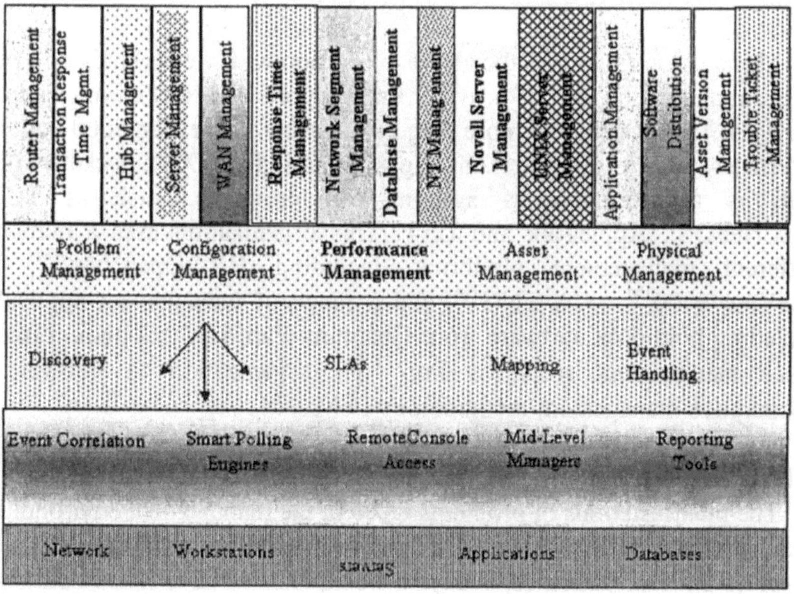

Figure 49. Management Application Environment[16]

The next level contains more sophisticated features (supported at platform level), such as auto-discovery (automatically identifying any new devices connected in the network), and mapping (establishing relationships between different elements in the system to link problems with their root cause).

The next level shows management functions (typically implemented as part of management application layer) that are classified by ISO under different categories; Fault management, Configuration management, Accounting management, Performance management and Security management (FCAPS). These functions were defined by ISO for network management. More functions (e.g., problem management, license management, help-desk management, and software distribution) have been added by the industry as part of systems management, applications management and service management. These functions are supported as part of a variety of different applications (shown at the next level) from multiple vendors, such as router management from CISCO (CISCOWorks™), and NTServer Management from Microsoft.

The next section illustrates these concepts over a real e-business management environment.

7.1.2 Modern E-business Infrastructure Scenario

This section illustrates the above discussion with a case study of a public telecommunication service provider that supports a variety of voice and data services. This system had more than 300 subnets, more than 5000 nodes and interfaces, nearly 170 routers/intelligent hubs and 225 X.25 packet switches. This is a heterogeneous system with protocols, such as TCP/IP, DECNet/OSI, AppleTalk and LAT. This organization uses a number of different management platforms, including HP OpenView™, IBM NetView/6000™, CA TNG™, and a range of management applications including help desk software from Quantum. Part 5 of this book discusses some management scenarios from this organization to illustrate our cooperative management methodology CoMENS.

7.1.2.1 Problems

The manifestations of problems faced in the management environment of the organization are illustrated in this section. The management typically involves 24-hour activities, 7 days a week, and we have listed below some problem manifestations. Each problem has been classified according to the ISO standard management functions abbreviated as F-Fault management, C-Configuration management, A-Accounting management, P-Performance management, X-Change management, and S-Security management.

- The NMS is giving alarms that the Silverwater site has become unreachable.[F]
- We've got to move 250 additional users from the Gordon Office to the Chatswood Office. Does the link have sufficient Bandwidth ?[C]
- One of the Production servers is giving db problems. Pls urgently remove it from the round-robin DNS.[A]
- Queues are building up at the Exchange Server in Brisbane, the Network is running like a dog - Pls do something [P, C]
- The NMS is giving alarms that a particular user device has been configured with the IP address of the router [F, A]
- Everybody seems to be getting a dedicated 100Mbps port for his workstation. When will I get mine ?[C]
- I'm leaving for the US & Europe tomorrow on official tour & want to be able to dial in to the network .[A]
- There are 65 new starters tomorrow and I need IP addresses. Of these 23 will need to pass through Firewall-A [A, S]
- We need a 100Mbps Dual Redundant Interconnect from the Admin Network to the OPS Network, & I'm doing the change at midnight. [X]
- I've connected a new Sun workstation, at my desk & it isn't talking to the network [A, S, F]

- After the network change last night I'm having problems with Appletalk™ but TCP-IP appears to be okay.[F, X]
- (And if it's going to be a really bad day for the NMC) The Data Center Site appears to have got segmented from the rest of the WAN. Help! [F]

7.1.2.2 Existing Management Environment

The implementation used is CA The New Generation (TNG), which is in turn connected to HP Open View and Internet service. E-business management platform monitoring may account for 75 per cent of total IT service monitoring. There are separate service centers for Network management(NMC), Systems management (SMC), and Application services (ASC). It is important to note that the management services are not integrated, as shown Figure 50.

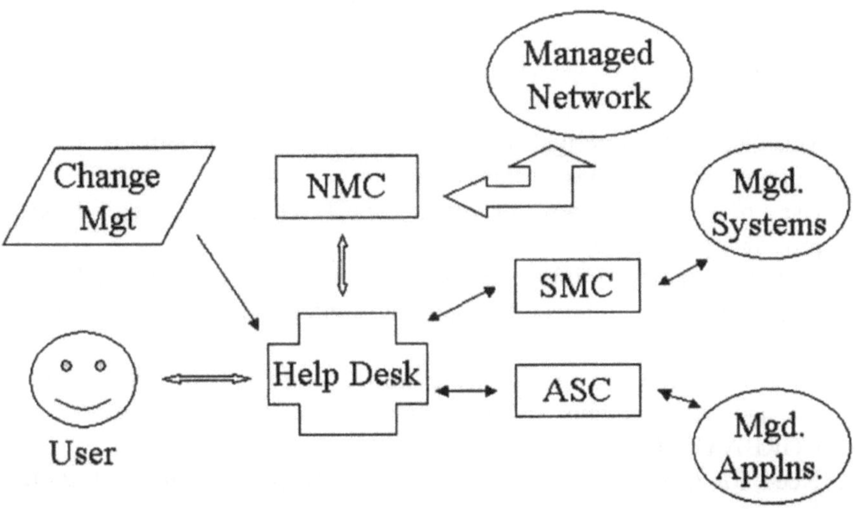

Figure 50. Modern E-business Management Environment

As shown in the Figure 50, the company adopted a distributed, CORBA based management platform - CA TNG™. At that time CORBA was only available in the element level managers. The common repository is the management database. This kind of management framework provides a hierarchy of multiple layers of management functionality. In this case SNMP agents provide the instrumentation, and CORBA Distributed Systems Managers (DSM) provide distributed management capability. The rest of the graphical reporting, analysis capabilities are provided at the service center , as shown in Figure 51.

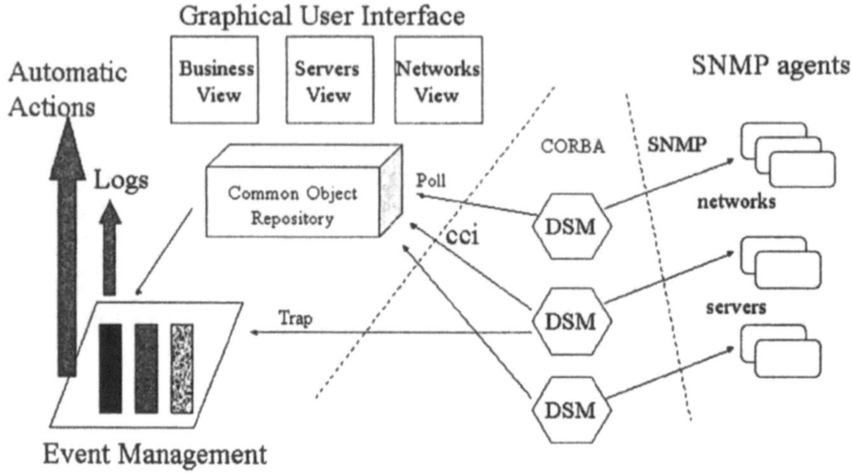

Figure 51. Distributed Management Platform for E-business Management

This discussion highlights the following aspects of modern management environment for e-business infrastructure:

1. Use of heterogeneous of management elements using different proprietary technologies
2. Need to support multiple instrumentation protocols including SNMP
3. Use of various architectural building conforming to different sets of standards
4. Need to divide the management infrastructure into different types of management elements (SNMP agents for network management, and CORBA DSMs for systems management)
5. Need for a variety of management services (e.g., event management, logs, etc.)
6. Need for a common management database (repository)
7. Need for different views of management information (network view, servers view, business view etc.). These views could be at different levels of e-business infrastructure.

In order to resolve the complexities, it is necessary to understand the different viewpoints of infrastructure management:

- Network management discussed in Section 7.2
- Systems Management discussed in Section 7.3
- Applications Management discussed in Section 7.4

Since most of the relevant technologies are originally based on network management technologies, we start the discussion with network management technologies.

7.1.3 Integrated Management Standards

The standards in this area are defined by a number of organizations, such as the Internet Engineering Task Force (IETF), International Standards Organization (ISO), Distributed Management Task Force (DMTF)[Error! Reference source not found.], International Telecommunications Union-Technical (ITU-T)[15], The Open Group (TOG)[21], World Wide Web Consortium (WWWC), TINA Consortium (TINA-C)[8], and Tele-Management Forum (TMF)[20].

The standards at the level of management of information infrastructure include IETF SNMP, ISO-OSI Mgmt (used for network management), DMTF Desktop Management Information (DMI) and Common Information Model (CIM), WWW, Extended Markup Language (XML) (used mainly for systems management), ITU-T Telecommunication Management Networks (TMN), ISO Reference Model for Open Distributed Processing (RM-ODP) (used for systems and service management), DMTF Web Based Enterprise Management (WBEM) and TINA (for application management)etc. Some of these technologies are used for multiple types of infrastructures, e.g., TMN used for all levels.

The other dimension used, with more practical effect, is that based on the integrated management framework discussed in the next section. The instrumentation technologies, concerned with providing hooks for getting management information from remote devices, include IETF SNMP, ISO Common Management Information Protocol (CMIP), and DMTF DMI. Many of these platforms have proprietary technologies. The DMTF CIM, WWW XML, and IETF Directory Enabled Networks (DEN) are bringing in standards for different platforms to interoperate. Technologies at the application level include ITU-T Trouble ticketing Interoperability Standard (X.790), TOG ARM, Application Integration and Control (AIC), and Software License Management (SLM).

It may be noted that this is a vast area. We have discussed some of the standards briefly in Part 3. Part 4 (Chapters 7 and 8) summarizes the remaining standards.

7.2 Network Management Technologies

Network management maintains the underlying physical connections of an e-business environment. Network management primarily involves the installation, configuration and monitored operation of hardware such as bridges, routers and servers, and ensures that systems and data remain available[10].

Many Integrated Management Technologies (e.g., SNMP) evolved from network management technologies. That is because networking is perhaps the most important factor contributing to the growth and hence problems in modern e-business systems. This section discusses the major network management technologies:

- Internet SNMP including SMI and MIBs
- Internet Remote Monitoring MIB (RMON)
- OSI Management including CMIP, and Guidelines Distributed Managed Objects (GDMO)

7.2.1 Internet SNMP

Internet standards are administered by an international body of professionals, called the Internet Engineering Task Force (www.ietf.org). It mandates that there must be substantial proof of the feasibility of practical implementation before any proposal is declared as an Internet standard. It may be noted that all Internet standards, called Request For Comments (RFCs) numbered chronologically, are available freely from this web site. This allows the process of standardization to be conducted through open discussions and over the Internet - one of the first practical implementations of e-business.

The Internet standard SNMP (RFC 1212 and RFC 1213) is based on the manager-agent model defined in Section 7.1.1. A manager entity repetitively polls an agent entity, which acquires management information from remote managed elements (devices, software, or applications) in the form of Management Information Base (MIB) variables. The manager-agent protocol, Simple Network Management Protocol (SNMP), uses get, or get-next commands to get information from remote managed entities. SNMP uses set command to control remote entities. Simplicity was the key to the standardization of SNMP MIB variables that are based on the following criteria[9]:

- Variables must be necessary for fault and configuration management
- Variables that can be derived from other variables can not be defined
- Instrumentation of variables in a managed entity shall take minimal software overhead
- Number of such MIB variables shall not be large

SNMP standards included the MIB-II based on the above principles. Major weaknesses of SNMP are lack of security, inefficiency due to polling based mechanism, unreliability, and lack of some functions, such as the ability to participate in a multiple manager cooperative management. SNMPv2 and SNMPv3 have been defined to overcome these limitations[9]. Local Area Networks (LAN) and Internet-based solutions and technologies have been most prominent in the corporate management information systems sector. This has resulted in the widespread adoption of Internet management technologies, including Simple Network Management Protocol (SNMP) and Internet MIBs as the network management framework for networking devices and equipment. This is mainly a standard at the instrumentation level of the integrated management framework, described in Figure 52.

According to the approach currently being taken, the management problem reduces to the development of MIBs for the managed elements. The IETF has defined a number of MIBs, such as Bridge MIB (for network bridges), Ethernet MIB (for manages Ethernet LANs), ATM MIB (for ATM networks), Printer MIB (for printers), and UPS MIB (for power supplies).

Although SNMP was primarily designed for network management, some MIBs help in systems management, such as Host Resources MIB (RFC1514), and RDBMS MIB (RFC1697).

The IETF has also developed a number of standards for the modeling and management of distributed applications and services in an e-business network. Some of these are Network Service Monitoring MIB (RFC 1565), Directory Monitoring MIB (RFC 1566), Mail Monitoring MIB (RFC 1567), and System Application MIB (RFC2287). Although these MIBs are useful for the identification of application attributes that need to be managed, the management framework of SNMP does not provide any means of expressing management as a distributed processing application.

More information and tutorials on Internet Management are available at [33].

7.2.2 Internet Remote Monitoring (RMON) MIBs

As shown in Section 7.2.1 Internet SNMP is a simple protocol based on polling of agents by manager entity. This leads to a substantial increase in traffic. Also the polling validity is critically dependent on the health of the agent that may be down. Hence RMON MIB (RFC1757) provides a decentralized mechanism for the reliable monitoring of a large number of managed network elements. An RMON MIB incorporates sufficient intelligence to filter and act on the information it collects without directly involving the managing station for every action or swamping the network with massive amounts of bulk data transfers.

Through preemptive monitoring, a sniffer (or probe) using RMON MIB continuously runs diagnostics on the network traffic, notifies the management station when a failure is detected, and provides useful information about the event. RMON MIB is organized into ten groups of variables, such as history, statistics, alarm, event, hosts, filter, capture etc. RMON-2 (RFC 2021) has added ten more groups to support end-to-end management of a large network, unlike RMON that deals with single network segment. RMON-2, probes are incorporated in network routers or hubs.

7.2.3 ISO/ITU OSI Management

ISO/ITU have jointly collaborated on producing OSI Systems Management standards (ISO-7498-4). These standards are aimed at the management of OSI communication systems. As mentioned before, OSI Management uses the manager-agent model, using a management communication protocol called Common Management Information Protocol (CMIP). The structure of management information in OSI Management uses an object-oriented view. Therefore, OSI MIBs are defined as managed object class libraries. Management functions have been classified into five categories; Fault management, Configurations management, Accounting management, Performance management and Security Management (FCAPS). A number of systems management functions have been developed to bridge the functionality gap between low-level managed objects and high-level FCAPS functions. OSI Management technologies including CMIP and MIBS are at the instrumentation level. However, agents here are much more powerful and intelligent than in SNMP

As in the case of the Internet SNMP, OSI management solutions largely depend on the development of appropriate managed objects. A number of such MIBs have been developed for telecommunication provider applications, such as Synchronous Digital Hierarchy (SDH) system and switch management. In the area of general e-business service/applications management, ISO/ITU have taken up work on some specific applications such as electronic mail (X.400) management. However, the focus of all these works is on the management of open communication systems as defined in OSI. They do not address issues related to a heterogeneous, distributed processing environment. Therefore, OSI management technologies may not be adequate for defining high-level distributed management services and applications.

Service and application management is supported in this standard framework as objects representing logical and other resources specific to a particular service. For example, in a toll free (800) service, the service contract involves logical telephone numbers or Advanced Numbers (AN) in addition to physical telephone numbers. The logical numbers are defined when a contract is defined, and deleted when the contract is cancelled.

OSI Management allows for the management of very complex and large networks and is therefore quite popular in the telecommunication industry. Other telecommunication management technologies, such as TMN use the OSI management model. However, its implementation is complex, unlike SNMP. The learning curve for people is rather steep. Hence OSI Management has not been deployed much in the corporate network management.

7.2.4 Standards at Platform and Application Levels

The above sections present Internet standards for network management at instrumentation level. These standards now enable the access of management information from heterogeneous e-business infrastructure elements.

SNMP is now a widely used standard at the instrumentation level, supported by most vendors of e-business infrastructure. However, there is a need to provide abstract models for the representation, aggregation and correlation of management information for solving management problems at the platform level. Therefore, SNMP has a limited utility in the development of distributed management applications. The IETF has been working on improving SNMP features for this purpose.

Vendors of network management platforms, such as HP, IBM, Aprisma, OSI, and AT&T have adopted proprietary models in their platform level products, leading to restrictions in the interoperability of management reports from different products. However, each of these vendors has defined Application Programming Interfaces (APIs) for the development of management applications by multiple vendors. There is now a trend towards standardizing the object models at platform and application levels by using standards, such as Common Object Request Broker Architecture (CORBA) from the Object Management Group (OMG) and Extended Markup Language (XML) from the World Wide Web Consortium (WWWC).

Section 7.3 discusses other successful developments (CIM and WBEM) in this area.

7.3 Systems Management Technologies

Systems management maintains the underlying logical connections of an enterprise's systems. Systems management primarily involves the installation, configuration, administration and monitored operation of operating systems and infrastructure services, such as file, directory and security services that support an application.

While network management concepts and technologies evolved from the traditional telecommunication carrier systems, systems management, of relatively recent origin, has grown with the proliferation of networked PCs in large enterprises. A discussion on integrated management technologies will be incomplete without mention of the recent developments in systems management technologies, initiated by the industry group Distributed Management Task Force (DMTF), consisting of major computer and software vendors. DMTF efforts originated from the need for controlling the Total Cost of Ownership (TCO) of PCs. While the hardware cost of PCs is falling, the TCO is increasing due to rising costs of tracking and updating software versions, licenses, and the support in a geographically distributed e-business environment. DMTF has announced a number of technologies:

- Desktop Management Information (DMI) at the instrumentation level
- Web-Based Enterprise Management (WBEM) at the platform level including Common Information Model (CIM), and Directory Enabled Networks (DEN)
- Combination with WWW, and TOG for application management (discussed in the next section)

DMTF standards are now being used for network, applications and service management (discussed in the next chapter), in addition to systems management.

7.3.1 DMTF DMI[1]

While SNMP and OSI Management have a number of MIBs for managing different types of networks and applications, these are too elaborate for the cost-effective management of PC components, such as VGA cards, monitors, SCSI disk drives, and PC-Windows software. For example, development of SNMP MIBs requires a good understanding of ASN.1 language, an expertise not commonly available amongst the manufacturers of PC components. SNMP agent software overhead (though much less than an OSI agent) requires a substantial amount of memory (approx 50kbytes). Many low cost PC components may not be able to provide that onboard local intelligence. Besides, SNMP is mainly designed to acquire management information from remote elements. It provides no support for the management of local components in a PC. Hence SNMP is not ideally suited to the management of PCs and their components.

Hence DMTF DMI (Figure 52) defines a simple management framework to support the management of PC components based on interfaces, called Component Interface (CI) and an ASCII Management Information Format.

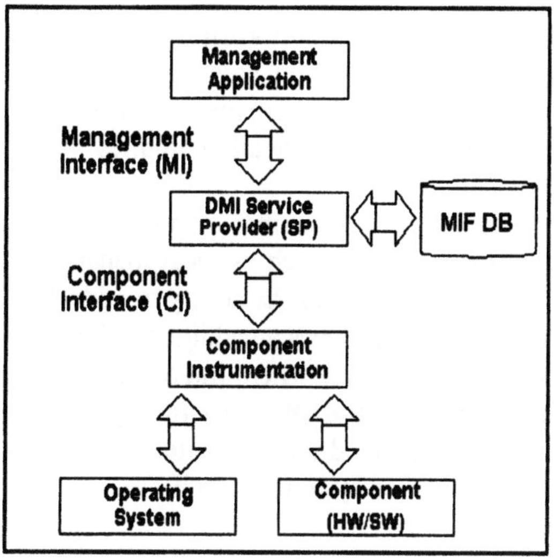

- Management Applications - can be local or remote
- Applications communicate with SP through MI
- Component Instrumentation - must be local

Figure 52. DMTF DMI Standard Framework[1]

A management software, called DMI Service Provider (SP), can support management applications through Management Interface (MI). This also provides mappings from SNMP (Figure 53). The main building blocks of DMI are Management Application (MA), Service Provider (SP), Management Information Format (MIF) and Component Instrumentation (CI).

DMI MAs manage compliant systems from a central location. They gain access and control to the PC hardware/software components through DMI SP using the Management Interface (MI). An MA provides the ability to monitor the status of a PC over time.

SP building block provides a central core standard management interface technology. It provides access/control to PC components (e.g., display, disk drive etc.) via Components Instrumentation (CI). Unlike SNMP, DMI SP allows a PC to signal unsolicited events.

Component Instrumentation (CI) allows real-time data to be collected from PC components. CI allows direct access and control to a PCs component, and enables a PC to report unusual conditions. So it is very useful for managing local devices as well as remote devices.MIF defines the management schema for a component in the form of a template with fields, such as name lists (names of variables), descriptions and formats, serial number list and software directory lists.

Like SNMP MIBs, DMI Management Information Format (MIF) database contains schema for management information structure provided for a PC component. Unlike in SNMP, MIFs schemas are available in self-describing ASCII format. DMI management information structure is compiled into the MIF database via an installation procedure. When you install your VGA card, the supporting disk has the necessary DMI information. Once the setup is done, MIF automatically compiles into the system.

It may be noted that DMTF DMI solves a number of problems at the instrumentation level for systems management, such as local management, small footprint, simple ASCII file based MIF, and the ability to address PC component management. However, DMI introduces an additional dimension of complexity at the management platform level where interoperability has to be provided with SNMP (Figure 53), OSI, and other proprietary formats.

DMTF DMI standard has now been accepted for distributed management not only for PCs but also for large networked systems as well.

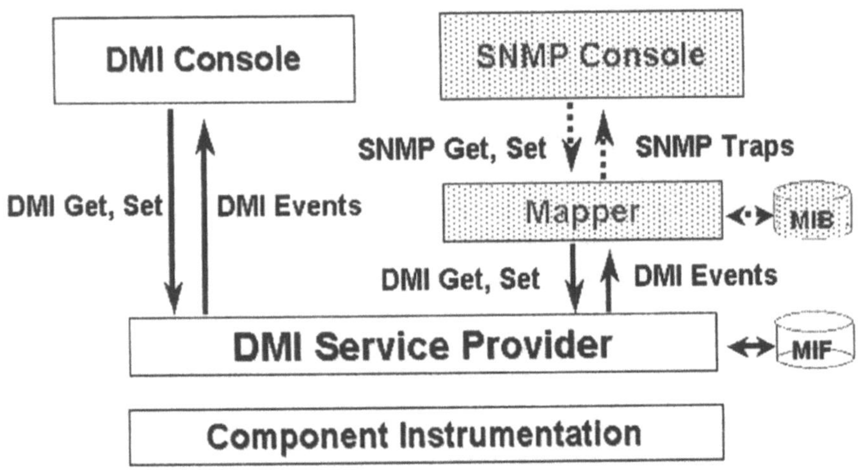

Figure 53. Interoperability of DMI with SNMP

While so far we have discussed standards at instrumentation level for systems management, the next sections discuss systems management at platform and application levels.

7.3.2 DMTF Common Information Model (CIM)[2]

As discussed earlier, a management platform integrates and aggregates management information from diverse instrumentation sources, including SNMP, OSI Management and DMI. Commercially available management platforms use proprietary object models for this purpose. The Object Management Group (OMG) CORBA provides a standard object for distributed computing. However, this model is not tuned for the peculiarities of a management application. For example, CORBA does not specifically address issues related to interoperability of management information available as SNMP MIBs, OSI GDMO, or DMTF MIF. This led to the definition of the Common Information Model (CIM) [25]. The Common Information Model (CIM) defines the Schemas used to represent the real-world objects being managed. CIM uses an object-oriented paradigm, where manageable objects are modeled using the concepts of classes and instances.It may be noted that CIM is the first management platform level standard. The salient features of CIM (Figure 54) are as follows[2]:

- CIM is an implementation neutral schema for describing overall management information
- CIM facilitates the integration of management information from different sources. It provides a high-level abstraction of management data to allow a common data interchange mechanism for multi-vendor management data
- An object-oriented data model that is a formalized representation and classification of the managed environment (hardware, software and networks)
- A new object syntax: MOF (Managed Object Format) to describe objects for CIM
- A new meta-model defining high-level concepts plus "common" models of systems, networks, devices and applications that provides a common vocabulary for management information
- Provides a model for both instrumentation and management and a way to subsume existing management information models such as SNMP MIBs, OSI GDMO, and DMTF DMI.
- CIM is a data model not an implementation

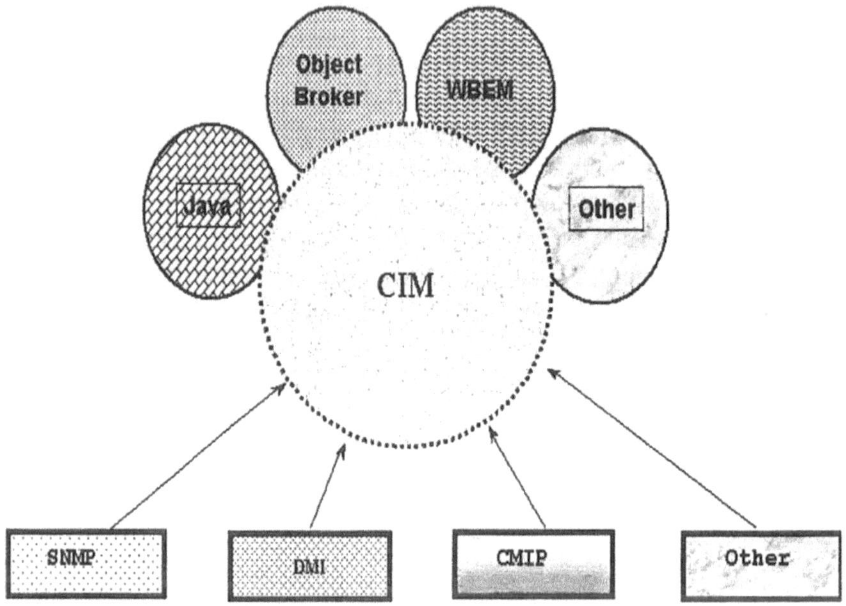

Figure 54. DMTF as the Common Object Model at Platform Level[2]

CIM comprises:
- A meta-schema to formally describe the model.
- Core schemas to capture notions that are applicable to all areas of management.
- Standard schemas to model vendor-independent information within a small number of specific areas of management (Networks, Applications and so forth).
- Extensions schemas to represent vendor-specific extensions of the standard schemas (for example, the Win32 schema).

Currently CIM schema (classes and instances) are expressed textually in Managed Object Format (MOF), a vernacular of Interface Definition Language (IDL), standard used in CORBA for the definition of interfaces for distributed objects.

Although the MOF describes the CIM schemas, it is necessary to define two aspects to make CIM usable over networks. Firstly, there is a need for a platform independent, universally available protocol to transport the CIM objects. The IETF Hypertext Transfer Protocol (HTTP) does the job. Here are the advantages of HTTP based CIM implementation[2]:
- Work on existing web servers
- Not mandate any new HTTP extensions

- Intuitively obvious to typical Web programmers
- Compatible with existing Web programming
- Simple in concept and implementation

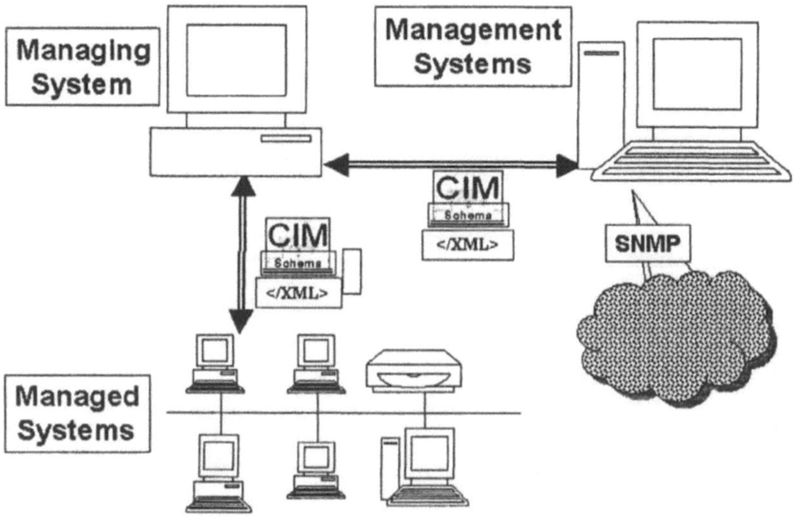

Figure 55. Distributed Management Interoperability based on CIM and XML[26]

Secondly, there is a need for the rendering of these objects in a platform independent manner- a job done by XML as shown in Figure 55[26]. CIM classes and instances are valid XML documents. This involves the definition of one XML Document Type Definition (DTD). An example is given below to define the disk storage information for management[2].

```
<CLASS Name="Disk">
<PROPERTY Name="Freespace">
200
</PROPERTY>
</CLASS>
```

The next sections describe how CIM is being integrated with standards from other standards bodies, such as IETF and WWWC.

7.3.3 Web Based Enterprise Management (WBEM)

Figure 55 shows the different elements of management in an e-business environment. Web-Based Enterprise Management (WBEM- an initiative now managed by DMTF) is a set of management and Internet standard technologies developed to unify the management of e-business computing environments. The objectives are to provide[3]

- Web access to management data
- Web access to managed elements
- Data Integration of management applications

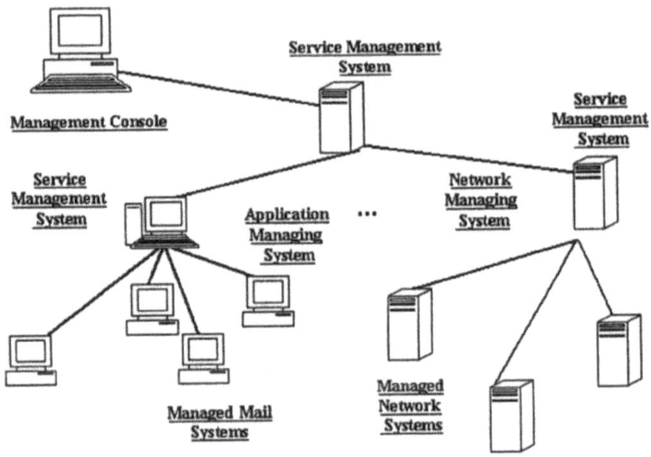

Figure 56. Integration of different types of management in WBEM[34]

While CIM provides the data content, HTTP provides the network protocol, and XML provides the platform-independent transport encoding language. In June 1998, the DMTF became the standards body for Web Based Enterprise Management (WBEM) and Directory Enabled Networks (DEN). WBEM is an umbrella initiative to link multi-vendor management applications using web WBEM (Figure 56) is expected to become the mother of all systems management technologies[3].

7.3.4 Directory Enabled Networks (DEN)

CIM is now tied to another, very interesting, standard called Directory Enabled Networks - DEN. DEN is useful to the management of large, networked systems. When we have to get data and we work on a system, we tend to go to directories on the PC. Similarly, when our system has to find another system on the Internet, it uses an online directory service, such as Internet Domain Name System (DNS). Similarly OSI X.500 directory services are used for locating matching services in many networked environments (e.g., Novell LANs). Therefore the directory is an integrating factor, which is required everywhere. The Internet has defined a simple protocol called Lightweight Directory Access Protocol (LDAP) for this purpose. If we can define the network resources and their relationships in the form of an extended hierarchy, then it should be possible to manage anything and everything using directory level networks. Anything we think of, whether we need applets, codes or documentation –can be placed and searched for on directories**Error! Reference source not found.**.

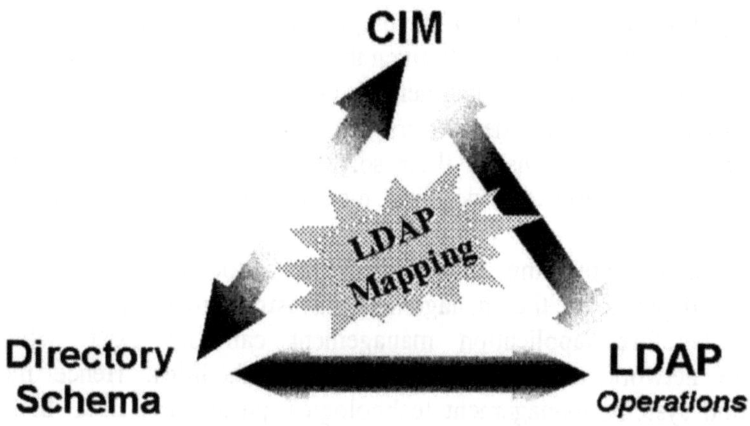

Figure 57. Integration of CIM with DEN[34]

So CIM and DEN together are now being suggested as the standard for platform level. This has the support of industry heavyweights, such as Microsoft. The Common Information Model (CIM) provides a mechanism for modeling various types of information. The model is independent of any implementation or repository. For a model or *schema* to be useful, it must be mapped into some implementation. Figure 57 shows the mapping of CIM schema to LDAP using Directory Schema. More details on CIM and WBEM can be found at [2,3].

7.4 Applications Management Technologies

Applications management is the next higher layer of the stack with management responsibility of keeping mission critical applications and data available and secure. Applications management primarily involves the installation, configuration, administration and monitored operation of e-business applications and their parameters, such as email, transaction processing and related parameters, like number of threads, number of connections, etc. Due to the increasing complexity of e-business applications, a number of middleware schemes have now emerged. Middleware management primarily involves the installation, configuration, administration and monitored operation of HTTP servers, database and transaction services, mail and community services and groupware services[10]. Since applications directly affect an e-business, application and middleware management are the major concerns for e-business infrastructure management today. Models and tools for application management are now emerging, unlike network management techniques that have matured to some extent over the past decade.

One might think that the task of developing a unified management for e-business applications is too difficult given the variety of applications and the number of ways they can be implemented. Fortunately, the task is not too difficult because software developers usually adopt some commonly understood informal patterns in their software. Hence the job involves identifying these patterns and defining models and tools based on such patterns.

Part 3 shows how the management infrastructure of networked applications depends on the management infrastructure of networks and systems. Therefore, application management can not exist without appropriate network and systems management facilities. Hence most network and systems management technologies, particularly IETF SNMP and DMTF WBEM are very relevant for application management. For example, IETF already has a number of draft standards for application management MIBs. They include Network Service Monitoring MIB, Mail Monitoring MIB, Directory MIB, and Application MIB. Similarly DMTF technologies are now being increasingly adopted for application management, as described in Section 7.4.1.

This section also discusses some emerging technologies on application management.

- The Open Group (TOG) Application Management standards, including,
  - Application Response Monitor (ARM)
  - Application Integration and Control (AIC)
  - Software Licensing Management (SLM)
- Java Management API (JMAPI)

7.4.1 DMTF Technologies for Application Management

DMTF technologies have led to products, such as Tivoli TME, which uses a format called Application Management Specification (AMS), based on DMI and MIF. As with Tivoli TME, a PC application, DMTF technologies help manage PC applications, topology, distributions, installation, checking, monitoring, control, security and performance management.

Application Management Specification (AMS) addresses the full lifecycle of an e-business application by supporting software distribution, application monitoring, event management and task automation (Figure 58).

One of the major challenges to application management is that management functions are usually overlooked when the application is designed. This leads to complications involving issues related to the security, performance and effectiveness of the application. AMS provides a non-intrusive (i.e., no code required) method to define management characteristics of an application using the Common Information Model (CIM), defined by the DMTF. Software development tools are provided to build CIM based files associated with the application. Management events and ARM (discussed in Section 7.4.2.3) transactions used by monitor agents may be referenced in AMS files. The systems management services interpret these AMS files to provide secure, efficient deployment, policy-based monitoring and event-driven problem resolution. AMS also includes a number of additional management functions[10].

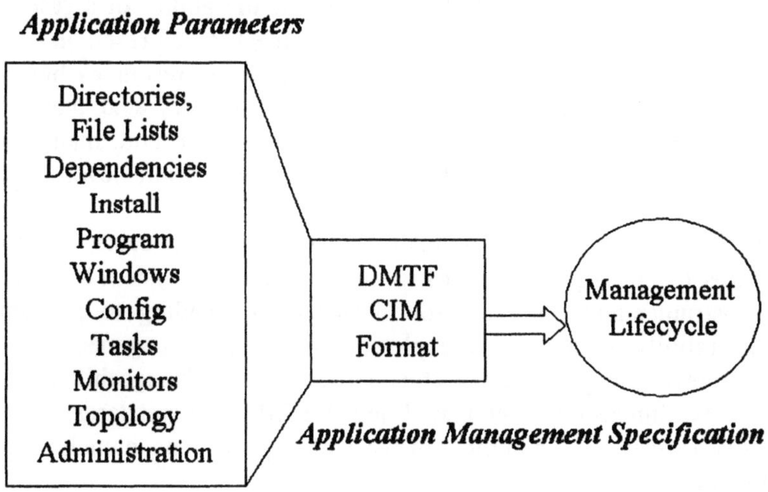

Figure 58. Tivoli Application Management Specification (AMS)[10]

Applications are further complicated by the existence of multiple, independently managed networks or administrative domains. For example, each participant in an e-commerce transaction controls a separate administrative domain - a collection of interconnecting hosts and routers, managed by a single administrative authority. This often results in a loss of functions, such as user administration and security, inventory management and performance management.

7.4.2 The Open Group (TOG) Manageability Initiative

Key objectives of The Open Group are to:

- Define an architecture that will drive effective manageability of applications
- Establish standards for a Management Service Provider layer of DMI
- Integrate existing specifications into a larger whole
- Provide an effective interface with Common Management Infrastructures (e.g., WBEM)
- Provide specifications for specific components of the manageability instrumentation

7.4.2.1 The Manageability Initiative[21]

The key distinction between TOG Management Initiative and the Manageability Initiative is that Management Initiative provides a high-level function that aggregates and interprets data, determining which actions need to be taken. Manageability Initiative refers to the ability of a resource to provide the data and control capabilities that need to be present in order for such data to be managed. Management depends on resources having the characteristics of manageability. In terms of the integrated management framework (described in Section 7.1) management and manageability initiatives correspond to platform and instrumentation level functions respectively.

In the case of current application management products, the lack of standards for manageability leads to the need for each system to provide its own instrumentation and control infrastructure, leading to problems of interoperability and a potential explosion of management agents.

As shown in Figure 59, The Open Group (TOG) Manageability initiative adds a new dimension to the DMTF led WBEM set of standards. This TOG initiative is relevant to a number of types of organizations, namely:

- Management system suppliers
- Software Providers (Applications and Middleware)
- OS suppliers

The Open Group has standardized Applications Management with the following three technologies[21]:

- Application Instrumentation and Control (AIC)
- Application Response Measurement (ARM)
- Software License Use Management (XSLM)

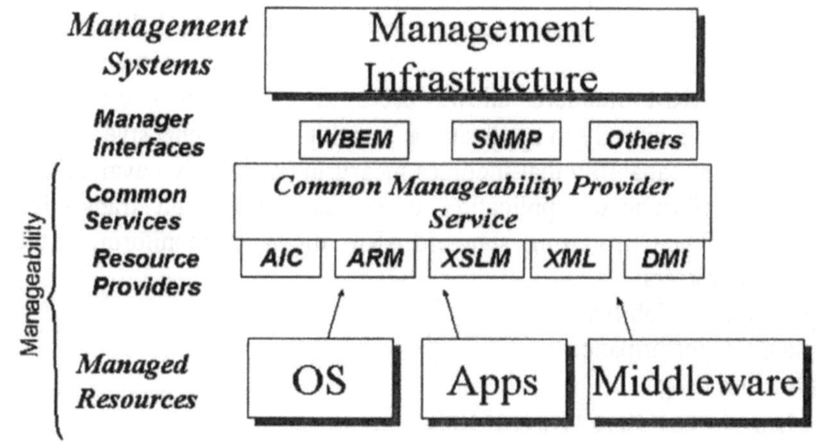

Figure 59. The Open Group Standards for Application Management[21]

7.4.2.2 Application Instrumentation & Control (AIC)[21]

The Application Instrumentation & Control (AIC) API provides the facility to instrument an application so that a user of that application will receive real-time information on the progress of work flowing through the application. It also enables the user to exercise control over the work being processed by the application. The objectives of AIC are:

- Get real-time information on the progress of work through an application
- Establish resource usage, transaction values
- Take business-critical decisions and actions

These facilities enable business managers to monitor the progress of work through their computing system applications, identify any problems with workflow through the application, for example, a particular item of work taking too long to complete a process and holding up processing of other high-priority work, or a need to switch more resources to processing a high priority workload.

This application management and control facility is particularly valuable to businesses that run mission critical applications, where smooth running of application processes and timely delivery of the results of transactions are key to the profitability and overall efficiency of the business. Obvious initial deployment has been in the financial (banking) sector, where even the briefest delay in completing a transaction on time can cost significant sums of money. However, the facilities AIC provides are also suited to many other types of business applications.

7.4.2.3 Application Response Measurement (ARM)

The Application Response Measurement (ARM) standard describes a common method for integrating e-business applications as manageable entities. The ARM standard allows users to extend their e-business management tools directly to applications creating a comprehensive end-to-end management capability that includes measuring application availability, application performance, application usage and end-to-end transaction response time. The Open Group standard ARM allows the monitoring of the following parameters:

- application availability
- application performance
- application usage
- end-to-end transaction response time

With the ARM API, sections of an application can be marked to define business transactions. By invoking ARM API function calls at the beginning and end of each transaction, the application can be monitored by any of the measurement agents that use data generated by ARM API. This provides a standard of application management instrumentation for client-server systems. Figure 60 shows how e-business management applications, measurement agents that implement ARM and business applications that call the ARM API, work together to provide a standard method to monitor application response.

Using ARM, e-business managers will be able to answer key questions such as:[21]

- Is the application working correctly (available)?
- How is the application performing? What is the response time? What is the workload throughput?
- Why is an application not available or performing poorly? What operation was the application performing when the problem occurred? Which remote application was being invoked when the problem occurred?
- Who is using the application, how they are using it, and what kind of operations are being performed? Which servers are providing the services?

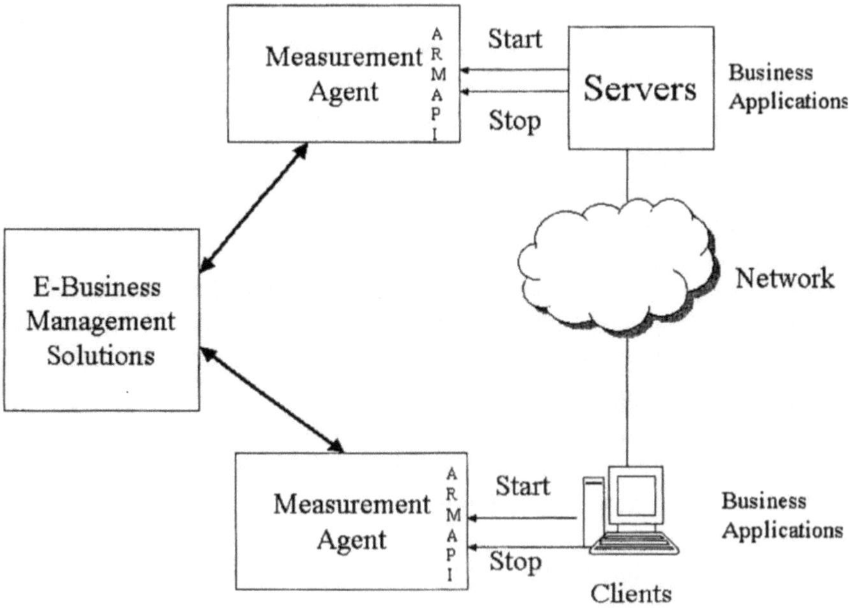

Figure 60. ARM in E-business Management[21]

7.4.2.4 Software License Use Management (XSLM)

The Open Group has published a technical standard for Software License Use Management (XSLM). XSLM defines the following:[21].

- Instrument applications for License management
- License characteristics and License server

Escalating software costs, the high administrative burden of license compliance control, the lack of effective customer control over their employees' use of licensed software and asset protection are all key business issues which led to the creation of this customer-driven project.

XSLM now provides an interoperable solution for monitoring the use of licensed software products in a business.

7.4.3 Java Management Extension (JMX)

Java Management Extension (JMX™) is the standard API for Java management. JMX™ provides the tools for building distributed, Web-based, modular and dynamic solutions for managing and monitoring devices, applications and service-driven networks[29].

JMX has defined an open component-based management platform based on Object Request Broker (ORB) based distributed objects, JavaBeans,

Enterprise Java Beans (EJB) and Java 2. It has Java beans in the client and EJB in the server. Java 2 serves as the management framework. The overall JMX architecture in bottom-up sequence consists of[23]:

1. Intelligent Java Agents, including Java agent, Native/SNMP agents
2. Multiple protocols support, including XML, RMI, CORBA IIOP, HTTP, SNMP and CMIP
3. Multiple Information Model Support, including CIM, SNMP MIB, DMI, OSI GDMO, CORBA and Java
4. Management Beans, and
5. Java 2 Management Framework consisting of JNDI, Persistence, XML, Management services, JDBC, ODMG, security, events, CORBA/RMI, Java Beans, EJB, AWT with links to LDAP directory, Management database and a repository

The Java Community Processes (JCP) initiative has made JMX the standard API for Java management. A number of e-business platforms (e.g., IBM Websphere™) now use JMX for management.

7.4.4 Industry Solutions

As discussed throughout this section application management is a very important part of e-business infrastructure management, but it is now in a nascent stage. Researchers and businesses are involved in identifying and generalizing some common patterns in e-business applications for management purposes. While some of these patterns have matured to standards, such as ARM, others have been incorporated in recent commercial application management products, described in[28]. Alternative approaches are:

- Custom Programmed Management Approach (used by many organizations)
- Traffic inference approach using RMON probes
- Client Agent Approach

Applications that aren't amenable to meaningful performance measurements based on generic measurements can only be measured and controlled with the custom-programmed management approach. The disadvantage is that few client-server or n-tier applications have been instrumented in this fashion. Even companies that are prepared to devote skilled programming resources to developing custom management solutions are unable to progress if the application wasn't created with management hooks and APIs. The other primary disadvantage of a custom approach is that skilled programming resources are rare, costly, hard to control and usually slower than expected.

The traffic inference approach has the big advantage of not requiring programmatic intervention in the target application. Probes or agents deployed on the local network close to the user may also be the simplest approach in terms of the number of computers and connections that must be modified.

The biggest disadvantage of traffic inference is that it's limited to only the least common denominators of application performance. Specific application behaviors, and. performance bottlenecks in the client may not be detected. Finally, the accuracy of a probe-only system may be questionable because the best the performance-management software can do is to make assumptions about the beginning and end of transactions and the makeup of packet flows.

The client-agent approach has the greatest possible proximity to the user. A client agent can readily distinguish user "think time" from client processing delays. By noting the beginning and ending time of transactions, a client agent is the only incontestable source of information about the total round-trip delay and the final word on whether a transaction concluded successfully.

The most significant disadvantage of client agents is the disadvantage of application-specific clients in general. It's hard to deploy software in mass quantities. Combinations of operating-system versions, hardware and application software are likely to have installation and compatibility problems with the agent.

Steinke in [28] has compared application management solutions being offered by a number of leading vendors as shown in Table 8.

Table 8. Selected Application Management Products[21]

Vendor	***Product***
BMC Software www.bmc.com/patrol	Patrol
Computer Associates www.ca.com/products/tng_application_response.htm	Application Response Option
Compuware www.compuware.com/products/ecosystems	EcoSystems
Concord Communications www.concord.com	eHealth
Dirig Software www.dirig.com	RelyENT xSpress
Hewlett-Packard www.managementsoftware.hp.com	OpenView VantagePoint
Lucent Technologies www.lucent.com/networkcare	VitalSuite
Manage.com www.manage.com	Frontline e.M

Vendor	Product
NetIQ www.netiq.com/products/network_performance	Pegasus
NetScout Systems www.netscout.com	ngenius
Tivoli www.tivoli.vom	Application Performance Management

7.4.5 Enterprise Systems Management

Enterprise systems management integrates the management functions across all the layers of the application stack to provide a consolidated view of an enterprise's business solutions, the applications they use and the underlying IT resources. The integrated management of applications, middleware, systems and networks using a single, comprehensive management system is important to maintain service levels and to keep the enterprise running efficiently. Consider a scenario where the failure of a network router causes apparent database and application failures. Determining the root cause of the failure using separate, non-integrated management tools results in additional effort on the part of both the database and application administrators. Mitropoulos illustrates the use of various standards mentioned in this chapter to implement an integrated management system for multimedia message handling systems[20].

This highlights the need for the integration of all e-business infrastructure management with e-business service and transaction management. Some standards in this area are now evolving, as discussed in the next chapter.

7.5 Chapter Summary

This chapter has discussed generic e-business infrastructure management technologies in a bottom-up manner in the sequence of network management, systems management, applications management, service management and business management. Other dimensions of technologies in e-business management include the framework (with instrumentation, platform and application levels), e-business perspectives (processes, transactions and infrastructure) and industry perspective (telecoms, e-healthcare).

Standards at e-business process management level are now evolving. Some business and service level standards, such as ITSM and ITIL were discussed in Part 3. XML is also now playing a major role in the definition of e-business management solutions.

Technologies at the infrastructure management level are manifested in the network management standards (e.g., SNMP, RMON and OSI Management), systems management standards (e.g., DMI, CIM, and LDAP.) and application management standards (e.g., ARM andJMX) described in this chapter. We also discussed how the Web Based Enterprise Management (WBEM) initiatiative that is bringing together standards from a number of standards bodies for the integrated management of e-business infrastructure. The next chapter will present a discussion of how these different technologies and standards can be integrated for effective management of e-businesses.

7.6 References

1. DMTF, *DMI Standards*, http://www.dmtf.org, June 2001
2. DMTF, *CIM Tutorial*, http://www.dmtf.org/spec/cim_tutorial/, March 2001
3. DMTF, *Web Based Enterprise Management (WBEM) Standards*, http://www.dmtf.org/spec/wbem.html, March 2001
4. DMTF, *DMTF-CSC Support Standards*, http://www.dmtf.org/spec/stan.html, March 2001
5. DMTF, *Service/Ploicy Model*, http://www.dmtf.org, June 2001
6. ETSI, Technical Activities, March 2001, http://www.etsi.org
7. Ghetie I.G., *Networks and Systems Management: Platforms Analysis and Evaluation*, Kluwer Academic Publishers, 1997
8. Hamada T., Kamata H. and Hogg S., "An Overview of TINA Management Architecture", *Journal of Network and Systems Management*, Vol. 5, No. 4, December 1997
9. Hidalgo J., "Introduction to Directory Enabled Networks", DMTF Developers' Conference, June 2000, http://www.dmtf.org
10. IBM, "An Open e-Business Foundation", *E-Business White Paper*, 1997
11. IT Service Management Forum (ITSMF), "ITSMF-DMTF Alliance", DMTF Developers Conference, June 2000, USA
12. Internet Engineering Task Force (IETF), *Requests For Comments (RFCs)*, 2002, www.ietf.org
13. ITU X.722 1992 | ISO/IEC 10165-4: *Information Technology - Open Systems Interconnection - Structure of management information - Guidelines for the definition of managed objects*, 1992
14. ITU-T Recommendation X.790 (11/95) - *Trouble Management function for ITU-T applications*, http://www.itu.int/plweb-egi/fasweb?getdoc+view1+5727++X.790.
15. International Telecommunications Union (ITU-T), "TMN Roadmap", http://www.itu.int/TMN/, 1997

16. ITU-T X.901 | ISO/IEC 10746-1: *Open Distributed Processing Reference Model - Part 1*, 1997 E
17. Kavanagh D., "Establishing an End-to-end Integrated Management Platform by Combining Network and Service Management with Operational Support Systems (OSS's)", *Forge Australia White Paper*, www.forge.com.au/products/Papers, December 1999Koehler D., "Service Level Monitoring", HP-OpenView'98 presentation, April 1998Lawrence D.G., "Service Incident and Knowledge Exchange", DMTF Developers Conference, June 2000, USA
20. Mitropoulos, S., "Integrated Enterprise Networking Management: Case Study in Intelligent Multimedia Message Handling Systems", *Journal of Network and Systems Management* (JNSM), Vol. 8, No. 2, March 2000
21. The Open Group, "Enterprise Management Forum Manageability Initiative", http://www.opengroup.org/downloads/index.htm, March 2001
22. Object Management Group (OMG), "Common Object Request Broker Architecture (CORBA) Common Facilities", http://www.omg.org
23. Orfali R., Harkey D. and Edwards J., *Client/Server Survuval Guide*, John Wiley & Sons, 1999, ISBN: 0-471-31615-6
24. Organization of Government Commerce (OGC formerly CCTA), "ITIL and BSI Code of Practice on IT Service Management", IT Service Management Forum (ITSMF) web site in UK, http://www.itsmf.com/itsmf/i2.htm, April 2001
25. Ray P., *Cooperative Management of Enterprise Networks*, Kluwer Academic/ Plenum Publications, May 2000, ISBN:0-306-46276-1
26. Sahai A., Machiraju V. and Wurster K., "Managing Next Generation E-Services", *HP Laboratories Technical Report* HPL-2000-120, September 2000, Palo Alto USA
27. Shrewsbury J.K., "An Introduction to TMN", *Journal of Network and Systems Management* (JNSM), Vol. 3, No. 1, March 1995
28. Steinke S., "The Well-Mannered Application", *Information Week*, USA, http://www.informationweek.com, January 29, 2001
29. Sun Microsystems, "Java Management Extensions (JMX)", http://java.sun.com/products/JavaManagement/index.html, May 2002
30. Tele Management Forum (TMF), "A Service Management Business Process Model", 1995.
31. TeleManagement Forum, "Smart TMN Technology Integration Map", GB909 issue 1.1, October 1998, http://www.tmforum.org/
32. Umar A., *Object-Oriented Client/Server Internet Environments*, Prentice Hall, 1997University of Twente Network management Center, "Tutorials on Network management", http://snmp.cs.utwente.nl, accessed June 2001Williams R., "DMTF Technical Roadmap for Enterprise

Management for e-business in the 21st Century", DMTF Developers Conference, June 2000, USA

Chapter 8. Integration of Technologies for E-Business Management

As discussed in Chapters 5 to 7, e-business management presents many different concepts, architectures, technologies and standards. To integrate these different paradigms it is necessary to think about the interoperability of different standards and technologies. Integration and interoperability of e-business management may be considered with respect to the following dimensions:

- Types of business (healthcare, telecommunications, finance etc.)
- Functions and Process (e.g., Business, Service, Infrastructure levels)
- Lifecycle (requirements, design, evaluation etc.)

Many e-business management issues are common across all industries (e.g., healthcare, finance and telecommunications). However, there are differences too depending on the nature of business. While we have used e-healthcare as the example in Parts 3, Parts 4 and 5 use case studies from the e-telco (telecommunications) sector. Integrated management is well developed in telecommunications service. However, the full potential of this e-business paradigm can only be achieved if all management functions in a telco (including finance, marketing, and personnel) adopt the e-business infrastructure. That would be the ultimate goal of an e-telco organization. This Chapter (and Appendix 2) discusse how the evolving standards and technologies can be integrated for the operation and implementation of e-business in telecommunication industry.

Like any software system, the lifecycle of e-business management is an important dimension. In Chapter 2 we discussed this dimension as part of methodology for e-business management. Part 5 will discuss the e-business management lifecycle in the context of cooperative management, which is particularly important in e-business.

This chapter starts with a general discussion of horizontal integration of management functions in multiple organizations in the cooperative e-business environment. This is followed by a discussion of "standards suites", which help with the vertical integration of a number of standards and technologies at different hierarchical levels with respect to one type of e-business. This is followed by a comparative evaluation of the interoperability of these different standards. Finally, we carry out a case study e-business management in the telecommunication service provider sector (e-telco).

8.1 Horizontal Integration

Part 1 of this book discusses many aspects of e-business management. The most important aspect is an organization's need to compete and cooperate with other organizations for the success of e-business. While organizations compete at the business level, they need to cooperate at the management technology level. This underscores the importance of horizontal integration of e-business management infrastructure across organizations. This section discusses horizontal integration with respect to the following issues [9,15]:

- Multi-domain management
- Cooperative Management
- Deployment
- Service Level Management
- Security

8.1.1 Multi-domain E-business Management

Businesses are rushing to take advantage of the benefits offered by the Internet: extended reach to new customers, improved service for existing customers, reduced cost of doing business, and continuous availability 7 days a week, 24 hours a day. However, doing business on the Internet forces companies to rely on systems, networks and people that they do not control and that do not necessarily function together.

Typically e-businesses span multiple service provider domains connected over the Internet. Hence effective e-business management requires multi-domain management in spite of differences in management policies and technologies in these different service provider domains. For example, one service provider may be using proprietary technologies over mainframes, while another might be using SNMP and a proprietary management platform technology (e.g., Aprisma Spectrum), and another might be using DMTF DMI and CIM (e.g., TIVOLI TME). Similarly there exist different types of help-desk technologies ranging from proprietary trouble-ticketing (used by some telecom carriers) to standard CSC SIS/SES based interoperable help-desk systems.

The complex infrastructure of Internet e-business applications, such as e-commerce, presents challenging management problems. As applications move across the Internet, attempts are being made to manage the issues of accountability and control that cloud Internet e business visibility. The failure of an application in one administrative domain might be the result of a problem in another administrative domain, but detecting and fixing the problem can be difficult when the cause lies outside the area to which the administrator has visibility and control.[9]

8.1.2 Collaborative Management

The success of e-business requires a new generation of management services and tools that provide end-to-end solutions designed specifically to manage widely dispersed, e-business applications. As activities cross administrative domains, the ability to synchronize application updates, manage availability and ensure security is compromised. E-business management services are being extended to address collaborative management. This means that the distributed object framework used by the various e-business management services needs to be extended to support formats and protocols that work across Internet firewalls in a secure fashion[9].

In general, cooperative management needs methodologies and tools to facilitate the cooperation of humans, and software elements within and across organizations. This topic is discussed in more detail in Part 5 of this book.

8.1.3 Deployment[9]

By their very nature, Internet e-business applications allow for pieces of the application to reside in multiple locations; components may be deployed not only at the hosting site, but also on customer and supplier's sites. As more applications reside beyond controlled firewalls, traditional management tools are not sufficient to ensure that applications are secure, properly deployed and available to all end-users. Hence horizontal integration is required to facilitate multi-domain management in spite of different security and licensing policies of different service providers.

To address these collaborative deployment requirements, modern management technologies utilize Internet software distribution technology whereby end users receive the appropriate applications and information by subscribing to *channels*. Channels are simply an abstraction that represents the executable and data files that comprise applications. The deployment server and deployment client work together to automatically keep channels current and reduce the complexity of delivering and maintaining applications across devices, platforms and networks[9]. To integrate with existing enterprise deployment schemes, channels may also be used to distribute files for application management (e.g., AMS files described in Chapter 7).

8.1.4 Service Level Management

Internet e-business applications also introduce another level of management complexity that is described as Service Level Management (SLM). Since the connection to partners and customers is through the Internet, performance problems due to bandwidth bottlenecks or availability problems due to improper server configuration or node failures can bring business to a standstill. Determining whose network or system is causing the problem requires collaborative collection and analysis of management information.

The application and systems monitoring agents used in the e-business management environment may be extended to adhere to cross-enterprise defined policies and procedures which can, for example, define agreed to performance thresholds as well as dictate which administrative domain and management system receives which messages[9].

8.1.5 Security

Ensuring the security of business-critical applications once they shift beyond an IT organization's control is also an important concern for the Internet e-business community. It is critical to safeguard information assets and protect the privacy of all parties in an e-commerce transaction because fraud, viruses, illegal intrusions, and unintentional corruption all pose serious threats. Also it is important to maintain an audit trail of transactions so that no party can later repudiate a transaction, asserting that it never took place. Even the perception of lack of security can cause businesses and consumers to become reluctant to use e-business.

The e-business management security services need to be extended to provide an enforceable security policy that ensures the extended enterprise remains inviolable. The extensions for cooperative management enable partners to manage their own security and, optionally, collaborate with key on-line business partners to manage access to their extranets. The extensions include [9,6]:

- An agent that detects external scans and intrusions (intrusion detector)
- A policy-based management console that scans the security infrastructure, collects data from intrusion detectors, initiates responses to security breaches and provides extensive reporting capabilities.

Security management is an important topic that has been addressed by a wealth of literature in the area [6,2]. This topic is beyond the scope of this book.

8.2 Vertical Integration

Since e-business services are dependent on networks, systems and applications. It is natural that service management would be very much dependent on the results of network management, systems management and applications management. This section presents a discussion of concepts and "standard suites" that provide a set of standards and concepts to integrate these different aspects of management covering business management, service management, applications management, systems management and network management. The prominent standards suites are:

- ISO Reference Model for Open Distributed Processing (RMODP)
- ITU-T Telecommunications Management Networks (TMN)
- TINA
- Tele-Management Forum (TMF) recommendations including TOM, Business agreements, and information agreements
- DMTF/CSC Problem Resolution Standards (PRS)

It may be noted that both TINA and TMF recommendations have strong implications for the business level management guidelines, such as ITSM and ITIL discussed in Part 3. We now discuss these standard suites.

8.2.1 ISO RM-ODP

The purpose of ISO's ongoing standardization effort, Open Distributed Processing (ODP), is to develop a framework that specifies an architecture integrating support for distribution, interoperability and portability. Fundamental to this reference model (RM-ODP) is the notion that distributed processing systems can be studied and described from several viewpoints, presented here with respect to the OSI Management model[14]. ISO ODP is the basis for telecommunication service technologies, such as TINA.

- The Enterprise Viewpoint studies organization-wide requirements and policies
- The Information Viewpoint addresses information structure issues of distributed applications
- The Computational Viewpoint expresses the functionality in distribution-transparent manner
- The Engineering Viewpoint describes mechanisms for providing distribution transparencies
- The Technological Viewpoint describes the implementation and testing aspects of a distributed system including relevant hardware, software and standards.

An enterprise viewpoint allows the description of the enterprise level view of a distributed system, encompassing human/organizational roles, their obligations, permissions and prohibitions. This helps in presenting a distributed network/systems management infrastructure in the context of the organizational business entities. This is very important from the point of view of providing a seamless integration between business management and network management.

An information viewpoint provides a mechanism to represent the structure of information in a distributed system, through schemas (state and structure of management information), relations (between managed objects) and a set of integrity rules (assertion about a schema). The information specification can be through a variety of methods (e.g., Entity-Relationship-ER diagrams and languages like ISO ASN.1).

A computational viewpoint shows the interfaces of objects participating in a distributed system. While network management technologies, such as SNMP and CMIP, define operational interactions between managers and managed objects, the ODP computational view allows other interfaces, such as streams. For example, multimedia objects may need stream interfaces for their management.

An engineering viewpoint describes a distributed system in terms of structural entities called objects, clusters, capsules, channels and functions. OMG CORBA has now become a standard for the implementation of object-based distributed systems. Therefore, RM-ODP has now adopted OMG CORBA as the infrastructure model at the engineering level. Hence, an ODP engineering viewpoint may be expressed in terms of CORBA Object Request Broker (ORB), stubs, skeletons, basic object adapters and CORBA clients/servers.

A technology viewpoint is concerned with the implementation of an object-based distributed system.

RM-ODP provides a conceptual framework for the study and development of distributed systems including management applications. Some of these concepts are used in evolving technologies in the area of distributed telecommunications, such as TINA.

However, ODP viewpoints do not provide adequate mechanisms to describe network management processes integrating business processes. For example, ODP viewpoints do not provide any model for describing human interactions as part of an organizational process.

8.2.2 ITU TMN

In addition to the instrumentation level network management standards discussed in Chapter 7, a telecommunication business requires a number of other management technologies at business and application levels. This realization resulted in the development of ITU-T Telecommunications Management Network (TMN) standards.

The telecom industry has embraced the TMN model as a logical way of viewing how the business of a service provider is managed. The TMN model consists of four management layers, usually arranged in a triangle or pyramid (Figure 61). Business management is at the apex, service management is the second layer, network management the third layer and element management is at the bottom. The idea is that management decisions at each layer are different but interrelated. For example, detailed information is needed to keep a switch operating (at the element management layer) but only a subset of that information is needed to keep the network operating (e.g., is the switch operating at full capacity).

TMN defines a layered logical architecture of management for services and systems for telecommunication described in a top-down fashion as follows (Figure 61)[27].

- Business/Enterprise Management Layer (BML) is concerned with the overall management of the telecom carrier business. Service Management Layer
- (SML) is concerned with the management of services provided on the network e.g., Intelligent Network (IN)
- Network Management Layer (NML) is concerned with a network with multiple elements
- Element Management Layer (EML) is concerned with individual network elements e.g., multiplexers and switches.

TMN defines an architectural framework consisting of reference points and interfaces between different building blocks of a telecommunication system, such as operations systems, workstations, mediation devices and network elements. Each reference point uses a manager-agent management model and OSI management standards (discussed in Chapter 7) for the modeling and exchange of management information between any two elements, one acting as a manager and the other as an agent. This allows the management of a complex chain of elements in a cascaded form.

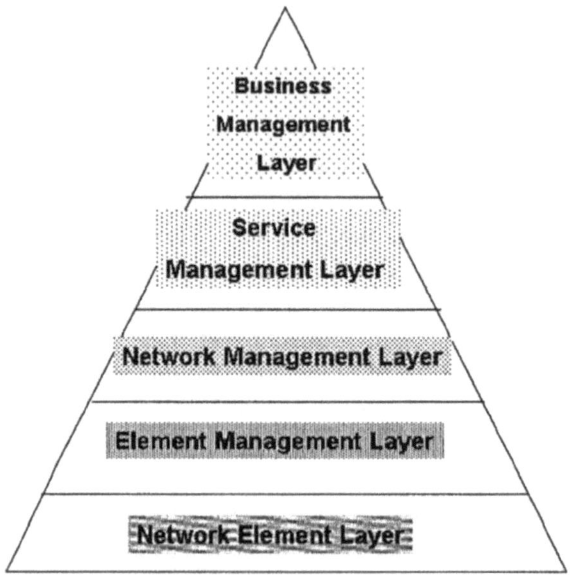

Figure 61. Telecommunications Management Network (TMN)

The focus of TMN is on the management of telecom equipment (switches, transmission gear etc.). Hence, most of the work has been done at the lower layers, i.e., EML and NML. Standards for higher layers are evolving[27].

Although the TMN covers all the management functions, it only provides a broad conceptual framework. It does not address the problems related to the interoperability of different types of management instrumentation, namely SNMP and OSI. Commercial management platforms, such as HP OpenView, Aprisma Spectrum and CA TNG have been traditionally handling this with proprietary object models. Consequently, processed management information at platform level may not be interoperable. Since management tasks need to utilize platform-level information from a number of systems, some platform vendors, such as HP and CA have incorporated the OMG CORBA object model at platform level. There is a management systems interest group in OMG that is working on the development of management oriented object architecture. However, the major thrust towards the standardization of platform level model has come from DMTF as discussed in Chapter 7.

The strengths of TMN are:

- TMN provides a stable reference model designed specifically for management system architects unlike RMODP that describes distributed systems in general
- TMN defines generic management services and comprehensive abstraction of managed resources for the layered implementation of FCAPS management functions
- TMN has been accepted widely in the telecommunication industry

The weaknesses of TMN are:

- Lacks support for top-down e-business management except for the hierarchical taxonomy
- Neglects general IT support, and lacks support for the interoperability of different management technologies
- Lack of support for cooperative management

Section 8.4 discusses the applicability of TMN in modern e-business environments in the telecommunication sector.

8.2.3 TINA

Telecommunications Information Networking Architecture (TINA) is the telecom domain consortium initiated by more than forty telecom carriers all over the world including AT&T, British Telecom, France Telecom, Telecom Italia, and Telstra, etc. TINA was born out of the need for the independent development of two aspects of telecommunication businesses:

- the commodity or transport business concerned with carrying bits over a network
- the growing value-added-service business, such as the Internet services.

The previous generation telecommunication infrastructure had both the above concerns addressed in a monolithic form of telecom switches. TINA provides architecture to develop and manage telecommunication services independent of the switching equipment. This architecture provides a multi-vendor software infrastructure to support properties; such as openness, flexibility against regulation, uniform support of management, support of multimedia services, mobility, scalability, separation of service from the telecom switch architecture, reusability of software, interoperability with various networks and services technologies. TINA provides a set of specifications for the deployment and management of scalable, multivendor, distributed services over a heterogeneous network. It uses the ISO ODP modeling concepts, the OMG distributed object model CORBA, and the ITU TMN management hierarchy[23].

TINA is the first attempt to define a business model for telecommunications in the context of e-business. It helps define the business interactions amongst interested parties through interfaces called reference points (different from TMN reference points). TINA business model and reference points provide business level interfaces between different business roles as shown in Figure 62. TINA defines interfaces (reference points) between the following telecommunication business roles[24]:

- consumers (i.e. end customer),
- connectivity provider (network operator),
- retailers (retail service provider)
- 3rd Party service providers (distributors) and
- brokers.

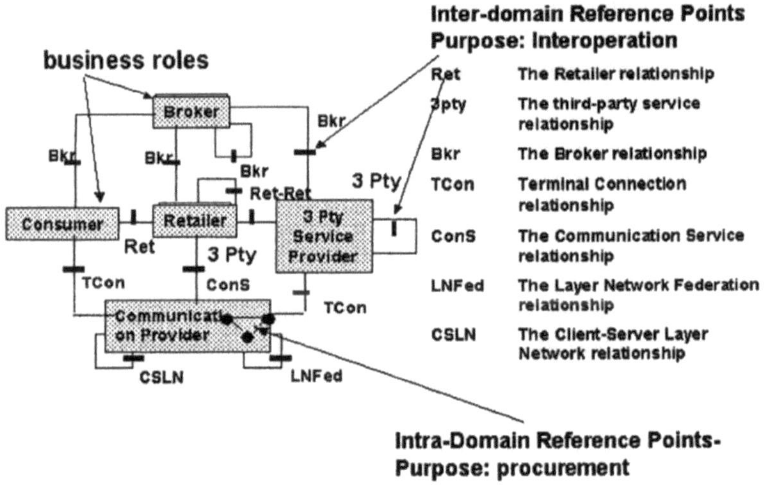

Figure 62. TINA Business Roles and Reference Points[23]

Reference points are specifications of interoperability between administrative domains. As shown in Figure 62, the following reference points are currently being specified in TINA.

- Retailer Inter-domain reference point (Ret)
- Broker inter-domain reference point (BKr)
- 3rd Party inter-domain reference point (3Pty)
- Retailer-to-retailer inter-domain reference point (Rtr)
- Connectivity service inter-domain reference point (Cons)
- Terminal connection inter-domain reference point (TCon)
- Layer network federation inter-domain reference point (LNFed)

TINA proposes an object-oriented model for integrating telecommunication service architecture with network resource architecture. Management and service could go hand in hand in a TINA object specification defined using an object oriented interface definition language called TINA Object Definition Language (ODL). ODL extends OMG CORBA Interface Definition Language (IDL) to specify services including multimedia streams, such as audio and video.

TINA object framework standardizes the management platform architecture around OMG CORBA and ODL specifications of management services of various types, hitherto implemented in proprietary fashion on commercial management platforms. Client-server layer network considers management from the perspective of FCAPS functions, TINA management architecture also considers a number of additional dimensions, namely:[8]

- Partitioning; TINA services and management are organized into three layers, namely service, resource and Distributed Processing Element (DPE)
- Computational: this dimension is concerned with the management of various aspects of DPE, such as event management.
- Life Cycle: this represents different phases of the service life cycle, such as conceived (not planned), not installed, installed and activated.
- TINA defines the object-oriented framework for the implementation of the middle three layers of TMN, i.e. service management layer, network management layer and element management layer.

TINA is the first attempt at integrating the management technologies for e-business in telecommunication sector. Although the TINA business reference model defines reference points for the interoperability of services across domain boundaries, TINA does not provide any methodology for the integration of business management with service/network management. In addition, substantial work needs to be done before TINA can be used for the development of service management solutions. Since business management issues have not been addressed in TINA, human and organizational factors have not been considered in the TINA framework. Unlike Internet SNMP and OMG CORBA, TINA has not been accepted yet in the integrated management and distributed systems industries.

8.2.4 Tele-Management Forum (TMF) Recommendations

Telecom service providers are investing heavily in the development or re-engineering of their processes and systems as their industry undergoes rapid change. Faced with a myriad of technology selections upon which to build their business solutions, telecom businesses needed a common direction that makes clear which technologies are best suited to different types of business needs. There are three key reasons for this[23]:

- The levels of investment are so large that service providers wish to lessen the risk of making choices that are either unsupported by industry or inadequate to the task;

- New technologies are being introduced at a pace that many service providers cannot cope with, and there is a desire both to take advantage of others' experiences and to 'future-proof' their decisions through group agreement;
- Increasingly, service providers are becoming just one part of an extended service delivery chain, with the consequent need to link systems across corporate boundaries. Mergers, acquisitions, alliances and partnerships all make clear the savings that can accrue by moving the industry toward some common technology ground rules.

The Network Management Forum (NMF), now known as Tele-Management Forum (TMF), is a telecom industry association involved in promoting the deployment of technologies for the sake of interoperability of telecommunication solutions. Almost all telecommunication related businesses are members of TMF now. The main objective of TMF is to define standards suites for the purpose of e-business in telecommunications. TMF has been developing best practices and guidelines to complement the existing standards for e-business infrastructure management for telecom service providers. It may be noted that TMF has done some pioneering work in the definition of standards at the e-business process level. Some of these are similar to ITIL standards discussed in Chapter 5. Strong backing from the industry makes TMF recommendations acceptable in telecommunications businesses today.

Some of the successful creations of NMF/TMF include:

- OmniPoint Integration Architecture for the deployment of OSI Management (1994)[25]
- A Service Management Business Process Model and SMART (1995)[20]
- Service Provider's Integrated Requirements for Information Technology (SPIRT)[27]
- Solution and Component Sets for Technology selection (1997)[27]
- SMART TMN Technology Integration Map (1998)[23]
- Business Agreements and Information Agreements
- Telecommunications Operations Map (TOM and eTOM) (2000)[29]

The TMF technology statement (Figure 63) suggests that they are going to adopt TMN guidelines wherever possible and integrate with other available standards, such as SNMP, CORBA, TINA, and SQL. Chapters 5 to7 discussed the needs for the different interfaces 1-4.

Interface	Type	Technology
1	Customer / Operational Staff access	Web browser / Java
2	Business Process interaction / Backbone distribution	CORBA (+ Workflow)
3	Business Process control of Network Resources	CMIP / GDMO SNMP / MIBs
4	Business Process access to Operational Data	SQL, SQL-Net, Data Distribution

Figure 63. TMF Technology Statement

The e-business of telecom operations is controlled by a software system called Operations Support Systems (OSS). Traditionally, each telecom carrier has had its own proprietary way of implementing OSS. But with the recent changes in telecom organizations (e.g., mergers and alliances), it is very important for the OSS of different telecom carriers to share information and processing. Hence standards have had different levels of impact on telecom businesses over the last decade[15].

The previous generation OSS is too clumsy, too complicated and too big for many of the present day solutions in view of the tremendous deregulation and the need for many smaller companies to come into the sector. TMF is coming out with a Next Generation Operating Support System (NGOSS) design, which is going to be a completely new way of designing OSS for applications service providers, internet service providers and telecom service providers.

Figure 64 summarizes the TMF guidelines and recommendations on e-business management from a telecommunication industry perspective. TMF guidelines are in the following major forms[30]:

- Telecommunications Operations Map (TOM) illustrates the various technologies and their relationships and assists in deriving a management solutions for a telecommunication industry
- Information Agreements deal with information models and formats for the exchange of information across different telecom service providers
- Business Agreements provide business workflows and contracts for the exchange of telecommunication service business (e-business) across organizations.

Appendix 2 describes the TMF recommendations for e-business management in the telecom industry, also known as Fulfillment, Assurance and Billing (FAB) processes.

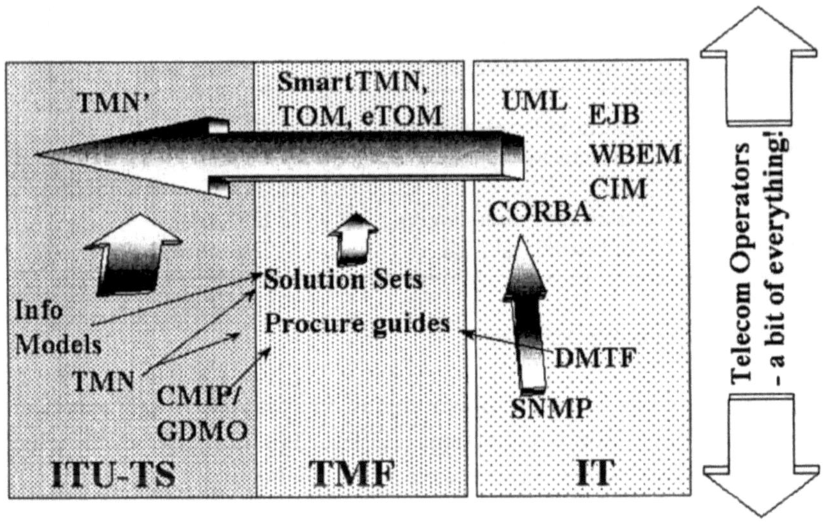

Figure 64. TMF Guidelines for Integrated Service Management

8.2.5 DMTF/CSC PRS based on CIM

Chapter 5 discussed support management standards called Problem Resolution Standards (PRS) that consists of SIS and SES. It may be noted that the main role of service support standards (PRS) is to resolve the semantic differences of stating a problem and its solutions. These standards help in automating the management of faults and their solutions. This section presents the vertical integration of PRS with DMTF CIM. This Section illustrates the use of DMTF CIM and XML for PRS as per the presentation by Chmaj and associates[2].

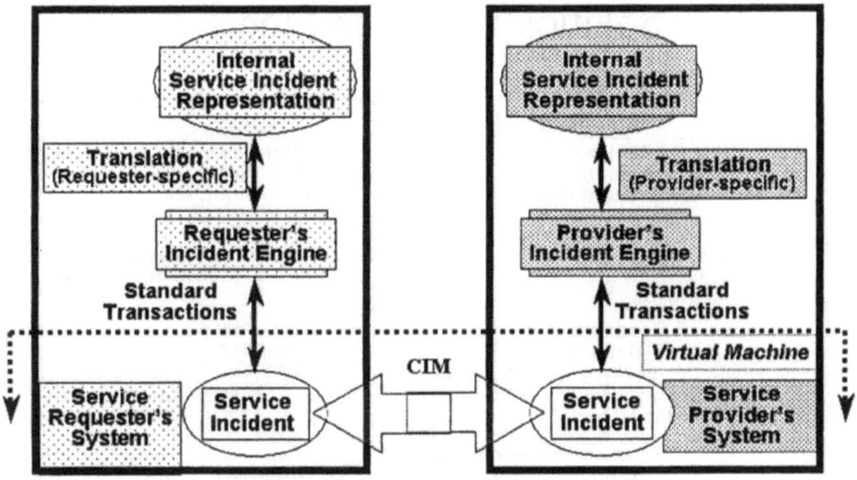

Figure 65. SIS based on CIM[2]

Figure 65 shows the framework for SIS based on CIM. This is presented in the context of service incidents (trouble-tickets) sharing across service providers, each having its own service incident representation. As discussed in Chapter 6, SIS provides a standard representation that enables the sharing of service incidents amongst these organizations. This, however, needs to be supported by appropriate management information models at the infrastructure management level (applications, platforms and instrumentation). Figure 65 shows the architecture of a virtual management platform using DMTF CIM for the exchange of management information at the platform level.

Service Incident transactions may include the following:

- Service Request
- Entitlement
- Problem Submittal
- Acknowledgment
- Problem Resolution
- Request Problem Information
- Provide Problem Information
- Provide Admin Information
- Query Incident
- Reject Resolution
- Reject Closure
- Confirm Close

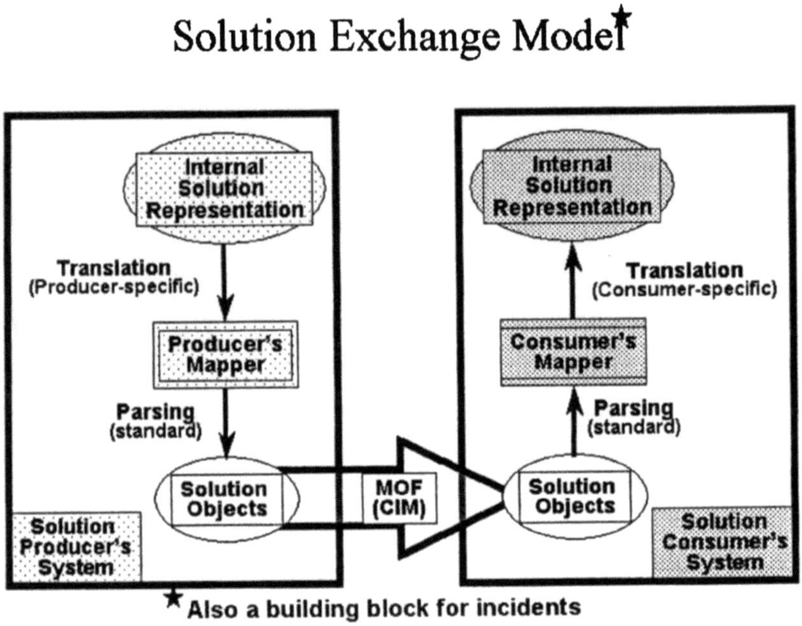

Figure 66. Solution Excahnge Standard (SES) Model

Figure 66 presents the Solution Exchange Standard (SES) in a similar context.

A Solution is subdivided into Problems, References and/or Resolutions. A Solution always has at least one of these elements and may have more than one. However, in the case of a Solution with multiple Problems, References and/or Resolutions, all of the elements always relate to a single issue. We now discuss the objects (Problems, Resolution and Reference) used for the definition of interoperable solutions based on SES and CIM[5].

A Problem is a description of a single issue. It may include symptoms, causes and other descriptive information, including product identification. **PRS_PROBLEM** is the aggregating object for a Problem.

A Resolution is used to describe how a Problem may be corrected. When a Solution contains a Problem, it typically contains one or more Resolutions. **PRS_RESOLUTION** is the aggregating object for a Resolution.

A Reference is used for general or non-diagnostic content that does not follow the Problem/Resolution paradigm. Solutions may be composed entirely of one or more References. This structure allows for non-diagnostic information to be exchanged. Examples of such information are: specifications, product documentation, FAQ's and similar reference material. References may also be used in combination with diagnostic content (Problems and Resolutions) when supplemental material needs to be provided with a Solution. **PRS_REFERENCE** serves as the aggregating object for a Reference[5].

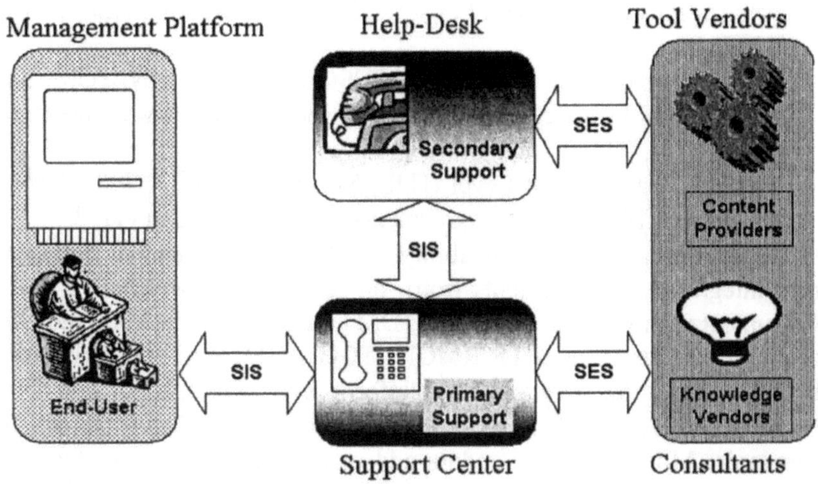

Figure 67. SES/SIS in the Context of E-Business Management [5]

Solutions, Problems, References or Resolutions may all benefit from classification. For example, a Solution may be related to installation issues, printing or specific functionality of a program.

Figure 67 shows the usage of SES and SIS in the process of e-business management involving a chain of support organizations, such as help-desk, primary support center, and other resources including vendor experts. Since help-desk-based trouble-ticketing provides the most well-understood model of e-business management, it is important to provide a linkage between DMTF standards and the ITSM guidelines discussed in Part 5. An industry body called It Service Management Forum (ITSMF) is now active internationally. Its charter advances ITIL process management guidelines to the IT industry.

8.3 Interoperability of Management Technologies

This book (Chapters 5-8) has presented standards at levels of network management, systems management, applications management, service and business management. This philosophy is partly supported by TMN layers. Some Standards support multiple levels as summarized below:

- Network Management Level (SNMP, OSI, TMN, RMON, WBEM, TINA, SPIRT)
- Systems Management Level (DMI, CIM, XSLM, JMAPI,LDAP, SNIA, WBEM)
- Applications Management Level (RM-ODP, ARM/AIC, XSLM, JMAPI, WBEM)
- Service Management Level (ITIL, SES/SIS, TINA, TMN, TOM, SPIRT, X.790, TMF Information Agreements) some of which were presented in Part 3
- Business Management Level (ITIL, SES/SIS, TOM, X.790, TMN, ISO XA/XA+, TMF Business Agreements) was presented in Part 3.

Table 9 presents the applicability of different management standards for the integrated management from an e-business perspective. At the instrumentation level, SNMP MIBs, DMTF DMI and OSI Managed Objects are now standardized. IETF RMON, TOG ARM, AIC standards are also being added at this level. At the platform level, TINA DPE, DMTF CIM, OMG CORBA and OSI System Management Functions are the major standards. Most platform vendors add many other proprietary features for effective management support. The management application level standards are now evolving. Some of the important evolving standards are TOG (ARM, AIC & XSLM), CSC (SES, SIS), and DMTF WBEM.

As there are so many different types of technologies in this domain of integrated management, it is quite possible that e-businesses will need to focus on management despite heterogeneity in standards used. Such a situation would be best handled from the fundamentals. A common mechanism is needed for:

- Shared data
- Shared business processes
- Shared semantics

Table 9. Comparison of Integrated Management Standards from e-business Perspective

Standards Body	**Standards/Support Mechanisms**	**Support for Distributed Management**	**Support for TMN Layers**	**Support for E-Business Management**
IETF	Protocol, MIBs	Limited	EML Only	None
DMTF	RPC,CIM, MIF, MOF,XML, LDAP	Yes, through CIM, XML and LDAP (WBEM)	EML, NML, SML	Yes, through WBEM, and joint efforts with CSC & ITSMF
ITU	OSI Mgmt, TMN hierarchy, reference points, X.790	Not Clear	EML, NML, SML	Limited, X.790 supports interoperability in telecom

Standards Body	Standards/Support Mechanisms	Support for Distributed Management	Support for TMN Layers	Support for E-Business Management
				business
ISO	OSI Mgmt CMIP, GDMO &, RM-ODP Distribution Viewpoints	Conceptual framework only	EML, NML	None
TINA-C	TINA Business Model, , Ref Points	Yes, ODP concepts +CORBA	NML, SML, BML	Models for telecom business,
CSC	SES, SIS	Yes, through CIM	SML, BML	Yes, CIM-based architectural framework
ITSMF	ITIL	NA	SML, BML	Yes, Best Practices
TMF	Guidelines-SPIRT, SMART, TOM etc.	NA	All	Yes, through guidelines, business and info. agreements
TOG	ARM, AIC, XSLM	Yes, through Special Agents	EML, NML, SML	NA

We have also seen the efforts towards horizontal integration and vertical integration of e-business management through standards suites, such as CSC/DMTF (PRS), ITU-T TMN, TINA, and TMF recommendations (eTOM).

The above sections have discussed the architectural perspective of integration and interoperability. However, it is important to bring these technologies together with software engineering methodologies, such as Unified Modeling Language (UML), for the development of future e-business service management solutions[17]. We discuss this topic in Part 5.

The next section illustrates the above concepts of integrated management of e-business from the perspective of a telecom service provider.

8.4 Discussion of E-business Management in the Telecom Industry

Many e-business service management technologies have to date evolved from the telecommunication world. Integration is a key driver within and between businesses. Telecommunication service providers (e-telcos) must cooperate to facilitate end-to-end solutions. As the number of such providers continues to grow at an ever-increasing rate, the imperative to inter-operate grows stronger. This need is driven by the customer demand for functionally rich end-to-end communications solutions. This section illustrates the concepts of e-business management (discussed all through Chapters 2-8) through a case study of e-business in telecommunication industry (e-telco).

In this decade of deregulation of telecommunication industry, integration is seen as the means by which e-telcos can improve the quality of customer service; introduce innovative new services; improve flow-through provisioning; lower costs; quickly develop business relationships with other parties; and use existing infrastrcuture and technologies where possible.

Firstly, we discuss the business characteristics of an e-telco organization. This is followed by a discussion of e-business management concepts, architectures and standards in terms of the four major management attributes (people, organization, process and technology). The discussion of management technology is organized along the main constituents of integrated management framework (instrumentation, platform and application).

8.4.1 E-Business in Telecommunication

The telecommunications industry is undergoing revolutionary change that is redefining the marketplace and creating lucrative opportunities for legacy and new players. Less than ten years ago, it was very easy to identify a telecommunications company. Primarily, telecommunications focused on telephony and providing telephone service, with data services only just beginning to gain in popularity. This section is largely based on the white paper from Entrust Technologies[6].

Today, there are hundreds of telecommunications companies thanks to rapid changes in the business environment as stated below[6]:

- The evolution of digital technology is enabling the convergence of all forms of information - email, video, audio, graphics and text - that must be communicated.
- The Internet has become a key communications medium and it has facilitated society's evolution as a global community.
- Deregulation is happening around the world. and legacy long distance carriers are reinventing themselves to address growing customer and competitive demands.
- New entrants are creating and packaging services that merge the ingredients of both communications and information technology (IT) and blur their boundaries.

An e-telco, therefore, offers voice, data communications and related services as its primary business. This industry definition then includes telecom carriers, cable providers, Application Service Providers (ASPs) and Internet Service Providers (ISPs).

8.4.1.1 Business Trends

Five key trends are impacting the telecommunications industry today[6]:

- *The rapid evolution of the Internet*: In the year 2000, it was widely reported that there were approx. seven billion people in the world and one billion web pages[34].Business-to-Business (B2B) revenue will approach $1.3 trillion in 2004[6]. Interest in the Internet already spans all customer markets and the one consistent concern is security, regardless of the customer's size or degree of activity.
- *The demand for data*: The demand for data is predicted to be much more than that for voice. One of the more pervasive examples of that demand is the customer's pursuit of high speed Internet access.
- *New and improving technology*: Although new technology is having an impact throughout telecommunications, one of the most visible areas is the wireless sector. According to industry estimates, by the year 2003, U.S. cell-phone penetration is anticipated to be 60%, with Japan approaching 70% and Europe over 80%[6].
- *Demand for services*: Business customers want to focus on their core business, and procure outside services for non-strategic functions. In addition, both businesses and consumers want to be empowered by having access to services and information when it is convenient to them, e.g., ordering and order status.
- *The changing regulatory environment*: Deregulation is encouraging telecommunications companies to enter each other's markets, resulting in increased competition from both traditional and new entrants. This increased competition further stimulates globalization, as companies move to add geography, customers, expertise and technology to their businesses.

8.4.1.2 Current Initiatives

In telecommunications, both new and legacy telecom competitors are reacting to this competitive environment and its trends by adopting a series of initiatives targeted to help them survive and thrive[6]:

- Build or acquire more network capacity to respond to universal demand
- Develop new revenue sources, businesses and environments
- Create and/or package new offerings
- Develop and/or package targeted "killer" applications to further drive Internet use and associated revenues
- Incorporate security into supporting IT infrastructure to address customer concerns
- Partner or acquire to provide "best of breed" integrated customer solutions and gain competitive advantage

- Sell services across all markets, prioritizing and packaging them differently for each market
- Develop and provide access services to support the user wherever s/he is, whatever communications device s/he is using, for voice and/or data
- Attract and retain more customers by improving customer service and aggressively cross selling
- Leverage the Internet to become a more efficient, profitable e-business

Leveraging the Internet will be key, since as predicted by the Gartner Group, the volume of business-to-consumer (B2C) transactions will reach $380 billion by 2003, and B2B will exceed $7 trillion by 2004[7].

8.4.1.3 Financial Benefits of E-business in Telco

If a company can provide this trusted environment, not only will business transactions be secure, but also it can:[6]

- Open new markets that can only be supported in a secured environment
- Improve cost effectiveness by better utilizing automated systems
- Build competitive advantage with accessible, user friendly customer services
- Shorten time to market by facilitating the introduction of new applications of services
- Forge closer, more productive business relationships with convenient efficient processes
- Mitigate risk using a secured transaction infrastructure

In addition to the business reasons for implementing a trust infrastructure, the financial benefits of becoming an e-Telco are also considerable[6]:

- *Procurement* - By moving procurement on-line, one leading Telco is expecting a transactions cost savings of 90% and a direct savings of $1 billion.
- *Customer Care* - On-line order management, customer self-services, help desk and technical support can dramatically decrease cost from over $700 for a field visit to $100 for a call center contact to $7.50 for a Web site interaction.
- *Billing*- One large global Telco has stated that services such as electronic billing and payment allow it to save $1 for every bill the customer pays on-line.

All of these savings add up. PricewaterhouseCoopers (PwC) evaluated a residential Telco with 10 million lines and a cost base of $5 billion. The potential savings were estimated as shown in Table 10[6]:

Table 10. Savings from e-business in telecommunication industry[6]

No	E-Business Initiative	Savings

No	E-Business Initiative	Savings
1	e-Procurement for all third party spending plus supply chain integration for major equipment purchasing	10-15%
2	e-Enablement (and potential outsourcing) of finance, HR and other back office functions	25%
3	e-Enablement (and potential outsourcing) of 20% IT Operations and development	20%
4	e-Enablement of customer acquisition, sales force operations and customer care	20-30%
5	Outsourcing of network construction (not including separate procurement opportunities)	10%
6	e-Enablement of field force operators and management (providing service and equipment	15-20%
7	e-Enablement (and potential outsourcing) of building/facilities management plus enabled remote working	20%

8.4.1.4 Management Strategy

A focused e-telco business delivers the following strategic message to its internal organizational, operational and technological departments:

- All processes of the business will be automated as much as possible.
- All processes of the business are on the road to integration. This will include integration with manual processes if automation is not an immediate possibility.
- All processes will be built to be adaptive.

The key attribute is "adaptability". This is the ability of an information system to participate readily in a re-organization of the business processes with minimal cost of effort to the business. E-business management systems that are adaptable must have the property of extendibility. The business needs to work towards building modular e-business management systems, how this is done will be discussed later.

Telecommunications Management Network (TMN) can be viewed as a vision that started with a narrower incumbent telecommunications provider focus that eventually evolved to a much broader concept. The trend for TMN standards has been towards technology-neutral models. They have evolved into a framework designed to ensure that both existing models and future models are reused as much as possible[11]. These models for e-business management in a telecom service provider are implemented through Operations Support Systems (OSS).

We now discuss the technologies and standards for e-business management at different architectural levels (similar to those defined in TMN). The levels in an e-telco environment are as follows:

- Business Process Level
- Service Level
- Infrastructure Level

- Network Management
- Systems Management
- Application Management

8.4.2 Management at Business Process Level

An e-telco can no longer model a business in isolation and needs to consider an ever-increasing number of external partners, including other service providers, suppliers of equipment and suppliers of management systems as discussed in Part 1. Management at business process level involves three types of factors, namely people, organization and process. We discuss these factors now starting with people issues.

8.4.2.1 People Issues

The skill sets required to achieve the delicate balance of taking the existing e-business management systems towards an integrated future are scarce at this time and concentrated in a few specialist software houses. Specialist software houses are going to be the key drivers in this market for the next few years because building adaptable e-business management systems for e-telco requires people with an understanding of TMN, RM-ODP, TINA, DPE (e.g. CORBA, EJB, RMI, CIM) Internet and Web technology blended with creativity and flexibility. It is a skill set hard to obtain and retain since most people with these skills have either formed new businesses to serve this market or have been recruited by such a business.

One of the really pressing issues for the telecommunication industry is to address the scarcity of skills in this area and the even scarcer fusion of skills required to blend these technologies with appropriate e-telco business acumen. This accounts for the current enthusiasm by both traditional network infrastructure creators and large solution houses for merger with, acquisition of and buy-in to smaller traditional OSS development houses. The race is on to acquire a limited skill set to the information required to run an e-telco business is most conveniently and cost effectively delivered over an Internet/Web based infrastructure. The only way the smaller e-telcos can harness these skills is to find reliable third party solutions and extensions on the open market either through acquisition, joint venture or partnership.

8.4.2.2 Organization Issues

ISO RM-ODP provides a great conceptual framework for the analysis of distributed systems. It considers different viewpoints, starting from the enterprise or organizational viewpoint that models distributed systems, such as an e-telcos, from a high level. RM-ODP also provides the mechanism for mapping the enterprise viewpoint to informational and computational viewpoints relevant to the development of software applications for e-business management.

An e-business organization is very much dependent on e-business processes. Hence we discuss the process issues next.

8.4.2.3 Process Issues

The TeleManagement Forum (TMF) describes Telecom Operations Map (TOM) as a high-level model of telecom operations that details key business and operational processes in service - Fulfillment, Assurance and Billing (FAB). It is a road map aimed at aligning the common processes performed by e-telcos. Without such an initiative beyond the business boundaries of each e-telco there would be little chance of the information and interfaces required to ensure the integration of information support systems ever happening. Where possible and as far as possible an e-telco should align its business processes with those identified in the TOM as described in Appendix 2. The TOM is being refined by TMF for e-business with eTOM.

Only with properly modeled business and operational processes and a clear understanding of the e-business management systems road map for business, will it be possible to move forward on integrating billing, customer care and network and service management functions. This will happen firstly, when the communication between these functions is improved by identifying and aligning with Business Agreements and Information Agreements. Such agreements are driven by organizations including the TMF, which now carry forward the TMN vision through Smart TMN. Secondly, new e-business management systems must be built using technologies designed to support well-defined transparent interfaces that can be distributed, published, subscribed and supported by authorization and authentication. Thirdly, the appropriate skill sets must be harnessed, developed and effectively applied.

8.4.3 Management at Service Level

The key to the future of the industry is in providing flexible services that can be found, used and successfully charged for. These services will, in turn, depend entirely on the e-business management systems that comprise and support them. Services must provide interfaces for their clients. These interfaces and hence information and services that can be traded for and used with appropriate authentication and authorization, are the key to a successful move to integrated and adaptive e-business systems. Key issues at this level are:

- Integration of technologies for Service Level Management (SLM)
- Help-Desk based SLM operations environment

- Deployment Strategies
- Security Framework

The notion of a service has been extended beyond the narrow use of the original TMN. TINA provides a clear separation between service interface and management interface using a. layered architecture, e.g., a service layer associated with Service Level Agreements (SLAs), etc. Service Level Management (SLM) systems automate service management by linking SLAs to underlying e-business infrastructure. Appendix 4 shows how existing standards, such as service monitoring MIB for SNMP from IETF are being used in the implementation of commercial SLM systems. In addition to these application-monitoring technologies, such as TOG ARM, are very useful for SLM. The use of intelligent agents is becoming more and more prevalent for service management as discussed in Chapter 7. Standards in this are expected to evolve with the increasing sophistication of e-business management.

Help-desk based trouble-ticketing forms the core infrastructure for service management in an e-telco. The telecommunication industry presently uses the ITU-T X.790 standards for sharing trouble-ticketing information amongst partner e-telcos, each having its own legacy, proprietary trouble-ticketing system This may be enhanced further using DMTF/CSC Problem Resolution Standards (PRS) consisting of SIS and SES that provide an object-oriented, system-independent framework.

A service can represent any capability that can be published and subscribed to. An instance of a recent application of this service concept with a low-level device focus is the Java Jini initiative. Jini is concerned with impromptu self-publication of services and devices so that they can be discovered and used by others. However, it is only available in a Java language environment. The act of acquiring a service may require that the entity making use of the service be authorized to use the service through a subscription. A subscription to a service may or may not incur costs, such as for maintenance of the service and for usage. The TINA Service Architecture presents a subscription model that covers charging for usage of services.

A key enabler for adaptive service management is free and unfettered public operational interfaces constrained only by authorization. This provides management information and service availability anywhere, any time to any suitably authorized party, which is easy to accomplish within an organization but nowhere near as easy to accomplish externally. Hence there is a major move towards the implementation of trusted and secure e-business environments with Public Key Infrastructures (PKI) provided by companies, such as Entrust Technologies[6].

8.4.4 Management at Infrastructure Level

Traditional OSSs have a history of development based on a mainframe centric, monolithic build for a small group of operational users in a heavily regulated industry. With de-regulation, more e-telcos and more service offerings over the number of traditional OSSs continue to grow at an ever-increasing rate. Hence TMF has defined an integrated set of standards for e-telcos called OMNIPoint[25]. These standards may be discussed in terms of the components of integrated management framework:

- Management instrumentation
- Management platforms
- Management applications

8.4.4.1 Management Instrumentation Level

The information that is currently available from traditional OSSs is still network-specific and based on manager/agent paradigms, CMIP/GDMO and SNMP/SMI, mediation or gateway conversion. TMN vision itself has evolved to a much broader ambit with RM-ODP, TINA and CORBA all within its scope. A new round of modeling with a set of more technology neutral objectives has seen a number of the earlier Guidelines for the definition of Managed Objects (GDMO) based models cast into more technology neutral models. Gradually, IETF SNMP based instrumentation standards are now proliferating.

8.4.4.2 Management Platform Level

The next consideration is at the platform level implemented as OSS in telcos. A combination of current technologies is considered by the TeleManagement Forum as necessary to building e-business management systems and this guideline is the impetus for their Technology Integration Map. The map is a pragmatic attempt to identify and document the technologies that will need to be mastered and understood to build integrated and adaptive OSSs from the current crop of OSSs and future OSSs. At the very least, three technology areas will need to be understood and integrated. These are:

1. Internet/Web based services
2. Object Request Broker (CORBA) based services
3. Telecom based Manager/Agent services (i.e. CMIP/GDMO and SNMP/SMI)

These services require a range of technologies, such as in the TMN, TINA and DPE (e.g., CORBA, EJB, RMI, CIM). TINA components all depend on an underlying Distributed Processing Environment (DPE) to function and communicate. The DPE includes the communications medium (e.g., CORBA) and services (e.g., lifecycle and persistence) that support the components. This infrastructure for distribution is a concept that has evolved from work on RM-ODP standards and has been a driver for many of the current crop of middleware offerings.

Object-oriented techniques were developed in response to the need to manage constantly changing requirements and the need to support adaptive modular designs. Enterprise models and operational models should be developed with a sharp focus on the principles derived from Object Oriented techniques. Using an Object Oriented approach eases the transition to modular information system designs based on open interfaces and open information models. Likewise, the newer technologies support Object Oriented information models and interfaces.

DMTF CIM with XML and DEN may be the future standard at the platform level for e-telcos.

8.4.4.3 Management Application Level

Standard and well-defined interfaces propel the existing body of information systems and new e-business management systems toward a modular component paradigm assisting future integration requirements and maximizing the chance for such integration. Integration cannot be achieved easily without modularity, and modularity cannot be achieved easily without an industry that is willing to forge the appropriate agreements between businesses. TMF has defined standard business agreements for e-telcos[30].

Management applications for OSS are mostly developed in-house by telecom service providers. Integration issues at this level are as follows:

- Legacy Applications
- Application Development Methodology
- Role of new distributed application concepts (e.g., Traders)

Since it is impractical to change all applications at the same time, it is important to work out the strategy for integrating legacy applications. A tactical consequence of the adaptive process strategy can be stated as follows:

- Existing "legacy" systems will be wrapped in such a way so as to present a standardized interface compliant with a well-embraced and supported industry Information Agreement. The agreement will be made available to all authenticated parties with the appropriate authorization. TMF standard information agreements may be used for this purpose.[26]
- New systems will present a standard operational interface.

We now consider the methodologies for management application development. RM-ODP standards attempted to clarify the means by which distributed management applications, and the services they offered, could be specified. TINA attempted to go beyond this but with a telecommunications emphasis, putting meat on the bones and identifying the additional services required to support robust and adaptable e-business management systems for telecommunications providers. A business in this situation needs to look outwards to organizations like the TeleManagement Forum for an integration road map and to software development houses with TMN, RM-ODP, TINA and DPE (e.g., CORBA, EJB, CIM) experience[26]. OMG standard object-oriented software development methodology Unified Modeling Language (UML) is now being used for e-telcos[19]. However, UML does not consider human cooperation aspects in the design of management applications. Part 5 of this book discusses this issue through CoMENS.

We now consider the role of *Trader*- a major concept in distributed applications that has been standardized by ISO, OMG and TINA. From the lowest to the highest levels within TINA, interfaces to services are published to a DPE service called a Trader. The Trader function is intended to be the "glue" that binds components together in that it is the way to discover other components that meet the need to provide a service. Services provided by components in TINA may be freely available in a given context. An example of this behavior is a set of components that interact with each other in a single system to provide a major service. These components would not necessarily be visible outside the system. TINA denotes these as "system services". In this case it is probable that only the interface to the major service would be published externally. Traders within a "TINA universe" would be federated (in effect making use of each other's data) to facilitate global service publishing and acquisition. As discussed above, Traders may only publish some interfaces, where it is the Trader that has overall responsibility for the security and validation (typing of interface, checking QoS values etc.) of the interfaces published to it.

Appendices 2 and 4 discuss more technical details on how integrated management (at business, service, and network levels) is being implemented for e-telco organizations.

8.5 Chapter Summary

This chapter presented the integration and interoperability of e-business management solutions in the context of emerging standards. We have seen some motivations and techniques for horizontal integration, i.e., integration across e-business partners. This was followed by a discussion of vertical integration, i.e., the integration of e-business at different layers in a top-down manner. We illustrated some standard suites, such as TMN (with OSI Management), TINA (with RM-ODP and CORBA), TOM (with ITIL), and PRS (with CIM) for this purpose.

The integration of these different standards and technologies for e-business management was illustrated through a case study of e-business management for telecommunication service providers (e-telcos). We discussed the trends and various applications of e-business applications for an e-telco. This was followed by a brief discussion of the applicability of different standards at various levels for e-telcos. Appendices 2 and 4 supplement this discussion.

The next part consisting of Chapters 9 and 10, will discuss e-business management from the lifecycle and methodology perspective through the discussion of our new Cooperative management Methodology for E-business Networks and Services (CoMENS).

8.6 REFERENCES

1. Chmaj J., "Customer Support Consortium Update", DMTF Developers Conference, May 2000, USA
2. Deitel H.M, Deitel P.J. and Steinbuhler K., *E-Business and E-Commerce for Managers*, Prentice Hall, 2001, ISBN:0-13-032364-0
3. DMTF, "CIM Tutorial", http://www.dmtf.org/spec/cim_tutorial/, March 2001
4. DMTF, "Web Based Enterprise Management (WBEM) Standards", http://www.dmtf.org/spec/wbem.html, March 2001
5. DMTF, "DMTF-CSC Support Standards", http://www.dmtf.org/spec/stan.html, March 2001
6. Entrust Technologies, "e-business Solutions for the Telecommunications Industry", http://www.entrust-technologies.com.au, Company white paper released in April 2001
7. Goldman and Sachs, "Where the Money Is: B2B-Money is in the profiling B2B buyers", 6 January 2000:30, http://www.iconocast.com/issue/20000010603.html
8. Hamada T., Kamata H. and Hogg S., "An Overview of TINA Management Architecture", *Journal of Network and Systems Management*, Vol. 5, No. 4, December 1997
9. IBM, "An Open e-Business Foundation", IBM E-Business White Paper, 1997
10. IT Service Management Forum (ITSMF), "ITSMF-DMTF Alliance", DMTF Developers Conference, June 2000, USA
11. Internet Engineering Task Force (IETF), "Application MIB", 1998, www.ietf.org
12. ITU-T Recommendation X.790 (11/95) - Trouble Management function for ITU-T applications, http://www.itu.int/plweb-cgi/fastweb?getdoc+view1+itudoc+5727+1++X.790

13. International Telecommunications Union (ITU-T), "TMN Roadmap", http://www.itu.int/TMN/, 1997
14. ITU-T X.901 | ISO/IEC 10746-1: Open Distributed Processing Reference Model - Part 1, 1997
15. Kavanagh D., "Establishing an End-to-end Integrated Management Platform by Combining Network and Service Management with Operational Support Systems (OSS's)", Forge Australia White Paper, www.forge.com.au/products/Papers, December 1999
16. Lawrence D.G., "Service Incident and Knowledge Exchange", DMTF Developers Conference, June 2000, USA
17. Lewis D., "A Review of Approach to Developing Service Management Systems", *Journal of Network and Systems Management (JNSM),* Vol. 8, No. 2, June 2000
18. Lucent Technologies, "Business Transaction Management", A Vitalsoft White Paper, August 2000, http://www.lucentservices.com/knowledge/whitepapers/index.asp
19. Object Management Group (OMG), "Common Object Request Broker Architecture (CORBA) Common Facilities", http://www.omg.org
20. Orfali R., Harkey D., and Edwards J., *Client/Server Survival Guide*, John Wiley & Sons, 1999, ISBN: 0-471-31615-6
21. Organization of Government Commerce (OGC formerly CCTA), "ITIL and BSI Code of Practice on IT Service Management", IT Service Management Forum (ITSMF) web site in UK, http://www.itsmf.com/itsmf/i2.htm, April 2001
22. Ray P., *Cooperative Management of Enterprise Networks*, Kluwer Academic/Plenum Publications, May 2000, ISBN:0-306-46276-1
23. Shrewsbury J.K., "An Introduction to TMN", *Journal of Network and Systems Management (JNSM)*, Vol. 3, No. 1, March 1995
24. Telecommunications Information Networking Architecture Consortium (TINA-C), "TINA Business Model and Reference Points", Version 4.0, May 1997
25. Tele Management Forum (TMF), "A Service Management Business Process Model", 1995.
26. Tele Management Forum (TMF), "OMNIPoint Integration Architecture", Forum TR114, 1994
27. Tele Management Forum (TMF), "Service Provider's Integrated Requirements for Information Technology (SPIRT)", http://www.nmf.org/books.htm#spirit, Jan 1996
28. Tele Management Forum (TMF), "Solution and Component Sets", http://www.nmf.org/sets.htm, 1997
29. TeleManagement Forum (TMF), "Performance Reporting Definitions Document", NMF701, April 1997

30. TeleManagement Forum, Telecom Operations Map (pdf version 1.3) GB910, October 2000, http://www.tmforum.org/
31. TeleManagement Forum, "Service Quality Management Business Agreement", http://www.tmforum.org/
32. TeleManagement Forum, "Smart TMN Technology Integration Map", GB909 issue 1.1, October 1998, http://www.tmforum.org/
33. Umar A., *Object-Oriented Client/Server Internet Environments*, Prentice Hall, 1997
34. Zhaner E., "Ahoy, Internet Companies", *USA Today*, 7 June 2000

PART-5

COLLABORATION VIEWPOINT

Chapter 9. Cooperative E-business Management

Part 1 presented a broad overview of e-business, including e-government, e-commerce and e-health, and a broad overview of various approaches to e-business management. Part 2 discussed the need for a methodology (with an illustrative example) for the development and management of services. The concepts of generic service design and management are illustrated with an e-health example. Part 3 provided a top-down discussion of the architectural aspects of integrated management of e-business (processes, transactions and infrastructures). Part 3 also discussed help-desk business processes and Service Level Management (SLM) platforms. We illustrated state of the art operations and implementation of e-business management. Part 4 presented a discussion of integrated management standards and technologies from the perspective of e-business infrastructure management.

Part 5, consisting of Chapters 9 and 10, combines all the knowledge from Parts 1 to 4 into a methodology for the development of integrated management solutions from a collaborative e-business perspective. This methodology called Cooperative methodology for Management of E-business Networks and Services (CoMENS), is a variation of the cooperative methodology, CoMEN, described in Ray's book[21]. CoMENS blends some recent developments in software engineering with CSCW concepts used in CoMEN. This chapter presents the software engineering and CSCW concepts underpinning CoMENS and the requirements analysis phase of the methodology. In Chapter 10 we discuss the design and evaluation of CoMENS. We illustrate CoMENS with management scenarios from telecommunication industry.

We begin with a discussion of the multi-disciplinary nature of e-business management processes. Then we discuss relevant concepts from software engineering and the role of CSCW in integrated management. This is followed by a description of CoMENS methodology, and its three major constituents, namely requirements engineering, design, and evaluation.

9.1 Multi-Disciplinary Nature of E-Business Management

As discussed in previous parts, e-business management presents a number of formidable challenges due to the following factors:

1. Efficient e-business management requires the understanding of a number of types of processes and concepts that originate from different disciplines, such as Sociology, Psychology, Computer Science, Software

Engineering, Telecommunication Engineering and Management Science. Hence it is not sufficient to present the problem and its solutions from a technical perspective with protocols and architectures.

2. It may be noted that almost all integrated management solutions are in software. Therefore, the development of an integrated management solution needs to use an appropriate software engineering methodology. Total Quality Management (TQM) theories suggest that the quality of a product depends on the quality of the process for making the product.
3. Since e-business management is critical for the survival and growth of many types of businesses, it is important that the e-business management strategies are understood clearly by people at higher levels of management.

For these reasons, we present e-business management development strategy from a high-level methodology perspective. The 8-stage service design and management model described in Part 2 is based on TQM theories. As discussed, this model is divided into two major phases - Design and Management. The management phase involves the following stages:

- Implementation and Deployment
- Measuring Performance
- Assessing Satisfaction
- Improving Performance

The first stage, Implementation and Deployment, is commonly used in the service design process in e-business as discussed in relation to ITSM in Part 3. We are mainly concerned with the last three stages in the development of a methodology for e-business service management.

Applying the same theory for software development, the development process becomes an important part of a development methodology. As discussed in Part 2, there could be five different approaches to systems development; development based on System Development Life Cycle (SDLC), prototype development (incremental development based on user participation), standard package-based development (depends on the availability of a package that would exactly fit the requirements), end-user development (user develops solutions using 4 GL tools, no programming involved) and outsourcing (development by third party).

Although SDLC is perhaps the most expensive (in time and cost) of all the above approaches, it is the most established conceptual framework for IS development and software engineering. However, it is a sequential process based on rigid deliverables after every stage. Hence it lacks the flexibility required to express deliverables for management solutions development that uses Commercial Of The Shelf (COTS) packages, prototypes to satisfy IKIWISI (I Know It When I See It), and outsourcing as used in modern e-businesses. Hence CoMENS uses an evolving model called Twin Peaks[18].

This model recognizes the practical reality that software solutions need to be developed incrementally in consultation with different groups of stakeholders (users, developers, business managers, etc.). Hence the 4-stage management development process described earlier can be adapted into the CoMENS software engineering methodology with three major stages:

- Requirements Engineering (for management measurements)
- Design (for management solutions and architecture)
- Evaluation (to assess user satisfaction)

The last stage of the Ramaswamy's model is concerned with improving performance - a generic management process as discussed in Part 2. This is not discussed as part of the software engineering methodology for e-business management solutions. On the other hand, it is important to discuss the methodology for e-business management software development from the perspective the cooperation of human, business and technical entities. That is best discussed using the concepts of CSCW.

9.2 Integrated Management as a CSCW Application

As defined in Part 4, integrated management is concerned with the integration of processes and techniques for network management, systems management, applications management, service management and business management. Although there have been substantial developments in techniques and protocols for integrated management at networks and systems levels, there has not been much work in integrating these techniques with management strategies at business and service levels.

This section discusses integrated management from the viewpoint of Computer Supported Cooperative Work (CSCW) and its constituents, such as workflows and groupware.

9.2.1 CSCW and its Evolution

J. Grudin, a well-known expert in this area, defines CSCW as "Computer-supported cooperative work, or CSCW, is the body of theory and practice which is concerned with the use of computers to support and enhance the work activities of groups. It involves work from a number of fields including: human-computer interaction, sociology, organizational psychology, user interface software, and distributed systems"[9]. This section will present a discussion on the evolution of CSCW systems from small local groups to larger wide-area and international networks - the common setting for the e-business environment.

9.2.1.1 Benefits of CSCW

The benefits of CSCW can be summarized as follows[9]:

- Efficiency
- Quality
- Networking
- Knowledge-sharing
- Better Customer Service
- Cost-Effective
- Concurrent Processes
- Control over Intellectual Property and Copyrights

A CSCW environment provides various tools to support joint working amongst co-workers at distance, in all phases of knowledge sharing, such as document preparation, consultation, joint design, contextual discussions and contextual evaluations. Since good management people are scarce, such tools are very useful in integrated management problems.

CSCW supports this through better tracking of customer information, using models, such as help-desk as discussed in Parts 3 and 4.

CSCW systems allow different team members to work concurrently in spite of differences in location and time zones. Since many mission-critical applications are now dependent on networks, cost of down time is very high. CSCW tools automatically keep track of any violations in copyrights or intellectual property rights. Busy management people do not need to worry about such issues.

9.2.1.2 Evolution of CSCW

Grudin describes the evolution of CSCW in terms of four concentric ellipses that characterise levels of cooperation required in various sizes of information system[9]. We present this from the perspective of enterprise network management processes (Figure 68). The innermost ring represents small networks managed by individual technicians. The outermost ring represents the management contexts of large network management organisations, such as telecommunication carriers and alliances for e-business. These are the two extremes of CSCW requirements. There has been a proliferation of networks in the inner two rings. For example, as small networks grow to medium size, management may require the cooperation of 4-5 persons located at different places (second innermost ring). On the other hand, many corporate networks now own fairly sophisticated management platforms, with multiple groups of people at different locations (second outermost ring). We now discuss cooperation requirements in these different network environments.

Large management organisations have people in multiple divisions/departments within the organisation, and people from external organisations, such as customers/vendors, cooperating to manage networks and their services. These organisations use a variety of platforms, and tools for the operation and management of their networks and businesses. People in these organisations are familiar with the interplay of social dynamics, organisational systems and human factors with network management processes[9].

Corporate enterprises may use formal network management platforms to manage their networks, perhaps spanning across continents. These organisations employ qualified network management personnel. However, there is now a tendency to use increasingly sophisticated help-desk systems to operate networks, using fewer skilled people. Such organisations therefore need cooperation across multiple groups of people with different levels of competence in network management.

Successful operation of CSCW systems requires effective communication at a number of communication interfaces. The major objective of this technological support is to diminish the cognitive gap between concepts easily understood by users and those used by system designers. The key elements of this support are as follows[23]:

- Easy Access to Information
- Improving Usability
- Maintaining Awareness

The implementation of CSCW systems involve the fusion of multimedia and wireless mobile communication technologies with businesses.

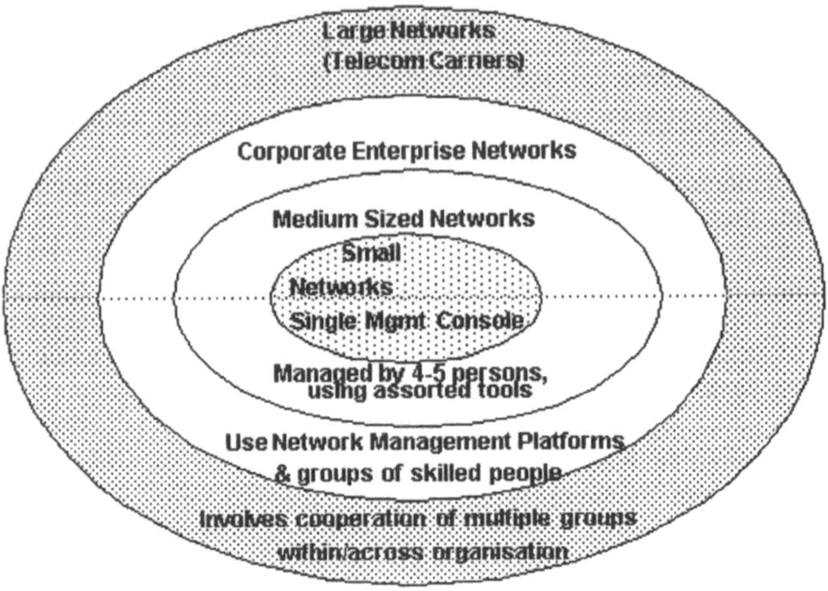

Figure 68. CSCW View of Integrated Network Management

The recent growth of multiple LANs and intranets have made many organisations critically dependent on a small group of say 4-5 support technicians. Such skilled people are scarce and must be adequately supported for the survival of organisational businesses. Therefore, small-group support is becoming more and more important for commercial network management product developers.

Computer Supported Cooperative Work (CSCW) facilitates cooperative activity involving groups of people interacting to achieve common goals. CSCW techniques can be broadly classified as:

- Groupware
- Workflows
- Communication Infrastructure (including mobile/multimedia)
- Autonomous Agents

Software tools, called "groupware", enrich a multiple user environment, such that users are aware of each others' activities.

Workflows and their support tools facilitate the definition, management and execution of work items involving human and software entitities to achieve a business process.

As discussed in Part 3 and 4, autonomous agents are intelligent agent software elements that can be invoked by certain events in a business process. Such agents are now extensively deployed over Internet search engines.

The next two sub-sections discuss the isues involved in the development of CSCW systems based on groupware and workflows.

9.2.2 CSCW in E-Business

CSCW techniques apply for business scenarios requiring the cooperation of human and software role for business tasks. Figures 69 and 70 shows the application of CSCW in telecommunication and healthcare industries.

Figure 69 depicts three management workflows in a telecom carrier[8]. The New Connection Provisioning Workflow captures the process of telephone service provisioning for a new customer. Task T0 involves an operator collecting line-provisioning activities. The objective of a provisioning activity is to construct a circuit from a customer location to the appropriate telephone, and to allocate equipment to connect the circuit. T2, T3 and T4 provide alternative means (in increasing order of cost) of achieving this objective. The manual work T5 is initiated by providing installation instructions (via hand-held terminals), and is completed when human engineers provide necessary work completion data. Task T6 involves changes in the telephone directory, while T7 updates the telephone switch to activate service and then generates the bill. Finally, task T8 involves a human operator who calls the customer to inform him of the establishment of the requested service and verify that the provided service meets the customer needs.

When sufficient customer data is collected, task T1 is performed to, (a) verify whether the information provided by the customer is accurate, and (b) create a corresponding service order record. On completion of T1, tasks T2, T3, and T4 are initiated to perform the tasks involved, the workflow defines the following task dependencies: (i) T1 starts after the completion of T0, (ii) T2, T3, T4, and T6 can be performed concurrently after task T1 is completed, (iii) T5 must start after the completion of T3 and T4, (iv) T7 is performed after the completion of T2, T5, and T6, and (v) T8 starts after T7 is completed.

Figure 70 illustrates CSCW in telemedicine as discussed in Chapter 4.

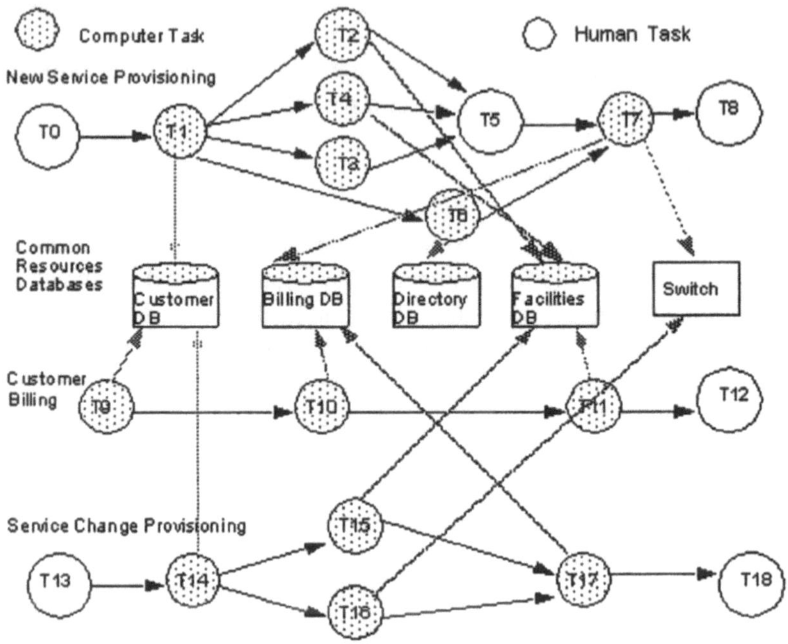

Figure 69. Workflows in Telecommunication Service Provisioning[8]

Figure 70. CSCW in Telemedicine

9.2.3 Groupware

While groupware is now being embraced in a variety of workgroup applications, it is important to be aware of some problems. Repeated, expensive groupware failures have resulted from not meeting certain challenges in design. Evaluation has identified a number of specific problem areas in the development of groupware as follows:

- Groupware applications often require additional work from individuals who do not perceive a direct benefit from the use of the application.
- Groupware may not enlist the "critical mass" of users required to be useful, or can fail because one individual in the group does not want to use it.
- Groupware can lead to activity that violates social taboos, threatens existing political structures, or otherwise discourages users crucial to its success.
- Groupware may not accommodate the wide range of exception handling and improvisation that characterizes much group activity
- Features that support group processes are used relatively infrequently, requiring unobtrusive accessibility and integration with more heavily used features.
- Intuitions in product development environments are especially poor for multi-user applications, resulting in bad management decisions and error-prone design process.
- Groupware requires more careful implementation in the workplace than single-used product developers have confronted.

While the first four points require better knowledge of the intended user's workplace, the final three require changes in the development process as discussed in a number of references on CSCW applications in telecommunications [2,9,11,19]. Some of these problems are explained below with particular reference to integrated management in Ray's book [21].

9.2.4 Workflows

Georgakopoulus and associates define workflows as "Workflow is a collection of tasks organized to accomplish some business process (e.g., processing e-purchase orders, e-provisioning of telecommunication services, e-healthcare insurance claims). A task can be performed by one or more software systems, one or a team of humans, or a combination of these. Human tasks include interacting with computers closely (e.g., providing input commands) or loosely (e.g., using computers only to indicate task progress)". Examples of tasks include updating a file or database, generating or mailing a bill, and laying a cable. In addition to a collection of tasks, a workflow defines the order of task invocation or condition(s) under which tasks must be invoked, task synchronization, and information flow[8].

It is possible to characterizes workflows along a continuum from Human-Oriented to System-Oriented as shown in Figure 71[8]. On the one extreme, Human-Oriented workflow involves humans collaborating in performing tasks and coordinating tasks. The requirements of workflow systems in this environment are to support the coordination and collaboration of humans and to improve human effectiveness. On the other extreme, System-Oriented workflow involves computer systems that perform computation-intensive operations and specialized software tasks. Real-life systems fall somewhere between the two extremes defined in Figure 71. While human-oriented workflow implementations often control and coordinate human tasks, system-oriented workflow implementations control and coordinate software tasks (typically with little or no human intervention).

Transactional workflows involve coordinated execution of multiple tasks that (i) may involve humans, (ii) require access to heterogeneous, autonomous and distributed systems, and (iii) support selective use of transactional properties (e.g., atomicity, consistency, isolation, and/or durability) for individual tasks or entire workflows. Unlike traditional Data Base Management Systems (DBMS) and Transaction Processing (TP) systems, workflow systems need to selectively use transactional properties. This is particularly true for integrated network and systems management systems.

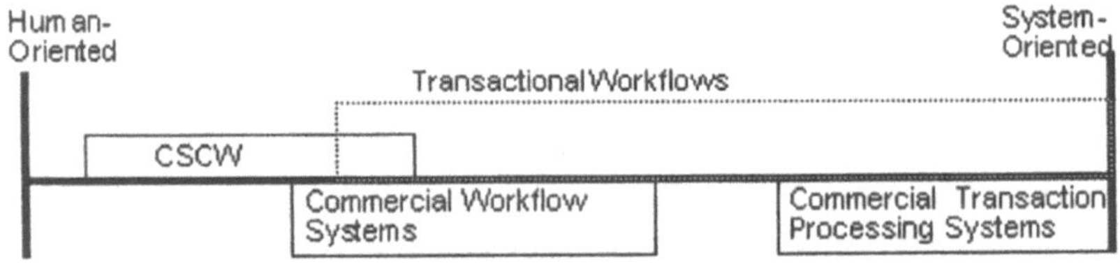

Figure 71. Workflow Types

9.2.4.1 Workflow Modeling

Modeling a process involves interviewing people with expert knowledge about the process. When enough knowledge about the process is obtained, workflow specification is performed to capture the process. For example, GTE (now part of Verizon) Telephone Operations undertook a large process engineering effort reported in[7]. According to that report, GTE Telephone Operations formed reengineering teams of 20-25 employees, to capture existing business processes. They conducted 1000 interviews and 10000 observations, and producing corresponding workflow specifications using a workflow specification tool.

In addition to understanding a business process, modeling the process involves workflow specification. There are different workflow specifications for different abstraction levels of a process. For example, a workflow specification may describe a process at the highest conceptual level necessary for understanding, evaluating, and redesigning the process. Another workflow specification may describe the same process at a lower level of detail required for performing workflow implementation.

Performing workflow specification requires a workflow model. A workflow model typically includes a set of concepts that are useful to describe processes, their tasks, the dependencies among tasks and the required roles (i.e., skills of the individuals or information systems) that can perform the specified tasks (Figure 72).

Workflow specification is typically performed using a workflow specification language. Workflow specification languages in commercial workflow systems use rules, constraints, and/or graphical constructs to describe the ordering and synchronization of tasks in a workflow. They also define task attributes in order to describe the tasks and their associated roles.

There are two basic categories of process modeling methodologies: communication-based (e.g., Action Workflow) and activity-based (GTE RAPID). Many commercial workflow systems use activity-based methodology, and consist of elements similar to the following:

- Workflows
- Tasks
- Manipulated Objects
- Roles
- Agents

Workflows are a partial or total ordering of a set of tasks:

Tasks are a partial or total order of operations, descriptions for human actions, or other tasks.

Manipulated objects are documents, data records, images, phones, fax machines, printers, etc.

Roles are a placeholder for human skill or an information system service required to perform a particular task.

Agents are humans or information systems that fill roles, perform tasks and interact during workflow execution.

The relationship between roles and agents is particularly significant during implementation. For example, the mapping of agents and roles helps to manage the work force and computing environment. In addition, it can facilitate load balancing.

9.2.4.2 Workflow Reference Model

Workflow Management Coalition (WMC) has developed a framework for the establishment of workflow standards. This framework includes five categories of interoperability and communication standards to allow multiple workflow products to coexist and interoperate within a user's environment. Figure 72 shows a reference architecture to facilitate the interoperability of workflows at different levels. This involves the identification of a number of generic components that are supported by different workflow products to different extents. Hence, this reference model provides a common architecture for the definition and implementation of workflow. The most important component is called a *Workflow Enactment Service* that may consist of one or more workflow engines in order to create, manage and execute workflow instances[24].

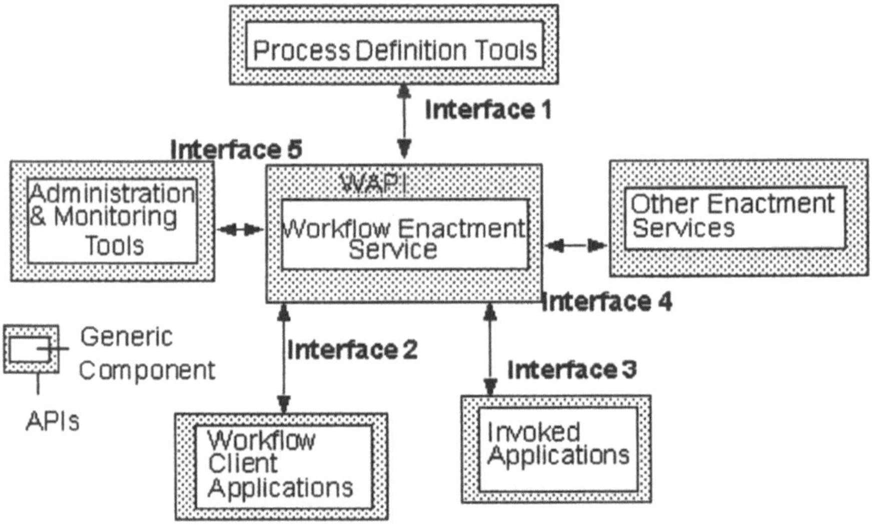

Figure 72. WFMC Reference Architecture[24]

A standardized set of interfaces (between generic components), and data interchange formats are defined for the interoperability between different workflow products. WAPI- Workflow APIs and Interchange formats, may be considered as a unified service interface, consisting of five interfaces to support management with five functional workflow management functions, namely[24]:

- Workflow Definition Interchange (Interface 1): a process definition import/export interface

- Client Application Interface (Interface 2): provides a set of commands for work list manipulation, and some functions, such as connection/disconnection, process control, data handling etc.
- Invoked Application Interface (Interface 3): supports additional functionality required for the interoperability with existing commercial workflow products that use other standards, such as OSI TP, X.400, etc.
- Workflow Interoperability Interface (Interface 4): allows different commercial workflow systems to pass work items seamlessly between each other.
- Administration & Monitoring Interface (Interface 5): includes CMIP and SNMP based MIBs for various aspects of management, such as user, role, audit, resources and process supervisory functions.

Some leading workflow software vendors, such as Staffware are developing products based on these standards[21].

In view of the growing adoption of distributed object models for distributed processing, CORBA and DCOM are expected to play more and more important roles in the implementation of future CSCW systems.

9.2.5 Autonomous Agents

As discussed in Chapter 1 and 3, agents play an important in web-based services and middleware. The field of agents evolved from the area of artificial intelligence. Agents are defined as complex, proactive software that is usually goal-driven, and it responds to events based on knowledge acquired continuously from the environment[16].

However, the term "agent" is used to mean different things in the field of integrated e-business management: For example,

- Agent software in the manager-agent model of network management acts as a simple software that mediates between a manager station and managed devices.
- More sophisticated version of agent is used for service management and application management as discussed in Chapters 5-7.
- Agents in e-business infrastructure assist in various ways, such as performing search according to a criteria, noting preferences, and making sense of huge amount of data.
- Agents in CSCW act as software assistants to human roles by providing the desired level of awareness for a successful interaction.

Therefore, agents play an important role in a cooperative management infrstructure as diuscussed in Chapter 10.

9.2.6 Role of CSCW in Integrated Management

It is now possible to obtain raw management data (using standard MIBs) from various network devices and applications. Increasing adoption of management standards like SNMP, mean that more and more components will become "manageable" from a remote console. However, "manageability" here means the ability to access certain pre-defined parameters from these devices and applications. This does not necessarily translate to an increase in management productivity. Therefore, much new research in network and systems management is concentrated on management applications that help assimilate vast amounts of network management data within a short time. Figure 73 shows a typical environment of integrated management in a large enterprise, encompassing multiple heterogeneous applications, multiple communication media/protocols, multiple groups of people across organizational boundaries and multiple types of software tools.

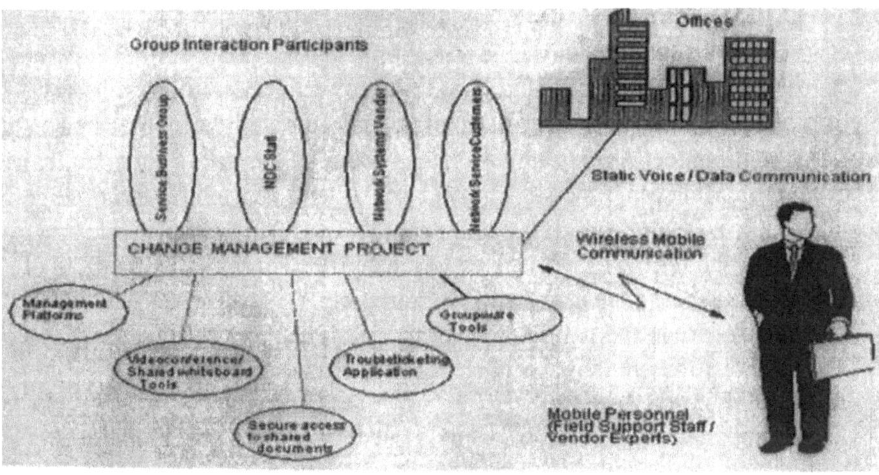

Figure 73. Cooperative Management Environment

Emerging e-business management solutions require a seamless integration of organisational business processes with the underlying IT infrastructure management. This necessitates the development of formal methodologies for integrated management solutions.Although there are a number of information system methodologies, they were designed mainly for large commercial data processing applications. These methodologies cannot be applied easily in integrated management, due to certain peculiarities of this fast developing area, such as requirements for real-time processing, heterogeneous elements and multiplicity of standards. However, cooperative systems methodologies incorporating human factors, are now evolving.

This chapter presents a new CSCW based methodology: Cooperative management Methodology for E-business Networks and Services (CoMENS) to illustrate the use of CSCW in integrated management. CoMENS is a new methodology for requirements gathering, analysis, design and evaluation of cooperative management solutions. This methodology is applicable to a wide variety of systems involving cooperation of people across distance, particularly in the e-business environment. This is illustrated in Section 9.4 and in Appendix 3.

9.3 Cooperative Management Methodology for E-Business

Before discussing the CoMENS methodology, let us discuss one of the proprietary software engineering methodologies for e-business solution development in use in the industry.

9.3.1 An E-Business Methodology

MindTree's e-Express™ methodology was developed to address the need for speed. Traditional, sequential approaches (based on waterfall model) to software development (i.e., requirements specification followed by conceptual design followed by detailed design) have failed to keep pace with the rapid changes demanded by e-business and system integration development. Even modern object-oriented approaches can prove inadequate for implementers struggling with business models that often evolve more quickly than the traditional development lifecycle can fulfill.

e-Express™ breaks down common barriers associated with the traditional approach. Specifically, this methodology (illustrated in Figure 74) comprises phases with parallel, integrated modules that incorporate business, creative and technical disciplines into one streamlined project. Because there is no "one size fits all" solution, the modular building blocks of MindTree's e-Express™ can plug and play in a variety of ways into an overall solution. This may be seen as an adaptation of the 8-stage service methodology (discussed in Chapter 4) for e-business management.

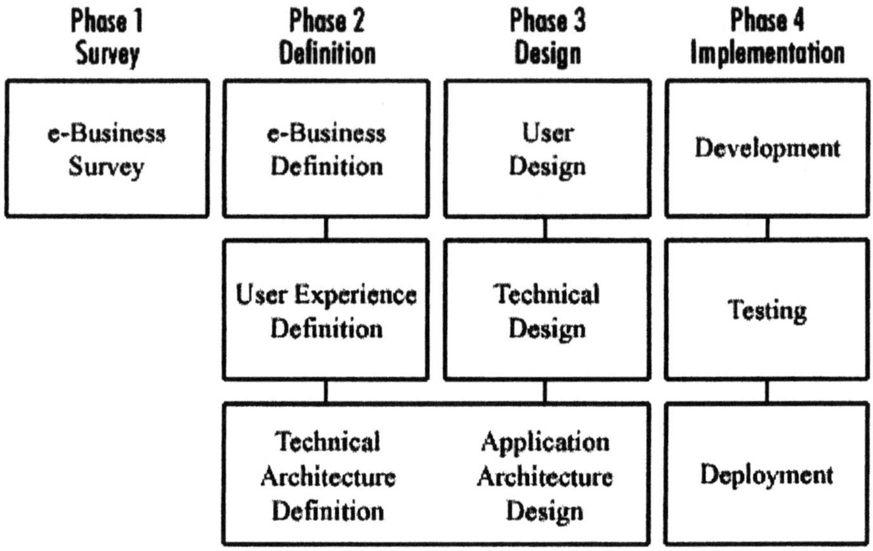

Figure 74. Cooperative Management in E-Business Environment[17]

The idea is to introduce as much parallelism as possible in the development process. For example, in phase 2, requirements engineering is done including e-business definition, user experience definition (using QFD matrices discussed in Chapter 4) and technical architecture definition in parallel. In phase 3, the design activities are performed including user design, technical design, and application architecture design in parallel. Finally in phase 3, implementation process involves parallel activities, development, testing and deployment[21]. As shown in this practical methodology, CoMENS treats requirements and architecture in parallel as discussed next.

9.3.2 CoMENS

As discussed in the beginning of this chapter, CoMENS is grounded on the philosophy that software development should consider requirements and architecture very closely in a fine-grained iterative process. This is illustrated in the Twin Peaks model (Figure 75) proposed by Nuseibeh in[18].

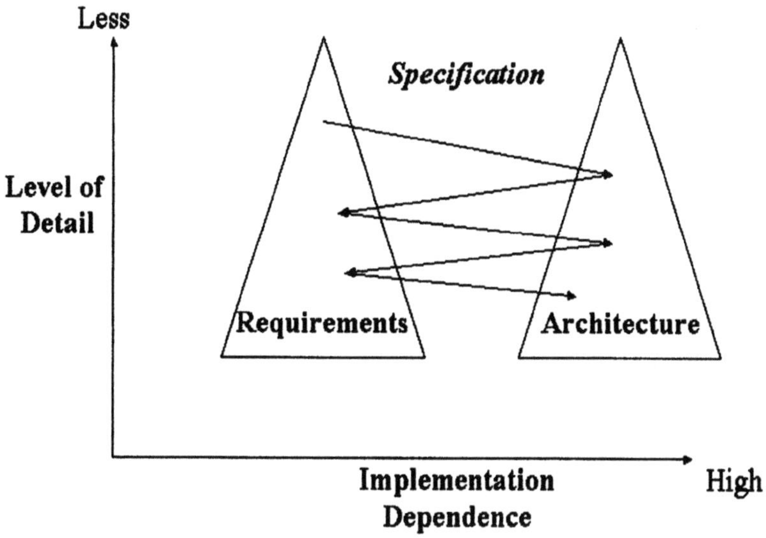

Figure 75. Twin Peaks Model[18]

As shown in Figure 75, the requirements are relevant at the early stages of a design, while the architecture is more implementation dependent as we saw in Part 3. However, it is important to take the architecture into consideration right from the beginnings of the design process, and the system is defined incrementally both for requirements and the architecture.

As discussed in the beginning of this chapter, CoMENS consists of three dimensions: requirements, design, and evaluation. Implementation comes partly in design and partly in evaluation. These three dimensions are related as shown in Figure 75. In the modern world, objects and components are becoming more and more prevalent in software development. Figure 76 also shows the process/artifacts used in the three dimensions of CoMENS, namely requirements process using scenario analysis, design process using patterns, and evaluation process using templates as described in subsequent sections.

Before we go further to discuss the three cornerstones of this methodology, we need to point out some major changes in the software engineering environment due to the proliferation of Commercial Off The Shelf (COTS) software packages. Hence the traditional Greenfield development based on SDLC is becoming less and less common. This necessitates a fresh look at the process of software development. Figure 76 shows the changed process of software development in light of COTS, a reality in all e-businesses and their management systems.

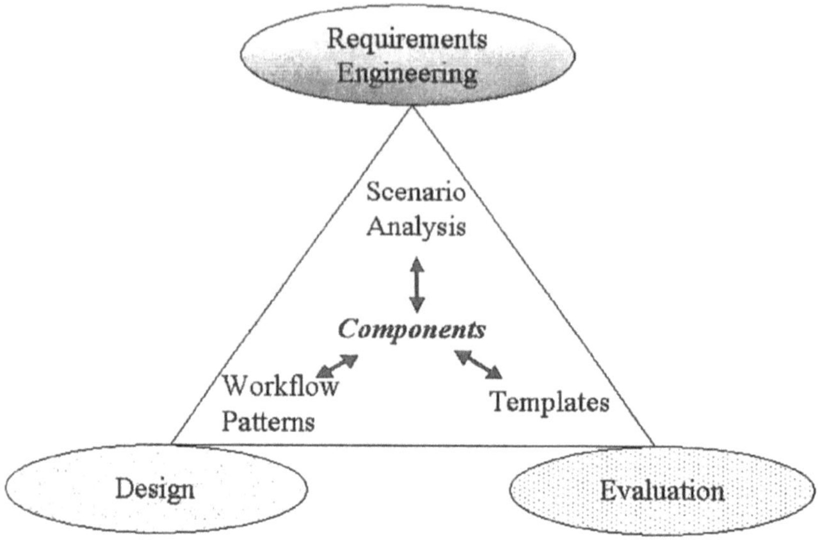

Figure 76. The Three major Dimensions of CoMENS

Therefore, we take the scenario shown in Figure 77 as the norm for integrated management software development that consists of three major overlapping processes[5]:

- Requirements, Architecture and COTS Selection
- Gluing and Tailoring (customization and integration)
- Maintenance and Management

Therefore, the process of management solution development is very much dependent on the three main processes; requirements, design/architecting, and evaluation, as discussed in the subsequent chapters.

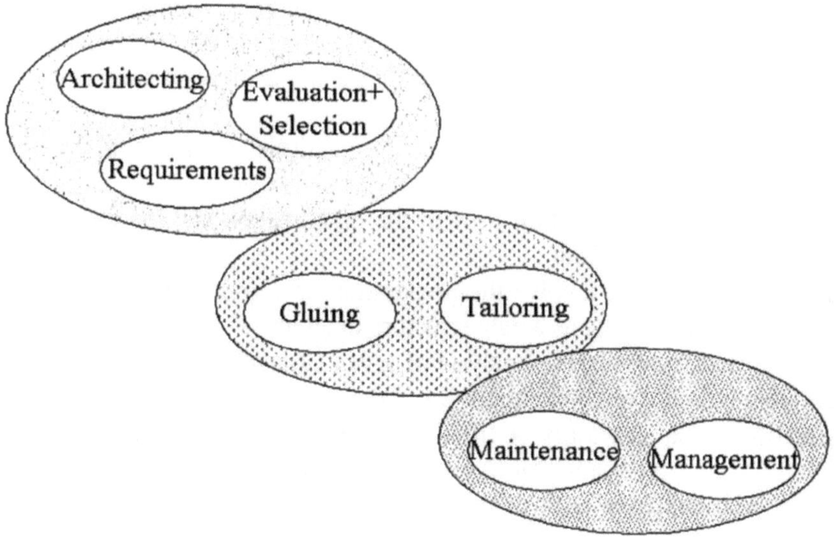

Figure 77. COTS-based Development Methodology[5]

9.3.3 Requirements Engineering (Scenario Analysis)

CoMENS uses a recent interdisciplinary technique called Scenario Analysis for requirements engineering. Recent research and practice demonstrate enormous interest in the software engineering and information systems community in scenario-based analysis[13].

9.3.3.1 Models and Processes

The requirement process is part of the first level of the cooperative management methodology. This level of the methodology is based on role theory, widely used for enterprise modeling. This theory postulates that individuals in an organization occupy roles, and there is authority, responsibility, functions and interactions associated with each role.

This section examines the process of arriving at the requirement specification based on organizational roles. This sub-process is concerned with the collection of information related to cooperative management problems from a real organization. This may involve the researcher getting hands-on experience with the environment and tools in the problem domain, and interviewing people with long experience in the given environment and tasks.

9.3.3.2 Techniques and Notations

Part 2 of this book described some general notations, such as Enterprise Analysis, that provide a formal methodology to carry out the first few stages of SSM. QFD matrices can be used to capture and analyze various types of organization-wide information.

In a typical information system, the analysis phase involves the following:

- The analysis of information flow in the organization and the associated analysis of material flow
- Data analysis could involve the preparation of a graphic representation, referred to generically as a data structure diagram

In this case, however, the analysis of given situations is performed with respect to a measure of cooperation. Since there are no available measures of cooperation, it is necessary to firstly define a measure of cooperation. Thereafter one starts analyzing given interactions with respect to this measure. The objective is to explain the existing problems on the basis of this measure.

This stage uses both graphical and tabular techniques, such as

- Process Diagrams, and
- QFD Matrices, discussed in Part 2

The technique of process diagrams is based on human computer interaction studies, called Activity Analysis. In this case, a CSCW activity is graphically modeled in terms of human roles and their interactions. While ellipses represent business roles, directed arrows represent interactions.

9.3.3.3 Scenario Analysis

CSCW brings together contributions from such diverse areas as Computer Science, Sociology, Psychology and Organisational Studies. Consequently, research approaches vary widely. In our CoMENS we use CSCW techniques, analysing practical scenarios based on human interaction concepts. Our methodology has two parts[21]: Part One - Scenario Analysis provides a method for the definition and analysis of scenarios of a cooperative management environment. This level encompasses activities relating to requirements study and analysis, and is based on Checkland's Soft Systems Methodology (SSM). SSM has laid the foundation for the holistic analysis of information systems, incorporating human factors. This part of the methodology uses new evolving techniques from CSCW.

Scenario Analysis involves a top down analysis of the cooperative system under study in the following stages (as shown in Figure 78):

1. Overall System Study (Step 1)
2. Process Study (Step 2)
3. Defining Collaborative Service Requirements (Step 3)

4. Analysis (Steps 4-5)

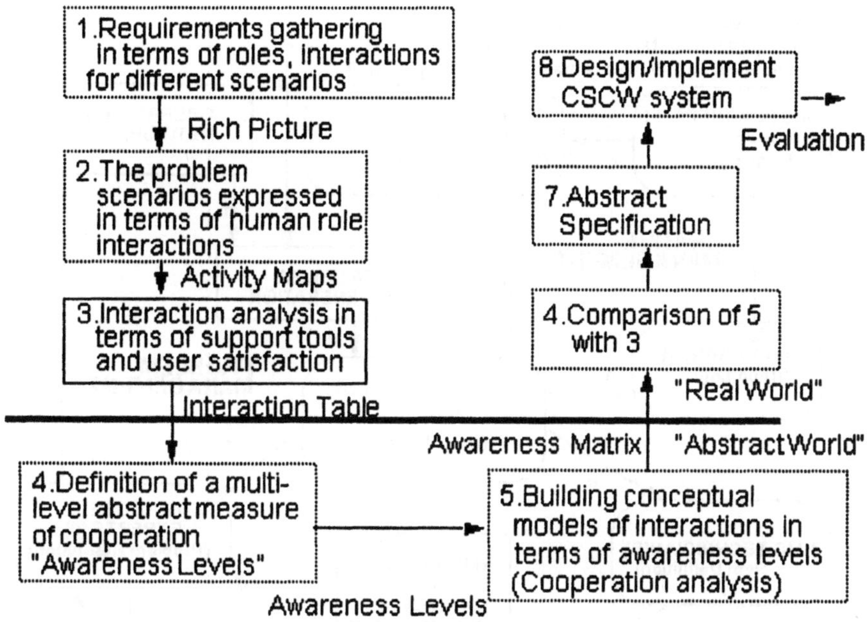

Figure 78. Requirements Analysis Methodology for Cooperative Management

Overall System Study presents the overall "big picture" of the system including the major human roles, activities and the environment. This produces a high-level description of the organisation view including some major management concerns in a graphical form. This stage produces a "Rich Picture" of the environment (Figure 79), including major human roles, their concerns and major interactions (using artifacts and tools) in the context of Integrated Management processes.

This step also involves the logical components identification for further detailed study. The major logical components are:

- Roles and Tasks: human roles and their major tasks.
- Activities and Interactions: this describes the dynamics of real life processes.
- Tools and Artifacts: some frequently used software, hardware and information structures in this system.

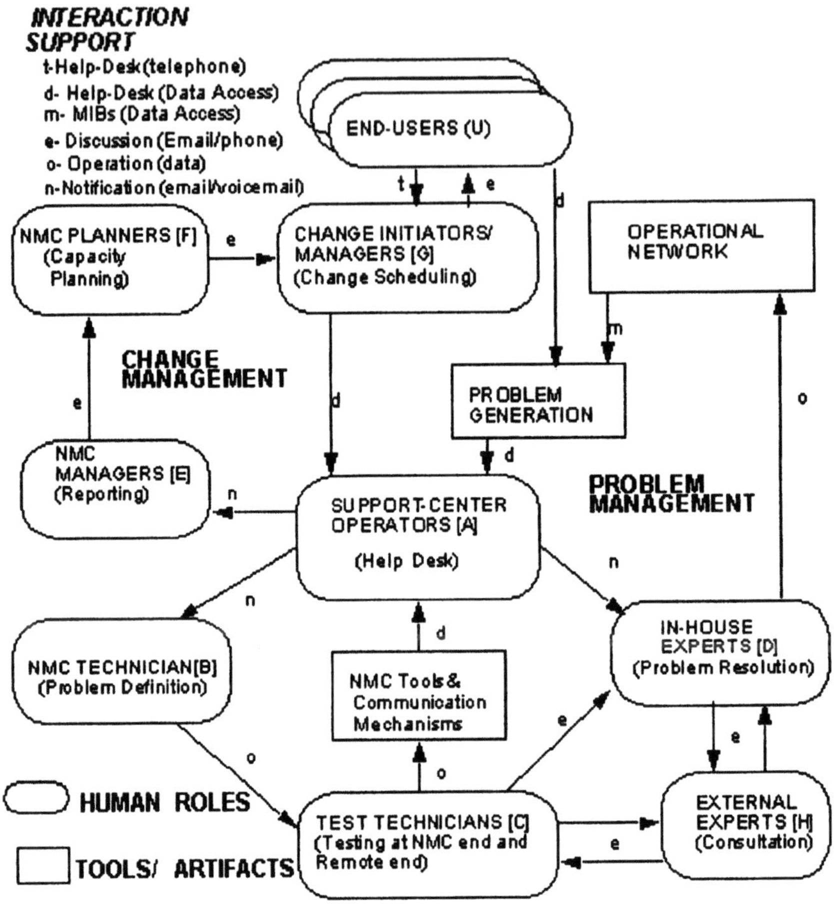

Figure 79. Rich Picture of a Cooperative Management Environment

Process Study involves a study of some sample scenarios in terms of human roles and their interactions. This study reveals certain generic process sequences that have a strong bearing on the efficiency of the process. This step produces graphical activity maps of the interactions of human roles in certain chosen scenarios at the workplace.

The next step, *Defining collaborative service requirements*, captures the availability or non-availability of collaborative service facilities in each of the scenarios under study. The collaborative facilities are categorised as repositories and communication tools as described below:

- Repositories: represent application services using data stores and associated processes.
- Communication Interfaces: mechanisms to access repositories, such as synchronous, asynchronous, remote conference, local meeting, etc.

This stage produces an interaction table that explicitly shows the existing collaborative facilities and possible future improvements for every interaction in a scenario.

Analysis involves the analysis of information collected at the above steps. We define an abstract model for measuring cooperation (awareness model) for this purpose. The analysis is based on this model. The idea is that eacg human role needs to have tools and communication mechanisms to support the desired awareness levels for an interaction. Typically the desired awareness level could be defined into a few (4/5) discrete levels depending on the context knowledge required (higher the context knowledge, higher the awareness level)[21].

The major tasks involve:

- Matching of scenarios to collaborative services (tools and group communication interfaces)
- Identification of gaps in collaborative services available on the basis of user satisfaction levels. We use an evolving CSCW awareness model to produce an awareness matrix for this purpose. The matrix contains the desired and actual awareness levels for each human role inviolved in an interaction in a cooperative management scenario.
- Analysis of the above information using abstract parameters, such as human role awareness levels. This leads to a conceptual design for a cooperative management System. The design objective is to provide appropriate awareness levels for all human role interactions.

Part two of the methodology is System Design Process, which starts from this awareness specification, a simple abstract measure that needs to be translated to a CSCW design[21]. The subsequent sections of this Chapter illustrate the CSCW based scenario analysis of CoMENS in the troubleticketing environment of a large telecommunication organisation.

9.4 CoMENS Requirements Engineering Case Study

This section presents requirements analysis for e-business management in the telecom service environment, using ethnography techniques that involve the *in-situ* study of enterprise management from an e-business perspective. We refer to studies carried out by this author in the network management center of a large telecom organization in Australia. This section discusses a scenario for the management of e-business networks. Appendix 3 applies the same methodology to a generic e-business management problem based on the e-service market model by Anna Durante et al from HP labs [6].

9.4.1 Overall System Study

A process chart of the system under study is shown in Figure 79. This is a simplified form of a Rich Picture diagram used to sketch an overall organisational context of an information system. Trouble-ticketing is a help-desk based Integrated Management application. In this case, management personnel cooperate to manage a problem using various network elements. Whenever there is a problem, the customer reports it to the help-desk. The operator then assigns a troubleticket to the problem and allocates it to the appropriate technical person. This person tries to solve the problem and escalates the alarm (calls the expert) if the problem cannot be solved within the stipulated time.

The troubleticketing environment in the organisation under study has many roles. Although trouble-ticketing is normally associated with fault management, in this book, we use the semantics of trouble-ticketing for both fault and configuration management purposes (Figure 79). Our example scenario, described below, involves Change Management with the following human roles:

1. The Change Manager (G)is responsible for successful operation of the given network changes in the given set of user organisations.

2. The NMC Technician (B) at the Network Management Centre is responsible for the technical aspects of this change.

3. *The In-house Expert* (D) provides technical consultation support on complex issues.

4. The Test Coordinator (C) assists the NMC technician with systems changes and testing in remote locations.

5. The Operator (A) at the Help-Desk is responsible for procedural communication amongst all concerned, and updates the repository available for this purpose.

6. The User(s) (U) represent contact persons in the user organisations where the network/systems change is being undertaken.

Figure 80 illustrates some typical interactions of these roles and relevant artifacts, with directed arrows. These roles can participate in a variety of interactions as discussed in the next section.

9.4.2 Process Study

We now illustrate this study with the analysis of a sample scenario of cooperative network management. This is a real change management scenario that was discussed with technicians in the organisation. An asterisk (*) with the interaction indicates that there are tools available to support the interaction.

The Sydney to Perth wide area link, which is on an existing 2 Mbps link on a lower version NTU, needs to be upgraded to a higher version NTU. For this an outage of 30 minutes is required. This involves the following interactions (Figure 80) amongst roles defined in the previous section:

1. The NMC Technician talks to a remote Test Coordinator about a suitable time (Role B<---> Role C)

*2. The NMC Technician/Expert places a change request with proposed time and user impact statement to the Change Manager (Role B/D ----> Role G).

*3. The Change Manager takes up with the affected Users (Role G -----> Role U). Only (G--->U1) is shown in the Figure 80.

*4. Related Users discuss impact and examine the proposed time (Role U1<--->Role U2<-- ->Role U3)

*5. The User resubmits a request to the Change Manager with possibly an altered schedule (Role U---->Role G)

*6. The Change Manager issues a Permit To Work to all concerned (Role G---> Role U,D). Only (G--->D,U1)

7. The Help-Desk Operator is notified before start of work (role G---->Role A).

8. The Help-Desk Operator alerts users regarding start of work (Role A---> Role U)

9. Work coordination between local and remote sites (Role B/D---->Role C, Role C---->Role D).

10. Proper completion of work is checked with (Role B/D----> Role U). Much of the time role D performs the role B also. Therefore, Figure 80 shows them in the same box to simplify the diagram.

11. The Help-Desk Operator is notified of completion.(Role D----> Role A).

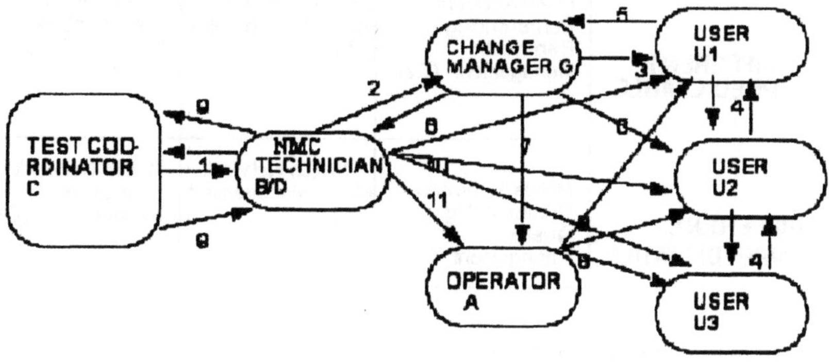

Figure 80. Cooperative Management Scenario

As shown in the list above, the majority of the interactions are not supported by existing automated tools and artifacts.. We now need to analyse the above interactions with respect to collaborative services available to support these interactions.

9.4.3 Collaborative Services Requirements

Collaborative services can be broadly classified as group support tools and group communication mechanisms.

The tools and artifacts used in an enterprise network management environment include help-desk system, Integrated Management platforms, change management systems, etc. These tools and artifacts need to be accessed using a variety of group communication techniques, such as wired voice telephone, email, cellular phones and pagers.

We present in the next section a sample, problem scenario that involves the upgrading of a network link at a remote site. This is an example of a number of scenarios we studied to arrive at a summary of requirements.

Group communication mechanisms depend on the nature of the collaborative task. Communication Mechanisms, in the context of cooperative management, can be classified as (Figure 81).

PLACE \ TIME	SAME	DIFFERENT, PREDICTABLE	DIFFERENT, UNPREDICTABLE
SAME	Network Management Centre(NMC) Monitoring & Control (C1)	NMC Working Shifts (C4)	NMC Expert Visits (C7)
DIFFERENT, PREDICTABLE	Fixed Network Conferencing Bandwidth Management (C2)	Fixed Network Alarm Management (C5)	Fixed Network Configuration Changes (C8)
DIFFERENT, UNPREDICTABLE	Mobile Network Conferencing Quality Management (C3)	Mobile Network Alarm Management (C6)	Mobile Network User Location Management (C9)

Figure 81. Group communication Requirements

The next step is to identify the problem areas in collaboration support. As discussed earlier, we studied a number of different, real Integrated Management scenarios in the organisation.

Table 11. Collaborative Service Evaluation

Inter-action	Tool Used	Communication Mechanism	User Satisfaction Level	**Remarks**
2	Change Mgmt System	Asynchronous Communication (C5)	3	Automatic Change Impact notification based on synchronous communication required
3	Change Mgmt System	Face-to-face / Asynchronous Communication (C1/ C5)	3	Automatic Change Impact notification based on synchronous communication required
4 & 5	Change Mgmt System	Voice Telephone Communication (C2)	3	Automatic Change Impact notification based on synchronous communication required
6	CiscoWorks on SunNet Manager	C5	2	No Ack. from users

9.4.4 Analysis

Table 11 describes the available automated support for some of the interactions in the sample scenario described in the previous section. The first column shows interaction numbers in Figure 80. Collaborative tools and communication mechanisms are classified according to the matrix in Figure 81. A user satisfaction level is also recorded on a scale of 0 to 10 (10 highest), on the basis of user interviews in the organisation under study. The information in Table 11 is presented with respect to only those interactions (leftmost column), that have satisfaction levels of 5 or below. Interactions with higher satisfaction levels are considered adequately supported, or not requiring any explicit group support mechanisms.

Although the data in Table 11 shows some correlation between user satisfaction levels and group communication support, the information is specific to the organisation under study. We need an abstraction based on a measure called "awareness level" to generalise this information across scenarios and organizations as discussed in [21].

It may be noted that many e-business systems now use intelligent agents for human and organizational roles. This adds another dimension to the scenario analysis representation. On the other hand, an agent-based model of role interaction would facilitate intelligent management by embedding substantial amounts of additional intelligence in the process components of e-business management. However, that may need more sophisticated representation and notation schemes as described in [4].

9.5 Chapter Summary

This chapter has discussed the problem of the integrated management of e-business from a multi-disciplinary perspective involving concepts from software engineering and CSCW. The Chapter began with a discussion of the main componets of CSCW, namely groupware, workflows and autonomous agents. We presented a methodology for the management of e-business services from the perspective of collaboration amongst different human and organizational roles, called Cooperative management Methodology for E-business Networks and Services (CoMENS).

CoMENS uses, the now evolving, iterative twin peaks model recommending design using requirements and architectures simultaneously. We presented the three dimensions of this methodology; Requirements, Design and Evaluation. This was followed by a discussion of each of these dimensions in terms of models and processes, and techniques and notations. This discussion brought together TQM techniques (e.g., QFD matrices), and CSCW techniques (e.g., rich pictures, scenario analysis). The requirements engineering (scenario analysis) dimension of CoMENS was illustrated through a case study in a telecommunication business.

Although the illustration shows human roles and their interactions in a B2C situation, the same methodology can be extended to a B2B environment where human roles are replaced by organizational entities, and human interactions are replaced by inter-organizational communications as shown in Appendix 3.

The next chapter will present the other two dimensions (design and evaluation) of CoMENS.

9.6 References

1. Aalst W.M.P. van Der, Hofstede A.H.M.ter, Kiepuszewski B. and Barros A.P., "Workflow Patterns", *Technical Report, Technical University of Einhoven (TUE)- CapacityGroup I&T, Netherlands*, November, 2000
2. Bouch A., Kuchinsky A. and Bhatti N., "Quality in the Eye of the Beholder: Meeting Users' Requirements for Internet Quality of Service", *HP Labs Technical Report HPL-2000-4*, January, 2000, Palo Alto, USA
3. Casati F., and Discenza A., "Modeling and Managing Interactions among Business Processes", *HP Labs Technical Report HPL-2000-159*, December, 2000, Palo Alto, USA
4. Chen Q. and Hsu M., "Inter-Enterprise Collaborative Business Process Management", *HP Labs Technical Report HPL-2000-107*, August 2000, Palo Alto USA
5. Dean J., An Evaluation Method for COTS Software Products", *Proceedings of the 12th Annual Software Technology Conference (STC), May 2000*, Saltake City, Utah, USA
6. Durante A., Bell D., Goldstein L., Gustafson J. and Kuno H., "A Model for the E-Service Marketplace", *HP Labs Technical Report HPL-2000-17*, February, 2000, Palo Alto, USA
7. Eckerson W., "Case Study: The role of IS in reengineering", *Open Information Systems*, 9(2) February 1994
8. Georgakopoulos D., Hornick M,, and Sheth A., "An Overview of Workflow Management: From Process Modeling to Workflow Automation Infrastructure", *Distributed and Parallel Databases*, 3 pp119-153, Kluwer Academic Publishers, the Netherlands, 1995
9. Grudin J., "Computer Supported Cooperative Work: History and Focus", *IEEE Computer Magazine*, May 1994
10. Holtzblatt K. et al., "Conducting and Analysing a Contextual Interview", *Readings in Human-Computer Interaction*, Morgan Kaufmann Publishers Inc., San Francisco, USA 1995

11. Ishii H., "Message-driven groupware design based on office procedure model", *Journal of Information Processing*, 1990
12. "Reference Model for Open Distributed Processing (RM-ODP) Parts 1,2, 3 and 4D. Avison and G. Fitzgerald, *Information Systems Development: Methodologies, Techniques and Tools*, McGraw-Hill, 1995
13. Jarke M. and Kurki-Suonio R., "Guest Editorial to the Special Issue on Scenario Management", *IEEE Transactions on Software Engineering*, Vol. 24, No. 12, December 1998
14. Laudon K. and Laudon J., *Management Information Systems: Organization and Technology*, Prentice Hall 1998
15. Lewis D., Wade V., and Bracht R., "The Development of Integrated Inter and Intra Domain Management Services", *Proceedings of the 6th IFIP/IEEE International Symposium on Integrated Network Management*, May 1999, Boston, USA
16. May P., *The Business of ECOMMERCE*, Cambridge University Press, UK, 2000
17. Mindtree, "E-Express Methodology", http://www.mindtree.com/about_us.html, 2000
18. Nuseibeh B,"Weaving Together Requirements and Architecture", *IEEE Computer*, 34 (3): 115-117, March 2001
19. Preece J., Rogers Y., Sharp H., Benyon D., Holland S and Carey T., *Human - Computer Interaction*, Addison-Wesley, 1994, ISBN 0-201-62769-8
20. Ramaswamy R., *Design and Management of Service Processes*, Addison Wesley, AT&T Engineering Process Improvement Series edited by J.W.Wesner, 1996
21. Ray P., *Cooperative Management of Enterprise Networks*, Kluwer Academic/Plenum Publications, May 2000, ISBN:0-306-46276-1
22. Sachs P., "Transforming Work: Collaboration, Learning, and Design", *Communications of the ACM*, Vol. 38 No. 9, September 1995
23. Tran V. and Liu D., "A Risk-Mitigating Model for the Development of Reliable and Maintainable Large-scale-Off-The-Shelf Integrated Software Systems", *In the proceedings of the 1997 Annual Reliability and Maintainability Symposium*, pp361-67, Jan 1997
24. Workflow Management Coalition, *Workflow and Internet: Catalysts for radical change*, available June 1998

Chapter 10. CoMENS Design and Evaluation

In Chapter 9, we discussed the three dimensions of CoMENS, namely requirements, design and evaluation. We also discussed and illustrated the requirements engineering (scenario analysis) dimension. This involved ethnographic techniques involving the identification of human roles and their interactions to identify gaps in CSCW support for a cooperative management process. The objective was to specify a cooperative e-business management from a high-level business perspective.

This chapter presents methodologies for the design and testing/evaluation of e-business management solutions. We discuss how the methodologies in the design and evaluation stages involve multi-disciplinary techniques from the areas of workflows, Commercial Off The Shelf (COTS) software, distributed systems and network and systems management. The techniques are illustrated with a case study in telecommunication support services. The case study is on trouble-ticketing application based on the help-desk based business model, used extensively for management (support) services in a wide variety of e-businesses.

10.1 Design

System design is based on a combination of design formalisms from distributed systems, CSCW and Integrated Management. This level encompasses the design, implementation and evaluation of the cooperative application design. Chapter 4 discussed an architecure-oriented e-business design process, consisting of the following stages:

1. Strategic Design
2. Organizational Architecture Design
3. E-business Technical Arcitecture Design
4. Information Architecture Design
5. Data Architecture Design
6. Application Architecture Design

The 8-stage Service Design and Management methodology discussed in Chapter 4 has shown some generic techniques for the selection of best alternative from a number of alternatives. Such techniques are useful in any management system. This may be called strategic design (step #1 above). Steps 2-6 are specific to information service management discusseed as part of CoMEN in this Chapter.

While Chapter 9 dealt with the CoMENS analysis stage, which encompassed the strategic design aspect, this chapter deals with the rest of the design stages. In order to integrate organizational design with system design, CoMENS incorporates methodologies for workflow specification, standards for distributed systems development, and standards for network and systems management. As discussed in Chapter 9, CoMENS recommends a Twin Peak model of software design. We present the process at two levels of design:

- Conceptual Design (encompassing step 2-3 of the above architectural design methodology) with deliverables, such as Workflows, UML use cases, and ODP viewpoints[11]. This Chapter uses workflows at this level.
- Detailed Design (encompassing step 4-6 of the above methodology) with the selection of group communication mechanisms, and group databases. Typically this stage of management design is heavily dependent on the CSCW platform used. We use Lotus Notes™ that provides a flexible platform for supporting a variety of: CSCW mechanisms, such as
  - Multimedia document database
  - Multiple autonomous agents and
  - Workflows.

CoMENS uses design patterns as a flexible notation for expressing cooperative management design at both conceptual and detailed design levels[26]. Design patterns are discussed in Section 10.2.

10.1.1 Conceptual Design Phase

The conceptual design phase covers the process of arriving at the design of a re-engineered management process. Considering the importance of workflow in this design, we describe our system design methodology as follows:

10.1.1.1 Workflow Specification and Design

There are existing techniques for describing workflows, such as Action Workflows, discussed in Chapter 3 and further detailed in Section 10.2.2. Our help-desk application design is expressed at the highest level, using Action Workflow Loops.

10.1.1.2 Distributed System Design

There are various ways of expressing design at this level. They include RM-ODP viewpoints, UML diagrams and Interfaces Definition Languages (IDL) for CORBA, Java or DCOM[11,15,30]. The choice depends on the suitability of the environment and the familiarity of the designer. CoMENS does not specify any particular choice. However, it is important that the design is as reusable as possible. Since this level is concerned only with an overall reusable framework, design patterns are used at this level.

This is the end of our conceptual design phase. It is necessary to consider the system development environment and its architecture before proceeding to the next level of design. At this stage, we are only concerned with the type of workflow design, automation tools, and repositories to search and reuse available patterns. CoMENS recommends that the output at this level be specified as new design patterns[26].

10.1.2 Detailed Design

This stage is concerned with the detailed design involving group databases, communication mechanisms, and protocols, software components, mapping to integrated management platforms/instrumentation.

The architectural environment at this stage is concerned with relevant patterns including case tools, class libraries, database design templates and communication interfaces. It may be noted that the design at this level depends on the type of middleware used. This could include emerging industry standards such as distributed objects (CORBA, DCOM, J2EE etc.), or proprietary systems, such as transaction processing systems (e.g., Tuxedo) and web systems (e.g., BEA Weblogic)[3].

This section discusses our prototype design for cooperative management using Lotus NOTES™[21].

10.1.2.1 Group Database Design

This is the beginning of our implementation design phase. In groupware systems, such as Lotus NOTES™, different application modules are designed as different databases. The designs are expressed in terms of Forms, Views, Macros, and database controls and structures.

10.1.2.2 Group Communication Design

In the absence of any formal notation to express group communication mechanisms, we use the time-space matrix of CSCW to specify communication mechanisms in our system [21].

10.1.2.3 Integrated Management Design

While the above steps define the application level of our integrated management framework, it may be necessary to define or tune managed objects at the instrumentation/native system level of our framework. These definitions need to use management object definition languages, such as OSI Guidelines for the Definition of Managed Objects (GDMO) based on ASN.1 specifications. We delegate this task to the next level of design, and will not be discussing it in this book.

10.2 Design Patterns

The paths to creating e-businesses are repeatable. Whether the company is a start-up or as extensive legacy applications, these patterns allow the reuse of existing technologies so that projects can be completed quickly. We have presented a discussion of high-level e-business patterns from IBM in Chapter 1. This section discusses patterns for the design of workflows as required in the development of management solutions based on[19].

One of the great values of object-oriented application development is the increase in the use of pre-built, tested, well-understood components. The proponents of this style of building code promised (and delivered) a great deal of reusability in their code and thereby shortened the development time for applications, reduced time to market for new products, and lowered the cost for both new development and maintenance.

One can extend these concepts of object-oriented applications to the development of e-business systems. If people working together can recognize the tasks they need to accomplish in familiar terms and understand how the desired application is composed of well-known parts, the specification of the new project is clear and the path to build the application can be mapped out in a set of known steps. In this sense the concept of patterns is closely related to that of methodologies used throughout this book.

A particular feature of patterns for e-business is that each business pattern has several logical patterns, or topologies, which might be thought of as variations on the main theme of the pattern. These topologies give a set of variations on how to fulfill a particular business need, based on the intent of the project and the starting point or existing infrastructure that must be incorporated into the final solution. For example, if the required data currently resides in a corporate database controlled by an existing transaction manager, then one must plan how to access and use this data.

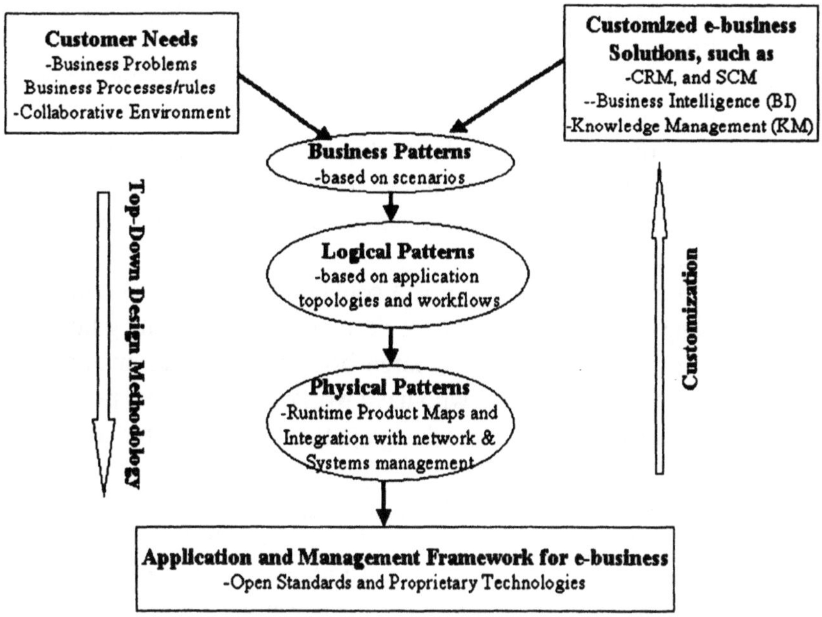

Figure 82. Use of Patterns in E-Business Development[19]

Patterns for e-business also provide a prescriptive approach. Physicians are formally taught a process to evaluate a patient and arrive at a treatment plan. They do this by quickly assessing the major systems, then honing in on the system or systems with problems. The physician can then follow a standard decision tree logic pattern to arrive at a treatment plan. In the case of the Patterns for e-business, one can start with the customer's wants and needs, their business problems, existing business processes and rules, and any existing systems, data, or infrastructure. One can then follow a structured approach to arrive at a customized solution for the customer that addresses the business functions (such as Customer Relationship Management, Supply Chain Management, Knowledge Management, Business Intelligence, Customer or Employee Collaboration, e-commerce, or others as shown in Figure 82).

The patterns work is intended to provide the smallest number of patterns for e-business that will let IT architects, in 80% of the cases, analyze their business problem and reuse 50 to 80% of proven architecture, design and product patterns and guidelines. While less complex projects may use single pattern or topology, more complex projects may use combinations of patterns. Patterns for e-business enable the development of an e-business infrastructure by the reuse of proven:

- Architecture patterns provide the configuration of building-blocks, such as SLM discussed in Chapter 5
- Design patterns provide the relationships between the building-blocks, as discussed in Chapter 6
- Runtime patterns provide the relationship between the software building blocks and their execution environment to be discussed in this chapter
- Design, development and deployment guidelines (design methodology under discussion here)

The patterns are not designed to be a cookbook or to give us a complete guide to building applications. They are designed to give strong guidance to designers and to provide links to a large body of reference material and experience from other developers who have worked on the same problem.

Table 12 shows some e-business design patterns and example usage.

Table 12. Examples design patterns for different E-Business Scenarios[19]

Business patterns	E-business solution areas
User-to-Business	CRM, customer self service
User-to-Online Buying	e-commerce
Business-to-Business	SCM, shipping, e-marketplaces
User-to-User	Collaboration, customer service
User-to-Data	Business intelligence, knowledge management
Application Integration	Business application integration (key for ERP package implementation)

The pattern names reflect the generalized nature of each of the patterns. The business solution areas are only examples of the general type of application solution provided by the pattern. This author and his students are working the developing hierarchical patterns e-business management as reported in [26].It should be clear that the patterns can be and often are combined to solve more complex business problems [17]. Similarly, design patterns can be defined as generic solutions to e-business management problems.

10.2.1 Workflow-oriented Design Process

Like any other heterogeneous distributed systems, workflow management systems need to deal with application integration, interoperability, and implementation correctness and reliability. Workflow management involves activities from modeling processes to synchronizing the activities of information systems and humans that perform the processes. As shown in Figure 83., management of workflow includes the following:[8]

10.2.1.1 Process Modeling and Workflow Specification:

This step requires workflow models and methodologies for capturing a process as a workflow specification.

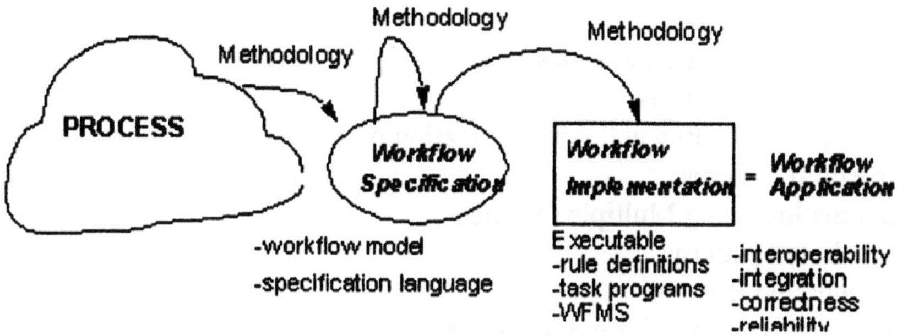

Figure 83. Workflow Development and Implementation Methodology[8]

10.2.1.2 Workflow Implementation and Automation

This requires methodologies/technology for using information systems, and human performers to implement, schedule, execute and control the workflow tasks as described by the workflow specification. Workflow specification and implementation can be loosely coupled (e.g., workflow specification and implementation are done by software engineers) or tightly coupled (e.g., workflow specifications are provided as direct input to workflow management systems that either generate code or interpret specifications for controlling workflow execution). Most commercial workflow systems are tightly coupled. In our illustration workflows are directly implemented on Lotus Notes.

10.2.2 Design Notations

We need a notation that can capture the high-level semantics, and graphically depict the workflows. It is also important to express the architectural aspect of the design. Hence we propose two types of notations in this stage:

- Workflow Design patterns
- Graphical Workflow Descriptions

As discussed in the previous chapter, design patterns have become a standard way of expressing distributed object-oriented architectural designs. Since most of the integrated management solutions use distributed objects, it would be natural to use design patterns. Design patterns are of various types, as discussed in the pattern literature[27]. Since our design is based on workflows, we are interested in workflow patters, as discussed in [1].

10.2.2.1 Workflow Patterns

This section is based on the recent work done by Aalst et al in the classification of workflow patterns, and a comparative analysis of commercial workflow products with respect to the support for these patterns[1].

Aalst and associates have classified workflow patterns as follows:

- Basic control patterns
- Advanced branching and synchronization patterns
- Structural Patterns
- Patterns Involving Multiple Instances
- State-based patterns
- Cancellation Patterns

These patterns are briefly discussed below:

As the name suggests *Basic Control Patterns* are the most commonly used workflow patterns that can be represented by some available workflow description techniques, such as Action Workflow. Some examples are:

- Activity execution in sequence (Sequence)
- Activity execution in Parallel (Parallel Split)
- Synchronization of two parallel threads (Synchronization)
- One execution path from many alternatives (Exclusive Choice)
- Merging two alternative paths (Simple Merge)

Advanced Branching and Synchronization Patterns are more complex. They are extensions of the above basic control patterns. For example, simple merge may be extended to multiple merge (merge several execution paths from many alternatives), and multiple choice (choice of several from many execution paths).

Some programming structures, such as loops are also used in workflows to repeat some basic workflows. *Structural Patterns* consider structures, such as execution of workflow graph without any restriction on loops (arbitrary loops), and terminate if nothing else to be done (implicit termination).

Patterns Involving Multiple Instances generate many instances of an activity based on existing knowledge (FOR loop), or no knowledge (WHILE loop) of the terminating condition.

State-based patterns allow the choice from multiple paths based on a system state. For example, deferred (implicit) choice allows the execution of one of the two alternatives threads based on system state.

Cancellation Patterns cancel or disable an enabled activity or process.

Each pattern is expressed in a descriptive format with the following headings:

- Description
- Synonyms
- Examples
- Problems
- Implementation

For example, the pattern ***Exclusive Choice*** can be described as [1]:

Description: A point in the workflow where, based on a decision or workflow control data, one of several branches is chosen.

Synonyms: XOR-split, conditional routing, switch, decision.

Examples:

- Activity contact help-desk is followed either problem-entry or contact operator is executed.
- Based on the workload, a processed tax declaration is either checked using a simple administrative procedure or a thorough evaluation by a senior employee.

Problem: Does not cause any specific problems.

Implementations: There are two basic strategies: some workflow engines provide an explicit construct (e.g. Staffware, Visual WorkFlo); while others (MQSeries/ Workflow, verve) need the workflow designer has to emulate this pattern by a selection of transition conditions.

This example has shown us the format for a simple pattern. Some patterns can be much more complex, requiring descriptions in languages, such as UML, in addition to the textual description.

There are two types of notations to express and design workflows:

- Activity maps
- Communication-based techniques (e.g., Action Workflow)

These graphical techniques are discussed next.

10.2.2.2 Process Activity Maps

This representation focuses on modeling the work instead of modeling the commitments among humans. For example, Figure 84 depicts the process "procure materials", composed of several tasks. The arrows indicate the sequential nature of the process map. "Procure materials" may be a task in another workflow, and tasks may nest arbitrarily deeply. Unlike communication-based methodologies, activity-based methodologies do not capture process objectives such as customer satisfaction.

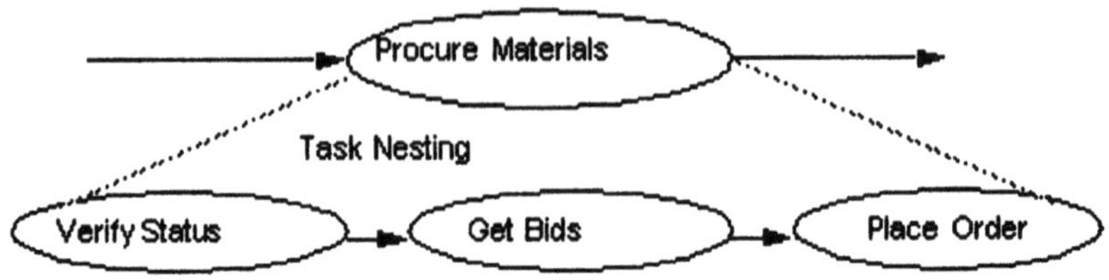

Figure 84. Material Procurement Workflow

Many commercial workflow systems provide activity-based workflow models. For example, GTE's RAPID methodology is activity-based and it provides two workflow models: a high-level model for performing conceptual business process analysis and a lower-level model for describing the corresponding information process[7]. In the high-level workflow model, workflows (referred to as process maps) contain tasks (referred to as steps) necessary to perform a particular business process. These steps can be partially or totally ordered as necessary to indicate alternatives or parallel execution of business process steps.

10.2.2.3 Action Workflow Diagrams

This methodology, as discussed in Part 2, assumes that the objective of business process re-engineering is to improve customer satisfaction. It reduces every action in a workflow to four phases based on communication between a Customer and a Performer (repeated in Figure 85 for completeness of the discussion).

- Preparation - when the customer prepares to ask for something and performer offers to do some work for the customer;
- Negotiation - the two entities agree on the work to be done and clarify the terms
- Performance - work is done to produce and deliver agreed results
- Acceptance - the customer reports satisfaction (or dissatisfaction) with the work

Each workflow loop between a customer and performer can be joined with other workflow loops to complete a business process. The performer in one workflow loop can be a customer in another workflow loop. The resulting business process reveals the social network in which a group of people, filling various roles, fulfills a business process.

Figure 86 shows a help-desk based, trouble ticketing application, using Action Workflow notation. Each loop shows an aggregate interaction that can be broken down into more specialized interactions. In this case, management personnel cooperate to manage a problem using various network elements. Whenever there is a problem, the customer reports that to the help-desk. The operator then assigns a trouble ticket to the problem and allocates it to the appropriate technical person. This person tries to solve the problem and escalates alarm (calls the EXPERT) if the problem can not be solved within the stipulated time. The trouble ticket is closed once the problem is resolved to the satisfaction of all concerned

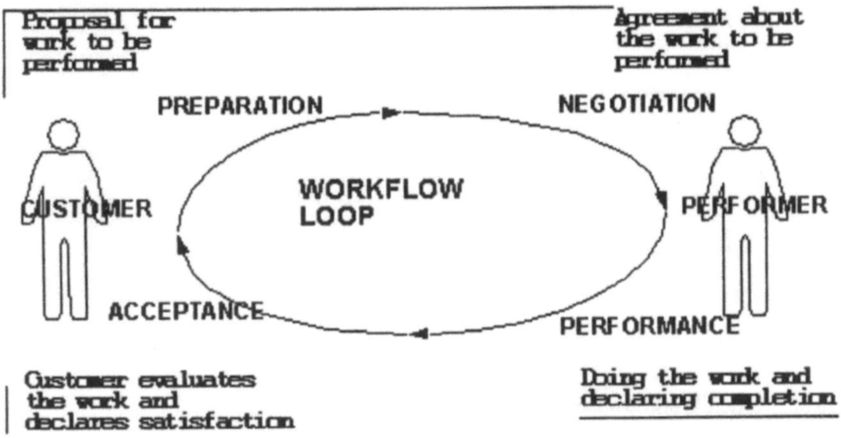

Figure 85. Action Workflow Loop

It may be noted that workflow specifications based on this Action Workflow methodology, do not indicate which activities can occur in parallel or if there are conditional or alternative actions. Since the objective is customer satisfaction, the emphasis is on the customer. However, there are business processes where the customer emphasis may not exist, e.g., if the objectives are to minimize information system costs or reduce waste in material in process. Therefore, this methodology may not be suited to objectives other than customer satisfaction. Also this methodology does not support workflow implementations.

The communication-based and activity-based workflow models can be combined when process re-engineering objectives are compatible with both models (e.g., satisfy the customer by minimizing workflow tasks and human roles). For example, a workflow model can be viewed as both activity-based and communication-based. Therefore, a cooperative management methodology will need to use both these models.

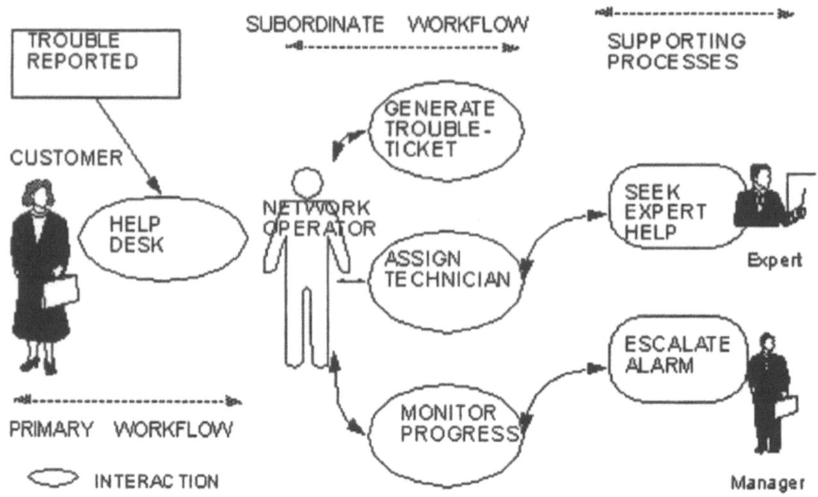

Figure 86. Action Workflow Loops in Trouble-ticketing

10.2.3 Management Policies

As discussed in Parts 3 and 4 of this book, the technology of integrated management is changing fast. It is however, necessary to develop and sustain a linkage between the business and technological perspective of management. We have seen how the concept of a business contract has been adopted so effectively for the management of workflows through Action Workflow loops. Similarly, the concept of management policy provides a flexible framework for the definition of management objectives, independent of underlying implementation mechanisms[28]. Policies help define responsibilities, obligations and relationships of different roles in the management context.

Management policies are broadly categorized into:

- Authorization policies - define the tasks that a management role may be allowed to perform.
- Obligation policies - define tasks that a management role must perform.

This field of policy-based management is one of the fastest growing areas of integrated management with a great deal of interest from industry as well as academia. Researchers in this area have developed certain representation mechanisms, tools and frameworks for the development and implementation of management policies[28]. They are likely to be very useful in the design of e-business management systems. As a matter of fact, policies could be a part of e-business management design patterns.

10.3 Evaluation

Although there are a number of integrated management systems in use today, there has been little work reported on the comprehensive evaluation of such systems. Czarnecki et al describe in[4] an evaluation criteria for management information models used in the instrumentation part of an integrated management framework. However, there is little reported work on the holistic evaluation of an integrated management system. Ray proposes a hierarchical model for the evaluation of integrated management systems in [21]. This uses inputs from the evaluation methodologies in a number of disciplines, such as telecommunications[10] and software engineering [1]. We propose a new template for the reporting and analysis of information for the evaluation of integrated management systems.

Since all e-business systems are based on software packages, it is important to first consider the recent developments in the area of the evaluation of systems designed using Commercial Off The Shelf (COTS) software packages. This area has seen some major developments thanks to the concerted efforts by many researchers in different parts of the world including the Software Engineering Institute (SEI) at Carnegie Mellon University and the US Department of Defense [2,5,20,17]. The next section presents a discussion of evaluation methodologies for systems using COTS.

10.3.1 Evaluation of COTS based Systems

As discussed in the beginning of this chapter, the software engineering landscape is now changing, particularly with the growth of COTS based systems. Recently, there have been some developments in the evaluation of COTS software that can be applied in the evaluation of integrated management systems from an e-business perspective. Here is a list of four evaluation methodologies for COTS, each of which emphasizes one or more critical aspects of COTS software evaluation[5]:

- COTS-based Integrated System Development Method (CISD)
- Off- The-Shelf-Option (OTSO)
- Checklist Driven Software Evaluation Methodology (CDSEM)
- Procurement-Oriented Requirements Engineering (PORE)

CISD model proposes a two-stage selection process as propose by Tran and Liu in [23]. The first stage identifies potential candidates based on vendor documentation, personal experience and other means. The second stage performs the evaluation of these candidates using prototyping. This stage involves evaluation with respect to three critical considerations; functionality, interoperability and performance. This methodology depends on a relatively complete predefined set of requirements, and is based on the

SDLC waterfall model, where each stage depends on the results of its predecessor. CoMENS uses the philosophy of the second stage of this methodology.

Kontio, Maiden and Ncube have defined OTSO by breaking it into three phases[14,20]; search, screening and evaluation, and analysis. The evaluations are performed against a set of criteria defined from requirement specifications, high-level design and project plan. The central theme of OTSO method is the construction of a product evaluation criteria hierarchy that is used in CoMENS (based on a set of criteria defined for integrated management). OTSO is an iterative process. The criteria are refined throughout the course of the evaluation.

Jeanrenaud and Romonazzi have defined a checklist-based evaluation methodology called CDSEM. It determines a quality metric for each item of the checklist, thereby producing a numerical result, which is so difficult in software evaluation. Many of the metrics are based on vendors disclosing some intimate information about the software (e.g., source code)[13,22]. CoMENS uses checklist evaluation as described in Section 10.3, but it produces a combination of qualitative and quantitative results of evaluation. Hence a numerical index is difficult to arrive at.

Maiden and Ncube define a template-based approach for the definition of requirements, and evaluation of software based on the template. Sometimes the requirements for the template are derived from a prototype[20]. CoMENS uses this template approach.

It is possible to use standards in management, distributed systems and software engineering, to define the evaluation process for integrated management systems. As discussed in the beginning of this chapter, CoMENS evaluation process caters for the last two stages of the Ramaswamy's service management model (assessing satisfaction, and improving performance). Hence CoMENS Evaluation methodology can be summarized by the following steps[5].

- Define Scenarios (from Requirements Engineering)
- Establish Basic Criteria
- Create Evaluation Templates
- Select candidates
- Perform evaluation until capabilities and requirements match (Contextual Evaluation via prototypes)
  - Determine Candidate capabilities
  - Redefine requirements and criteria
  - Perform Evaluation
- Submit Results
- Selected System
- Refined Requirements for Improved Performance

The next section uses these concepts to define the Evaluation Template for CoMENS.

10.3.2 Evaluation Template

This section presents a suggested template for CoMENS evaluation. The next section presents a generalized approach towards hierarchical evaluation criteria for integrated management systems. Finally, this evaluation methodology is illustrated by its application in the heuristic evaluation of an enterprise management system.

There has been substantial work on the formulation of metrics for the evaluation of software systems.[2] However, these metrics do not address the specific needs for integrated network management. ISO Basic framework for Quality of Service ISO QoS framework has addressed in [10], many of the metrics related to an e-business network. Therefore, the proposed evaluation framework is based on[10]. This template may be viewed as a formal structure for expressing technical design attributes discussed in the Ramaswamy's 8-stage methodology in Chapter 4.

In this framework the evaluation parameters are defined as quantitative items (subjective or measured). These items are specified by the user and they need to be monitored by some means (real-time or off-line). The parameter values may include numbers (e.g., boolean, integer, real, complex numbers etc.), vectors, matrices, ranks and names of states. Efforts are required to achieve maximum consistency of definition across different parameters by defining generic parameters, specializing them for particular environments and deriving others from them. We now define a template for defining and evaluating an integrated management system.

A definition of an evaluation parameter needs to include the following information:

- NAME: of the parameter
- DEFINED AS: explains its purpose and intended usage
- TYPE: Subjective/ Measurable/ Enumerative
- QUANTIFIED AS: how the parameter is quantified, giving units in which values are expressed
- CATEGORISED AS: which broad category the parameter falls into
- DERIVATION: if there is a derived parameter
- OPTIONAL FURTHER INFORMATION

Each of the metrics listed in the previous section can now be described in the above template. For example, Response Time of a management application can be described as follows:

- NAME: Response Time

- DEFINED AS: an average of time taken in getting a response after a command is given
- TYPE: Measurable
- QUANTIFIED AS: time value in seconds
- CATEGORISED AS: Application Performance
- DERIVED PARAMETER: Application throughput

This type of template is useful for the recording and subsequent automated analysis of evaluation data. The next section discusses the application of this evaluation framework to our research.

Section 10.3.4 presents an overall methodology for the evaluation of network management systems, using the hierarchical evaluation criteria described earlier, and the template for definition described in this section.

10.3.3 Evaluation Criteria

System evaluation is an important area of information systems development. Any evaluation framework needs appropriate metrics for comparing various solutions/systems. Therefore, we need evaluation criteria appropriate for e-business management that depends on the underlying network and systems management. In Chapter 4 we discussed some evaluation criteria for measuring a service performance from a business perspective. Lawliss and Associates have discussed some evaluation criteria for COTS products from the perspective of software engineering. CoMEN has developed evaluation criteria for network and systems management[21]. CoMENS extends these criteria as discussed below: It may be noted that the discussion in this section uses technical parameters for network management. However, a hierarchical model has been prescribed to express e-business management evaluation criteria at various levels as shown in Figure 87:

- Enterprise and Business Level (Level 1)
- Management Architecture Level (Level 2)
- Management Function Level (Level 3)
- Technical Attribute Level (Level 4)

As expected, level 1 criteria capture the business level issues. This will be illustrated with relevant questionnaire in Section 10.5[21].

Now we discuss the evaluation criteria at level 2. Due to the absence of any other guidelines for this purpose, we decided to use the integrated management framework described in Part 4. Therefore, we define evaluation criteria in terms of instrumentation, platform and applications aspects of the framework (Figure 87). We need to add to this, some evaluation metrics at the human user level to cater for cooperative enterprise processes in an e-business organization.

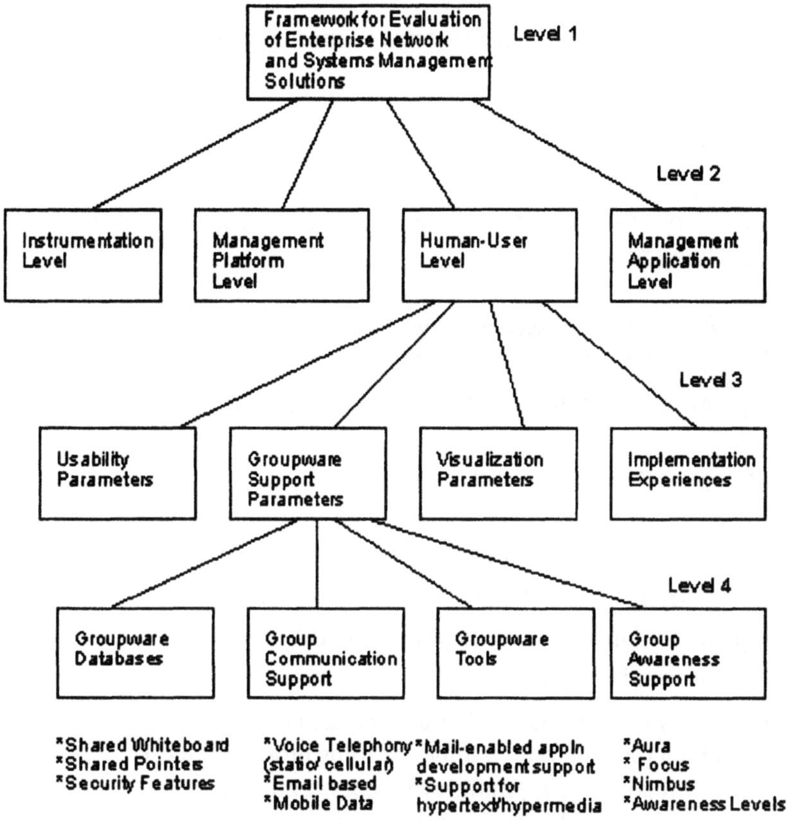

Figure 87. Hierarchical Evaluation Criteria for Cooperative Management

Level 3 criteria drill down to the function level in each of the aspects at level 2. For example, issues at the human user level could be usability, visualization, groupware support and implementation experiences. Level 3 attributes of other aspects of level 3 are not shown in Figure 87 due to space constraints[23].

Finally, at level 4 one can define technical attribute level parameters for each of the functions in level 3. For example, attributes at groupware level could be groupware database characteristics, communication tools and explicit awareness support mechanisms. Some CSCW researchers are experimenting with new parameters, such as focus and nimbus[21].

We now discuss possible technical attributes in terms of the various aspects of the level 2 of the hierarchical evaluation criteria of Figure 87.

10.3.3.1 Evaluation Criteria at the Instrumentation Level

- Management Information Level

- Structure (OO vs. Table-driven)
- Types of managed devices/systems supported (types of MIB available)

• Protocol Level

- Type of Standard (CMIP/LLC, SNMP over IPX etc.)
- Flexibility of Access (precise addressing, scoping/filtering etc.)
- Robustness (authentication/access control)
- Efficiency (implementation code size, execution speed, load on underlying network etc)

10.3.3.2 Evaluation Criteria at the Platform Level

• Management Communication level

- Support for multiple management communication protocols (e.g. SNMP, RPC)

• Management Database Level

- Database Access (proprietary, standard SQL support)
- Database Access performance

• Distributed Processing Environment (DPE) Level

- Support for Open Standards (e.g., CORBA)

• Management Services Level

- Scalability (e.g., number of nodes managed)
- Efficiency (polling rate, number of traps processed etc.)
- Security features (e.g., multilevel access control)
- Functionality with APIs (object management, inference engines, relationship modeling etc.)

10.3.3.3 Evaluation Criteria at the Management Application Level

• Support for Heterogeneous Platforms

- Object model level
  Distribution Transparency
- Conformance to RM-ODP, CORBA, Java RMI, DCOM and TINA
  Application Functionality
- OSI Management Functions Supported (fault, configuration, accounting, performance, security mgmt)
- Support for evolving network user services (mobile services, multimedia systems etc.)

These parameters are defined with respect to our integrated management framework. However, it is possible to define the parameters with respect to some other model, such as TMN hierarchy.

10.3.3.4 Evaluation Criteria at the Human User Level

Evaluation criteria at this level are quite significant for enterprise management in view of the growing scarcity of skilled network management professionals and the need for such people to cooperate within and across organizations. It draws input from research in CSCW and Human Computer Interaction[23]. The complexity of the task of visualization of a large amount of management data with respect to abstract management models, underscores the importance of virtual environments. Some of the parameters are:

- Usability
  - Ease of learning
  - Ease of use and flexibility
  - Documentation support
  - Conformance to ISO Usability Standards
- Groupware Support
  - Awareness (levels of awareness, focus, nimbus etc.)
  - Group Decision Support Systems (shared workspace, shared pointers etc.)
  - Group Communication Support System (asynch email vs. synch conference call, mobile/multimedia communication etc.)
  - Visualization (layered visual models such as TMN, web based management, multisensory interfaces such as virtual reality)

Each of the above categories needs some measure of implementation experience for procurement purposes. The above list is by no means exhaustive. However, this gives us an indication of the complexity of the task of defining standard evaluation criteria for integrated management systems.

Management applications vary widely depending on the type of network/system/services, organization, user and other environmental factors. Hence it is not feasible to define a standard set of measurement parameters for the evaluation of all integrated management systems. However, it is possible to select a subset of evaluation criteria for any specific enterprise network management systems or, parts thereof. These evaluation criteria can lead to the formulation of experiments or questionnaires for evaluation, depending on our method of evaluation.

It may be noted that it is not possible to describe all metrics exhaustively in this book due to space constraints. However, this Section has shown how any new evaluation criteria could be derived from this hierarchical model. Also similar hirearchies of evaluation criteria may be defined for other business domains. We now need a formal notation for presenting evaluation criteria. This is described in the next section.

10.3.4 Evaluation Methodology

The proposed methodology consists of the following steps:

10.3.4.1 Prototype Implementation

Since our research is concerned with a new design framework, a prototype implementation is necessary. However, this step is not required for the evaluation of commercially available products.

10.3.4.2 Development of Metrics for Evaluation

This involves the selection of an appropriate set of evaluation criteria from our generalized hierarchical model described earlier. These criteria are of various types. Some of them require quantitative performance measures to be extracted from performance reports generated from management platforms. There are now many tools commercially available for this purpose. However, many parameters can be evaluated only in qualitative form. This requires a user or an expert in the application to perform this evaluation. To guide such an evaluation, it is necessary to develop a broad questionnaire that can be addressed through a structured interview or any other form of data collection.

10.3.4.3 Development of Questionnaires relevant to the Evaluation

This phase develops a broad questionnaire to address the appropriate criteria for evaluation. Depending on the objectives of evaluation, these questionnaires can be answered in various ways. For performance evaluations, various machine performance measured need to be entered in response. Since our research involves cooperative management of human users, we need to conduct interviews for this purpose.

10.3.4.4 Heuristic Evaluation by Contextual Interview

This type of evaluation requires a few experts in the area to be interviewed in a laboratory environment, with the help of implementation of the systems under evaluation. This is called a contextual interview[8]. It helps interviewees to quickly grasp the purpose, look and feel of the features proposed.

This stage requires the development of a questionairre (for interview) based on the evaluation criteria and the template. More details on heuristic evaluation and illustrative questionairre are available in [25].

10.4 Illustration of Design and Implementation

In our design, we need to demonstrate schemes to overcome generic weaknesses in the existing collaborative services for the management of enterprise networks. The next section summarizes some major problems observed (as part of Requirements Engineering dimension of CoMENS) in support of group cooperation in existing integrated management environment.

10.4.1 Architectural Framework

Having arrived at the workflow model, our next step is to design and implement the software. A groupware-integrated solution requires the following major components:

1. A CSCW platform that has integrated applications support, such as object-oriented database, mechanisms for designing input forms/output reports, autonomous agent designs, and workflows. An example of commercial CSCW platforms is Lotus NOTES™.
2. A management platform with support for a standard network management protocol, such as SNMP, and related MIBs. Examples of commercial network management platforms include HP OpenView, TIVOLI TME™ and Aprisma SPECTRUM™.
3. A cooperative management application for integrating the above two major components. Although the widely used, help-desk based trouble-ticketing application is used for illustration, this methodology would work for any other cooperative management application. The next section presents the proof-of-concept implementation.

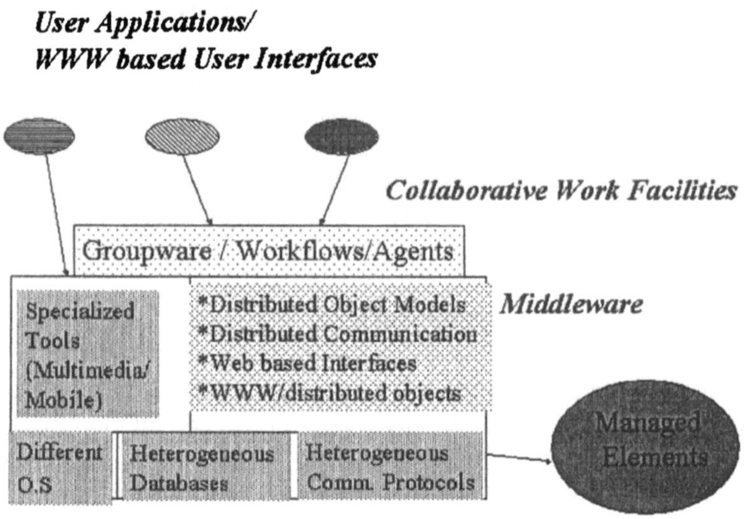

Figure 88. Architectural Framework for Cooperative Management

The existing integrated management frameworks are not capable of handling such a wide range of dynamic management requirements involving people and equipment. This requires an integration of integrated management platforms, mobile/multimedia communication systems, and sophisticated business workflow/groupware tools. The heterogeneous nature of multivendor, telecommunication solutions necessitate the use of distributed object modeling. We present an architectural model (Figure 88) that incorporates recent advances in object modeling and communication technologies (e.g., mobile, multimedia) and intelligent agents.

The above illustration shows how a cooperative e-business management system could be designed. However, the actual architecture will depend on the type of business. For example, an e-telco management system would use e-TOM recommendations and a variety of management platforms, as discussed in Chapter 8 and appendices 2 and 4.

10.4.2 Workflow Design

Figure 89 describes the overall re-engineered workflow of this application, using Action Workflow notation. It is not possible to present the detailed process due to space limitations. This overall picture presents the interaction amongst a number of related workflows loops as per the Action Workflow notation described earlier.

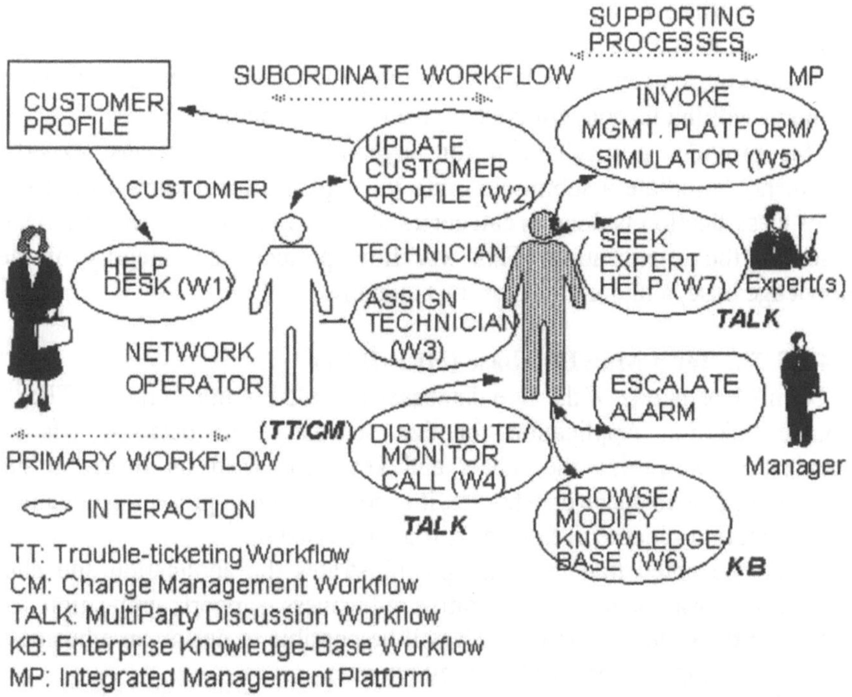

Figure 89. Detailed Workflow Design based on Action Workflow

10.4.2.1Trouble ticketing Database (TT)

This is a repository for handling all customer calls and information related to customer organizations, their people, contracts, configurations, etc. It allows different views for pending calls in terms of various organizations, callers, etc. Also there is a facility for the escalation/reassignment of calls to different skill groups.

10.4.2.2 Change Management Database (CM)

This repository assists in the planning, execution and support of various change management activities.

10.4.2.3 Multiparty Discussion Database (TALK)

This allows discussion amongst all concerned on various issues related to network management. These discussions are organized in various threads according to topics of interest.

10.4.2.4 Knowledge-Base (KB)

This workflow allows the technician to browse the technical documentation and the knowledge base for any clues to solving the problem. It also integrates different tools, such as integrated management platform and simulator within this cooperative management environment.

This provides a mechanism for anybody (e.g., technicians, experts, customers) to initiate a submission into the organizational knowledge base, but its classification is done in categories of rules and notes by an authorized person in the organization. This workflow protects the integrity of the knowledge base, a major asset for the company.

10.4.2.5 The Term Map Database (HLP-DSK)

Term Maps is one of the five databases included in our Lotus NOTES™ Trouble ticketing Application for this purpose. This database lets an organization customize the labels and keywords used on forms in the application. Due to space constraints, it is not possible to present the detailed implementation scheme in this book. It is discussed in [21].

It may be noted that this example illustrates the application and data architecture designs for a cooperative e-business support application for using help-desk model. Similarly, it will be possible to design an e-business management application for other requirements.

In addition to these there are supporting processes to call other human roles, such as seeking expert help and escalating a call to a higher level of management.

It may be noted that this workflow design may be similar to many existing trouble ticketing systems. However, the workflow diagrams capture the design considerations for any re-engineering required in the future. Many existing telecommunication trouble-ticketing systems are now facing problems with their systems due to the changing telecommunication business environment (e.g., due to mergers and sell-offs).

10.5 Illustration of Evaluation Methodology

This phase evaluates the resulting framework. Depending on the type of project, the evaluation may involve the testing of the framework and/or the prototype against evaluation criteria for cooperative management. These evaluation criteria depend on the type of problem domain. While some areas have well-defined evaluation criteria, other areas, like e-business management, do not have any commonly agreed evaluation parameters. Therefore, it is necessary to devise an evaluation strategy for this project.

While there are a number of techniques for the evaluation of human-computer systems,[23] this book uses the heuristic evaluation technique, involving the interviewing of experts in e-business management on the basis of the prototype and framework description.

The results of this evaluation process will depend very much on the interest and background of experts being subjected to the contextual interview. Since our design framework is expected to be applicable to enterprise networks in general, we chose three network and systems experts with at least 10 years' experience in the technical and management functions in a variety of businesses, such as telecommunication carrier, government networks and banks. These experts are called EXPERT1, EXPERT2 and EXPERT3, respectively, in our evaluation results presented in the last section.

The following sub-sections illustrate the application of this methodology. Since our research involved a new design framework for cooperative management, a prototype was implemented using Aprisma SPECTRUM™ network management platform and Lotus NOTES™ groupware platform to show the integration of business processes with network management.

10.5.1 Evaluation Metrics

The first step of the above methodology involves the development of appropriate metrics. Table 13 illustrates a template for defining evaluation metrics as per the hierarchy shown in Figure 87.

Table 13. Development of Evaluation Metrics

Name:	Categorized As:	Defined As:	Type	Quantified As:
Ease-of-use	Usability	User effort required for fault-free operation	Subjective	Graded user opinion (scale 1-10)
Support for standard user interface	Usability	Whether any user interface standard (e.g. Motif) supported; if yes what are they	Boolean;Enumerative	Boolean value with values "true" or "false"
Group Communication Support	Groupware Support	Whether any group communication support systems are supported; if yes what are they	Boolean;Enumerative	Boolean value with values "true" or "false"; list
Hypertext/	Visualization	What hypertext/	Enumerative	List

Name:	Categorized As:	Defined As:	Type	Quantified As:
Hypermedia Support		hypermedia facilities are supported to assist in the browsing of management information		
UI Implementation Experience	Visualization	How much Implementation experience exists (years, installations); quality	Number; Subjective	number/fractions; Graded user opinion (scale 1-10)
Support for new network service	Application Functionality	Is there support for new network services (e.g., mobile multimedia); if yes what are they	Boolean;Enumerative	Boolean value with values "true" or "false"; list
Response time	Application Performance	Average response time for a set of critical commands to execute	Measurable	Quantitative value in time (seconds)
Load on the distributed infrastructure	Application Performance	System load in terms of network bandwidth required at all interfaces	Measurable	Quantitative values (Mbits/sec)

10.5.2 Checklist-Evaluation of Architectural Features

In order to address some of the above evaluation metrics, we firstly need to examine the architectural features as shown in Table 14. This is followed by the heuristic evaluation by experts.

Table 14. Evaluation Template Applied for Architectural Evaluation

Name:	Categorized As:	Defined As:	Type	Value
Support for CORBA	Platform	Whether the platform supports OMG	Boolean	FALSE

Name:	Categorized As:	Defined As:	Type	Value
		CORBA object model		
High Performance Computing Functions	Platform	Whether the platform supports mobile / multimedia computing functions; If yes, what are they?	Boolean; Enumerative	TRUE; SPECTRUM Mobile phone interface for alarms and messages, NOTES selective replication
Support for CORBA	Platform	Whether the platform supports OMG CORBA object model	Boolean	FALSE
High Performance Computing Functions	Platform	Whether the platform supports mobile / multimedia computing functions; If yes, what are they?	Boolean; Enumerative	TRUE; SPECTRUM Mobile phone interface for alarms and messages, NOTES selective replication
Support for standard user interface	Usability	Whether any user interface standard (e.g. Motif) supported; if yes what are they	Boolean;Enumerative	TRUE; Motif, Microsoft Windows 3.1
Group Communication Support	Groupware Support	Whether any group communication support systems are supported; if yes what are they	Boolean;Enumerative	TRUE; email, static and mobile phones, WAN
Hypertext/ Hypermedia Support	Visualisation	What hypertext/ hypermedia facilities are supported	Enumerative	NOTES supports hypertext/hypermedia

It may be possible to analyze this information further if a large number of responses can be obtained. However, it may not be of much use in this particular case due to the small number of responses.

This Section has briefly illustrated the process of the evaluation of e-business management solutions. It may be noted that this illustration has used criteria, and templates tailor made for cooperative management of e-business infrastructure. This methodology can be adapted for other types of e-business management evaluations.

10.6 Chapter Summary

This chapter has discussed and illustrated the methodologies for the design and the evaluation of e-business management solutions as part of the Cooperative management Methodology for E-business Networks and Services (CoMENS).

The design dimension of CoMENS uses workflow design and automation techniques. We discussed high-level descriptive notations (e.g., design patterns), and graphical notations (e.g., workflow loops) that clearly captured the business aspect of the requirements, and allowed the definition of design and architecture iteratively as per the twin peaks model described in the previous chapter. The iterative nature was illustrated by the design of a trouble-ticketing system in two stages; conceptual level and detailed design level that involve different architectural considerations.

Finally this chapter presented the evaluation dimension of CoMENS. We started the discussion with some recent advances in the evaluation of COTS systems, and that of integrated management systems. The three major components of this evaluation methodology are; a template, a hierarchical criteria and heuristic evaluation. While templates were used as the notation to capture the wide variety of metrics for evaluation of integrated management systems, a hierarchical model is used to derive the metrics for evaluation at different architectural levels.

This work lays the foundation for further work in the formal design and evaluation of integrated management systems from an e-business perspective. More work is required in testing and evaluating CoMENS in the changing, real e-business environment. We hope more such testing will lead to refinements, and variations of this methodology that will be applicable to different types of e-business environments, including e-health, e-govt, e-commerce and e-banking.

10.7 References

1. Aalst W.M.P. van der, Hofstede A.H.M. ter, Kiepuszewski B., and Barros A.P., "Workflow Patterns", Technical Report, Technicl University of Einhoven (TUE)- CapacityGroup I&T, Netherlands, November, 2000

2. Boloix G.and Robillard P.N., "A Software System Evaluation Framework", *IEEE Computer*, December 1995
3. Casati F. and Discenza A., "Modeling and Managing Interactions among Business Processes", *HP Labs Technical Report* HPL-2000-159, December, 2000, Palo Alto, USA
4. Czarnecki P., Jajszczyk A., and Wilkosz M., "Comparison Criteria for GDMO-Based Network Management Information Models: A Step towards the Integration of Management Systems," *Journal of Network and Systems Management* Vol. 4, No. 1, March 1996
5. Dean J., "An Evaluation Method for COTS Software Products", *Proceedings of the 12th Annual Software Technology Conference (STC)*, May 2000, Saltake City, Utah, USA
6. Eckerson W., "Case Study: The role of IS in reengineering", *Open Information Systems* 9(2) (February 1994)
7. Georgakopoulos D., Hornick M., and Sheth A., "An Overview of Workflow Management: From Process Modeling to Workflow Automation Infrastructure", *Distributed and parallel Databases*, 3, pp.119-153, Kluwer Academic Publishers, Netherlands, 1995
8. K. Holtzblatt et al., "Conducting and Analysing a Contextual Interview", *Readings in Human-Computer Interaction*, Morgan Kaufmann Publishers Inc., San Francisco, USA 1995
9. IETF, Host Resources MIB, Internet RFC1514, 1993
10. ISO JTC1.21.57.2/ ITU-T Q19/7 &Q27 CD, "QoS - Basic Framework", Interim Meeting Output, Toronto Canada, January 1995
11. ISO 10746-X, "Reference Model for Open Distributed Processing (RM-ODP)" Parts 1,2, 3 and 4
12. Avison D. and G. Fitzgerald G., *Information Systems Development: Methodologies, Techniques and Tools*, McGraw-Hill, 1995
13. Jeeanrenaud J. and Romanazzi P., "Software Product Evaluation: A Methodological Approach", *Software Quality Management*, II: pp.59-69, 1994
14. Kontio J., "A Case Study in Applying a Systematic Method for COTS Selection", *Proceedings of the 18th International Conference on Software Engineering*, pp.201-209, 1996
15. Larman C., *Applying UML and Patterns: An Introduction to Object-Oriented Analysis and Design*, Prentice-Hall, 1998,
16. Laudon K. and Laudon J., *Management Information Systems: Organization and Technology*, Prentice Hall, 1998
17. Lawliss P., Mark K., Thomas D. and Courtheyn T., "A Formal Process for Evaluating COTS Software Products", *IEEE Computer*, Vol. 34 No. 5, May 2001

18. Lewis D., Wade V., and Bracht R., "The Development of Integrated Inter and Intra Domain Management Services", *Proceedings of the 6th IFIP/IEEE International Symposium on Integrated Network Management*, May 1999, Boston, USA
19. Lord J., "Patterns for e-business: Lessons learned from building successful e-business applications", *IBM White Paper*, http://www-106.ibm.com/developerworks/library/lessons/, June 2000
20. Maiden N. and Ncube C., "Acquiring COTS Software Selection Requirements", *IEEE Software*, 15(2): 46-56, Mar 1998
21. May P., *The Business of ECOMMERCE*, Cambridge University Press, UK, 2000,
22. McDougall A., and Squires D., "A Critical Examination of the Checklist Approach in Software Selection", *Journal of Educational Computing Research*, Vol. 12 (3): 263-274, 1995
23. Preece J., Rogers Y., Sharp H., Benyon D., Holland S. and Carey T., *Human - Computer Interaction*, Addison-Wesley, 1994, ISBN 0-201-62769-8.
24. Ramaswamy R., *Design and Management of Service Processes*, Adison Wesley AT&T Engineering Process Improvement Series edited by J.W.Wesner, 1996.
25. Ray P., *Cooperative Management of Enterprise Networks*, Kluwer Academic/Plenum Publications, May 2000
26. Ray. P., CoMENS: Cooperative management Methodology for E-Business Networks and Services, *submitted for publication*, May 2002
27. Riehl D. and Zulinghoven H., "Understanding and Using Patterns in Software Development": *Theory and Practice of Object Systems* 2(1): 3-13, 1996
28. Sloman M.(Ed), *Network and distributed systems management*, Addison Wesley, Workingham England; Reading MA USA, 1994
29. Tran V.and Liu D., "A Risk-Mitigating Model for the Development of Reliable and Maintainable Large-scale-Off-The-Shelf Integrated Software Systems", In the *Proceedings of the 1997 Annual Reliability and Maintainability Symposium*, pp.361-67, Jan 1997
30. Umar A., *Object-Oriented Client/Server Internet Environments*, Prentice Hall, 1997

APPENDICES (1-4)

Appendix 1. BPM: A Case Study

ICS GmbH, Munich, Germany © May 2000
http://www.ics.de/

This appendix supplements the discussion in Parts 1 and 2 of this book with a real case study of the implementation of an e-business management solution as reported by Intelligent Communication Software (ICS), Germany. This case study presents an e-business management problem from the perspective of a global IT service provider. The document highlights the multi-vendor nature of e-business management using a product .of ICS called CONTINUITY™ and a number of commercially available products.

Today, the end-to-end monitoring of business processes based on service level agreements and applications, system and infrastructure performance in the IT management environment is usually little more than a vision. The idea of business process management is to use IT-oriented performance variables and proven service level management concepts to draw conclusions as to the availability of business processes and if necessary, trigger alarms about business continuity

Particular problems, which have arisen in the past with implementing this thinking, are as follows:

- The fact that it is often almost impossible to map processes in individual systems to infrastructure resources (mainly many to many relations)
- The complexity of the processes themselves (i.e., logical connections between process steps, interaction with external processes, etc.)
- Assessing infrastructure faults, which usually occur in parallel in terms of business continuity (correlation, business impact)
- A lack of sufficiently detailed, consistently documented business process models.

This case study aims to present a successful project, which addresses precisely these problems. This is the first time the approach and the technologies employed were applied in this form. Explicit details are given of the initial situation, the approach used and the tool portfolio employed. The resulting financial benefits are also assessed. Figure 90 shows the core solution approach and the main results achieved.

A1.1 Background

The organization in question is a globally operating IT service provider of an international group. The IT services are provided centrally by a business unit consisting of several thousand staff, which supports all the divisions of the company and many external clients. In its IT operations to date, the company has followed a strategy of deep vertical integration, which is completely normal within the industry. Over the years, this has led to a totally non-transparent portfolio on both the applications and on the administration and management side. Increasing staff turnover on the development side was putting the quality and 100% availability of applications at risk, and with it the long-term competitiveness of the business as a whole.

The IT infrastructure was set on a multi-layered regional basis, with different regional IT management servers at state level together with local networks. Most of the business processes involved infrastructure components with differing regional areas and layers. Global processes, using a large number of distributed resources, had to be examined.

In such an environment, proactively managing or measuring the IT operating risks was seen as too expensive and impossible. Ultimately however, the IT goal was defined as introducing a business process management concept with tool support.

In concrete terms, the goals are as follows:

- Using early-warning mechanisms on selected business processes
- Consistent monitoring of infrastructure elements, systems, SLAs and business processes
- Significant reductions in downtimes
- Increasing value added through quantifiable service improvements

An enterprise management project was set up as the platform for achieving these goals. There is no room to examine all aspects of the project here, because of its size and that of the business. This case study will therefore limit itself to looking at:

- The initial situation of the company
- The tool portfolio used
- How the project was conducted, and
- Quantifying the benefits generated in selected processes

It does not include:

- The basic methods and tools of process modeling
- Basic concepts of IT management, such as ITIL
- A detailed account of the service level management[1] field
- The process of selecting tools
- The characteristics or individual requirements of individual SLAs and/or business processes.

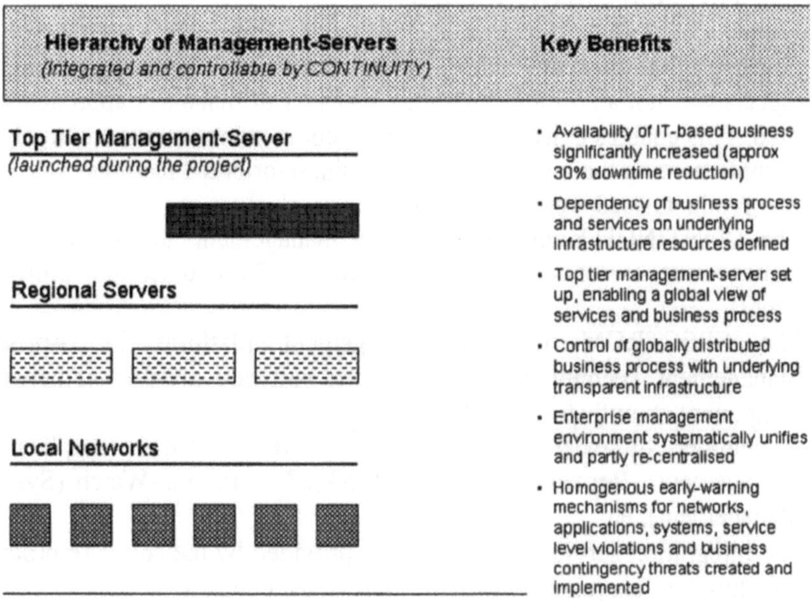

Figure 88. Benefits of Business Process Management

A1.2 Initial Situation

The infrastructure of the company comprised :

- Around 35,000 endpoints worldwide
- Around 2,000 servers (more than half of them applications servers)
- A three-layer system of regional management servers and local networks for supporting globally distributed business processes
- Around 3,500 central IT staff, with a total of some 7500 worldwide
- Virtually all the standard hardware and software platforms including a monolithic back-end system (fully developed in-house)
- Approximately 20 SLAs at technical level.

Before the project started, the company was using all the current system management platforms commonly in use at the time, but did not have a holistically designed overall solution. The core business processes had been modeled and largely optimized in a recent Business Process Reengineering (BPR) initiative.

The timeframe for solving the tasks set was at around six months.

A1.3 The Tool Portfolio Used

Because of the company's size, using just a single product for managing all aspects was not an option. Instead, a manager of managers approach was adopted. This enables existing management components to remain largely in use, supplementing them with primarily business-oriented features.

The products used were as follows:

- The CONTINUITY business process management and service level management system from ICS Intelligent Communication Software GmbH
- The SPECTRUM network management platform by Aprisma Management Technologies, formerly the software division of network component manufacturers Cabletron Systems
- A number of existing tools, such as BMC Patrol (Application Management), Remedy ARS (Help Desk), Metrix Win-Watch (System Management), etc.

The integration services required were provided by the software product manufacturers in conjunction with the staff of the company.

A1.4 Implementing the Project

The project was implemented in four rough work packages:

- The "processes" package:
  - Establishing the existing process models
  - Mapping the infrastructure resources and services on the process step level to correlate alarms at process level
- The "technology and services" package:
  - Recording the existing infrastructure
  - Defining the services/SLAs to be supported
  - Modeling the services, interdependencies between resources and services; implementing the interfaces with existing components and systems
  - Integrating and testing service and process models
- The "organizational anchoring" package:
  - Training the core team in implementing and supervising further work
  - Training users across the board
- The "rollout" package: implementing the tool portfolio at production level.

Figure 91 shows the overall project schedule.

Process mapping and infrastructure and services modeling were operated in parallel to handle all these packages within the time allowed. They were combined in the sub-steps of "process mapping" and "modeling".

In view of the size of the project, consideration was also given to using a pilot project in an isolated business unit of the company; but this was rejected, again to save time.

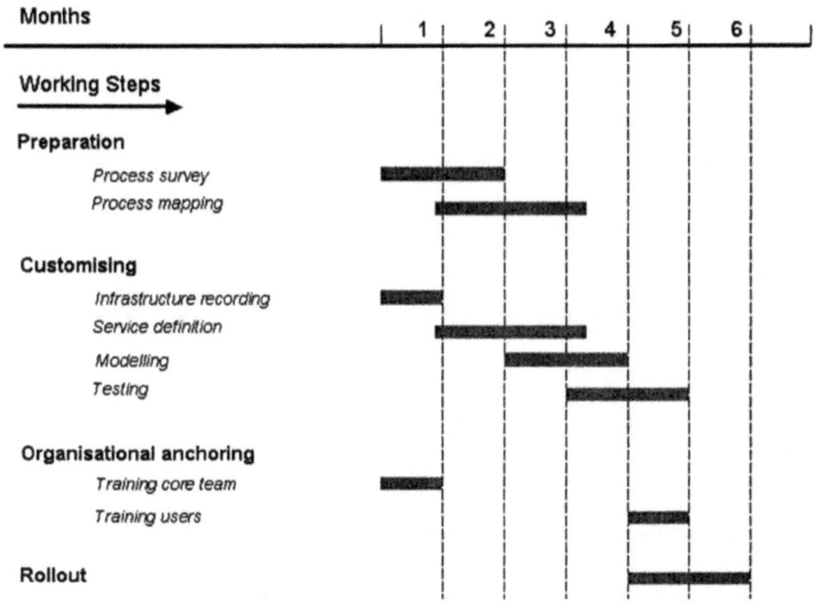

Figure 89. Business Process Management Project Schedule

The process models submitted at the start of the project included many workflow concepts reflecting the logical links between sub-processes and activities. To make the models less complex, these links were ignored when modeling and correcting faults in CONTINUITY. The monitoring concentrated on the dependency of individual processes on service level agreements, which in turn depended on the availability and performance of the underlying services, applications and infrastructure resources. The underlying strategy is shown in Figure 92.

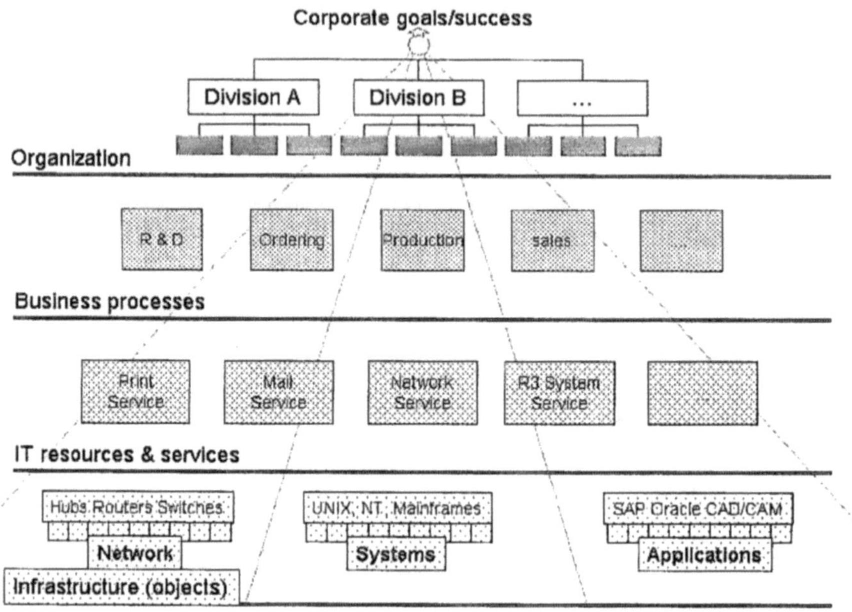

Figure 90. Corporate Goals of Business Process Management

The work packages described above were implemented with the aid of the following team structure:

- ***Project Steering Committee***: met regularly to examine the progress of the project and accept results at critical milestones
- ***Project management***: the sub-team which handled the operational management of the day to day project business
- ***Processes and organization team***: handled the process mapping and analyses and anchored the overall solution in the organization, including training and implementation required
- ***Technology and services***: a sub-team, which handled the technology side of the project.

The biggest challenge proved to be getting company commitment to the project. At the start of the project, responsibilities for certain technologies had created "fiefdoms", which the project dealt with and in some cases re-centralized.

It also became relatively clear that implementing a business process management project in an organization of this size could not cover all processes. As the project progressed, its scope was limited to certain core processes whose availability was the main cause of the IT operating risk.

The central approach was to set up an overall top-tier management server, which would make it possible to monitor global services and business processes across regional servers. The core elements of this solution were CONTINUITY and SPECTRUM.

A1.5 Quantifying the Benefits

The financial benefits of the project were estimated and verified on the basis of the value added through better process continuity. The quantification started with the hourly costs, which the company incurred if certain business processes failed. These costs were estimated internally in some cases, and taken externally from industry benchmarks in others. From historical monitoring data, it was possible to tell what the non-availability of each process cost the company a year, which also made it possible to determine the annual benefits (assuming a certain reduction in downtimes).

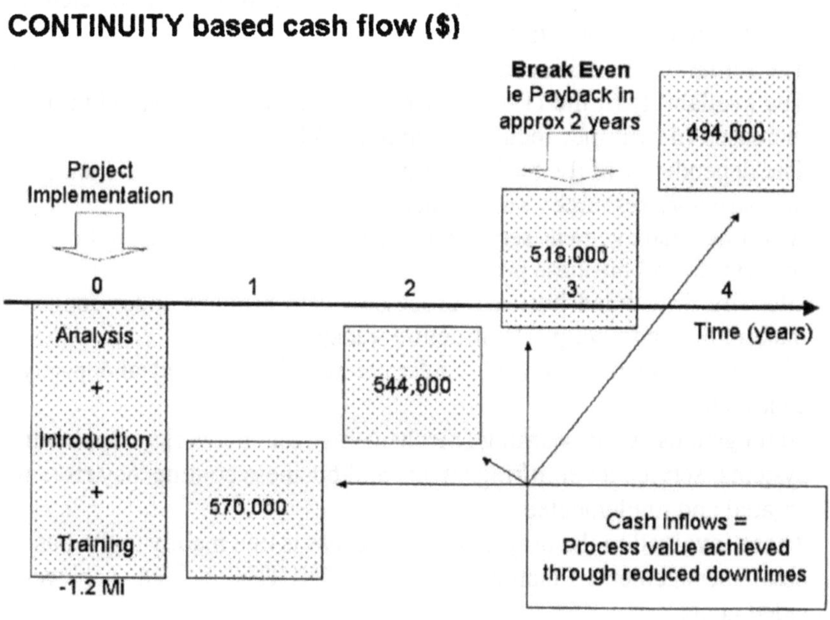

Figure 91. BPM Project Cash flows

It was assumed that the benefits of the solution would last forever, this meant that the project could be allocated a total cash inflow (by discounting). When the inflow was set against the project budget, it showed a clear positive net present value.

In terms of time, it was also apparent that the payback period for the investment in the project was about two years. There is no way of making such statements in most IT management projects to date. This could only be done through referring explicitly to business processes.

The payback calculations are shown in Figure 93 (actual values changed).

Assumptions:

- CONTINUITY worth $ 600.000 a year (based on underlying process values and actual downtimes)
- Annual cash flows discounted at 5% p.a.
- Project investment volumes and process values assumed

A1.6 Assessment of The Project

Implementation of the software components had been completed at the time of writing this Appendix, and the business processes selected were being monitored at production level.

The actual results achieved are as follows:

- The availability of the IT-supported business processes was significantly increased (downtimes reduced by approx. 30%)
- The dependency of the business processes and services on the underlying infrastructure resources was defined
- A top tier management server was installed, enabling a global overview of services and business processes
- Globally distributed business processes were brought under control, by making the underlying infrastructure transparent
- The enterprise management landscape was harmonized and partly re-centralized
- Homogenous early-warning mechanisms for networks, applications, systems, service level infringements and business contingency risks were created and implemented.

Those involved in the project say its success is due mainly to the business process management functions of CONTINUITY helped achieve the intended goals.

A1.7 Discussion

This project involved a new approach to implementing business process management in practical terms. This approach is not widely used yet; but it can be expected that the success of this project will push developments further and make business process management attractive to a wide range of organizations.

Another major factor in implementing the processes described here is inherent in the organizational changes as required by business process management. The strictly functional structure of many large IT organizations should be replaced by clearly defined organizational units with end-to-end responsibility for business processes ("process owners") or at least services ("service managers").

This case study has briefly presented the business perspective of e-business management, and supplements the discussion in Part 1 of this book.

Appendix 2. TMF Guidelines for FAB

This appendix illustrates the use of TMF guidelines for major e-business processes in telecommunication service providers. This case study also supplements the discussion of standards-based e-business management of e-telcos in Chapter 8. The document is based on the standardization of telecom service Fulfillment, Assurance and Billing (FAB) processes, as defined by Tele-Management Forum (TMF) in the Telecom Operations Map (TOM) version 2.1, GB910 dated March 2000

A2.1 Introduction

TM Forum uses a business and customer services driven approach to achieving end-to-end automation using integrated Commercial Off-the-shelf (COTS) software. It enables product availability, along with development specifications needed to produce management systems that can work together to produce the operational results needed by service providers and network operators. TM Forum makes use of international and regional standards when available, and provides input to standards bodies whenever new technical work is done. The TM Forum focus is on providing pragmatic solutions to business problems and is based on the business layering principles articulated in the ITU-T layered TMN model.

The TM Forum approaches automation from both a business context and a systems context. Through the work in business context areas, members define the business process, requirement models and both technology-neutral information models, as well as technology-specific information models. This work is directly related to key market segment issues. The projects that develop the business context work can be both Process Automation (requirement and information modeling focused) projects and catalyst (implementation focused) projects.

The systems context work is done under the umbrella of TM Forum's drive to create a New Generation of Operations Systems and Software (NGOSS™) that more truly delivers Plug and Play environments. NGOSS™ is driven by the business context work and requirements for systems infrastructure. It includes business case development for NGOSS™, the development of detailed requirements for NGOSS™, the development of the application component design and the infrastructure into which applications can plug and unplug. The NGOSS™ infrastructure is being developed as a technology-neutral architecture with associated technology-specific architectures and technology selections.

This approach integrates the following major aspects of telecom service specification and realization.

1. **Process-**A common business process framework
2. **Information-**Common information models to link processes
3. **Systems** Implementation-'rules' for plug and play 'Off-the-shelf' products that work together
4. **Products-**Commercial Off The Shelf (COTS) products

A2.2 Telecom Operations Map (TOM)

The Telecom Operations Map serves as the blueprint for process direction and the starting point for development and integration of Business and Operations Support Systems (OSS). Now, it also helps to drive TM Forum members work to develop NGOSS™. For service providers, it provides a neutral reference point as they consider internal process reengineering needs, partnerships, alliances and general working agreements with other providers. For suppliers, the Telecom Operations Map outlines potential boundaries of software components, and the required functions, inputs, and outputs that must be supported by products. It consists of:

- A description of the role of the Telecom Operations Map
- A high-level view of Communications Operations processes, sub-processes and activities that is top down, customer-centric, and end-to-end focused
- A high-level identification of the primary end-to-end processes of fulfillment, assurance, and billing, and sub-processes within each Illustrative examples of process flows that show end-to-end process
- A more detailed view of the functions of each sub-process, including activities of each sub-process box, as well as its inputs and outputs to other sub-process boxes

The basic model continues to be stable even as the Telecommunications industry continues to change, largely because the Telecom Operations Map:

- Uses a high level and generic approach
- Reflects a broad range of operations views
- Reflects the way service providers run and are architecting their businesses
- Is widely used

TOM is the 'de facto' standard for operations management processes for the industry.

A2.2.1 TOM Objectives

Whether incumbent providers or new entrants, service providers continue to urgently require well-automated operations processes, since they are faced with ever-increasing competition and a market experiencing dramatic change at an unprecedented rate. Many are struggling to move from a manual-intensive, inconsistent, inflexible environment to one that provides significant improvement in customer focus, service quality, costs and time to market. They have to pervasively do business electronically with trading partners, suppliers and wholesale and retail customers. For the growing Mobile, Wireless and IP Services markets, these SPs are focused on quickly provisioning new customers and supporting service quality issues. For all service providers, the drive to introduce both new value-added services and dramatic improvements in customer care is intense.

For the full range of service providers and network operators, the leading focus of the

TM Forum's mission is to enable end-to-end process automation of telecommunications and data services operations processes. The Telecom Operations Map is the framework for accomplishing this mission.

The purpose of the TOM is to continue to set a vision for the industry for competing successfully through the implementation of process driven approaches to operations management. This includes ensuring integration among all vital operations support systems concerned with service delivery and support. The focus of the Telecom Operations Map document is on the business processes used by service providers, the linkages between these processes, the identification of interfaces, and the use of Customer, Service, Network, and other information by multiple processes. Exploitation of information from every corner of the business will be essential to success in the future. The objectives of the Telecom Operations Map are to continue the progress made in establishing:

- An 'industry owned" common business process model.
- Common definitions to describe processes of a service provider.
- Agreement on the basic information required to perform each process, sub-process and process activity, i.e., sufficient high level information to serve as the starting point for business requirements and information model development, and the satisfaction of those requirements through industry agreement and products.
- A process framework for identifying which processes and interfaces are in most need of integration and automation, and most dependent on industry agreement.

This document describes the processes and their points of interconnection that make up the end-to-end process flows for Fulfillment, Assurance and Billing across the process layers of the Telecom Operations Map. It identifies the major processes and interfaces that make up an end-to-end process. Service providers need this common map of processes to enable doing business efficiently and effectively with other entities and to enable the development and use of third-party software without the need for major customization.

A2.3 Business Drivers

The communications industry is rapidly changing with new rules, new competitors, new customers, unprecedented demands and the emergence of requirements for e-business. Service providers worldwide all face similar challenges, risks and struggles to remain profitable in the face of more competition, higher customer expectations, falling market share and price pressures. As the providers face these challenges, their suppliers must find innovative ways to deliver value or they may also risk going out of business.

Service providers face very different regulatory environments and their business strategies and approaches to competition are quite distinct. In general however, service providers share several common characteristics:

- Heavily dependent upon effective management of information and communications networks to stay competitive
- Adopting a service management approach to the way they run their business and their networks.
- Moving to more of an end-to-end Process Management approach developed from the customer's point of view
- Automating their Customer Care, Service and Network Management Processes
- Need to integrate new OSSs with legacy systems
- Focusing on data services offerings and Focusing on total service performance, including customer satisfaction
- Integrating with current technology (e.g. SDH/SONET and ATM) and new technologies (e.g., IP, DWDM)
- Emphasizing more of a "buy" rather than "build" approach that integrates systems from multiple suppliers

A2.3.1 The Importance of Service

The core of a service provider's success is rapid response to the service needs of the customer. As the market develops the key objectives are 'more for less' -- faster service introduction, improved quality of service at a lower cost. Achieving these objectives requires automation of Customer Care and the supporting Operations.

Some service providers choose to operate their own network infrastructure, while others choose to outsource this segment of their business. The effective exploitation of this network infrastructure, whether directly operated or outsourced, is an integral part of the service delivery chain and directly influences the service quality and cost perceived by the end customer. Service providers will need to become skilled at assessing outsourcing opportunities whether in network infrastructure areas or other areas and then, be skilled at integrating and managing any outsourcing arrangements.

With the growth of data services, it is becoming evident that the end customer perception of quality requires service providers to expand traditional measures of quality and to move more to proactive Service Management and interactive Customer Care. Customer applications now inherently provide sophisticated measures of quality. Service providers have to go beyond network-centric views of Quality of Service and support to meet customer's expectations. It means pushing the limits of service and Customer Care processes performance.

Keeping up with quickly escalating customer service expectations, requires integrated and flexible process and system architectures that allow more off the shelf solutions and reduced dependence on customized solutions.

A2.3.2 Linking Objectives and Requirements

Making a link between communications business objectives and the requirements typically stated for operations management systems is a challenge. Systematic process models are an essential source of solutions to this challenge. They can be used to positively influence a service provider's organization in many ways such as:

- Simplifying internal communications and communications with suppliers or other outside parties
- Revealing the way the organization performs, particularly from a customer point of view
- Identifying process, sub-process and process activity interfaces, particularly at or supporting all points of contact between the service provider and its customers
- Identifying control points and critical performance metrics
- Targeting productivity and quality improvements
- Providing a framework to assess automation opportunities
- Allowing less experienced staff to be quickly effective
- Maintaining gains and enabling continuous improvement

Operations management systems and third party applications, becoming available in the market place today, are maturing in terms of their ability to support these business process models and needs.

A2.3.3 Business Process Models

The use of systematic business process models, like the TOM, also makes it easier to evaluate and improve the processes themselves. Employing business process modeling techniques contributes to the goals and profitability of service providers. Using consistent modeling techniques for business development and information system development brings noticeable efficiency improvements and removes barriers within those organizations and across cooperative, inter-corporation projects.

Service providers that use systematic business process modeling to manage and improve their businesses have a much greater chance of success in today's and tomorrow's marketplace.

A2.4 Business Relationship Reference Model

The global nature of today's emerging telecommunication services is not only multi-national, but is also becoming multi-corporation as companies extend their reach to serve larger geographical areas or to increase the range of services they can offer to their customers. Although one route to accomplish this extended reach is through direct expansion of networks and development of new service capabilities, another route is via formal or informal relationships with other providers.

A2.4.1 Management Value Chain

With emerging e-business requirements and the structural transformation it requires, the demands on the service provider enterprise for automation and integration in processes and applications will be an ongoing concern. The relevant business relationships of a simplified Business Relationship Reference Model are between:

- Customers and Service Providers
- Service Providers and Service Providers
- Service Providers and their Suppliers

The process interfaces inherent in these relationships are part of the 'management value chain' from supplier to network operator and service provider through to customers. These automation and integration requirements involve the total depth and breadth of the service providers' business, including:

- Enterprise Management
- Customer Relationship Management
- Selling Chain Management
- Service Management

- Supply Chain Management
- Procurement Management.
- Network and Element Management

A2.4.2 A Business Reference Model

The Business Reference Model shown in Figure 94 is the foundation for the management value chain and illustrates the principal points of contact between a service provider, its customers, its suppliers and other service providers. A wide range of automation and integration opportunities exists among the business roles and relationships shown. Each has a specific business objective dictating the level and type of management information exchanged, the robustness required of the management interface, and the priority with which industry agreements are pursued in the area concerned.

This model realizes the business reference involving a value chain of service providers where one service provider becomes the customer for another service provider, and an outsourced service provider becomes the supplier for another service provider. The chain ends at the end customer.

There are many implications of this business model. In the past, there was a singular relationship: between the service provider and the customer. With this current view, there are more relationships and there is more complexity:

- The interfaces to suppliers, third party applications vendors and other providers/operators are external. These are initially 'procurement' interfaces, but after deployment, become an integrated part of a service provider's service delivery and support.
- To effectively manage the value chain, standardized internal interfaces and functions to support common or widely implemented management capabilities will be required.
- From the perspective of system software life cycle costs, it is not enough just to outsource custom development. Applications such as trouble ticketing provide opportunities to share a common system model for use within the enterprise versus developing a custom trouble ticketing system for use within the enterprise. It has the added benefit of simplifying the management of trouble ticketing across interfaces to external entities of the management value chain.

The business model interfaces are the points at which different applications vendors' software need to be able to exchange information. This may involve agreeing to a common applications component infrastructure, within which the applications will reside, as well as agreeing on the information to be exchanged. There are potential benefits to all by agreeing upon an open set of processes and information flows. For the service provider, it reduces development cost, enlarges the source of potential suppliers and the product functionality available. For the supplier, it creates a larger potential customer base for their products.

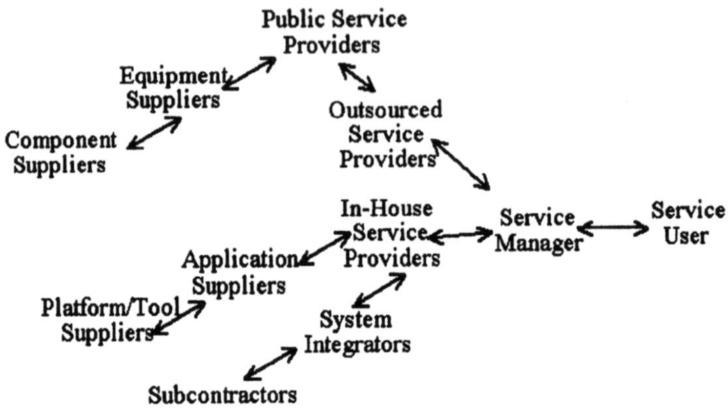

Figure 92. Value Chain based Business Model

A2.4.3 Establishing Common Specifications

Today, the exchange of management information still has significant manual elements or involves proprietary, low-level interactions. There is a continuing need to establish common specifications and agreements to allow providers, their customers, and their suppliers to work together more effectively than is currently possible.

Achieving this goal depends first on identifying the business objectives and the business process framework related to the value chain.

Today, the processes of most service providers remain very manual. No one has fully automated end-to-end processes across the majority of the functions depicted on the Telecom Operations Map, or has fully automated for all the services a service provider offers. Some processes may never be candidates for extensive automation. For example, the Service Development Process, except for Project Management aspects, will likely have a minimum of automation and is based on highly proprietary processes.

A2.5 Telecom Operations Process Model

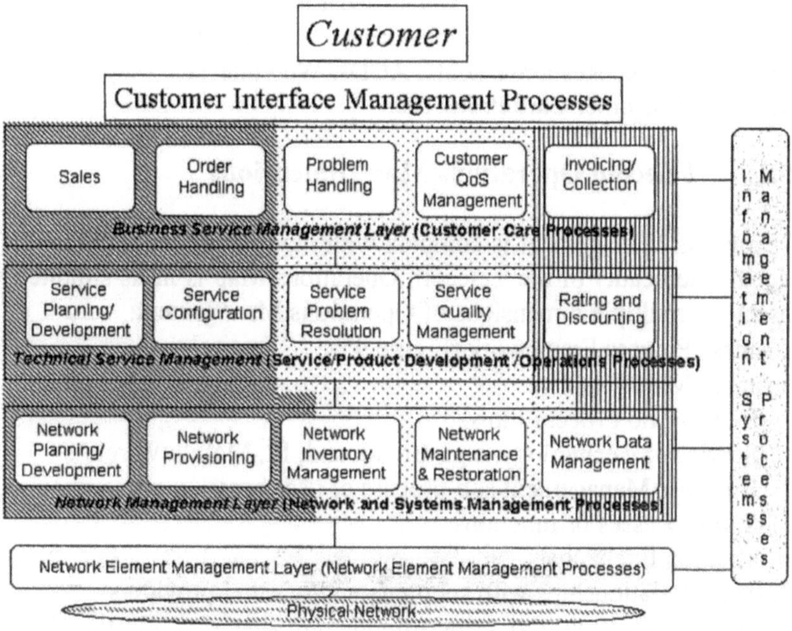

Figure 93. *TOM Common Process Model*

Service providers must apply a customer-oriented and service-management approach, using business process management methodologies, to cost effectively manage their businesses and deliver the service and quality customers require. To manage within a service provider's value chain, a common process framework is required. Figure 95 shows the Telecom Operations Map, the communications industry's common process framework for understanding the relationships among individual process flows.

The Telecom Operations Map uses the layers of the ITU-T TMN model to organize core business processes, but divides the Service Management layer into 2 parts: Customer Care and Service Development and Operations Processes. In the simplest sense, the division reflects differences between processes triggered by individual customer needs from those applied to a group of customers subscribed to a single service or service family. It also reflects the accountability for direct customer contact handling in Customer Care Processes and the critical need to focus on integration and automation of and in support of Customer Care Processes. As Web-based interfaces continue to emerge and e-business concepts are implemented, the integrated Customer Care interface is an essential service differentiator. For this reason, Customer Interface Management is also separately delineated and represents the customer interfacing functions (e.g., integrated customer contact management, Voice Response Units, ACDs, Web interface support) that are supported by Customer Care Processes.

A2.5.1 Telecom Operations Map Dimensions

Operations Management is complex with many dimensions that must be managed. The beauty of the Telecom Operations Map is in its simplicity to represent the multiple dimensions of Operations Management:

- Business Process Framework (Figure 95).
- Business Management
  - •End-to-End Process Flows
  - •Service or Technology, e.g., Broadband, IP, Mobile/Wireless
  - •Business Management sub-process or use cases
  - •Sub-processes or functions
- Information Exchange
- Business Relationships with suppliers and/or other providers
- Systems/Application and Data Architecture that supports the Business Processes

A2.5.2 Business Management Views

Business Process Management is the systematic design and definition of a company's processes and information, including the supporting data and systems structure, to meet its mission, goals and customer requirements. Business Process Management starts with a Business Process Architecture designed to accomplish a specific company's objectives. A company will then define the detail of its end-to-end processes to deliver to customers and to meet its business requirements. The aspects of Business Management highlighted here provide direction on applying the Telecom Operations Map to support process management.

A2.5.2.1 End-to-End Process Flow

The objective of service providers is to automate their processes to deliver value to their customers. Therefore, the most critical process work is the design and definition of the end-to-end process flows for providing services to customers. The Telecom Operations Map approaches this as three basic end-to-end processes common to any service oriented business:

1. Service Fulfillment (timely and correct provisioning of what the customer ordered)
2. Service Assurance (maintaining the service--timely response and resolution of customer or network triggered problems, tracking, reporting, managing and taking action to improve performance for all aspects of a service)
3. Service Billing (timely and accurate bills, knowledgeable and responsive Billing collections)

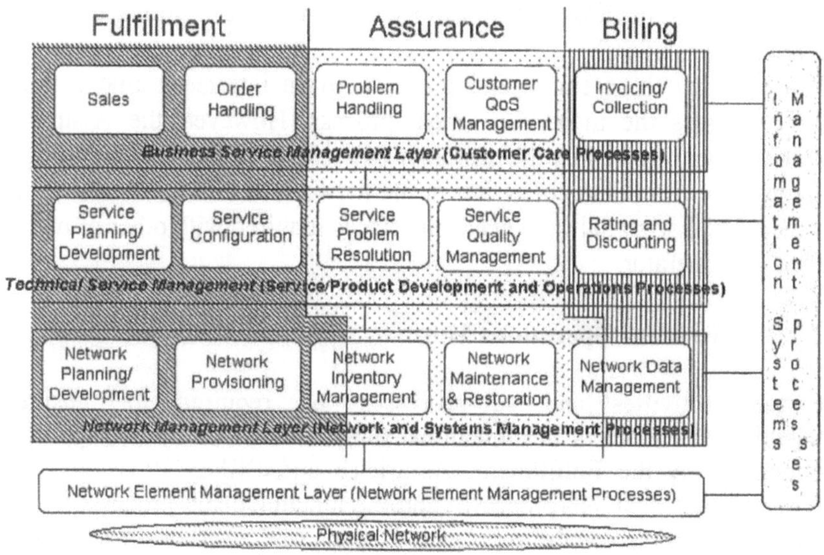

Figure 94. *Fulfillment, Assurance and Billing Processes in TOM*

Figure 96 shows a broad breakdown of the TOM framework into the three customer focused activities (Fulfillment, Assurance and Billing). The purpose is to show in more detail the predominant processes that need to be involved—integrated and automated to support the end-to-end, customer support processes.

The Network Inventory Management and Network Data Management boxes are split to display their significant role, more than an information input or output function, in both end-to-end processes depicted. For example, Network Inventory Management, which includes physical implementation activities in the network, is important to both the Fulfillment and Assurance processes for final installation of the service and restoration and repair of a service.

A2.5.2.2 'FAB' End-to-End Process Flows

The 'FAB' end-to-end process breakdown in Figure 96 does not get across the dynamic, *end-to-end process flow* required to support Service Fulfillment, Assurance and Billing. It involves three essential flow elements that boils down to three flows from top to bottom (customer to network equipment) for each of the sub-processes; fulfillment, assurance and billing:

- Between the customer interface and support in a network element
- From sale through billing
- Between other providers and network operators

And a horizontal flow from left to right (fulfillment to billing though to other service providers).

However, all three end-to-end processes have interfaces among many processes across the map. Fulfillment process. However, the Assurance process can be triggered by the customer or network elements and Billing is predominantly from data collection in the network to bills presented to the customer. The horizontal flow needs interfaces required with other providers and network operators.

A2.5.2.3 Telecom Operations Map

Certain activities and sub-processes are required for business management processes or are functional sub-processes that must support or be supported by the Fulfillment, Assurance and Billing Processes. The business management sub-processes and the functional sub-processes or set of process activities can be represented in a '3-D' overlay diagram. One diagram example is shown Figure 97 for Service Level Agreement Management mapping on FAB matrix.

The service provider needs to meet market demand for service quality and procedures for assuring contracted service quality. The Service Level Agreement (SLA) is a statement of the contracted quality of service levels between the service provider and the customer. The Management of the SLAs must consider all the business activities from identifying and defining SLA parameters, release management, configuring of the operational processes and systems to support and report life-cycle management of the agreements.

The SLA is part of the service offering and, therefore, is developed in the Service Development Process, as shown by the SLA Engineering overlay box. In some cases, a customer sale negotiation may result in a new SLA requirement. In that case, the Service Development Process is employed to establish the new requirement, if appropriate for the business.

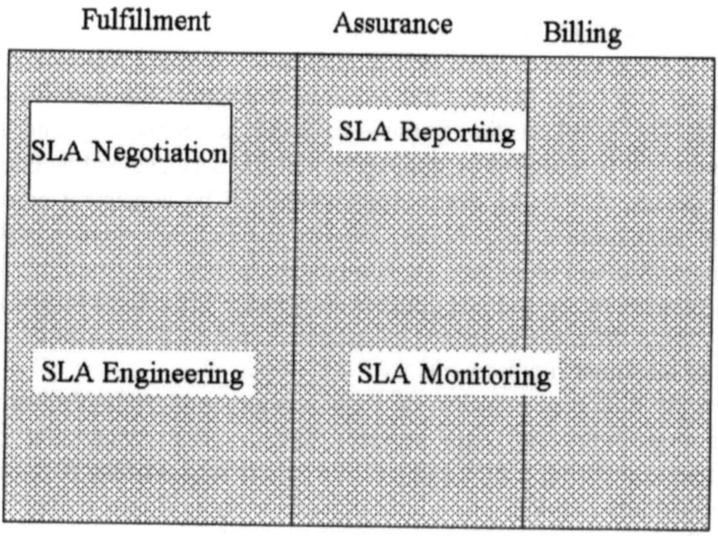

Figure 95. *SLA Management in FAB*

To support existing SLA offers, the SLA Engineering box also indicates that the Service Configuration Process may need to be involved. Once the specific SLA offer is available, the Fulfillment Process triggers the Assurance process to manage SLA performance through monitoring and reporting. An SLA may include measures for performance, pricing, installation intervals, billing timeliness, time to repair, call handling and other metrics or requirements.

This overlay approach can also be used to look at functional sub-processes or capabilities required across the map. Test Management is an example of a functional sub-process that must support several framework processes, e.g., Service Configuration during Fulfillment, Problem Handling in Assurance, Rating and Discounting as part of Billing, Network Maintenance and Restoration as part of Assurance or Billing. Test Management capability support is managed either within the specific process or as a competency/capability function available to any process.

A2.5.2.4 Service and Technology Specific Dimensions

Common processes across services and technologies are essential to:

- Deliver to process cost targets and process performance improvement
- Provide a consistent customer service experience

- o Enable cost effective and fulfilling people management
- o Enable cost effective process automation

Services are differentiated in the common processes by differences in process activities and information required to support the specific service. Although the TOM at the framework level is technology and service independent, it is meant to be applied to real life services and technologies. The processes, flows and basic information will be consistent across two different technologies or services, but the detailed information will have differences. Certain activities or sub-processes may be required for one service or technology and not another. A Service Provider's business rules may dictate a different sequence of activities due to the nature of specific service or customer requirements.

There is a constant influx of new services and technologies in the telecommunications and data services industry that bring new process requirements or bring a new perspective to existing process requirements. Mobile/Wireless Services provide examples for both of these cases:

- o Roaming Management--new process requirements
- o Fraud Management extended to address new requirements in support of roaming capabilities--a new perspective on existing sub-process requirements

Roaming Agreement Management is an important aspect of Mobile Services. Roaming is a service provided by mobile service providers, where customers of a home service provider may use the infrastructure of another. To make this happen, the home service provider and the serving service provider negotiate and enter into a contractual relationship, called a roaming agreement, either directly or through a clearinghouse. The development and implementation of this contractual arrangement is managed as part of the Service Planning and Development Processes. The management of roaming agreements and the associated operational processes is complex, consisting of interfaces across all layers of the map. Mobility and roaming add to the complexity and difficulty of detecting and preventing fraud and are crucial considerations for managing Mobile Services.

A2.5.2.5 Business Relationships with Suppliers and/or Other Providers Views

Joint service arrangements are increasingly becoming the norm to support interconnection due to the huge growth in partnerships, alliances, mergers/acquisitions, new entrants--competitive access providers, and regulatory requirements. To provide service, one service provider will need to interface with one or more service providers and/or network operators. Service providers may interface with different functions at multiple layers of the Telecom Operations Map, when providing a joint service or subcontracting services. For example, the interface points vary depending on:

- o The degree of process automation of the service providers involved
- o The service or technology being supported
- o Whether an SP is acting in a wholesale or retail role
- o Whether an SP is acting on behalf of their network infrastructure or in support of a specific customer service instance

Increasingly a service provider's processes have to be viewed as part of an overall value chain and, therefore, it is critical to understand the interfaces required with suppliers, other providers and network operators. Since many processes that have been internal may now have external aspects, it is critical now to also understand the relationships of a service provider's internal processes. The onset of e-business demands it.

A2.5.2.6 Service Provider TOM Application

The service and network management structure and the process design of a service provider depend on their corporate mission, target markets and strategies. The basic operational functions identified within the Telecom Operations Map are process blocks that can be applied to various service providers' infrastructures and organizations. It is important to recognize that the specific process boundaries shown in the model do *not* correspond to organizational boundaries. In one service provider, a single work group may have responsibility for order taking and receipt of problem notification from a customer. Another work group might be responsible for tracking the progress of an order/trouble and reporting its completion. Another company might conduct all customer contact through one group, with all other processes providing input and taking instruction from that group. In each case, the basic function being executed is similar. To succeed a service provider must incorporate critical aspects from the views highlighted above, and effectively translate business mission, goals and strategies into Business Process Management architecture along with an organizational structure. The Process Architecture must be supported by an integrated and automated Systems/Application and Data architecture, as well as an operational environment that executes these processes with high quality.

Figures 98 through 100 (the FAB process diagrams) provide rough illustrations of the principles of process flow by depicting segments of a process or one instance of the application of the process flow. Developing process flow diagrams is one of the first steps in Business Process Mapping showing the relationships of service provider business needs to the identification of information, requirements, and sequencing required to drive automation.

A2.5.3 A Service Fulfillment Process Flow Instance

The Service Fulfillment process starts with pre-sale activity and ends with:

- On-time and correct installation of a customer's requested service-- as well as a satisfied customer.
- The output of information required to manage the SLA, to provide problem/trouble management and to provide a correct bill.

A2.5.3.1 Order Request and Installation Example

This example of a fulfillment process (Figure 98) shows a possible sequence of activities to support a customer inquiry, subsequent order for service, the configuration of the service, and the installation and completion of the request. Depending on the service provider process, orders can be placed through the sales process and/or directly through the order management process. For a specific service provider, some customers may be supported by a specific sales team that places some, or all orders for the customer and tracks them to completion.

The complete fulfillment flow-through may not actually be required every time for some simple services, which have pre-assigned service capacity. For example, the flow for an instance of a service set-up could be bypassed at Network Provisioning, when configured and tested facilities have been pre-provisioned. This depends upon a particular provider's operational process and policy. It will also impact the timing of interactions with Network Inventory Management; hence, the interface sequence number has been omitted.

In other cases, more process activities may be required for a variety of reasons, e.g., due to the complexity of the service being offered, due to a new SLA requirement, etc. Interfaces to the customer are shown, as well as the output interfaces required to support Service Assurance and Billing processes, i.e., trouble/problem management, SLA management and billing. Interfaces are required with other service providers or network operators when the service offered to a customer involves joint service arrangements.

As mentioned in the diagram note, security is critical and applied at every interface. Security, like test management, may be a functional sub-process applied across the map or be managed as part of the specific process and handled as requirements for the process and system involved.

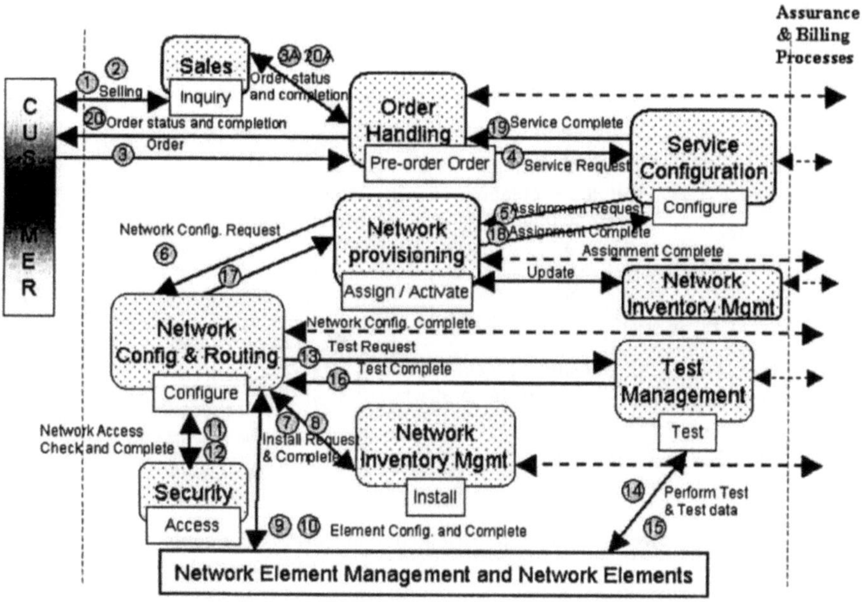

Figure 96. *Fulfillment Process Example*

A2.5.4 A Service Assurance Process Flow Segment

The Service Assurance process starts with registering SLA terms by specific customer and updating trouble/problem management systems for specific service and customer instance. It ends with: Identification of an SLA or QoS violation, reporting, managing improvement and providing information to Billing, if there is a bill impact.

Identification of a trouble from the customer or identification of a trouble triggered by network or information technologies through fast isolation, restoration, repair and providing information to Billing for credits, if there is a bill impact—and a satisfied customer.

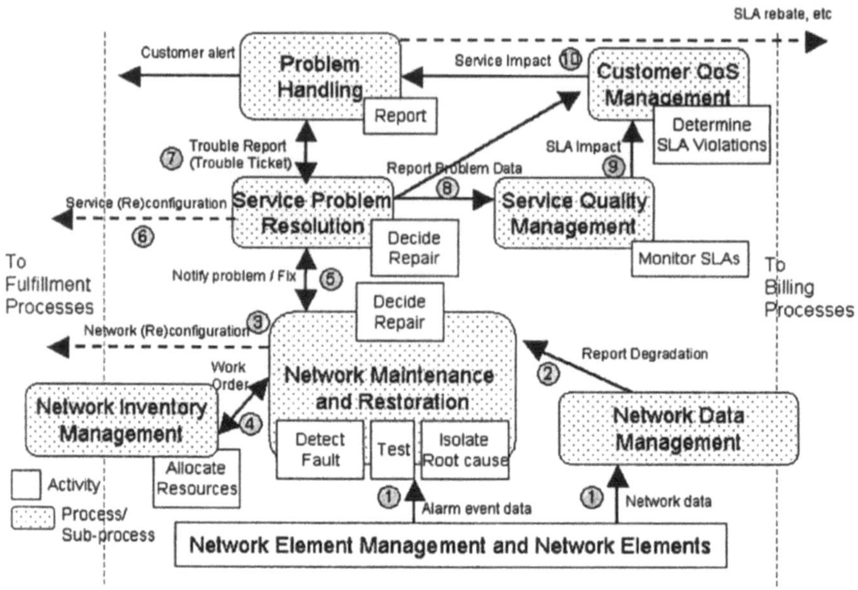

Figure 97. *Assurance Process Example*

A2.5.4.1 Network-Detected Fault / Quality of Service Problem Example

Figure 99 shows a possible sequence of activities in response to a *network-detected* problem. The problem could be non-service-affecting because of inherent 'self healing' capabilities in the underlying network and information technology infrastructure (for example, SONET/SDH networks have some instant redirection capabilities). The service provider's policy could be to decide on how to repair the problem at the network layer and, subject to 'no-break in service', may not even inform the service layer of the event.

The figure 99 shows two ways a potential service-affecting problem could be identified, i.e., by either an 'alarm event' or by synthesis of network data, through Network Data Management. Neither is exclusive. Network Data Management collects and processes performance and traffic data, as well as usage data. The usage data is used in the Billing Process.

Most service providers are driving their Service Assurance processes to become primarily proactive, meaning triggered by automation rather than triggered by the customer. This is important for improving service quality, customer perception of service and for lowering costs. Customer Care Processes have been reactive until recently. The extreme pressure to reduce cost, customer demand for more control and customer demand for more proactive, customer-enabled service support are driving a major shift to interactive support through automation. With the advent of Internet access, interactive customer-enabled service includes giving the customer the ability to see and act on service performance or the performance of 'his/her network.' Superior companies are also recognizing the value of customer provided information at each customer interface point. They are capturing that information for use in other ways across the enterprise, e.g., to customize offers to customer needs, to relate to the customer in future interactions, etc.

If the service provided is a joint service type arrangement, the main service provider must interface with other service providers or network operators to monitor and support the service provided.

A2.5.5 A Service Billing Process Flow Instance

The Service Billing process starts with creating and updating customer accounts, as well as registering SLA terms by specific customer. It ends with a satisfied customer and:

- Correct and on-time issuance of bills, including application of outage credits and SLA violation credits.
- Customer Account or Billing Inquiry support.
- Timely and accurate bill adjustment.
- Management of accounts receivable, including payment collections from customers.

A2.5.5.1 Flat Rate, Usage and SLA Element Bill Generation Example

Figure 100 shows a typical sequence of activities to generate a bill that has flat rate elements (e.g., one-time installation, monthly recurring charges), usage charges and possible SLA adjustments. Service providers may also choose to apply discounts or rebates (for outages and/or Service Level Agreement breaches) to a specific customer's bill, according to service type, by promotion, by customer relationship, according to its policy or customer contract.

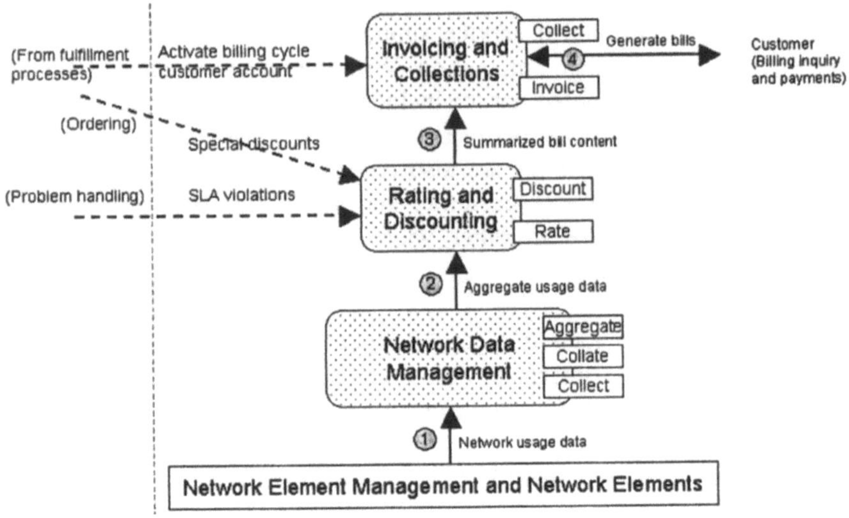

Figure 98. *Billing Process Example*

When a service is provided by a combination of different service providers, usage and/or other billing data may be aggregated by the 'main' service provider from input by other 'secondary' service providers' and one bill presented to the customer. This is a trend, but depends on the service provider billing strategy, customer wishes, the actual service arrangement provided, and/or service provider process capability and policy.

A2.6 Conclusion

This appendix has provided a general introduction to the Fulfillment, Assurance and Billing processes, part of the Telecom Operations Map (TOM), defined by Tele-management Forum to facilitate the interoperability and reuse of e-business management in the telecommunication business sector.

The author acknowledges the contribution of Simon Znaty of Effords, France and Albert Fuss of ICS Germany in developing some of the content in this appendix as part of a joint course offered to telecom professionals.

Readers interested in more details may like to see the latest version of TOM called eTOM and the application notes available from the web site of Tele-Management Forum- http:// www.tmforum.com.

Appendix 3. CoMENS for E-Business Management

This appendix shows how the CSCW-based CoMENS requirements engineering techniques may be used to analyze a typical e-business management problem. Some of the ideas and roles have been taken from the work of Anna Durante and her colleagues "A Model for the E-Service Marketplace" in the Software Technology Laboratory, HP Labs, Palo Alto, USA, as published in HP labs report HPL-2000-17 dated Feb 2000.

This document supplements the discussion of CoMENS in Chapter 9 of this book.

A3.1 Overall System Study

E-business management involves interactions amongst roles in the context of various types of e-businesses, such as:

- Business-to-business
- Consumer-to-business
- Consumer-to-consumer

While the last two types of interactions have been illustrated in Chapter 5 on CoMENS scenario analysis, this document extends those concepts to a typical business-to-business model. A generic role-interaction model for e-business needs to consider a variety of possible roles that can be classified as:

- Transaction Participants (e.g., Buyer, Service Provider etc.)
- Mediators (e.g., Advertiser, Finder Agent etc.)
- Market makers (e.g., Contract Enforcer, Auditor, Trusted authority etc.)
- Lifecycle Managers (e.g., Composition Manager, Operations Manager)
- Financial Managers (e.g., Bid Manager, Billing Manager etc.)

These roles participate in a the following phases of a typical e-business service scenario:

- Service Creation phases involves the composition of a service by the aggregation of a number of outsourced services
- Service Discovery phase has two views, one for buyer and other for service provider
  - Buyer side involves the preparation of Request for Proposals (RFP), and its dissemination/matching through advertiser and finder agent
  - Service Provider side involves matching the RFP to a possible offer involving multiple service providers
- Negotiation and Contract phase involves the finalization of the Service Level Agreements (SLA) based on buyer specifications and service provider specifications. It also involves, the checking and formalization

of financial credentials of all concerned parties through a trusted third party, or Certification Authority (CA).
- The Monitor and Manage phase involves the monitoring and control of SLAs through appropriate agents
- Finally the Fulfillment and Payment phase involves the payment from buyer to service provider as per the contracted SLA

A3.2 Roles and Tasks

Although it is possible to involve the various types of roles discussed earlier, we consider a simple scenario with the following roles:

☐ Buyer is responsible for

- Creating RFPs
- Commissioning of advertisers and finder agents
- Evaluation and negotiation of offers through agents
- Participate in SLA management
- Provide appropriate notifications to service providers, and human users

☐ Service Provider (SP) is responsible for

- Specification of protocols for initiation, termination, and interfacing
- Participate in negotiations and finalization of SLAs
- Negotiate with other SPs
- Deliver the contracted SLA

☐ Advertiser is responsible for

- Maintaining reference to registries for RFPs, and offers
- Advertising RFPs or offers
- Accept notifications

☐ Finder Agent is responsible for

- Maintain reference to registries with RFPs and offers
- Search for offers
- Match RFPs to offers
- Present matches to buyer
- Accept notifications

☐ Negotiator is responsible for

- Drawing up the contractual SLA
- Coordination with concerned parties (e.g., buyer and SPs)
- Managing the information, agreement and Settlement phases of the negotiation

- ☐ Trusted Authority is responsible for
  - Checking the financial credentials of concerned parties (e.g., buyer, and SPs)
  - Certification of signatures
  - Guaranteeing payment to SPs
  - Providing necessary insurance
- ☐ Operations manager is responsible for
  - Monitor SLAs
  - Raise Alarms if there are performance issues
  - Correct performance situations
  - Ensure delivery of service

A3.3 Process Study

Figure 101 shows the typical process scenario of e-business management, where a buyer wants to explore, negotiate, contract and pay for a product/service over the network. The roles are shown as ellipses with full and abbreviated names. The Contractual SLA has been shown as the only artifact in view of its high importance in such a scenario. Other artifacts will be discussed in the next section with tools and communication mechanisms.

The above numbered interactions can now be described as follows:

1. Buyer (b) initiates advertisement of RFP through Advertiser (a) and Finder Agent (f).

2. Advertiser (a) send the RFP to Finder Agent (f) who initiates the search for an SP

3. Finder Agent (f) notifies the Buyer (b) of any matching offers

4. Finder Agent (f) contacts a potential SP.

5. The SP discusses the RFP with other SPs (SP1-3) for a possible composite offer

6. A potential SP sends a matching offer to Finder Agent (f)

7. Trusted Authority (ta) checks the credentials of Buyer and SPs

8. ta confirms the signatures and payment guarantees through a certificate into SLA

9. Buyer (b) commissions a Negotiator (n) for contract and discusses contents

10. SP discusses the composite contract with Negotiator (n)

11. Buyer, SP and N provide their inputs to finalize the contractual SLA

12. Operations Manager (O) gets SLA inputs from the contractual SLA to set the monitoring specifications

13. N notifies SP in case of any performance problems

14. N alarms b in case of any SLA violations

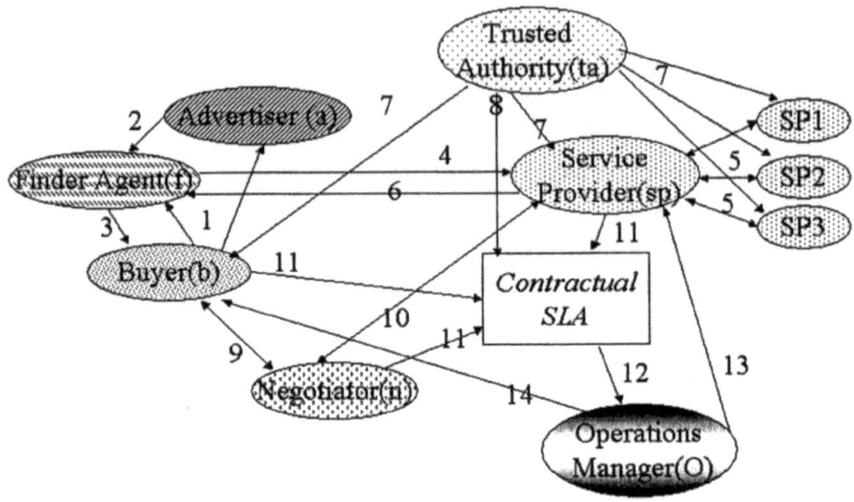

Figure 99. *E-Business Management Scenario*

A3.4 Collaborative Service Evaluation

This section discusses the artifacts including tools for each interaction. It may be noted that objects are perhaps the most generic way to describe these artifacts. These are now listed in the Table 15.

It is now possible to carry out an analysis of the gaps in these artifacts as per CoMENS Requirements Engineering methodology described in Part 5 of this book.

Table 15. Listing of Artifacts for E-Business Scenario

Interaction Number	Artifacts Used
1	Buyer Specification, RFP
2	RFP
3	RFP Matches
4	RFP
5	RFP, and Composite Offer

Interaction Number	Artifacts Used
6	Composite Offer
7	Public Keys of SPs, and b
8	Ta Certificates
9	RFP
10	Composite Offer
11	SLA
12	SLA
13	SLA, Perf Results
14	SLA, and Monitoring Results

A3.5 Conclusion

This appendix has used the CoMENS methodology to describe an e-business management scenario using generic roles found in a typical a B2B transaction environment for e-business services. It may be noted that this discussion may be extended to illustrate all stages of CoMENS up to the design of cooperative management of e-business. More details are available in the publication:

P. Ray, *Cooperative Management of Enterprise Networks*, Kluwer Academic/ Plenum Publications, 2000

Appendix 4. Service Level Management (SLM)[2]

This case study supplements the discussion of standards-based Service Level Management (SLM) implementation in Chapter 6. The discussion is based on an ITIL (discussed in Chapter 5) compliant product called CONTINUITY from Intelligent Communication Software (ICS) Germany. Most of the material is from Intelligent Communication Software (ICS), "A Definition of Service Level Management", A White paper, November 2000, http://www.ics.de.

A4.1 SLM SYSTEM REQUIREMENTS

The main requirement of a Service-Level Management system is an integrated toolset built around a configuration management database, which is used as a central, common data repository by each of the following disciplines involved in IT service delivery:

- Availability management
- Capacity management
- Problem & change management
- Contingency planning

The service delivery disciplines avail of the configuration management database, which itself contains all the models that comprise the IT infrastructure and functions as the central element in the support of a fully integrated solution based on the following components and concepts:

1. *IT-Infrastructure modeling catalog* – in the form of a modeling database containing an extensive catalog of fully developed models.
2. *IT Infrastructure Topology Views* – these views provide a means of generating a working model of the IT infrastructure using the catalog mentioned above.
3. *SLA View* – this view is used to hold explicit SLA models, groups of SLAs, or a combination of both.
4. *Service Catalog View* – The service catalog view fulfills a template function and contains service-specific generic model types.
5. *Service View* – this view is used to model and display the actual services.
6. *Business Function View* – The business function view fulfills a template function by providing already modeled structures for typical business functions.
7. *Business Views* – views tailored to the individual needs of specific organizations or departments. The business view is meant to contain

[2] Adapted with permission from ICS Intelligent Communication Software GmbH. White paper "A Definition of Service Level Management", http://www.ics.de (2001).

models of business functions (organizational units such as marketing, sales or training) as well as the business processes that make up these units.

8. *Scalability* - A true client/server architecture in which multiple display stations can attach to management servers that host the modeling database and contain the polling, event-handling and alarm-correlation capabilities. Since these servers will probably be located across a wide geographical area (i.e. across a WAN) the system must provide *Manager-to-Manager* support.
9. *Alarm Correlation* - A mechanism for correlating polled, event and alarm information, processing it and making some decision based on the relative importance of the processing results.
10. *Distributed Service Link Environment* – This functionality supports service related alarm correlation across different management servers.
11. *Alarm Roll-up and Suppression* – To complement the correlation techniques mentioned above, the system needs to support a mechanism for filtering or suppressing alarms based on attributes such as alarm severity and the location of failed components in the view hierarchy.
12. *Reporting* - An effective reporting utility is a significant requirement for an efficient Service-Level-Management system. This utility must provide reporting capabilities, not just for IT resources, but also for service related attributes such as quality-of-service.
13. *Advanced Service Management Applications* - Efficient service management is directly dependant on the accuracy and content of the modeled service views. However, the construction and maintenance of these views is the most challenging part of implementing service management. CONTINUITY™ provides three advanced applications designed to reduce the overhead in constructing service and business views. These are:

- A modeler application to actually map the IT resources to services and business processes.
- A Viewer to be used by the operations personnel responsible for IT management
- An analyzer to calculate parameters such as availability and the impact of component failure on business processes.

A4.2 CONTINUITY™ FROM ICS

CONTINUITY™, a product developed and marketed by ICS GmbH of Munich, Germany, enables its users to realize their management goals in a pro-active fashion, and thus significantly reduce their expenditure on IT management. CONTINUITY™ is based on the ITIL Service Management philosophy in which different products from different vendors are seamlessly integrated into one homogenous system management environment and it provides support for the following management functions:

- Service-Level management
- Availability management
- Business Continuity management
- Business process management
- Configuration & change management
- Capacity management

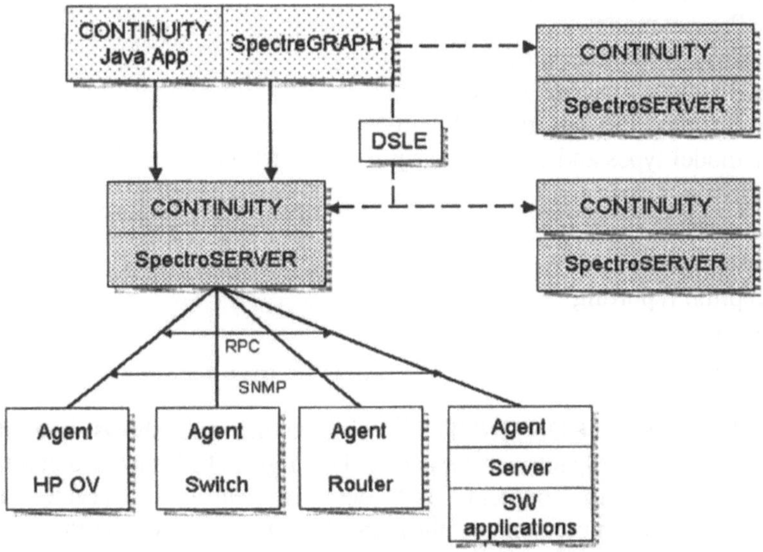

Figure 100. SLM Implementation

CONTINUITY™ uses modeling and AI techniques, such as model-based reasoning and correlation, to manage the IT infrastructure and to mold its disparate parts and their various interdependencies into cohesive IT services and business processes. In order to avail of the benefits of the common configuration management database, CONTINUITY™ has been embedded into Cabletron Spectrum™ at the database level and can thus reap the benefits of Spectrum™'s modeling techniques (that use AI based Inductive Modeling Technology).

CONTINUITY uses the infrastructure and functionality, which is already available in Spectrum™ and it is styled in compliance with the Spectrum™ style guide. These are factors, which have considerable significance during the initial rollout of the product. Personnel who have been working with Spectrum™ and are already familiar with its modes of operation already have the knowledge and skills needed to master the new system.

CONTINUITY™ includes a modeler, a viewer, an analyzer and a reporter, as well as a complete new set of model types, which are added to the Spectrum™ system at installation time. These new model types are:

__ The SLA model
__ The SLA Container model
__ The Service model
__ The Mirror Service model
__ The ReqResource model
__ The Project model
__ The Project Member model
__ The Business Function model
__ The Business Process model

The model types and applications provide functionality in the areas of:

- Modeling
- monitoring
- measurement
- exception reporting
- analysis
- statistics
- reporting

Figure 102 depicts CONTINUITY™ architecture and shows how it is integrated into the Spectrum™ system. The figure 102 shows a multiple SpectroSERVER environment and demonstrates how service level management is implemented through the Distributed Service Link Environment (DSLE). The SpectroGRAPH and Java clients run on separate machines and communicate with the servers using standard TCP/IP methods. The servers communicate with the various managed objects via the SNMP management protocol or in the case of application management, via either SNMP or by using RPC based functions.

A4.3 IT-Infrastructure Modeling Catalog

The modeling database, which comes with the Spectrum™ system at installation time, provides a large catalog of management modules. These modules contain approximately 500 fully functional model types representing nearly every IT related component currently in widespread use. This ensures that the system can be put into operation in most environments almost immediately. This is one of the key differentiating factors that set Spectrum™ apart and place it clearly ahead of competing enterprise management frameworks. Management modules contain *model types, which* are fully functional, logical representations of physical entities. A model type has attributes, which describe the entity's configuration and it has intelligence, which reflects the actual functionality. Model types are associated with each other by the mechanism of creating *relations* between them, e.g., Model X *connects to* model Y, or Model A *contains* Model B. There are numerous other relations in the database, such as that between a hub chassis and any of its modules. In this case the boards would be associated with the chassis via the *has part* relation. Discrete IT resources are gathered underneath logical models by creating a *collects* relation between them.

The concept of a model-based system has distinct advantages over a rule-based system. The rules are already a part of the model types and do not have to be modified each time the network infrastructure changes, thereby considerably reducing the configuration overhead of the management system itself.

The core database includes model types for standard network distribution components such as routers, bridges, hubs and switches in addition to server class components such as Network File Servers or Database Servers, and network host class components such as NT workstations and desktop PCs. System specific model types such as file systems, disk partitions, system logs, process tables and print queues as well as a number of complete application model types such as SAP R/3™ or Oracle™ are also available. Non-standard, or less widely used devices can be integrated into the catalog quickly and easily by the process of deriving them from existing types. Powerful development toolkits are included to facilitate the integration process. Non-IT devices like PBXs or air-conditioning systems, which do not use standard management protocols can also be integrated using the toolkits.

Third-party management systems such as HP Openview™, Tivoli TME10™, Sun Solstice™ or CA Unicenter TNG™ .can be integrated into modeling catalog by installing a specialized module which includes its own generic management agent and provides support for a wide variety of operating systems. The generic agent's configuration can be set up using a GUI, which is included with the management module. The GUI allows the agent to be deployed, configured and operational for all supported platforms with a minimum of effort.

A4.4 Management Views

The need for different viewpoints of a distributed system has been established through the development of five viewpoints in the ISO standard

Reference Model for Open Distributed Processing (RM-ODP). This major concept is heavily used in the presentation of management information by management platforms, such as Aprisma SPECTRUM. This section discusses the different views involved in SLM.

A4.4.1 IT Infrastructure Topology Views

The actual network infrastructure model is presented in a "Topology" view, which can be constructed either manually or automatically by the process of "autodiscovery". This model is stored in the SpectroSERVER's configuration management database. The actual network devices are created in the topology hierarchy by the process of "instantiating" the model types from the catalog described above. Once a model has been created it begins to interrogate the device it is modeling and then configures itself in accordance with that device's configuration. In other words, the model of the device assumes the real device's actual current state. A device model can be in any one of 5 possible states: reachable, unreachable, marginally defective, defective or maintenance. When these devices are subsequently associated with service models, CONTINUITY™ begins to monitor their states and records each state - change that occurs in a model. The topology view can display two categories of models – discrete and logical. Discrete models represent actual network distribution components such as routers or hubs, whereas logical models represent *collections* of networked devices like: LAN, WAN, Wide-Area-Link, FDDI-Ring, LAN_802.3 or LAN_802.5. Relationships between device models or between logical models are displayed as *pipes*, which connect them together. These pipes dynamically change color to indicate the status of the connections they are showing. Networked class components such as servers or workstations are modeled using icons, which have a hierarchical structure. Applications and system specific models - e.g. file systems or disk partitions that are located on these components are modeled within this hierarchical structure.

A4.4.2 SLA View

The SLA view is used to create and manage the model types that represent the actual Service-Level-Agreements. There are two model types from the above list, which can be placed in this view. These are: the "SLA" model and the "SLA Container" model. The SLA Container is a composite model used to group SLAs together. The SLA model itself provides attributes to define, manage and monitor the Service-Level- Agreements in real-time.

The functions and configuration fields are accessed via point-and-click options attached to the SLA icon. The supported parameters include, activating and de-activating the SLA, defining the service hours, and entering the textual form of the agreement. The icon has a color-coded indicator to provide "at-a-glance" real-time status of the services covered by the SLA. A mechanism to measure service reliability over a specified time period has been implemented in the SLA model by ensuring that the model remembers its alarm history and notifies the help desk only after one or more disruptions.

Repair time is measured by monitoring the length of time a service has been in a specific condition, for example, when a disrupted service has not been restored to operation within a specified period during peak service hours. Condition and state-change monitoring is one of the key capabilities of the SLA model. This has been implemented as a real-time function whose purpose is to continually monitor the state of each service covered by the SLA. It does this by keeping an on-going log of all the condition changes that have occurred since the service went into operation.

Services can have one of five possible conditions: available, degrading, degraded, unavailable or maintenance. A single display window presents the observer with a service's "condition history" in the form of both a pie chart and a numerical table showing exactly when the service entered a particular state, and the length of time it remained in that state. Finally the model maintains a "change log" which is an inventory of the service's components. If the service is modified in any way e.g. by adding or removing components, .an event will be generated and the support group or the service maintainer will be informed of the change.

A4.4.3 Service Catalog View

The Service Catalog view provides a template service hierarchy analogous to the model catalog discussed in the "IT-Infrastructure Modeling Catalog" above. It provides the capabilities to create "Generic Service" templates that can be used by a department to either jump-start the modeling process or for the purpose of availability planning for future IT projects. The generic services make it possible to create complete model hierarchies of IT-services generally provided to a customer by an external or internal provider. Generic hierarchies have been pre-modeled for various services typically used in Corporate networks: e.g., for corporate e-mail services, for WWW services or for environments using Lotus Notes SAP R/3 or Novell NetWare. The WWW service template for example, is a model hierarchy designed to represent the complete structure of a Corporate Web Service. The following core components (Table 16) are critical to all smoothly running Websites and are modeled as "services" and "required resources" in the Web Service template:

Table 16. Implementing the Web Infrastructure Management

Machines	Network	Files
Name Server	Access ports (dial ups)	Log files(sizes)
Database Server	Router	tmp files(sizes)
File Server	Hub	

- Processes Web site
- Ftp Server CGI sub system
- Proxy Server Pages
- e-mail Server External links
- News Server

Service templates are categorized according to specific "types" and a template of type "Web Server" to be used to model several different machines without the overhead of re-creating the entire hierarchy for each machine.

A4.4.4 Service View

Creating Services is achieved by logically grouping models of the various managed objects and gathering them into composite models, which we call "Required Resources". The "Required Resource" model is in turn placed within a Service model, thereby associating all the components and applications underneath it, with that specific Service. IT components are associated with the ReqResource models by a one-to-many relation and they can therefore be used in several services simultaneously. The ReqResource has intelligence and functionality, which allow it to display the cumulative status of all the entities located within it *in real-time.* The benefit of modeling resources in this way is that it supports *Availability-Management* by allowing techniques such as the end-to-end modeling of *all* the components within an IT service, by providing a basis for functional paradigms, such as component-redundancy, and by providing a means of pinpointing potential single points of failure. This concept can be used to define modeling structures according to arbitrary criteria, such as vendor types or hardware/software types , or even service supplier types. For example, it can be used to gather all the disks from a particular manufacturer into a ReqResource model or all the frame-relay links provided by a particular service provider for purposes of comparing them to each other or to competitive products with the emphasis on reliability, availability or MTBF.

Service reliability has been implemented in the concept of a "rolling window", which is a user-definable time period during which alarms for specific devices are collected and *remembere*d. If a pre-configured number of alarms for a managed object have been fired within the rolling window period, the support group receives a notification that the service is degrading. A *recovery* mechanism for services has been implemented as follows: as soon as a service becomes unavailable through loss of one or more of its sub-components, the software starts a recovery timer which can be set in either hours, minutes or seconds.

If a specified number of the service's components have not been restored to full operation before the timer expires, an alarm is generated and the support group is notified. These functions allow a high level of differentiation between the various IT Services based on their relative importance.

Service availability in CONTINUITY™ is indicated by one of five possible states. These are: Available; Degrading; Degraded; Unavailable and Maintenance. "Quality-of-service" thresholds in the form of percentages (%) can be applied to the service models and configured to fire alarms if a service begins to degrade. A service is considered to have a 100% "Quality-of-Service" rating when all of its sub-components are fully functional.

A4.4.5 Business Views

CONTINUITY™ supports Business Function oriented views aimed at providing specific departments or external organizations with a customized window into the IT services which they are either using themselves, or are providing to yet other organizations, or to end customers. Business view hierarchies can be constructed in a top down fashion and in accordance with departmental or organizational structures using the model types "BusinessFunction", "BusinessProcess", "Project" and "ProjectMember". "Service" models, which would have been created in advance, can be associated with each business process by actually placing them inside the process models. From this moment on, all the condition states of the business process models will be rolled up through the hierarchy, showing both the real-time status of the business functions and the impact that a component failure would have on them.

A4.4.6 Business Function View

The business function view provides a template hierarchy analogous to the service catalog discussed in paragraph 4 above. It provides the capabilities to create generic business process models in the form of templates that reflect the real business functions frequently used by an enterprise.

A4.5 Scalability

Spectrum™ is implemented in a client/server architecture and the client application is known as the "SpectroGRAPH©". The SpectroGRAPH application provides all the graphical display functionality *locally* – the only communication between the client and the server is the transfer of control information used to update the display. Unlike other management implementations, there is no transfer of graphical data across the wire. This means that the client can connect to the server across a WAN connection thereby enabling the system to realistically support the notion of an enterprise-wide "client/server" system.

The client can be installed anywhere across the enterprise and can be configured to attach to any amount of management servers. This allows great flexibility when implementing security and access rights to the different views. The client also provides an integrated alarm view with alarm suppression and filtering on model names, alarm severity or date/time as well as the capability of assigning alarms to specific users.

A separate, optional application, the "Alarm Notifier" provides advanced, policy based alarm management. Also supported is view-only, or read-only access to the alarm database using any HTML-based browser.

A4.6 Alarm Correlation

Spectrum™ provides alarm correlation functionality to facilitate the systematic processing of resource data from the management server. CONTINUITY™ uses this functionality to perform alarm correlation within its own model hierarchy. Due to the sheer magnitude of present-day, corporate networks and the volume of the event and alarm data flowing into the management system, it is necessary to correlate this flood of data and condense it down to only the most important information for presentation on the display console. Consider the example of a failure in a network distribution component, such as a router or a bridge. If it is a component which happens to segment the management station itself from a large part of the network, the failure will cause an avalanche of events from every model located on the effected segment.

Evaluating these events with the intent of locating the real source of the problem is a next to impossible task for the operator alone. In a case such as this, AI capabilities are indispensable for sorting through the alarm flood and attempting to prioritize and nail down the real problem cause. The event and alarm lists need to be analyzed, the insignificant data eliminated and the most likely offender – in this case the link element, identified.

A4.7 Distributed Service Link Environment

CONTINUITY™ is designed to operate in a large distributed processing setup. To this end it provides alarm correlation capabilities that can traverse an environment containing multiple management servers. The task of managing the IT infrastructure can be transparently distributed across the various servers, thus reducing the risk of processing bottlenecks while at the same time providing increased redundancy in the management environment.

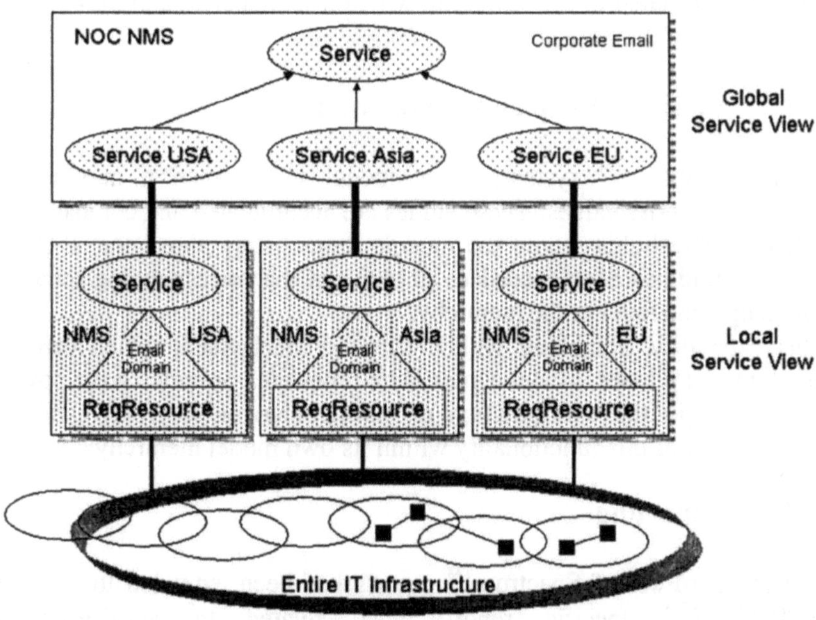

Figure 101. Multi-domain Management

Service models can be constructed to span multiple management servers, irrespective of geographical restrictions, yet still be fully monitored and controlled from a client workstation located at some central point in the organization, typically the NOC.

Services controlled by distributed management servers can logically be grouped into services and sub-services.

The notion of an entire service model composed of services containing several sub-services, is realized through the implementation of a functional paradigm called "distributed service link environment". This concept, as it is implemented in CONTINUITY™, allows alarm correlation across management servers, and the availability of an entire service can then be monitored even if that service transcends geographical boundaries. We refer to the above mechanism as a "correlator of correlators" function.

The Figure 103 shows a CONTINUITY™ service hierarchy consisting of a service that contains 3 sub-services. Each sub-service is modeled on a separate NMS and is being monitored and controlled by that NMS. Alarm correlation for the sub-services is occurring on each of the NMSs.

The NMS, which resides at the *top* level of the architecture is collecting alarms from each service underneath and is carrying out service alarm correlation across the whole management environment. This will ensure that a failure in a resource, irrespective of that resource's physical location, will be properly correlated to the service in which it is modeled, and thus reflect the availability of the overall service.

A4.7.1 Alarm Roll-Up and Suppression

In the Spectrum™ system, every model is assigned a number of configurable severity values. These values are accumulated and compared to user-defined thresholds set on the models immediately above them. Once such a threshold has been exceeded, an alarm of the corresponding severity is "rolled up" one level in the hierarchy.

This capability, combined with a filtering mechanism, which can be keyed on model classes, model names, date/times etc., provides great power and flexibility in the configuration of alarm behavior. CONTINUITY™ takes advantage of this functionality within its own model hierarchy.

A4.7.2 Reporting

The standard set of Spectrum™ reports has been extended to include CONTINUITY™ specific report types related to Service-Level-Management. ReqResource, Service and SLA models all have formats for both graphical and textual report types built into them. Some examples of reports shipped with the system are:

- Quality-of-Service reports
- Service Condition-Times reports
- SLA Condition-Times reports
- Req-Resource .Condition-Times reports

All relevant attributes that are associated with the CONTINUITY™ model types are logged in the events and statistics database, thereby providing support for the data-warehousing capabilities offered by the Spectrum™ system.

A4.8 Advanced Service Management Applications

ICS CONTINUITY™ is a product, which is designed to be used by end customers, support organizations and service providers alike. As such, it needs to provide a user interface, which allows great diversity and power while still remaining flexible and easy to operate. The user tools, which make up the product should be identical and easily supportable on each of the platforms on which they run. These were the considerations, which influenced the decision to develop CONTINUITY™'s configuration applications and analysis tools in Java.

These tools have been developed to support the service management disciplines in a more task-oriented fashion. The following list illustrates the tasks, which the applications are designed to address:

- which component(s) belong to which service(s)
- if the service is currently in use
- Impact on a service through loss of a component
- If there are times when a component could possibly be turned
- .off - e.g. for maintenance
- or whether a service is covered by an appropriate SLA

The "**Service Configuration**" utility uses a two-pane configuration window showing managed objects in one pane and the IT services in the other. The managed objects can be selected either individually or in bulk and placed into the appropriate service using a drag-and-drop operation.

The **"Component Failure Impact Analysis"** utility is a program designed to produce an analysis of critical components based on the following criteria:

- If a component failure does not effect a service in any way
- If a component failure causes a service to become unavailable
- If a component has automatic failover capabilities.
- If a component has manual failover capabilities

Components, which fit into any of the above categories will be flagged appropriately and an analysis of the flagged components will indicate the degree of impact that a failure would have on a particular service. For example, a component that is modeled in several services and belongs to category 2 can be classified as a high-risk device.

The **"Business Impact Analysis**" utility is an application which is designed to assist the user in: identifying critical business processes showing the potential damage incurred by a business process through loss of a critical IT service. This is achieved by selecting either a conceptual model, such a ReqResource *or* a discrete managed object, and using it as an entry point to begin the analysis. The object's availability status is now set to "off " to simulate a component failure. The analysis utility is then started against the selected object, and will present the user with a graphical display showing all the services and business processes which would be impacted by the failure.

The **"Maintenance Window Analysis"** utility is designed to present information on possible maintenance windows for IT resources. Any given resource is likely to be part of more than one service and may therefore be covered by more than one SLA. The utility locates all the services in which the selected resource is modeled and analyzes the service times of all the SLAs associated with those services. The user can then determine when a particular device can be brought down for maintenance, e.g., a hub card being used by some department, is to be replaced.

The utility will use the card model as the starting point for an analysis of all the services using the card. It will then analyze the service times of the SLAs for each of those services and compute the maintenance window. If the hub provides hot-swap functionality, the board can be swapped out at the convenience of the maintenance team. If the hub needs to be switched off in order to swap the card, then this can only be done at a time when the hub and all its other cards can be taken offline.

More details on CONTINUITY and SPECTRUM are available from the company web sites http://www.ics.de and http://www.aprisma.com respectively.

Index

MIX
Papier aus verantwortungsvollen Quellen
Paper from responsible sources
FSC® C105338

If you have any concerns about our products,
you can contact us on
ProductSafety@springernature.com

In case Publisher is established outside the EU,
the EU authorized representative is:
Springer Nature Customer Service Center GmbH
Europaplatz 3, 69115 Heidelberg, Germany

Printed by Libri Plureos GmbH
in Hamburg, Germany